Story of God Bible Commentary
Series Endorsements

"Getting a story is about more than merely enjoying it. It means hearing it, understanding it, and above all, being impacted by it. This commentary series hopes that its readers not only hear and understand the story, but are impacted by it to live in as Christian a way as possible. The editors and contributors set that table very well and open up the biblical story in ways that move us to act with sensitivity and understanding. That makes hearing the story as these authors tell it well worth the time. Well done."

Darrell L. Bock
Executive Director of Cultural Engagement, Howard G. Hendricks
Center for Christian Leadership and Cultural Engagement,
Senior Research Professor of New Testament Studies
Dallas Theological Seminary

"The Story of God Bible Commentary series invites readers to probe how the message of the text relates to our situations today. Engagingly readable, it not only explores the biblical text but offers a range of applications and interesting illustrations."

Craig S. Keener
Professor of New Testament
Asbury Theological Seminary

"I love the Story of God Bible Commentary series. It makes the text sing, and helps us hear the story afresh."

John Ortberg
Senior pastor of Menlo Park Presbyterian Church

"In this promising new series of commentaries, believing biblical scholars bring not only their expertise but their own commitment to Jesus and insights into today's culture to the Scriptures. The result is a commentary series that is anchored in the text but lives and breathes in the world of today's church with its variegated pattern of socioeconomic, ethnic, and national diversity. Pastors, Bible study leaders, and Christians of all types who are looking for a substantive and practical guide through the Scriptures will find these volumes helpful."

Frank Thielman
Professor of Divinity
Beeson Divinity School

"The Story of God Bible Commentary series is unique in its approach to exploring the Bible. Its easy-to-use format and practical guidance brings God's grand story to modern-day life so anyone can understand how it applies today."

Andy Stanley
Senior Pastor
North Point Ministries

"I'm a storyteller. Through writing and speaking I talk and teach about understanding the Story of God throughout Scripture and about letting God reveal more of His story as I live it out. Thus I am thrilled to have a commentary series based on the Story of God—a commentary that helps me to Listen to the Story, that Explains the Story, and then encourages me to probe how to Live the Story. A perfect tool for helping every follower of Jesus to walk in the story that God is writing for them."

Judy Douglass
Author, Speaker, Encourager
Office of the President, Cru
Director of Women's Resources, Cru

"The Bible is the story of God and his dealings with humanity from creation to new creation. The Bible is made up more of stories than of any other literary genre. Even the psalms, proverbs, prophecies, letters, and the Apocalypse make complete sense only when set in the context of the grand narrative of the entire Bible. This commentary series breaks new ground by taking all these observations seriously. It asks commentators to listen to the text, to explain the text, and to live the text. Some of the material in these sections overlaps with introduction, detailed textual analysis and application, respectively, but only some. The most riveting and valuable part of the commentaries are the stories that can appear in any of these sections, from any part of the globe and any part of church history, illustrating the text in any of these areas. Ideal for preaching and teaching."

Craig L. Blomberg
Distinguished Professor of New Testament
Denver Seminary

EPHESIANS

Editorial Board
of
The Story of God Bible Commentary

The Story of God Bible Commentary

EPHESIANS

Mark D. Roberts

Tremper Longman III & Scot McKnight
General Editors

ZONDERVAN®

ZONDERVAN

Ephesians
Copyright © 2016 by Mark D. Roberts

This title is also available as a Zondervan ebook.

Requests for information should be addressed to:
Zondervan, 3900 *Sparks Dr. SE, Grand Rapids, Michigan 49546*

ISBN 978-0-310-32723-3

Cover design: Ron Huizinga
Cover image: iStockphoto®
Interior composition: Matthew Van Zomeren

Printed in the United States of America

16 17 18 19 20 21 22 23 24 /DHV/ 20 19 18 17 16 15 14 13 12 11 10 9 8 7 6 5 4 3 2 1

This commentary is dedicated to three men who have helped me understand and live the story of God in Ephesians.

To Don Williams,
my uncle and lifelong role model, whose seminary lectures first stirred my passion for Ephesians and who modeled its truth through his own imitation of Christ.

To Lloyd Ogilvie,
my pastor and mentor, whose preaching of Ephesians proclaimed the ministry of all of God's people and who profoundly shaped my identity as a Christian, a pastor, and a theologian.

To Howard E. Butt, Jr.,
my inspiration and friend, whose lifelong zeal for the good news of Ephesians now lives in me and who motivated me to believe that God can indeed do immeasurably more than all we ask or imagine.

Old Testament series

New Testament series

Contents

Acknowledgments

I am thankful to Scot McKnight, series senior editor, for the invitation to write this commentary and for his consistent encouragement. Lynn Cohick, editor of this volume, and Katya Covrett of Zondervan have also been helpful throughout the project. Thanks to Scot and Lynn, and also to Pete Santucci, Tod Bolsinger, and Marcus Goodyear, for their critical comments and insightful suggestions.

Thanks to Harvard University, where I did much of the research for and writing of this commentary.

Although I moved on from Irvine Presbyterian Church in 2007, much of this commentary reflects what I learned through my sixteen years as pastor of this beloved congregation. I'm thankful for the partnership in Christ we shared, learning together how to live "worthy of the calling" that is ours in Christ.

I'm grateful for the support, suggestions, and comments from the readers of the Daily Reflections I wrote while working for The H. E. Butt Family Foundation. For more than two years, my reflections were drawn from Ephesians. During this time, I received more than a thousand notes filled with encouragement, illustrations, questions, and insights. These helped me understand Ephesians more truly and convey its truth more vividly.

I could not have written this commentary apart from the support of the Foundation. When I was invited to write this volume, Foundation leaders Howard E. Butt, Jr. and David Rogers gave their thumbs up. Because Howard's life and ministry had been shaped so much by Ephesians, he was "over the moon" about the potential for me to help others encounter the life-changing, church-changing, and world-changing truths of this letter. As I labored slowly and painfully on this project, David saw that I needed extended time away from ordinary work in order to focus on research and writing. The Foundation made this possible.

This book is dedicated to three men who helped me understand and live the story of God in Ephesians. The example, teaching, and praying of Don Williams, Lloyd Ogilvie, and Howard E. Butt, Jr. have transformed my life. My gratitude to God for them is immense.

My children, Nathan and Kara, stood with me through thick and thin as I was writing this commentary. They made room in their busy lives for their dad when I was in Cambridge, working in the Harvard libraries. They allowed me to come up for air while enjoying their company. Thanks, Nathan and Kara!

I can't imagine how I would have completed this project apart from the encouragement, patience, and sacrificial support of my wife, Linda. Her partnership with me in all things is reflected throughout this commentary, even if I don't footnote her wisdom on every page. In particular, my understanding of how to live the story of God in Ephesians 5:21–6:4, the passage on family life, has been deeply informed by what I have experienced with Linda in our marriage and parenting. Thanks, Linda, for all of this and so much more.

Finally, thanks be to God for showing me once again, through the writing of this commentary, that he is indeed "able to do immeasurably more than all we ask or imagine, according to his power that is at work within us." To God be all the glory!

The Story of God Bible Commentary Series

The Word of God may not change, but culture does. Think of what we have seen in the last twenty years: we now communicate predominantly through the internet and email; we read our news on iPads and computers; we can talk on the phone to our friends while we are driving, while we are playing golf, while we are taking long walks; and we can get in touch with others from the middle of nowhere. We carry in our hands small devices that connect us to the world and to a myriad of sources of information. Churches have changed; the "Nones" are rising in numbers and volume, and atheists are bold to assert their views in public forums. The days of home Bible studies are waning; there is a marked rise in activist missional groups in churches, and pastors are more and more preaching topical sermons, some of which are not directly connected to the Bible. Divorce rates are not going down, marriages are more stressed, rearing children is more demanding, and civil unions and same-sex marriages are knocking at the door of the church.

Progress can be found in many directions. While church attendance numbers are waning in Europe and North America, churches are growing in the South and the East. More and more women are finding a voice in churches; the plea of the former generation of leaders that Christians be concerned not just with evangelism but with justice is being answered today in new and vigorous ways. Resources for studying the Bible are more available today than ever before, and preachers and pastors are meeting the challenge of speaking a sure Word of God into shifting cultures.

Readers of the Bible change, too. These cultural shifts, our own personal developments, the progress in intellectual questions, as well as growth in biblical studies and theology and discoveries of new texts and new paradigms for understanding the contexts of the Bible—each of these elements works on an interpreter so that the person who reads the Bible today asks different questions from different angles.

Culture shifts, but the Word of God remains. That is why we as editors of The Story of God Bible Commentary series, a commentary based on the New International Version 2011 (NIV 2011), are excited to participate in this new series of commentaries on the Bible. This series is designed to address this generation with the same Word of God. We are asking the authors to explain what the Bible says to the sorts of readers who pick up commentaries so they can understand not only what Scripture says but what it means for today. The Bible does not change, but relating it to our culture changes constantly and in differing ways in different contexts.

When we, the New Testament editors, sat down in prayer and discussion to choose authors for this series, we realized we had found fertile ground. Our list of potential authors staggered in length and quality. We wanted the authors to be exceptional scholars, faithful Christians, committed evangelicals, and theologically diverse, and we wanted this series to represent the changing face of both American and world evangelicalism: ethnic and gender diversity. I believe this series has a wider diversity of authors than any commentary series in evangelical history.

The title of this series, emphasizing as it does the "Story" of the Bible, reveals the intent of the series. We want to explain each passage of the Bible in light of the Bible's grand Story. The Bible's grand Story, of course, connects this series to the classic expression *regula fidei*, the "rule of faith," which was the Bible's story coming to fulfillment in Jesus as the Messiah, Lord, and Savior of all. In brief, we see the narrative built around the following biblical themes: creation and fall, covenant and redemption, law and prophets, and especially God's charge to humans as his image-bearers to rule under God. The theme of God as King and God's kingdom guides us to see the importance of Israel's kings as they come to fulfillment in Jesus, Lord and King over all, and the direction of history toward the new heavens and new earth, where God will be all in all. With these guiding themes, each passage is examined from three angles.

Listen to the Story. We believe that if the Bible is God speaking, then the most important posture of the Christian before the Bible is to listen. So our first section cites the text of Scripture and lists a selection of important biblical and sometimes noncanonical parallels; then each author introduces that passage. The introductions to the passages sometimes open up discussion to the theme of the passage while other times they tie this passage to its context in the specific book. But since the focus of this series is the Story of God in the Bible, the introduction leads the reader into reading this text in light of the Bible's Story.

Explain the Story. The authors follow up listening to the text by explaining each passage in light of the Bible's grand Story. This is not an academic series, so the footnotes are limited to the kinds of texts typical Bible readers and preachers readily will have on hand. Authors are given the freedom to explain the text as they read it, though you should not be surprised to find occasional listings of other options for reading the text. Authors explore biblical backgrounds, historical context, cultural codes, and theological interpretations. Authors engage in word studies and interpret unique phrases and clauses as they attempt to build a sound and living reading of the text in light of the Story of God in the Bible.

Authors will not shy away from problems in the texts. Whether one is examining the meaning of "perfect" in Matthew 5:48, the problems with Christology in the hymn of Philippians 2:6–11, the challenge of understanding Paul in light of the swirling debates about the old, new, and post-new perspectives, the endless debates about eschatology, or the vagaries of atonement theories, the authors will dive in, discuss evidence, and do their best to sort out a reasonable and living reading of those issues for the church today.

Live the Story. Reading the Bible is not just about discovering what it meant back then; the intent of The Story of God Bible Commentary series is to probe how this text might be lived out today as that story continues to march on in the life of the church. At times our authors will tell stories about what this looks like; at other times they may offer some suggestions for living it out; but always you will discover the struggle involved as we seek to live out the Bible's grand Story in our world.

We are not offering suggestions for "application" so much as digging deeper; we are concerned in this section with seeking out how this text, in light of the Story of God in the Bible, compels us to live in our world so that our own story lines up with the Bible's Story.

SCOT MCKNIGHT, general editor New Testament
LYNN COHICK, JOEL WILLITTS, and MICHAEL BIRD, editors

Abbreviations

AB	Anchor Bible
ABD	*Anchor Bible Dictionary*
ACCS	Ancient Christian Commentary on Scripture
APOT	*The Apocrypha and Pseudepigrapha of the Old Testament* (Charles)
BDAG	W. Bauer, *A Greek-English Lexicon of the New Testament and Other Early Christian Literature*, trans. and rev. W. F. Arndt, F. W. Gingrich, and F. W. Danker. 3rd ed. Chicago: University of Chicago Press, 2000.
BDB	Francis Brown, S. R. Driver, and Charles A. Briggs. *A Hebrew and English Lexicon of the Old Testament*. Oxford: Clarendon, 1907.
BECNT	Baker Exegetical Commentary on the New Testament
CEB	Common English Bible
DLNT	*Dictionary of the Later New Testament and Its Developments*
DPL	*Dictionary of Paul and His Letters*
ESV	English Standard Version
KJV	King James Version
LCL	Loeb Classical Library
LSJ	H. G. Liddell, R. Scott, and H. S. Jones. *A Greek-English Lexicon*. 9th ed. Oxford: Clarendon, 1996.
LXX	The Septuagint, the Greek Old Testament
NICNT	New International Commentary on the New Testament
NIDNTT	*New International Dictionary of New Testament Theology*
NIDOTTE	*New International Dictionary of Old Testament Theology and Exegesis*
NIGTC	New International Greek Testament Commentary
NLT	New Living Translation
NRSV	New Revised Standard Version
OTP	*Old Testament Pseudepigrapha* (Charlesworth)
PNTC	Pillar New Testament Commentary
WBC	Word Biblical Commentary
ZECNT	Zondervan Exegetical Commentary on the New Testament

Introduction to Ephesians

The story of God in Ephesians will change your life if you let it. It will astound you, encourage you, challenge you, comfort you, instruct you, admonish you, and inspire you. It will open your eyes to seeing God, your life, the church, and indeed the entire universe in a whole new way.

The story of Ephesians is truly the story *of God*, a drama in which God is the primary *actor* and the entire cosmos his *stage*. God is also the primary *author* of this story, though it comes to us in human words. It begins before creation and ends in eternity. God's story touches individual lives, to be sure, but it encompasses far more than just personal transformation. In Ephesians, God is gathering a people for himself and his purposes. He's building the church as the body of Christ and the temple of his Spirit. And through this church, that is, through us as a community, God is at work, doing more than we could ever imagine so that the entire cosmos might see the glory of his gracious plan. According to this plan, God is uniting all things in heaven and on earth in Christ, restoring and renewing the whole creation.

If you think that last paragraph promises too much, just wait until you have read Ephesians!

The Best Introduction to Ephesians Ever Written

I have read a dozen introductions to Ephesians in Bible dictionaries, commentaries, and introductions to the New Testament.[1] And now I want to invite you to read the very best introduction to Ephesians ever written. I'm not

---

1. Among the many scholarly commentaries, I have found the most helpful to be: Clinton E. Arnold, *Ephesians*, ZECNT (Grand Rapids: Zondervan, 2010); F. F. Bruce, *The Epistles to the Colossians, to Philemon, and to the Ephesians*, NICNT (Grand Rapids: Eerdmans, 1984); Andrew T. Lincoln, *Ephesians*, WBC 42 (Dallas: Word, 1990); Frank Thielman, *Ephesians*, BECNT (Grand Rapids: Baker, 2010); Markus Barth, *Ephesians*, 2 vols., AB 34, 34A (New York: Doubleday, 1974); Harold W. Hoehner, *Ephesians: An Exegetical Commentary* (Grand Rapids: Baker, 2002). Less technical, but academically solid and pastorally relevant commentaries include: Thomas R. Yoder Neufeld, *Ephesians*, Believers Church Bible Commentary (Waterloo, Ontario: Herald Press, 2002); Lynn H. Cohick, *Ephesians*, New Covenant Commentary (Eugene, OR: Cascade, 2010); Peter T. O'Brien, *The Letter to the Ephesians*, PNTC (Grand Rapids: Eerdmans, 1999); Peter S. Williamson, *Ephesians*, Catholic Commentary on Sacred Scripture (Grand Rapids: Baker, 2009). I have also been informed by classic insights found in John Calvin's *Commentary on Galatians and Ephesians* (Amazon Digital, 2010), Kindle edition; and in selections gathered in Mark J. Edwards, ed., *Galatians, Ephesians, Philippians*, ACCS 8 (Downers Grove, IL: InterVarsity Press, 1999).

referring to what I've written here. Rather, the best introduction to Ephesians *is the letter itself.*

I urge you to put down this book in a moment and take a half hour to read the whole letter we call Ephesians. As you read, don't get caught up in details; there will be time for them later. Rather, take in the grand story of God in this letter. When you finish a chapter, stop for a few moments to reflect on the narrative you have just read. What has happened in this chapter? Who did what and why? What are this chapter's high points, major themes, and points of tension? How does this chapter relate to the rest of Ephesians?

So, stop reading this book and turn your attention to the best introduction to Ephesians you'll ever read.

Some Distinctive Features of Ephesians

A Real Story about God. Perhaps one of the first things that struck you as you read Ephesians is that it tells a real story, especially in the first three chapters. Embedded within a prayer of blessing (1:3), the story of Ephesians recounts what God has done, beginning "before the creation of the world" (1:4) and ending in eternity (1:10; 6:24). God, who is identified as our Father and the Father of Jesus Christ (1:2–3), is the primary actor in his story.

The Centrality of Christ. In Ephesians, Christ plays a co-starring role. Not only is Christ the agent of crucial events in the story—such as reconciling Jews and Gentiles through the cross (2:16)—but God is often said to act "in Christ." This phrase or something similar, such as "in him," appears some twenty-eight times throughout the letter.

The Spiritual Powers in the Heavenly Realms. Someone reading Ephesians in the twenty-first century, especially within Western culture, might stumble over references to supernatural powers. Even if we're comfortable with the existence of God, we may not be so sure about "all rule and authority, power and dominion" that dwell in "the heavenly realms" (1:20–21). We may not envision one's life apart from God as servitude to some "ruler of the kingdom of the air" (2:2). But we can't evade the heavenly powers in Ephesians. They are, in fact, the primary audience for the church as it makes known God's wisdom (3:10). Moreover, in the conclusion of Ephesians, Paul claims that our struggle is not against human opponents, but "against the rulers, against the authorities, against the powers of this dark world and against the spiritual forces of evil in the heavenly realms" (6:12). How in the world—how in the heavens!—are we going to make sense of a story that includes mysterious, otherworldly beings?

Lofty Style. Even when read in translation, Ephesians features a writing style that is more exalted than what we find in most of the rest of the New

Testament. Words are stacked upon words to convey the majesty of the subject. Sentences are long and complicated, even in translation. In fact, Ephesians 1:3–14, eight complex sentences in English, is one long sentence in Greek; spanning 202 words, it is the longest sentence in the Greek New Testament. The following sentence, 1:15–23, comprises "only" 169 words. In his other writings, Paul can use long sentences and complicated phrases at times, but Ephesians stands alone in its grandeur.

No Obvious Setting in the Life of the Early Church. Paul's letters usually reflect a life setting in a particular church or collection of churches. Thus, he wrote Galatians because of theological problems plaguing the churches in Galatia. He wrote 1 Corinthians in response to divisive issues in the Christian community of Corinth. So it goes throughout the Pauline corpus, until we get to Ephesians. This letter shows almost no indication of any distinct situation in the life of any definite group of disciples. Paul never mentions members of the Ephesian church. He makes almost no reference to what's going on among the letter's recipients, other than a vague comment about their faith and love (1:15). Plus, there is little in Ephesians that particularly concerns the city of Ephesus, such as a reference to the nearby temple of Artemis and her worshipers, which surely affected the Christians there (see Acts 19). One could argue that the emphasis in Ephesians on cosmic powers is a response to the worship of Artemis. This is possible, though the challenge of pagan gods and goddesses would be found in every city in Asia Minor. Thus, Ephesians was relevant for any first-century church throughout the Roman Empire.

Absence of Familiar Pauline Perspectives. If you've read Paul's other letters, you might be concerned about what's missing in Ephesians. Many interpreters are perplexed, for example, because this letter does not mention justification by faith. Instead, Ephesians features the language of *salvation by grace through faith.* Moreover, given that Paul had advised the Corinthians to remain single rather than get married, "For this world in its present form is passing away" (1 Cor 7:31), the teaching on marriage in Ephesians 5:21–33 seems better suited to a world that goes on and on. The eschatological urgency of Paul's other letters is missing here. It has been replaced by a striking new perspective in which we have already been raised with Christ to heaven (2:6).

Writing for Gentiles Who Don't Know Paul. Though Ephesians tells us very little about the life setting of the ones to whom Paul wrote, we get an occasional glimpse of the recipients. In 2:11, he refers to his readers as "Gentiles by birth." In 3:1 he speaks to "you Gentiles." Nothing in Ephesians suggests that any of the readers were Jewish Christians, even though Ephesus had a large Jewish population, and it's highly likely that this church had Jewish members. Furthermore, Paul hints that the letter's recipients do not know him personally (3:2). This would explain the lack of personal details in the letter, but it makes little sense if Paul were writing to the Ephesians, with whom he had recently spent more than two years (see Acts 19:8–10).

The Mystery of the Missing Phrase "in Ephesus." You would not have seen this in your quick read through of Ephesians unless you were reading the oldest Greek manuscript of the letter. This document, known as Papyrus 46, was written around AD 200. Though its page bears the title "To the Ephesians," the opening greeting reads (in translation), "Paul, an apostle of Christ Jesus by the will of God, to God's holy people who are also faithful in Christ Jesus."[2] The words "in Ephesus" (the Greek is *en Ephesō*) are missing. This is true in several of the oldest and best manuscripts of Ephesians, though most manuscripts of the letter, including ancient, reliable ones, contain *en Ephesō*. There is a complicated scholarly debate about how to explain this odd difference, as we shall see further on.

Without question, the letter we know as Ephesians is distinctive in many ways. It would not be an exaggeration to say it is unique among the letters attributed to Paul. If we are going to understand Ephesians rightly, if we are going to hear its story accurately, then we need to examine its uniqueness in a bit more detail, beginning with the question of authorship.

Who Wrote Ephesians?

If you've recently read through Ephesians, you might think this is a needless question, since in the first verse, the author identifies himself as "Paul, an apostle of Christ Jesus by the will of God" (1:1). Later, he refers to himself as "I, Paul, the prisoner of Christ Jesus for the sake of you Gentiles" (3:1). There then follows an autobiographical section in which the author, who portrays himself as Paul, speaks of his personal calling to make known to the Gentiles the mystery of Christ. In the closing verses of the letter, the author does not identify himself by name, but he does refer to Tychicus, who will let the recipients of the letter know how the writer is doing. Tychicus is known from other New Testament writings as Paul's companion and messenger.[3]

On the surface, therefore, Ephesians appears to have been written by Paul, the same "apostle of Christ Jesus" who wrote other letters with the same opening identification (see 1 Cor 1:1; 2 Cor 1:1; Col 1:1). Beneath the surface, too, there is much other evidence in favor of Pauline authorship. For example,

2. For a photo of this manuscript, see http://quod.lib.umich.edu/cgi/i/image/image-idx?rgn1=apis_inv;q1=6238;size=20;c=apis;subview=detail;resnum=39;view=entry;lastview=thumbnail;cc=apis;entryid=x-3595;viewid=6238_146.TIF.

3. See Acts 20:4; Col 4:7; 2 Tim 4:12; Titus 3:12.

the author is clearly an expert in Pauline theology, one who not only can write like the apostle but also whose theological vision spans the cosmos, just like Paul's does. The author of Ephesians is also deeply versed in the Old Testament, knowing both its grand story and many particular passages. This writer, like the writer of Romans, Galatians, and the other letters of Paul, is convinced that Christ is the focus of God's work throughout the creation.

For the first eighteen years of my life, it never occurred to me that Paul might not have written Ephesians. But in my freshman year at Harvard I took "Introduction to Early Christian Literature" taught by George Mac-Rae, a world-renowned biblical scholar and a learned and engaging lecturer. He didn't appear to have an axe to grind when it came to questions like the authorship of Ephesians. Rather, he presented the evidence in a calm, convincing manner, making a strong case for the authorship of Ephesians by someone other than Paul, presumably by one of Paul's closest disciples.

I had never heard anything like this before, and I found it quite upsetting. I wondered if Prof. MacRae was some sort of radical thinker, given his denial of Pauline authorship. I discovered that he was not. For seventeen centuries Christians had assumed that Paul wrote Ephesians. But in 1792 an English pastor named Evanson expressed his conviction that Paul did not write this letter. Few agreed with him until the late nineteenth century, when many scholars argued against the traditional view of Pauline authorship. From that time onward, New Testament scholarship has been split down the middle on this issue.[4]

Why did Prof. MacRae believe that Ephesians had been written by a follower of Paul, but not Paul himself? He pointed to some of the data we have already noted: the lofty writing style that differs from Paul's other letters; the lack of an obvious life setting for the letter; and the absence of familiar Pauline perspectives, as well as the introduction of unexpected theological emphases (such as what is called "realized eschatology"; see comments under "The Context and Purpose of Ephesians"). Moreover, Prof. MacRae pointed to other factors: the use of language in Ephesians that does not appear in Paul's other letters; greater emphasis on the resurrection-exaltation of Christ than on the cross; and the unusually close relationship of Ephesians to Colossians, which Prof. MacRae took to be solid evidence for the fact that a disciple of Paul copied from Colossians when writing Ephesians. More generally, I learned in class that the overall tone, theology, and vantage point of Ephesians reflects a time after the death of Paul when the church was more established, when Christ's return did not seem as imminent, and when the founders of the church could

---

4. See Hoehner, *Ephesians*, 6–20.

be identified as "God's holy apostles and prophets" (3:5)—something the real Paul would not have said, according to Prof. MacRae.

Nevertheless, said Prof. MacRae, the possibility that Ephesians is "pseudonymous," that is, written by someone who appropriated the name of Paul, does not undermine its authority. He explained that in the Roman world people commonly wrote in the name of someone else. Such a practice was not considered to be dishonest but was a way for a writer to honor some more famous thinker, to develop that thinker's ideas in creative ways, and to gain credibility for a new document. Since we have many examples in early Christian literature of pseudepigrapha (people writing books and using the name of a more famous person as its supposed author), Prof. MacRae argued that we should not be scandalized by the non-Pauline authorship of Ephesians.[5]

So during my years at Harvard, both as an undergraduate and a grad student in New Testament, I assumed that Paul did *not* write Ephesians. I did not know a single professor or fellow student who believed otherwise. It made sense to me that one of Paul's brilliant disciples, seeking to apply Paul's theology for a new day, took Colossians as his model and wrote the letter we call Ephesians. He wrote as if he were Paul, not intending to deceive anyone, since his readers would have known who actually wrote the letter. The writer of Ephesians did such a fine job that, before long, Christians who did not know the real origins of the letter thought Paul had written it himself.

Since my days at Harvard, my view on the authorship of Ephesians has changed again. There are several reasons for this. Partly, I no longer find the arguments against Pauline authorship of Ephesians to be persuasive. Plus, I find the arguments for his authorship to be more reasonable, though I recognize that wise scholars and godly Christians can disagree about this.[6] One of the problems with the question of who wrote Ephesians is that, in the end, it involves a subjective judgment. Yes, that judgment should be based on objective evidence. But when all is said and done, each scholar has to come to his or her own conclusions: "This just doesn't sound like the real Paul to me," or "I hear the genuine voice of Paul in this letter."

I don't mean to imply that there are no decent arguments for and against Pauline authorship. There are. Yet some of the main arguments against Pauline authorship of Ephesians clearly beg the question. Consider this point made by Andrew Lincoln, who believes Paul did not write Ephesians: "Apart from the

---

5. This view of pseudonymous writing in early Christianity has met with opposition in the last couple of decades. For a concise, readable summary of the arguments for and against the practice of pseudonymity in the early church, see Cohick, *Ephesians*, 5–27.

6. Tom Yoder Neufeld, one of my dearest friends in grad school, a Christian scholar for whom I have the utmost respect, and a true lover of Ephesians, argues in his commentary that authorship by a follower of Paul makes the most sense of the evidence. See Yoder Neufeld, *Ephesians*, 24–28.

fact that the undisputed letters of Paul (including Romans) are addressed to specific concrete needs of his churches, whereas Ephesians is far more general, there are some other major reasons for thinking that the case for pseudonymity is the stronger one."[7] Lincoln assumes that one major argument against Pauline authorship is the fact that Ephesians "is far more general" than "the undisputed letters of Paul." He recognizes that other reasons are needed. But he doesn't acknowledge the fallacy of one of the most common arguments against Pauline authorship. The argument goes like this: The real Paul wrote to his churches, addressing specific, concrete needs. Ephesians is general, not addressing specific needs of churches. Therefore, Paul did not write Ephesians. Of course, this argument completely begs the question. It simply assumes that Paul *never* wrote general letters, an assumption for which we have absolutely no evidence. In fact, one could well argue that we have a major piece of contrary evidence, namely, Ephesians itself. But many scholars simply assume that Paul did not write general letters, so they dismiss the evidence that disproves their assumption. This kind of methodology prevents many scholars from seeing Ephesians in its uniqueness as a general letter from Paul, and therefore a letter that is different from the others in many ways.[8]

In addition to seeing the flaws in many of the arguments against Pauline authorship of Ephesians, my personal perspective on communication in ministry settings has changed since my days in grad school. At that time, like most biblical scholars, I spent countless hours poring over ancient texts. I saw the world of early Christianity mainly in terms of the relationships between texts. So, if Ephesians is curiously like Colossians, then, surely, one of the letters must be dependent on the other. And if some words in Ephesians don't show up in Paul's other letters, then this odd phenomenon is best explained by the hypothesis of a different writer for Ephesians. From the perspective of a person studying the Bible in a library, this made sense.

But then I left the university and entered the "real" world of pastoral ministry. During my twenty-three years as a parish pastor, I gave several thousand speeches (teachings, sermons, lectures). I preached in academic settings that required learned rhetoric, in children's sermons that called for colorful simplicity, in traditional worship settings that required mature wisdom, and in cutting-edge worship services that demanded spontaneity and casual speech. Every weekend during my last three years at Irvine Presbyterian Church I

---

7. Lincoln, *Ephesians*, lxii.

8. If you are interested in the complex arguments for and against Pauline authorship of Ephesians, I would recommend two sources. Lincoln is an evangelical scholar who once affirmed Paul's authorship but later changed his mind. You can find his reasoning in his commentary (*Ephesians*, lix–lxxiii). An extraordinarily detailed case in favor of Pauline authorship is found in Hoehner, *Ephesians*, 2–61.

preached basically the same sermon in four different settings (baby-boomer contemporary service, two traditional services, one millennial-edgy service). Yet each version of the sermon differed from the others in style, language usage, and occasionally, theological insight. By my fourth version, sometimes I had seen something new in the text and added that point to my sermon. If, in a hundred years, a library-bound academic were to study transcripts of my sermons, I'm quite sure this scholar would conclude that the same person did not preach all of these sermons. There would be way too much divergence in language, style, illustrations, and even theological nuance. That scholar would probably conclude that, in addition to the authentic Mark Roberts, there were several others who based their preaching on mine and, for some reason, attributed their sermons to me.

I realize the analogy between my sermons and Paul's letters is imprecise. But my point is that Paul and his disciples were not sitting in libraries, studying texts and writing papers. They were out preaching, teaching, founding churches, and pastoring them. They were continually facing new challenges, confronting new philosophies, hearing new words, discovering new truths, and seeing with new eyes. They held fast to the same core truth, the *regula fidei* or "rule of faith" based in the gospel. Yet they expressed this truth in various ways, sometimes repeating things they had said or written before, sometimes creating new ways to say the same things, sometimes saying altogether new things they had recently discovered.

So when I now read Colossians and then Ephesians, I have no trouble imagining that the same person wrote both of these letters, most likely through the use of a secretary, as was common practice in that day. Because they were written at about the same time, they are quite similar in many ways. But Colossians addresses a particular challenge in a particular church, like most of Paul's letters; Ephesians does not. Yet it sounds very much like Colossians in places, sometimes using the same words in the same order. On the one hand, Ephesians is innovative and creative in ways Colossians is not. If you sit down and imagine someone actually trying to write Ephesians on the basis of Colossians, even Paul himself, you end up with a project that could happen only in some quiet library filled with obscure texts and few distractions. On the other hand, if you envision a busy church planter and pastor trying to write one specific letter to a hurting church and one general letter to many churches, it's easy to imagine Paul writing both. The approach we will take in this commentary is that Paul himself wrote Colossians and Ephesians.[9]

---

9. I will not devote much space in this commentary to analyzing the close relationship between Colossians and Ephesians. The reader can find this kind of analysis in all recent scholarly commentaries on Ephesians.

The Context and Purpose of Ephesians

Though I believe Paul wrote Ephesians, clearly it is different from his other letters, and these distinctives help to reveal the context, message, and purpose of the letter. We need to ask questions like: When and where was Ephesians written? To whom was it written, and why? Other commentaries lay out in detail the possible answers to these questions and the evidence supporting them. I do not have the space for such analysis here. Rather, the reader may consult other, more technical commentaries. For my part, I will tell a story that should account for the particular content and unusual characteristics of Ephesians.

This story begins in Acts 19 with Paul's visit to Ephesus in Asia Minor (Acts 19:1). He began preaching there in the Jewish synagogue, but some (not all) of the Jews refused to accept his message and "became obstinate" (Acts 19:9). As a result, Paul moved the location of his preaching from the synagogue to a private lecture hall. There, he proclaimed the gospel for two years, "so that all the Jews and Greeks who lived in the province of Asia [in western Asia Minor] heard the word of the Lord" (Acts 19:10). Many Jews and Greeks held the name of Jesus "in high honor" because of miraculous deeds done in his name (Acts 19:17).

Later, Paul decided to go to Jerusalem and from there eventually to Rome (Acts 19:21). His departure from Ephesus was hastened by a "great disturbance" in the city, led by craftsmen who made money selling trinkets in honor of Artemis and who rioted because the success of Paul's ministry was negatively affecting their bottom line (Acts 19:23–29). When a Jew named Alexander tried to defend Paul to the mob, he was shouted down (Acts 19:33–34). Finally, the uproar ended and Paul departed.

Paul traveled to Macedonia and Greece on his way to Jerusalem, accompanied by several companions, including a man named Tychicus (Acts 20:2–6). On a short return trip to Asia Minor, Paul decided to bypass Ephesus because he figured he'd be slowed down in his effort to get to Jerusalem (Acts 20:15–16). He did take time, however, to meet with some of the elders from the Ephesian church while in nearby Miletus (Acts 20:17–38).

Finally, Paul arrived in Jerusalem, where he was warmly welcomed (Acts 21:17). Yet when some Jews who were visiting from Asia Minor saw Paul in the temple, they stirred up the crowd, accusing Paul of opposing the Jewish people and bringing Gentiles into the temple, thus defiling it (Acts 21:27–29). As a mob was trying to kill Paul, the Roman commander in Jerusalem intervened. He arrested Paul, but gave him time to make his defense to the crowd (Acts 21:33–22:21). When the crowd began to riot, the commander gave the order that Paul be flogged (Acts 22:22–24). But when he learned

that Paul was a Roman citizen, he backed off (Acts 22:29). Once again, Paul's
Jewish opponents tried to kill him, so the commander sequestered Paul in the
barracks (Acts 23:10). The following night, the Lord appeared to Paul in a
vision and said, "Take courage! As you have testified about me in Jerusalem, so
you must also testify in Rome" (Acts 23:11). As he continued to be harassed
and threatened by his Jewish opponents, Paul appealed to Caesar, a request
that meant he would be transferred to Rome under house arrest. Finally, after
many adventures, Paul made it to Rome where he lived along with a soldier
to guard him (to whom he was chained; Acts 28:16). He remained in Rome
for two years, where he "welcomed all who came to see him" and "taught
about the Lord Jesus Christ—with all boldness and without hindrance" (Acts
28:30–31).

Among the visitors Paul received while in Rome were people from Asia
Minor, including Tychicus and Epaphras, who was from Colossae (Col 4:7–
13). No doubt these two men and others informed Paul of what was happening in the churches of Asia Minor. It's likely that Epaphras and Paul prayed
together for these churches (Col 4:12–13).

During this time Paul felt a need to write to the churches in Asia Minor.
He dictated the letter we know as Colossians in order to help that church in
a time of theological confusion. He wrote the letter to Philemon, a Christian
in Colossae, to appeal for Onesimus, one of Philemon's slaves. Both of these
letters were typical of the Pauline letters we know since they were addressed
to specific people in reference to specific problems. Paul wrote another letter
at this time to the church in Laodicea (a nearby town in Asia Minor; see Col
4:16). This letter has apparently been lost.

In addition to the letters to Colossians, Philemon, and Laodicea, Paul
decided to write another letter to Asia Minor; he would send it with Tychicus
when he traveled there. This letter would be different from Paul's usual cor-
respondence. It would not be a response to a particular situation in a specific
church but rather a general letter meant for several. It would be written in a
more thoughtful, elevated style, since it would have wide readership, perhaps
even beyond a first reading in the churches to which it would be sent. To
give this letter the solemnity it deserved, Paul drew upon traditional sources,
including the Old Testament and material from early Christian worship: he
borrowed phrases from Christian hymns, even quoting a whole line in one
place (Eph 5:14). He wanted to model for the recipients of the letter how
they too might speak to each other "with psalms, hymns, and songs from the
Spirit" (5:19).

Because there was not one specific destination for this letter, Paul did not
follow his standard approach and identify the recipients by their location.

Rather, he left a blank that Tychicus would fill in with the appropriate place name, "to the saints in Colossae," "to the saints in Laodicea," "to the saints in *Ephesus*." If a church wanted to save a copy of this circular letter for later use, then they could make a copy, penning in their location in the opening address. At least one church did this, the church in Ephesus. Thus, from the beginning, at least one copy of Paul's letter mentioned the Ephesians, while other manuscripts did not.

Like all of his letters, Paul's circular letter was centered in the gospel and its implications. It told the story of what God had done in Christ. It spelled out the ethical implications of this story with practical exhortation that flowed from the narrative and didactic parts of the letter.

Yet this letter was different, not only in its style and not only because it lacked specifics of a community-based letter, but also because it included some of Paul's more recent reflections on God's purposes for the world. This letter centered in God's intention "to bring unity to all things in heaven and on earth under Christ" (1:10). The theme of unity permeated the letter, influencing how Paul told the story of Christ's saving work on the cross (2:11–22) and how he talked about the purpose of the church (3:9–10). The essential importance of unity was the core of Paul's ethical instruction (4:1–6), and it shaped his teaching on how Christians are to live with each other as members of Christ's body (4:7–5:2). A focus on unity also gave Paul a unique way to talk about marriage and the obligations of wives and husbands, and to see in marriage an illustration of the unity between Christ and the church (5:21–33).

Paul also determined to develop in this circular letter some reflections on eschatology. He still saw all of history heading in the direction of God's glorious future (1:10, 14, 18; 2:7; 4:30; 6:24). Yet Paul wanted to explore some ideas he had hinted at in his other letters, thoughts about how Christians can experience the reality of God's grace and power right now. Even though the final resurrection of believers is still in the future, in a sense believers have already been raised with Christ (2:4–6). This unusual use of resurrection language gave Paul a new way to develop the vision of life he had shared in 2 Corinthians 5:17: "Therefore, if anyone is in Christ, the new creation has come: The old has gone, the new is here!"

So with the letter he had dictated to the Colossians still ringing in his ears, perhaps even with a copy nearby, Paul dictated another letter, the circular letter that Tychicus would deliver and read in the churches of Asia Minor, including the congregation in Ephesus. Even though this letter was rather impersonal, the Ephesian Christians regarded it as a message written for them, and so they added in to their copy, "To God's holy people *in Ephesus*" (1:1). The rest, as they say, is history.

The Story of God in Ephesians

It's not hard to imagine why Paul might have written the letter we know as
Ephesians. (By the way, though this letter was not originally intended only
for Ephesus, from now on I will call it Ephesians, rather than "the letter we
know as Ephesians." I will also refer to the letter's recipients as "recipients" or
"readers," even though most of them heard the letter read in church gatherings.) Paul wanted to tell the story of God in a new way and from this story
draw out implications for how his readers might live out the story. I use this
language of story not just because this commentary is part of The Story of
God series but also because what we find in Ephesians, especially chapters
1–3, is literally a *story of God*.

In this story, God has done the following: blessed us in Christ, chosen us
in Christ, destined us through Christ, bestowed grace on us in the Beloved,
redeemed us, forgiven us, lavished grace on us, made known the mystery of his
will to us, set forth his will in Christ, marked us with the Spirit, raised Christ
from the dead, seated Christ in the highest heavens, put all things under Christ's
feet, made Christ head of the church, loved us greatly, made us alive with Christ,
raised us with Christ, seated us with Christ in heaven, saved us by grace, created
us anew in Christ, gave us good works to do, brought us near in Christ, built
us into his temple, commissioned Paul as a steward of the gospel, revealed the
mystery of the gospel, acted according to his eternal purpose, called us, gave us
grace for ministry, and made us light in the Lord. If we were to add to this list
the actions that God will do in the future, plus actions in which Christ is the
stated actor, plus other implied actions, the list might be twice as long.

The story begins before the creation of the world (1:4), and it ends in
God's glorious future, when he will unite all things in Christ (1:10). In that
future day, God will fully inherit his people as his prized possession (1:14,
18), and he will show "the incomparable riches of his grace, expressed in his
kindness to us in Christ Jesus" (2:7). The story of God is centered in Christ,
in whom God acts and who died on the cross to bring unity and peace to
broken humanity (2:11–22). God, who is identified as our Father and the
Father of Christ (1:2–3), is also manifested in the activity of the Holy Spirit
(1:13; 2:18; 3:5, 16; 4:3, 30; 6:17). Though Paul does not refer specifically
to "the Trinity," the roots of what would later be called Trinitarianism grow
deeply into the soil of Ephesians.

God is the primary actor in the story of Ephesians. In the narrative of the
first three chapters, human beings receive the benefits of God's gracious election, adoption, redemption, and reconciliation. Perhaps the most famous verse
in Ephesians crowns this story, "For it is by grace you have been saved, through
faith" (2:8).

From this perspective, it might almost seem as if we are mere pawns in God's giant chess game rather than people who participate actively in the game. Yet, even though chapters 1–3 focus on God's activity, they also reveal our involvement in God's story. God chose us to be holy, that is, to be set apart for him and his work (1:4). God predestined us so that we might exist "to the praise of his glory" (1:11–14). As God saved us by grace, he also created us anew in Christ, giving us good works to do (2:10). We, as the church together, are to make known God's wisdom to the spiritual powers in the heavenly realms (3:10). God is "able to do immeasurably more than all we ask or imagine, according to his power that is *at work within us*" (3:20, emphasis added).

Ephesians 4–6 spells out the nature of our participation in greater detail, urging us to live our lives worthy of the calling that was revealed in Ephesians 1–3 (see 4:1). At the heart of this calling, we are told to maintain the unity of God's people that is forged by the Holy Spirit (4:3). Moreover, we are to participate together with Christ in unifying and building his body (4:7–16). In every part of life, including our family and work life, we are to live the story of God (5:21–6:9).

Ephesians reveals that God has drawn us into his work of uniting all things in Christ. The good works he has prepared for us involve nurturing the unity of God's people and participating in the growth of Christ's body (4:1–16). As we live out and proclaim the good news of God's work in Christ, the spiritual powers of the cosmos will see God's wisdom in us (and so will our fellow human beings). As people who have been changed from darkness to light, we have the opportunity to shine the light of Christ into the darkness, thus exposing the darkness and giving those who still live in it the chance to become light themselves (5:8–13). To them we say, as the old hymn goes, "Wake up, sleeper, rise from the dead, and Christ will shine on you" (5:14). Yet, because of the spiritual nature of our battle to reclaim the darkness for God, we must put on God's armor and fight with his strength. We fight by sharing the good news of God's word and by praying all the time for all of God's people.

Thus, we are not incidental to God's story. Nor are we merely those upon whom God acts. Rather, we are, by grace, participants in God's story, sharers together in his work of redemption in Christ.

The Essential Role of the Church

Notice that I said "sharers *together* in his work of redemption in Christ." The theme of togetherness fills the story of Ephesians, underscoring the essential role of the church in the plan of God.

The "together" aspect of our life in Christ is seen in a striking stylistic and linguistic feature of Ephesians. Unfortunately, this might be missed in our English translations, but in the Greek it stands out clearly. In the letter Paul uses ten different words that begin with some version of the Greek word *sun*, which means "with." These words convey the following:

God *made us alive* together with Christ (2:5)
God *raised us* together with Christ (2:6)
God *seated us* together with Christ (2:6)
We are *citizens* together with the saints (2:19)
We are *joined* together with other parts of God's building (2:21)
We are *being built* together with other parts of God's building (2:22)
We are *heirs* together with Israel (3:6)
We are *members* together with each other in the body (3:6)
We are *sharers* together with each other in the promise (3:6)
We are *joined* together with each other in Christ's body (4:16; see also 2:21)
We are *held* together with each other in Christ's body (4:16)

The unusual inclusion and combination of these words underscores the "together-with-ness" of the Christian life. We are together with Christ and therefore together with each other.

One of the salient features of the story of God in Ephesians is the central role of the church in his plan. When Ephesians refers to the church, it is what we sometimes call the "universal church," namely, the gathering of all Christians everywhere and at every time. Because we are all "in Christ," there is a sense in which we are all together in one cosmic congregation. This is unusual language for Paul, who generally prefers to use "church," *ekklēsia* in Greek, to refer to particular congregations. Generally, but not always: 1 Corinthians shows that he can also think of the church as inclusive of all believers (see 1 Cor 1:2; also 12:27–28).

In part, the unusual use of "church" in Ephesians has something to do with the fact that the letter is not intended for a single church, but for multiple congregations. Yet beyond this, Ephesians offers a deeper and wider insight into the nature of the people of God united in the church. The church is Christ's "body, the fullness of him who fills everything in every way" (1:23). The church is the demonstration of the gospel to the cosmic powers (3:10). The church as the body of Christ grows as all members participate (4:15–16). The church is loved by Christ, who seeks to present the church to himself as a radiant, holy, blameless bride (5:25–27). The church is profoundly united to Christ, even as a husband and wife are united in marriage (5:31–32). The church, along with Christ himself, is the locus of God's glory on earth throughout all generations (3:21).

The essential role of the church in Ephesians reminds us not to read this letter as if it were addressed only to separate individuals. To be sure, the good news of Ephesians transforms our personal lives, and each of us should individually follow its exhortations. Yet Ephesians is written not just to a bunch of disconnected, solo Christians but to Christians unified "through the bond of peace" (4:3). The work of Christ saves each one of us individually, thanks be to God (2:8). But the cross also breaks down "the dividing wall of hostility" between groups of people, so that Christ can unite people together into one new humanity (2:14). Such unity is not just some unintended benefit of the gospel; it is an essential part of Christ's saving work.

For those of us who were raised in North American culture, which places a high premium on individualism, we tend to read Ephesians as if Paul were speaking just to each of us as *individuals*. Yet the text continually invites us to see ourselves and God's work among us as a *community* of people. In a day when Christians are seeking new forms of corporate life, in a time when traditional church structures are failing right and left, in a time when Christians are wondering what it really means to be church and do church, Ephesians speaks to us with as much power and relevance as it once spoke to the churches of Asia Minor.

The Story of God in Human Stories

I am glad that about a third of this commentary, like others in the Story of God series, is dedicated to how we might "live the story" today. Because of this focus, I have seen many things in the text that I would otherwise have missed. But God's story is not only to be read, understood, and believed. It is also to be lived by God's people.

In the "Live the Story" sections of this commentary, I tell stories of people who are seeking to live God's story as told in Ephesians. Many of these stories are from my own life. I tell them, in part, because I am convinced that preachers and teachers in the church should share their lives, not just the content of their teaching, with those they teach. I got this idea from Paul, by the way: in describing his ministry among the Thessalonians, he writes, "Because we loved you so much, we were delighted to share with you not only the gospel of God but our lives as well" (1 Thess 2:8). Thus, after he finished writing Ephesians, Paul sent it with Tychicus, who not only delivered the letter to various churches but also told them "everything, so that you also may know how I am and what I am doing. I am sending him to you for this very purpose, that you may know how we are, and that he may encourage you" (Eph 6:21–22). I hope that by sharing my own example of living the story of God in Ephesians, you will indeed be encouraged to do so yourself. Should you ever want to share with me your own cases of living the story of God in Ephesians, I'd be delighted to hear them.

CHAPTER 1

Ephesians 1:1-2

📖 LISTEN to the Story

¹Paul, an apostle of Christ Jesus by the will of God,
To God's holy people in Ephesus, the faithful in Christ Jesus:
²Grace and peace to you from God our Father and the Lord Jesus
Christ.

Listening to the text in the Story: Exodus 19:5–6; Leviticus 19:1–2; Acts
9:1–19; 2 Corinthians 1:1–2; Galatians 1:1–17; Colossians 1:1–2.

The opening section of Ephesians reflects the standard form of a personal letter in the Greco-Roman world of the first century. Paul adapts this basic form
to set the stage for what is to come, introducing not only himself but also the
principal characters of the story told in the letter, God the Father and the Lord
Jesus Christ. Moreover, he uses the greeting in verse 2 to present theological
concepts, grace and peace, that will figure prominently in the rest of Ephesians.

🔦 EXPLAIN the Story

The Letter Writer and Recipients (1:1)

Letters written in Greek ("Hellenistic" letters) from the time of Paul began
with a basic form: name of writer, name of recipient, and greeting. Sometimes
this introduction was followed by a prayer to the gods, either as a thanksgiving or as a wish. So, for example, a third-century AD writer began his letter,
"Aurelius Dius to Aurelius Horion, my sweetest father, many greetings. I make
supplication for you every day before the gods of this place."[1]

Paul, an apostle of Christ Jesus (1:1) Though many scholars believe this
letter was actually written by a disciple of the apostle Paul, there are good
reasons to believe that Ephesians was, in fact, written (or composed and

---

1. "137. From a Student to his Father," *Select Papyri, Volume I: Private Documents*, trans. A. S.
Hunt and C. C. Edgar, LCL 266 (Cambridge: Harvard, 1932), 343, 345.

dictated) by Paul himself. (See Introduction for more detail.) The basic meaning of "apostle" in Greek is "envoy" or "messenger."[2] Apostles were authorized by someone and given authority to carry messages on the sender's behalf. So Paul's authorization came from "Christ Jesus by the will of God." In some of his letters Paul emphasizes his authority as an apostle (2 Corinthians; Galatians), but he does not do so in Ephesians. In fact, the other three uses of the word "apostle" in Ephesians are plural, including other people besides or in addition to Paul (2:20; 3:5; 4:11). In his self-introduction as an apostle, Paul underscores the fact that he has this role not by his own choice but because God chose him.

To God's holy people in Ephesus, the faithful in Christ Jesus (1:1). Ephesus was among the cities for which this letter was written. Yet as we saw in the Introduction, the words "in Ephesus" do not appear in several of the most important ancient manuscripts of Ephesians. Given the uncertain tie between the letter of Ephesians and the church of Ephesus, and given the unusual lack of detail in the letter related to any specific congregation in a particular location, it seems wise to interpret this letter without overemphasizing its connection to Ephesus.

The English phrase "God's holy people" translates a plural form of the Greek word *hagios*. Typically, *hagioi* is rendered as "saints" (ESV, NRSV, KJV), but "God's holy people" faithfully captures the meaning of the original. Paul typically addresses the recipients of his letters with this designation. Given our contemporary use of the word "saint," it's important to remember that *all* believers, not just special Christians, are saints. (For further detail, see commentary on 1:4 below.)

Those who receive Paul's letter are not just holy people, but also "the faithful in Christ Jesus." Though "faithful" in Greek could mean "trustworthy," here it probably refers to those who believe in Christ (see 1:13, 1:15). The phrase "in Christ Jesus" is pregnant with meaning that will be explored further (see discussion of "In Christ" in reference to 1:3).

The Greeting (1:2)

The greeting in verse 2, "Grace and peace to you from God our Father and the Lord Jesus Christ," is the standard Pauline salutation, found with exactly the same Greek words, and in the same order, in six other Pauline letters.[3]

Grace and peace (1:2). With the word "grace," Paul employs a curious play on words. Usually, first-century Greek letters began with *chairein*, the infinitive of the verb "to rejoice," which means "greetings" (for example, Acts

---

2. BDAG 122.
3. Rom 1:7; 1 Cor 1:3; 2 Cor 1:2; Gal 1:3; Phil 1:2; Phlm 3.

23:26; James 1:1). Paul chose instead to use the word *charis*, which means "grace" and sounds like *chairein*. To this he added the word *eirēnē*, which means "peace" in Greek and echoes the traditional Hebrew greeting, *Shalom*. So, "grace and peace" is a Christianized greeting that combines both Greek and Jewish elements. As far as we know, Paul himself coined this particular greeting, which shows up in several later New Testament letters (1 Pet, 2 Pet, Rev). Paul's invention is rather like when a Christian ends a letter with "Yours in Christ" rather than the common secular ending "Yours truly." Paul took that which was culturally common and tweaked it to carry a new message. Though we who know the collection of Paul's letters are not surprised by the phrase "grace and peace," his original readers (rather, listeners, since his letters were read in churches) might have been surprised by what they heard. It sounded familiar, yet curiously different. They might have wondered why Paul made this unusual rhetorical move. What is so special about grace and peace?

In fact, the letter to Ephesians will explain in depth the extraordinary importance of grace and peace. These major themes of the letter are central to the good news. Moreover, at the end of the letter Paul will once again bring up the subjects of peace (6:23) and grace (6:24). In between the beginning and the end, he will mention grace or peace an additional sixteen times.

Grace and peace come not from Paul or his good wishes but "from God our Father and the Lord Jesus Christ" (1:2). God is not some distant, impersonal being, but rather one who can be known intimately as "our Father." Jesus is called "Christ," a term which, in Ephesians, may or may not still echo its Semitic source, "Messiah," the anointed one of God. Jesus Christ is "the Lord," a term often used by Jews for God. Thus, verse 2 reveals a striking partnership between God and Jesus, one in which Jesus is pictured as divine, not merely human.

LIVE the Story

Often, the opening scene of a story introduces one or more of the main characters. In the first chapter of Charles Dickens's classic novel *Great Expectations*, for example, we are introduced to the protagonist, Philip Pirrip, better known as Pip, as well as a convict who seems relatively inconsequential at first but who turns out to play a pivotal role in the narrative. Right from the start, we know two of the major players in Dickens's story.

Ephesians begins in a similar way. The opening verses introduce the main characters of the story found in this letter. Yes, these characters include Paul, the apostle who writes the letter, as well as its recipients, who are believers in

Christ. Both Paul and the recipients figure prominently in the story told in the letter.

But if we pay close attention to the first two verses of Ephesians, and especially if we compare these with other Hellenistic letters written around the same time, we are struck by the repetitive appearance of two other main characters. Paul is named once. The saints who are receiving the letter are named once. But Christ is named three times, and so is God, who is identified as "our Father" (1:2).

The starring role of these two divine persons (the Spirit is introduced later, in 1:13) is seen not only in how often they are named but also in their function. Paul is an apostle because God willed him to be so (1:1). Grace and peace come "from God the Father and the Lord Jesus Christ" (1:2). Thus, in a short introduction we are introduced to the main actor of the drama that will soon unfold: the God whose will defines the center of the narrative (1:9–10) and from whom comes the grace that changes everything (1:6–7; 2:5–8) and the peace that results from the grace given through Christ (2:14–17).

Thus, the opening verses of Ephesians do not just parrot the words of a first-century form letter. Rather, they introduce the main characters and begin to reveal ways in which these characters determine the narrative that follows. The grace that transforms our lives and the peace that comes as a result of grace are not things we produce through our own ingenuity and effort. Rather, they are gifts "from God our Father and the Lord Jesus Christ" (1:2). Ephesians is, more than anything else, the story *of God*.

CHAPTER 2

Ephesians 1:3-14

📖 LISTEN to the Story

³Praise be to the God and Father of our Lord Jesus Christ, who has blessed us in the heavenly realms with every spiritual blessing in Christ. ⁴For he chose us in him before the creation of the world to be holy and blameless in his sight. In love ⁵he predestined us for adoption to sonship through Jesus Christ, in accordance with his pleasure and will—⁶to the praise of his glorious grace, which he has freely given us in the One he loves. ⁷In him we have redemption through his blood, the forgiveness of sins, in accordance with the riches of God's grace ⁸that he lavished on us. With all wisdom and understanding, ⁹he made known to us the mystery of his will according to his good pleasure, which he purposed in Christ, ¹⁰to be put into effect when the times reach their fulfillment—to bring unity to all things in heaven and on earth under Christ.

¹¹In him we were also chosen, having been predestined according to the plan of him who works out everything in conformity with the purpose of his will, ¹²in order that we, who were the first to put our hope in Christ, might be for the praise of his glory. ¹³And you also were included in Christ when you heard the message of truth, the gospel of your salvation. When you believed, you were marked in him with a seal, the promised Holy Spirit, ¹⁴who is a deposit guaranteeing our inheritance until the redemption of those who are God's possession—to the praise of his glory.

Listening to the text in the Story: Genesis 1–3; 12:1–3; Exodus 1–20; Psalm 103; Mark 1:9–11; Romans 8; 2 Corinthians 5:16–21.

Ordinarily, Paul follows his greeting by offering thanks to God for the recipients of the letter. In the case of Ephesians, however, an extensive section comes before the thanksgiving, which begins in 1:15. The section that stretches from verse 3 to verse 14 commences and concludes with praise to God, and might rightly be called a doxology or even a eulogy (see commentary on 1:3). The whole section comprises a 202-word sentence in Greek, the longest in the New Testament. English translations divide the Greek sentence into several smaller sentences; the NIV uses eight. But it's not just the length of the Greek sentence that impresses the reader. Its words and images are also grand, stretching our minds to consider the greatness of God, the riches of his grace, and his stunning plan for the cosmos.

Ephesians opens by telling the story of God, quite literally. God the Father is the chief author and actor in the story of Ephesians as he acts in and through Christ. The Holy Spirit is mentioned as well (1:13–14). The story of God in 1:3–14 begins "before the creation of the world" (1:4) and ends with the consummation of history (1:10).

The narrative in this section focuses on God's activity in Christ but includes us Christians as those whom God writes into his story. Thus, the divine story becomes our story as well. It shapes our fundamental identity and purpose. Everything about our lives can be governed and transformed by the story of God in Christ. The more we reflect on this story, the more we will see ourselves differently and live differently. Yet, the goal of 1:3–14 is not to make us self-aware but rather to point us to the knowledge of God that inspires us to praise him.

⚡ EXPLAIN the Story

Summary of Ephesians 1:3–14

Ephesians 1:3–14 lavishly praises God for his gloriously gracious work in the world. Though the words of this sentence are woven together in an almost seamless narrative, for ease of interpretation we can break up this passage into three sections. Verses 3–6 bless God for his manifold blessings to us, which include choosing us to belong to him as his holy children. Verses 7–10 celebrate our redemption in Christ and the revelation God has made to us of his plan to unite all things in Christ. Verses 11–14 spell out the chief purpose of our lives: we exist for the praise of God's glory. Ephesians 1:3–14 begins and ends with praise and could be called a "blessing,"[1] "eulogy,"[2] or "opening worship."[3]

This passage tells the story of what God has done, beginning before creation and ending with the summing up of all things at the end of history. God, identified as the "Father of our Lord Jesus Christ," does not act alone,

---

1. Barth, *Ephesians*, 76; Lincoln, *Ephesians*, 7.
2. O'Brien, *Ephesians*, 88; Cohick, *Ephesians*, 40.
3. Yoder Neufeld, *Ephesians*, 36.

however. What God does, he does "in Christ," a phrase repeated in one form or another eleven times throughout 1:3–14. Moreover, God's praiseworthy deeds draw human beings into the story as receivers of God's grace who, chosen by God, exist "for the praise of his glory" (1:12, 14).

Blessed Be God Who Has Blessed Us (1:3–6)

Praise . . . blessed us . . . blessing (1:3). Ephesians 1:3 begins with an expression of praise. Beneath the NIV's "Praise be to" God lies a Greek adjective, *eulogētos*, which can be translated as "blessed be" or "praise be to."[4] Yet "praise be to" unintentionally obscures the intended parallelism in verse 3. This verse contains three uses of words from the Greek root *eulog-*, which means "good word" and is related to the English word "eulogy": "Praise be to [*eulogētos*] the God and Father of our Lord Jesus Christ, who has blessed [*eulogēsas*] us in the heavenly realms with every spiritual blessing [*eulogia*] in Christ." Our action in blessing God is a result of God's prior action in blessing us. We bless God by speaking good words about him in response to how God has blessed us by doing good things for us. The threefold use of *eulog-* words establishes a pattern of God's action and our response, and it is seen throughout Ephesians. In fact, this pattern pervades the Bible, especially in the often repeated Hebrew blessing found, for example, in Psalm 72:18: "Blessed be the Lord, the God of Israel, who alone does wondrous things" (NRSV).

In the heavenly realms (1:3). Given the popular tendency to think of heaven as the abode of God "up there," not to mention the tendency to think of spiritual things as separate from the physical world, we might conclude that the blessings of God in verse 3 are saved up for our postmortem existence. Yet this misses the nuances of "heavenly realms" and "spiritual blessing." The Greek phrase translated in the NIV as "in the heavenly realms" is *en tois epouraniois*. It is literally "in the heavenlies," with "places" or "realms" implied. The plural may reflect the fact that the standard Hebrew word for heaven or sky is plural (*shamayim*). Moreover, the apocalyptic visionaries of intertestamental Judaism pictured heaven as being multilayered.[5] These heavenly realms were the domain of supernatural beings, including God.

---

4. BDAG 408.

5. 2 Cor 12:2–4. See also the Jewish writing T. Levi 3:1–8: "Listen, therefore, concerning the heavens which have been shown to you. The lowest is dark for this reason: It sees all the injustices of humankind and contains fire, snow, and ice, ready for the day determined by God's righteous judgment. In it are all the spirits of those dispatched to achieve the punishment of mankind. In the second are the armies arrayed for the day of judgment to work vengeance on the spirits of error and of Beliar. Above them are the Holy Ones. In the uppermost heaven of all dwells the Great Glory in the Holy of Holies superior to all holiness. There with him are the archangels, who serve and offer propitiatory sacrifices to the Lord in behalf of all the sins of ignorance of the righteous ones. They present to the Lord a pleasing odor, a rational and bloodless oblation. In the heaven below them

The phrase *en tois epouraniois* appears in the New Testament only in Ephesians, where it shows up five times: the heavenly realms are the place of spiritual blessing (1:3); the place where God and Christ are seated, above other supernatural powers (1:20–21); the place to which Christians have been raised and seated with Christ (2:6); and the place in which supernatural "rulers and authorities" dwell (3:10), including the "spiritual forces of evil" (6:12). In Ephesians, Satan is the "ruler of the kingdom of the air" (2:2), and Christ, who descended to the "lower, earthly regions," also "ascended higher than all the heavens [*ouranōn*]" (4:9–10). Drawing together all this evidence, we learn that the "heavenly realms" are the place where God is seated (in the highest level). Yet other supernatural beings, both good and evil, dwell in the heavenly realms. Human beings are influenced by what happens in the heavenly places, and, in fact, we who have received God's grace through Christ are already seated, in some sense, with Christ in the heavenly realms. Thus, the blessings God has given us "in the heavenly realms" are not something we enjoy only after we die or in rare moments of spiritual delight during our earthly existence; since we have already begun to live in the heavenly realms in Christ, we have already begun to experience God's blessings while we live in this world.

Spiritual blessing (1:3). Similarly, the word "spiritual" should not suggest something like "immaterial and otherworldly" and therefore irrelevant to everyday life. As we'll see when we get to the final verses of 1:3–14, we who have heard and believed "the gospel of [our] salvation. . . . were marked in [Christ] with a seal, the promised Holy Spirit" (1:13). Thus, our blessings are "spiritual," not because they are vague and intangible but because they are mediated by the Holy Spirit.

What are these blessings? They surely include the gracious gifts of God mentioned in 1:3–14: God chose us, predestined us, gave us his grace, redeemed us, forgave us, made known to us his plan for the cosmos, sealed us with the Holy Spirit, and gave us our true purpose for living. Paul will enumerate more of God's blessings throughout the rest of Ephesians, and even then he will only begin to identify the ways in which God has blessed us.

In Christ (1:3). God has blessed us "in Christ" (1:3). This phrase, or something similar, appears eleven times in verses 3–14. God blessed us "in Christ" (1:3) and chose us "in him" (1:4). God has given his grace to us "in the One he loves" (1:6). "In him" we are redeemed (1:7). God purposed his will "in

---

are the messengers who carry the responses to the angels of the Lord's presence. There with him are thrones and authorities; there praises to God are offered eternally" (*OTP*); also Apoc. Mos. 37:4–5: "[Adam] lay three hours, and so the Lord of all, sitting on his holy throne, stretched out his hands and took Adam and handed him over to the archangel Michael, saying to him, 'Take him up into Paradise, to the third heaven, and leave (him) there until that great and fearful day which I am about to establish for the world'" (*OTP*).

Christ" (1:9), which is to "bring unity to all things under Christ," including things in heaven and on earth "in him" (1:10).[6] "In him" those who were first to hope "in Christ" were chosen by God (1:11–12). Moreover, we who came to believe "in him" were also "included in Christ" (1:13).

What does the phrase "in Christ" mean (*en Christō* in Greek)?[7] "In Christ," "in the Lord," and similar phrases appear often in the letters of Paul, though rarely in the rest of the New Testament. The word *en* permits a wide array of interpretations. Many scholars argue that "in Christ" should be thought of in terms of *location*: believers in Jesus, though dwelling in this world, are also living "in Christ" as if he were a kind of place. Thus, Paul can write to "all God's holy people in [*en*] Christ Jesus at [*en*] Philippi" (Phil 1:1). Moreover, because we are *en Christō*, we have already been raised with Christ and live in the heavenly realms in him (Eph 2:6). But the Greek word *en* can also have an *instrumental* meaning, such as in 2 Corinthians 5:19: "God was reconciling the world to himself in Christ"; Christ was the agent through whom God was reconciling the world. *En Christō* can also be used to describe the *manner* in which something is done, such as in Romans 9:1, where Paul speaks the truth *en Christō*.

Constantine R. Campbell has shown that the phrase "in Christ" describes our union with Christ and participation in his life.[8] Being "in Christ" therefore is more than living in a new region. It is our sharing in a new life, the very life of Christ himself. Therefore, God's blessings come to us *en Christō*, not just through the agency of Christ, not just because we somehow live in the space defined by Christ, but also because we live in Christ, united with him, sharing in his life and love.[9]

He chose us. . . . predestined us (1:4–5). God's blessing us in Christ is illustrated by the fact that God "chose us in him before the creation of the world to be holy and blameless in his sight. In love he predestined us for adoption to sonship through Jesus Christ, in accordance with his pleasure and will" (1:4–5). For centuries these two verses have stirred up vigorous theological debate. Calvinists see these verses as demonstrating the truth of God's election and predestination of some to salvation and (in some Calvinist systems) others to damnation. For advocates of free will, these verses show that Christ is the chosen one and that

6. My translation varies from the NIV, which does not accurately represent the use of "in Christ" and "in him" in 1:10.

7. For a quick overview of the options, see M. A. Seifrid, "In Christ," *DPL* 433–36.

8. Constantine R. Campbell, *Paul and Union with Christ: An Exegetical and Theological Study* (Grand Rapids: Zondervan, 2012).

9. James D. G. Dunn, in his discussion of "Participation in Christ," writes that, for Paul, the phrases "in Christ" and "in the Lord" represent "Paul's perception of his whole life as a Christian, its source, its identity, and its responsibilities." See *The Theology of Paul the Apostle* (Grand Rapids: Eerdmans, 1998), 399.

we who choose to believe in him participate in the benefits of his own election and sonship. I would suggest that verses 4–5, though relevant to theological debates about election, predestination, and free will, do not serve as an invitation to debate but to worship. When we realize that God has chosen us to belong to him because of his love for us, our hearts pour forth blessing.

In accordance with his pleasure and will (1:5). Our worshipful response to God is accentuated by the fact that God has chosen us, not because something forced him to do it nor because something in us deserved it. Rather, God chose us "in accordance with his pleasure and will" (1:5). To put it simply, God chose us because that's what he decided to do, and doing so gave him pleasure. The more we consider God's delight in us, the more we will be drawn to worship.

To the praise of his glorious grace (1:6). Moreover, God's choosing and predestining us is an expression of his "glorious grace, which he has freely given us in the One he loves" (1:6). We belong to God not because of anything we have done to earn God's favor but because God is gracious, giving us that which we do not deserve and sparing us from that which we do deserve. (For more on grace, see commentary on 2:8.) God has predestined us "in love"[10] to share in the grace given "in the One he loves." Again, the response to this good news in Ephesians 1 is praise, not theological debate. God has chosen and adopted us "to the praise of his glorious grace" (1:6).

Though allowing for a variety of interpretations of God's choosing and predestining, we should attend to the storyline of these verses. To put it simply, God has been at work for our benefit. God has blessed us, chosen us, and predestined us. God has done all of this because it gives him delight and because it leads to "the praise of his glorious grace" (1:6). Though nothing in this passage necessarily denies human freedom, the dominant theme is God's sovereignty, grace, and action. If this passage were all we had when it comes to the doctrine of election, we would surely believe that God chose us on the basis of his sovereignty and grace, not because of anything we have done or would do. Yet this passage does not begin to address the tricky issues associated with election, such as the status of those who are *not* "in Christ."

Holy and blameless (1:4). God has chosen us to be "holy and blameless." Both of these terms reflect Old Testament themes. To be holy is to be set apart from the world by God for a relationship with and service to God. We are to be holy because God is holy (Lev 19:2). Our holiness has to do not only with our intimate relationship with him but also with living in countercultural ways that honor God. The use of "holy" for the Gentile recipients of Ephesians underscores

---

10. Though scholarly arguments are inconclusive, I'm inclined to see "in love" as going with "predestined" rather than "holy and blameless."

their inclusion among God's people. The Greek word translated in 1:4 as "blameless" literally means "unblemished."[11] It functions in the Septuagint (the Greek version of the Old Testament that was in popular use in Paul's day) to describe sacrificial animals that are "without defect."[12] But it also can be used for blameless human behavior.[13] Thus, God has chosen us to be set apart for him and his purposes and to offer our lives as a perfect sacrifice for him (Rom 12:1–2; 15:16).

The relational nature of our election and predestination is underscored by a phrase in the Greek original of Ephesians 1:5 that is not translated by the NIV. Where the NIV has "predestined us for adoption to sonship through Jesus Christ," the Greek reads more literally, "he predestined us for adoption to sonship through Jesus Christ *into him* [*eis auton*]." This additional phrase, in which "him" probably refers to God,[14] accentuates that fact that our adoption by God brings us into an intimate relationship with him. The language of verse 5 is reminiscent of the story of the baptism of Jesus, where the voice from heaven says, "You are my Son, whom I love; with you I am well pleased" (Mark 1:11). Similarly, we are adopted because God loves us and because of God's own pleasure (1:4–5). Through Christ, the unique Son of God, we become sons and daughters of God, entering into a relationship with the Father that is similar in many ways to that of Christ himself.

The account in Ephesians 1:3–6 of God's blessing and choosing us to be "holy and blameless in his sight" echoes two major stories from the Old Testament. In Genesis God chooses Abram, promising to bless him and through him to bless "all peoples on earth" (Gen 12:2–3). God's choice depends on God's own will, not on Abram's worthiness. Then in Exodus God graciously delivers his people from bondage in Egypt. He chooses them "out of all nations" to be his "treasured possession." They will be for God "a kingdom of priests and a holy nation" (Exod 19:4–6). Again, God's choice of Israel does not depend on their impressiveness or righteousness but rather on God's sovereign will (see Deut 7:7; 9:4–6). Now, in Christ, God blesses us as he once did Abram. Now, in Christ, God has set us apart to be holy, as he once did with Israel. Now, in Christ, God treasures us as he treasured Israel.

Redemption, Revelation, and Unification (1:7–10)

God's blessings, introduced in verse 3, continue in verses 7–10, which describe God's redemption of us, his revelation to us, and his plan to unite all things in Christ.

---

11. BDAG 56.
12. For example, *amōmos* in Exod 29:1 LXX; Lev 1:3 LXX; etc.
13. Ps 14:2 LXX (15:2 in the NIV: "The one whose walk is blameless").
14. In Greek "him" could refer either to God or to Christ.

We have redemption through his blood, the forgiveness of sins (1:7). Redemption (*apolutrōsis* in Greek) referred to "manumission" (the technical term for freeing slaves) or setting someone free by paying a ransom.[15] In the New Testament it functions metaphorically for our redemption or deliverance from sin, guilt, and death, thus bringing us forgiveness. The relationship of redemption and forgiveness to "blood" draws upon the Old Testament practice of sacrificing animals to signify God's forgiveness. Yet unlike the priests in the temple, Christ offered not "the blood of goats and calves" but rather "his own blood, thus obtaining eternal redemption" (Heb 9:12).

Furthermore, the connection of redemption and blood alludes to one of the most formative Old Testament stories, the redemption of the Israelites from Egypt. The Lord promised to "redeem" his people from their slavery in Egypt "with an outstretched arm and with mighty acts of judgment" (Exod 6:6). These mighty acts culminated in the Passover, when the Israelites put the blood of sacrificed lambs on the doorframes of their homes (Exod 12:7). When God struck down the firstborn of Egypt, he "passed over" the houses that had blood on their doorframes (Exod 12:12–13). Thus, the sons of Israel were spared because of the blood that had been shed, and the Israelites were redeemed. In the case of our redemption through Christ, the blood that redeems us is not that of lambs but of Christ himself. He is the "Passover lamb," sacrificed for us (1 Cor 5:7). He is the "Lamb of God, who takes away the sin of the world" (John 1:29).

The allusion to Exodus suggests what will be made clear later in Ephesians, namely, that we too were in bondage, not to Egyptian tyranny but to "the ways of this world" and "the ruler of the kingdom of the air" (2:2), as well as to "the cravings of our flesh" (2:3). We were deserving of God's wrath (2:3). Thus, we were in need of redemption, which could only be accomplished through the shedding of Christ's blood.

The riches of God's grace (1:7). Why did God choose to forgive us in such a costly way? It came about not because of some worth of our own but "in accordance with the riches of God's grace that he lavished on us." Verse 6 identifies God's grace as "glorious." In verses 7–8 it is rich and abundant. This description anticipates what we will see in 2:7, which speaks of "the incomparable riches of his grace, expressed in his kindness to us in Christ Jesus." The "in him" that begins verse 7 continues to describe this lavish outpouring of grace. In many ways, all human beings have known God's grace. We experience "common grace" in the beauty of nature, the tenderness of familial love, and the fulfillment that comes from good work. These are gifts available to all human beings. Yet God's grace, though experienced in part by all people, is

---

15. BDAG 117.

showered upon us through Jesus Christ, especially through his death, which purchased our redemption and brought us forgiveness.

With all wisdom and understanding (1:8). This phrase could go either with what precedes it, thus "he lavished on us with all wisdom or understanding," or what follows, "With all wisdom and understanding, he made known to us . . ." The NIV prefers the latter option. The verse numbers, along with many other English translations, assume the first rendering (CEB, NLT, KJV). The Greek grammar allows for either possibility. Both opinions make good sense of the text. Perhaps, as Yoder Neufeld suggests, "The phrase *with all wisdom and insight* is cleverly placed to relate equally well to both grace and revelation."[16]

[God] made known to us the mystery of his will (1:9). The word for "mystery" in the Greek (*mustērion*) conveys a sense of secrecy, not unlike the English word "mystery." But in the case of verse 9, this secret is not withheld but revealed. Some members of the original audience of Ephesians may have once participated in the so-called mystery cults of the Greco-Roman world. In these secret societies, people supposedly gained access to arcane information about the cosmos. Yet the notion of divine mysteries was also common in aspects of Judaism, including the Wisdom writings; we might mention the apocryphal Wisdom of Solomon 2:22 (NRSV)—"and they did not know the secret purposes of God"; and again in 6:22—"I will tell you what wisdom is and how she came to be, and I will hide no secrets from you, but I will trace her course from the beginning of the creation, and make knowledge of her clear, and I will not pass by the truth." The idea is also common in the apocalyptic writings: for example, God is the one who "reveals mysteries" hidden in the heavens to special people like Daniel (Dan 2:28, 47).[17] But now, in Christ, God's mystery is revealed, not just to cultic initiates but to all people. In fact, in Ephesians 3 we'll learn that God's mystery is being made known to the whole cosmos (3:9–11).

Paul explains God's actions in terms of God's own pleasure, as was true of his act of predestination in 1:5. God has made known "the mystery of his will according to his good pleasure" because it delights him to do so.

When the times reach their fulfillment (1:10). The Greek reads more literally of a plan "for the fullness of the times" (*tou plērōmatos tōn kairōn*). This is the first use in Ephesians of the Greek word *plērōma*, which means "fullness, sum total, or fulfilling."[18] The phrase "fullness of the times" suggests that when

16. Yoder Neufeld, *Ephesians*, 48 (emphasis in the original).

17. See the classic study of Raymond E. Brown, *The Semitic Background of the Term "Mystery" in the New Testament*, ed. J. Reumann, Facet Books: Biblical Series 21 (Philadelphia: Fortress, 1968), 56–66.

18. BDAG 829–30.

God ordered all of history, he picked the perfect moment to implement his plan of salvation. The CEB captures the sense of the Greek by saying, "This is what God planned for the climax of all times."

To bring unity to all things in heaven and on earth under Christ (1:10). Other English translations prefer, "to bring all things together in Christ" (CEB); "to unite all things in him" (ESV); "to gather up all things in him" (NRSV); to "bring everything together under the authority of Christ" (NLT); "the summing up of all things in Christ" (NASB); "gather together in one all things in Christ" (KJV). These translations iron out the wrinkles of the Greek of verse 10, which could be translated literally, "to sum up everything in Christ, things in the heavens and things on the earth, in him."

The verb translated as "bring to unity, sum up" is *anakephalaioō*, which has the basic meaning, "to sum up, recapitulate."[19] It can be used in Greek for summing up a verbal case or argument, as in Romans 13:9, its only other appearance in the New Testament. Or it can be used for adding up a column of numbers. Its theological use in Ephesians is different: it is reminiscent of the use of reconciliation language in 2 Corinthians 5:16–21. There, the new creation has come "in Christ" (2 Cor 5:17). God has reconciled himself to us through Christ and has given us the ministry and message of reconciliation (2 Cor 5:18–20). Reconciliation involves bringing together those who have suffered brokenness in relationship. It is a form of uniting, focusing on estranged people or groups of people, including humans and God.

In Ephesians 1:10, the uniting of all things in Christ includes the sort of relational reconciliation found in 2 Corinthians 5. But it reaches much further, encompassing not just human beings but "all things." In Greek, "all things" is *ta panta*, a phrase that appears several times in Ephesians.[20] In 1:11, for example, God "works out everything [*ta panta*] in conformity with the purpose of his will." In 3:9 God created "all things [*ta panta*]." The neuter form of *ta panta* in 1:10 suggests that God is unifying not just people but everything in the universe. This is clarified and reinforced by verbal repetition that is not apparent in the NIV. Verse 10 could be rendered more literally, "to bring unity to all things in Christ, the things in the heavens and the things on the earth, in him." "All things" means *all* things: the whole universe and everything it contains.

Notice that this cosmic unification happens "in Christ," emphasized by the addition of "in him" at the end of verse 10 (not shown in the NIV). This could be an instance of the instrumental usage of *en Christō*: God is uniting all things by means of Christ. Yet there is a strong local sense as well. Everything

---

19. BDAG 65.

20. *Ta panta* occurs in 1:10, 11, 23; 3:9; 4:10, 15.

in the universe will be put back in its right place when the whole universe finds its rightful place within Christ.

The Story Behind the Story. Those of us who are familiar with the story of God in Scripture may take for granted the need for God's blessings spelled out in 1:7–10. Of course we need redemption and forgiveness. Of course we need divine revelation. Of course all things need to be unified in Christ. We can take all of this for granted because, like Paul, we understand the story behind the story of 1:7–10. This backstory is even more foundational than the story of God redeeming his people from Egypt, which underlies verse 7. It is the most elemental of all biblical stories, the story in Genesis 1–3 of the creation and the fall.

In Genesis 1 God creates all things in a carefully ordered way. He sees that his creation is good, even "very good" (Gen 1:31). God creates humankind in his own image, as male and female, delegating to them authority over his good creation (Gen 1:27–30). The relationship between the man and the woman is unique in that they share the same substance as well as the same role of stewardship (Gen 2:23–24). The man and woman enjoy unhindered intimacy together (Gen 2:25).

Yet, God had given to human beings the power to reject his intentions for them (Gen 2:16–17). In Genesis 3 they succumb to temptation and do the one thing God told them not to do (Gen 3:6). To use the theological term, they sin.

As a result, God's perfectly ordered world is shattered. The first evidence of this brokenness comes in the relationship between the man and the woman, who try to hide from each other (Gen 3:7). Then they try to hide from God (Gen 3:8). When God finds them, they try to avoid the blame that is rightly theirs (Gen 3:12–13). Human sin leads to brokenness in the world, as natural processes malfunction and human work becomes painful and difficult (Gen 3:16–19). God's world is broken, though not completely dysfunctional or destroyed, because its created order continues to underlie all things. Nevertheless, like Humpty Dumpty, the world had a great fall, and "all the king's horses and all the king's men couldn't put the world together again."

But in this case, the King could put the world together again, and that's exactly what we see in Ephesians 1:10. Part of this restoration includes reconciliation between God and human beings. It also involves the repairing of relationships among people. It affects all things, *ta panta*, everything in the heavens and everything on earth. Nothing is exempt from God's unifying work in Christ.

Thus, when we read Ephesians 1:7–10 in light of the fundamental story of creation and the fall, and when we read all of Ephesians in this light, and indeed, when we read all of Scripture in this light, we see God's wider, deeper purpose for the cosmos. God is not just saving souls, as essential as this is to his plan. God is not just forming community, urging righteousness, and doing justice, as significant as all of these activities are. Rather, God is putting all things back together in Christ. As we continue our study of Ephesians, we must always keep in mind the central purpose of God as revealed in this letter: "to bring unity to all things in heaven and on earth under Christ."

The Praise of God's Glory (1:11–14)

The basic storyline of 1:11–14 is clear: In Christ God acted according to his will so as to form a people who exist for "the praise of his glory" (1:12, 14). Thus, the sentence that began in verse 3 by praising God ends, some two hundred words later, by highlighting God's praise as our reason to live.

We. . . . And you (1:11, 13). Several of the details in this passage are not so clear, however. First of all, there is a curious shift in subject in verse 13 from "we" to "you." "We" means, first of all, Paul and those who are reading (or hearing) his letter. Yet the shift in verse 13 to "you"—"And you also were included in Christ"—suggests a different sense of "we" in the previous two verses. "We" in verses 11–12 are those "who were the first to put [their] hope in Christ." "You" in verses 13–14 are not these earliest believers but rather those who "heard the message of truth" and "believed" in Christ some time later. Commentators debate whether "we" and "you" means "first ones" and "later ones" or perhaps "Jews" and "Gentiles." The fact that, historically speaking, the first believers were Jewish and the latter ones Gentiles means that both options make sense. It is striking that the Gentiles, who were formerly excluded from God's people (2:12), are now included among the people God possesses through Christ without having to become Jewish. Moreover, the main point of 1:11–14 is that God has set apart a people who exist for the praise of his glory. This is applied in the text both to the first believers (1:12) and to the later believers (1:13). The point, therefore, is not the difference between the groups but rather what they share in common in Christ.

We were also chosen (1:11). This verb for "chosen" (*klēroō*) appears only here in the New Testament. It is related to the word *klēros*, which means "lot, portion."[21] The verb means either "appoint by lot" or "obtain by lot." In one case, God appoints us to receive an inheritance. In the other, it is God who receives an inheritance, namely us. The NIV prefers the latter sense in its use of "we were also chosen," which is to say, "we were obtained by lot [by God]." This interpretation is consistent with the Old Testament story of God's relationship with Israel. In Deuteronomy 9:29 LXX, for example, Moses says to

21. "*klēroō*," BDAG 548–49; and "*klēros*," BDAG 548.

the Lord, "But they [the Israelites] are your people, your inheritance [*klēros*] that you brought out by your great power and your outstretched arm." This may now be said as well of those who belong to God in Christ.

Yet other interpreters prefer the "appointed by lot" sense of *klēroō*. The ESV, for example, reads: "In him we have obtained an inheritance." (The CEB and the NRSV have similar translations.) The sense here is that we were appointed by God to receive our own *klēros*. This reading is more consistent with the immediate context in Ephesians. In verse 14 the Holy Spirit is "a deposit guaranteeing our inheritance." This seems to point to that which we will inherit in the age to come.

What makes all of this so perplexing is the nature of the vocabulary involved here and the fact that both options are theologically true. In the age to come we will receive an inheritance from God. And in the age to come we will be God's own inheritance. Moreover, the storyline of Ephesians 1:3–14 could support the weight of either position: on the one hand, this passage tells the story of God's actions, which lends support to the "we are God's portion" interpretation. On the other hand, God's actions are described as blessings given to us, one of which could include our inheritance in the age to come. This supports the "we will inherit our portion" interpretation. Thus no matter which position one takes, it will be both linguistically possible and also theologically true.

Were marked in [Christ] with a seal, the promised Holy Spirit (1:13). The verb "marked with a seal" is the language of ownership. In the first-century world, people marked their possessions with distinctive wax seals. Slaves and cattle would be branded. So when believers in Christ are given the Holy Spirit, they are sealed in Christ, and therefore they know that they belong to God (see also 2 Cor 1:22).

A deposit guaranteeing our inheritance (1:14). The Greek text of verse 14 uses the word *arrabōn*, which could be translated "first installment, deposit, down payment."[22] It is used two other times in the New Testament, in both cases in reference to the Spirit as proof that our future in God is secure and that the Holy Spirit reassures us of this future blessing (2 Cor 1:22; 5:5).

The praise of his glory (1:12, 14). Twice in 1:11–14 we find the phrase "the praise of his glory" in reference to God. Verse 12 reveals that he predestined those who were the first to hope in Christ so that they "might be for the praise of his glory." Similarly, all who respond to the "the message of truth" (1:13) by putting their trust in Christ exist (the verb is implied) "to the praise of his glory" (1:14). Grammatically, "his" in vv. 12 and 14 could refer either to God the Father or to Christ. But the use of "glory" in Ephesians tips the scale in favor of

---

22. BDAG 134.

a reference to the Father's glory: 1:6 speaks of God's "glorious grace," 1:17 refers to God as "the glorious Father," and 3:21 offers glory to God "in the church and in Christ Jesus." In the Old Testament, God's glory is often associated with his weighty importance, as well as with his radiance or splendor. The New Testament Greek word for glory, *doxa*, can also mean "fame, recognition, honor."[23]

How can we live for the praise of God's glory? It could include praising God along the lines of Ephesians 1:3–14. It could also mean living in such a way that God is glorified in us in all we do and say (see 2:10; 3:21; 4:1–6:24). No matter how, we ought to be astounded by the notion that our purpose in life, our very reason for being, is the praise of God's glory. We'll consider this question more fully in the "Live the Story" section.

LIVE the Story

Ephesians 1:3–14 tells a mind-expanding, heart-stirring, praise-inspiring, life-transforming story of God. In this story God has blessed us beyond measure because of the riches of his grace. This blessing began even before creation, when God chose us to belong to him and to be devoted to his purposes. God's blessing did not stop even when human beings harmed his creation through sin. Rather, God redeemed and forgave us. He revealed his no-longer-secret plan: to bring unity to everything in heaven and earth. God did and is doing all of this in Christ. When we believe in him, we step into God's story, accepting our special relationship with God and our divinely established purpose: to exist for the praise of God's glory.

The Story *of God*

Ephesians 1:3–14 is the story of God in two main ways. First, it is a story that is authored by God, who through Paul "made known to us the mystery of his will" (1:9). In chapter 3, Paul explains that "the mystery" was "made known to [him] by revelation" (3:3). So, God is the primary author of the story. Everything that happens in this story is an expression of God's will as its author (1:6, 9).

God is also the primary actor in the story; thus it is, in a sense, God's autobiography. God is the one who blessed us, chose us, predestined us for adoption, freely gave us his grace, redeemed us, forgave us, made known his will to us, sealed us with the Holy Spirit, and gave us our purpose for living.

As the author and actor of this story, God gets all the credit, all the "glory" for it. If a human being were to write a story and star in it primarily to be

---

23. BDAG 256–58.

praised by others, we would say this person is sinfully egotistical. But with God it's different. God is worthy of all praise, deserving every bit of it and more. Plus when we live for the praise of God's glory, we discover the core reason for our own existence.

Who is the God who authored and starred in this story? As we have seen in "Explain the Story," much of the narrative takes shape in light of formative Old Testament stories: the call of Abram, the redemption of Israel from Egypt, the choice of Israel as God's holy people, and most of all the creation narrative in Genesis along with its account of sin and its consequences. So, we begin to answer the question "Who is God?" by saying that God is the God of the Old Testament, the God who created all things, chose his people, and redeemed them. We will never rightly understand God's story, nor will we ever rightly know its author and principal actor, unless we ground our knowledge in the story of the Old Testament.

Yet, the God of Ephesians 1:3–14 is also the God who has acted and continues to act *en Christō*, in Christ. God is the "Father of our Lord Jesus Christ" (1:3). This title "Christ" comes via the Greek word *christos*, which renders the Hebrew word *mashiach*, meaning "anointed one" or "messiah." The Christ through whom God acts is God's anointed one, the Messiah, the rightful king of Israel. Jesus the Messiah/Christ inaugurated the kingdom of God through his words and deeds, through his death and resurrection. God blessed us in Christ, chose us in Christ, predestined us for adoption through Jesus Christ, and gave us his grace in his beloved Christ. God redeemed us in Christ, established his will in Christ, and is bringing unity to all things in Christ. When Paul speaks of Christ, he envisions the living, reigning Lord in whom we trust and live.

The interconnection of God the Father and the Lord Jesus Christ in Ephesians 1:3–14 points to the fact that Jesus, the Christ, was and is more than a mere human being. Though Paul does not use the language of later Christian Christology, Ephesians does provide a solid foundation for the formulation that Christ is at once fully God and fully human. Moreover, the mention of the Holy Spirit, who guarantees our inheritance and through whom we receive "spiritual" blessings, prefigures later Trinitarian thought.

Thus, Ephesians 1:3–14 reveals that the story of God is, indeed, the story *of God*, authored by God, filled with God's actions, governed by God's will, and told for God's glory.

Given the self-preoccupation instilled by our culture and the extent to which many Christians are captive to this cultural obsession, not to mention the way many versions of the gospel cater to a me-centered reality, the fact that God's story is really God's own story may be unsettling to us. We may have been led to believe that being a Christian is about the divine improvement of our personal story. Of course, God does make our individual stories better, though not necessarily in ways applauded by our culture. But what matters most is not the betterment of our stories so much as our knowing, telling, and living in God's own story.

Rick Warren gets it exactly right in the opening lines of his bestselling book, *The Purpose-Driven Life*:

> It's not about you.
> The purpose of your life is far greater than your own personal fulfillment, your peace of mind, or even your happiness. It's far greater than your family, your career, or even your wildest dreams and ambitions. If you want to know why you were placed on this planet, you must begin with God. You were born *by* his purpose and *for* his purpose.[24]

Finding Our Place in God's Story

One of the ways we discover and live for God's purposes is by discovering our place in his story. According to Ephesians, God wrote us into his script even before creation: God chose us to be set apart for him and his purposes. The "eulogy" helps us discover that we play a crucial role in God's story. Though God is the primary actor, we are supporting players, written into the text by God's own hand. In many ways, we're rather like Frodo in J. R. R. Tolkien's *The Lord of the Rings* trilogy. As the story begins, Frodo is an apparently insignificant hobbit, living his own unremarkable story. Yes, he happens to own an unusual ring given to him by his uncle Bilbo, but initially Frodo has no idea of how this ring will draw him into a much larger story, a story of the epic battle between good and evil. Through the revelation of the wise wizard Gandalf, Frodo begins to understand that his part in the grand story will change his life forever, and perhaps even all of life in Middle-earth.

As Frodo starts to live into this bigger story, what he does matters immensely. His choices and efforts turn the tide of good against evil. So, though the story is not primarily Frodo's story, his participation is crucial. In our case, we are not the ones who defeat evil through our efforts. The task of vanquishing sin, death, and demonic dominion is Christ's alone. Yet as people set apart by God for his purposes, as people who exist for the praise of God's glory, we will play an essential—though not a starring—role in God's story.

Moreover, the more we let God's story fill our minds and enlarge our hearts, the more God's story becomes the framing story of our lives. The

---

24. Rick Warren, *The Purpose-Driven Life: What on Earth Am I Here For?* (Grand Rapids: Zondervan, 2002), 17 (emphasis in the original).

narrative of God becomes the "metanarrative," that grand overarching and controlling story that gives meaning to our own stories. As we understand, tell, and live this story, it transforms us, giving us new vision for life. It gives us a whole new sense of who we are and why we matter. God's story tells us what examples we should imitate and what values we should embrace. His story reframes our view of the world. In time, as we let the story of God form us, our own story will begin to look more and more like God's story.

A striking example of this sort of transformation can be found in the life of Louis Zamperini. His story is captured in Laura Hillenbrand's gripping biography, *Unbroken*, which was the basis of the feature film directed by Angelina Jolie. As a child, Louie's headstrong resistance to authority was the guiding principle of his life. But when he discovered that he could run competitively, Louie channeled all of his vehemence into winning races. And win he did, becoming the fastest high-school-aged miler in the world in 1934. Two years later he became one of the youngest Olympians in American sports history. He competed at the Berlin Olympics, where he met Adolf Hitler and managed to make off with a Nazi flag as a souvenir.

Louie's promising track career at the University of Southern California was cut short by World War II. Enlisting in the Army, he was soon deployed in the Pacific theater. After his plane was shot down over the ocean, Louie spent forty-seven days adrift on a raft, with hardly any food or water. Badly dehydrated, Louie promised God, in whom he barely believed, that if he would save him, he would serve God forever. Amazingly, rain came and Louie's life was preserved. But he soon forgot his promise.

When Louie's raft washed up on an island, he was taken captive by Japanese soldiers, who beat him savagely before delivering him to a prisoner-of-war camp. There, he was horribly treated, most of all by a Japanese sergeant nicknamed "the Bird." Enduring extreme abuse because of his Olympic fame and resilient will, Louie managed to survive two years of deprivation and sadistic treatment at the hands of the Bird. During all of his body-and-mind-fracturing torture, Louie remained "unbroken."

When he was finally rescued by the American army and sent home, Louie was celebrated as a war hero. He married Cynthia and seemed to have a blessed life in Southern California. But the unbroken man was broken inside, and soon that brokenness permeated his life. Tormented by dreams of his captivity, Louie experienced what we would now call extreme post-traumatic stress disorder. In an effort to find the peace that eluded him, Louie began drinking heavily and acting irresponsibly. Cynthia initiated divorce proceedings, and Louie's life was in shatters. He believed that he would only experience peace if he could get back to Japan and kill the Bird.

At that time, Billy Graham was holding a crusade in Los Angeles. Because Louie refused to have anything to do with religion, Cynthia went alone. She gave her life to Christ. For weeks she tried to get Louie to visit one of the crusade meetings, but his unbroken resistance remained firm. Finally, near the end of the crusade, Louie agreed to attend. At first he felt only rage when he heard Graham's preaching. But one night, as Louie began to leave during the altar call, he remembered for the first time in years the promise he had made to God to serve him if God rescued him. Louie went forward to receive Christ.

Thereafter, God began to unite the pieces of Louie's broken life. He no longer suffered with nightmares of captivity. He lost his desire to drink and threw away his stash of alcohol. The morning after his conversion, he felt a peace he had not known before. "When he thought of his history, what resonated with him now was not all that he had suffered but the divine love that he believed had intervened to save him. He was not the worthless, broken, forsaken man that the Bird had striven to make of him. In a single, silent moment, his rage, his fear, his humiliation and helplessness, had fallen away. That morning, he believed, he was a new creation."[25]

From that point onward Louie began to live as part of a larger story. The forgiveness of God in Christ, which Louie felt in his own life, inspired him to forgive the Japanese guards who had afflicted him so mercilessly. Many of these guards he was able to forgive face-to-face when he visited Japan.[26] Louie did truly begin to serve the Lord as he had promised on that raft in the Pacific Ocean. He devoted much of his life to helping children at risk. In his later years he served on the staff of the First Presbyterian Church of Hollywood, overseeing a meal program for senior adults. It was during those years that I got to know Louie as a friend. Aware of his life story, I was always amazed by how thoroughly he loved life. I can still picture the seventy-year-old Louie skateboarding like a teenager all over the church campus. I have often referred to Louie as the happiest person I have ever known.

If ever there was a man who had been living his own story, it was Louie Zamperini. Though his personal story was compelling, it was ultimately inadequate. By God's grace Louie came to see his life as part of a larger story, a redemptive story, a story of God's love in Christ. He experienced God mending his brokenness, and he dedicated his life to helping others experience the same.

Our personal stories may never be the subject of a bestselling biography or a major motion picture. Yet we can all experience the transformation that

25. Laura Hillenbrand, *Unbroken: A World War II Story of Survival, Resilience, and Redemption* (New York: Random House, 2010), 376.

26. The Bird refused to meet with Louie, but he may have received a letter Louie wrote, forgiving him.

comes when God's story becomes our story. We too can experience the divine love that saves us and gives us a new reason to live. We too can respond to the story of God by allowing God to rewrite our story so that we might live for the praise of God's glory.

How Do We Live for the Praise of God's Glory?

How do we live for the praise of God's glory? As a young pastor, I thought I knew the answer to that question: living for the praise of God's glory meant valuing worship above all things. This was worship by my own definition, by the way, meaning what Christians did when we gathered on Sunday mornings in order to sing, pray, listen to a sermon, and celebrate the sacraments. I echoed preachers I had heard who said that the hour we spend worshiping in church on Sunday morning is the most important hour of our week. Everything we did, I was told, was preparation for the single most important activity of our lives, namely, worshiping God along with our fellow Christians.

I still believe that what happens in worship services is absolutely crucial. Yet I no longer believe that living for the praise of God's glory happens only (or even mainly) in these settings. Rather, I am persuaded by Scripture that living for the praise of God's glory can and should happen throughout the week in everything we do. Our weekday activities have potential to be worshipful not only as they prepare us for Sunday morning but also as we offer them and ourselves to God.

This truth permeates Ephesians. In 2:8–10, God's salvation by grace includes being newly created "to do good works, which God prepared in advance for us to do." In the last three chapters of Ephesians, these good works of course include what Christians usually call worship. As we are filled with the Spirit, we will be "speaking to one another with psalms, hymns, and songs from the Spirit" (5:19). We will "[s]ing and make music from [our] heart to the Lord, always giving thanks to God the Father for everything" (5:19–20). Yet according to the broader scope of Ephesians, everything we do in all of life can and should be for the praise of God's glory.

Many Christians miss this life-changing insight because we assume that what we call the "spiritual" part of life is all that ultimately matters. In this view, physical reality is, at best, a stage for the nonphysical stuff God *really* cares about. God's plan for the cosmos is focused in the salvation of human souls and that's it. Corporate worship counts because it focuses our hearts and minds on God and eternal, spiritual things. It allows us to turn our eyes upon Jesus and look full in his wonderful face, so the things of earth will become strangely dim.

Yet if we take the story of God in Ephesians seriously, we discover that things on earth are not "strangely dim" to God. Yes, God's plan includes saving human beings from sin and death (2:1–10). But there is much more. Ultimately, God intends to unite all things in Christ, including "things in heaven and on earth" (1:10). This means God cares about earthly things and plans to redeem them as a part of his mending our broken world.

This is not surprising if we remember that Ephesians has roots in the Old Testament story of God. After all, God created all things, a fundamental truth that proves their value in his eyes. Moreover, God delighted in what he created, calling it good and even very good (Gen 1:31). When sin broke God's good creation, he did not abandon what he had made but rather began to implement his plan for restoring everything. The centerpiece of God's plan was to affirm the creation through the incarnation of Christ: God became part of it in order to redeem it (John 1:14).

Thus, we can live for the praise of the God who made all things and who is uniting all things in Christ, not only in our corporate worship, not only as we lead Bible studies, serve on church boards, and go on mission trips, but also as we coach soccer teams, serve on the school board, and go to the office. What we do in corporate worship primes our hearts and sets our compass so that we might worship God at all times and in everything we do (see Rom 12:1–2).

When I think of people who live for the praise of God's glory each day, my mind turns to Michelle. Michelle is a housekeeper at Laity Lodge, a retreat center I once directed. She does an outstanding job cleaning rooms there. Throughout the year, she cleans bathrooms hundreds of times. I once asked Michelle what keeps her going in such humble work. She answered quickly, "That's easy. I want to serve the guests well. But mostly I think, I'm cleaning this bathroom for God."

I also think of Don, who sells cars for a living. More accurately, Don is the owner of a major automobile sales company. He is also a Christian who seeks to live for the praise of God's glory in every part of life, including his work. Over the years, Don has carefully considered everything he does and everything his company does in light of the story of God. He has thought about what it means for his company to treat customers and employees in a way that reflects God's work in the world. For example, Don discovered that customers who were least able to pay for a car tended to pay the most because they were not skilled at negotiation. So he changed from using the typical model of "haggling" to a set-price model. The potential loss of profit was, in time, made up by an increase in customer loyalty.[27] But Don made this change

---

27. To learn more about Don Flow and his efforts to serve Christ through his business, see "Don Flow: Ethics at Flow Automotive" (http://ethix.org/2004/04/01/ethics-at-flow-automotive) or "Don Flow: How do you live faithfully?" (http://www.faithandleadership.com/qa/don-flow-how-do-you-live-faithfully).

not primarily as a way to increase profit but as a way of living out God's story in his business.

Whether your work involves cleaning bathrooms like Michelle or leading a major company like Don, whether your work is focused on raising children or fighting the trafficking of children, whether your work is leading worship in a church or leading the choir in the local high school, Ephesians invites you to do it all for the praise of God's glory, allowing his story to shape the story of your whole life as you share in God's work of uniting all things in Christ, things in heaven and things on earth.

Ephesians 1:15–23

📖 LISTEN to the Story

¹⁵For this reason, ever since I heard about your faith in the Lord Jesus and your love for all God's people, ¹⁶I have not stopped giving thanks for you, remembering you in my prayers. ¹⁷I keep asking that the God of our Lord Jesus Christ, the glorious Father, may give you the Spirit of wisdom and revelation, so that you may know him better. ¹⁸I pray that the eyes of your heart may be enlightened in order that you may know the hope to which he has called you, the riches of his glorious inheritance in his holy people, ¹⁹and his incomparably great power for us who believe. That power is the same as the mighty strength ²⁰he exerted when he raised Christ from the dead and seated him at his right hand in the heavenly realms, ²¹far above all rule and authority, power and dominion, and every name that is invoked, not only in the present age but also in the one to come. ²²And God placed all things under his feet and appointed him to be head over everything for the church, ²³which is his body, the fullness of him who fills everything in every way.

Listening to the text in the Story: Exodus 3:1–15; Psalm 110; Matthew 25:31–46; 28:18–20; John 1:14–18; Romans 5:1–5; 1 Corinthians 12; Philippians 1:3–11; 2:5–11; Colossians 1:3–14; 1 Thessalonians 1:2–10; Revelation 5:1–14.

Following the expansive doxology of 1:3–14, Ephesians 1:15–23 summarizes Paul's prayers of thanksgiving and intercession for the letter's recipients. In Greek, this prayer report is a single, complex sentence of 169 words (a little shorter than the 202-word sentence in 1:3–14); English translations divide 1:15–23 into several sentences. After a short description of his thanks for the recipients, Paul tells them what he is asking God to do for them. This leads into an extensive reflection on the resurrection and exaltation of Christ, which sets the stage for the introduction of the church as the body of Christ. The chapter ends in an intriguing fashion, by identifying the church as "the fullness of him who fills everything in every way" (1:23). Ephesians 1:15–23 introduces several major themes of the letter, including the importance of knowledge, the role of spiritual powers, and the church as the body of Christ.

EXPLAIN the Story

Summary of Ephesians 1:15–23

After mentioning the faith and love of the letter's recipients, Paul reports on his prayers for them. Verse 16 acknowledges his sustained thanksgiving and transitions into the next section of the report. Verses 17–19 record Paul's request that those who read Ephesians be given deeper knowledge of God and his blessings. The first two blessings focus on the future: "hope" and "glorious inheritance" (1:18). The third blessing is experienced in the present: God's "great power for us who believe" (1:19). The reference to this power, which was demonstrated in the resurrection and exaltation of Christ, leads to a proclamation of the sovereignty of Christ over all spiritual entities "in the heavenly realms" (1:20–21). In light of this divine victory, the church is introduced as Christ's "body, the fullness of him who fills everything in every way" (1:23).

Sustained Thanksgiving (1:15–16)

Hellenistic letters commonly began with a short prayer to the gods, including a thanksgiving. Paul follows this practice, though he says much more than was typical. As he does in several letters (for example, Phil 1:3–11), Paul begins Ephesians by sharing his gratitude to God before reporting on his supplication for those who will read his letter.

For this reason (1:15). This phrase connects the prayer report in 1:15–23 with the extensive eulogy that celebrates God's blessings for those who are in Christ (1:3–14). Several emphases from the eulogy are picked up in the prayer report, including belief, the Spirit, inheritance, and God's glory. Paul is grateful, ultimately, for what the gracious God is doing in their lives.

I heard about your faith in the Lord Jesus and your love for all God's people (1:15). "I heard about" suggests that Paul does not know at least some of the recipients of his letter. Yet he is grateful because they are strong in two of the essentials of the Pauline triad: faith, hope, and love (1 Cor 13:13; 1 Thess 1:3). In fact the second element, hope, will appear in 1:18 as something Paul prays that the recipients will come to know.

The phrase "faith in the Lord Jesus" can mean either faith that has "the Lord" as its object (we trust in the Lord) or faith we have within the sphere of life defined by Christ (as those who exist in the Lord, we have faith). Arguments can be made for either option, though I find the first more likely.

In Greek, *en* can specify the object of belief, as in Mark 1:15, "Repent and believe [in] the good news [*pisteuete en tō euaggeliō*]." Moreover, in Ephesians 1:15 faith that is directed at the Lord seems consistent with what follows: love that is directed toward all of God's holy people.

I have not stopped giving thanks for you (1:16). Hellenistic letter writers sometimes claimed to "pray without ceasing" for their addressees; Paul follows this practice (for example, Col 1:9; 1 Thess 1:2). He hardly means that he has been praying for them every second. Rather, using a common figure of speech, Paul indicates that he has been praying regularly and consistently for them. Thus, he affirms his relationship with them and models a life of consistent prayer.

Remembering you in my prayers (1:16). This phrase is dependent grammatically on "I have not stopped giving thanks," and it serves as a bridge to the intercession that follows. Paul models what he commands in Philippians 4:6, mingling supplication with thanksgiving.

Knowing God and His Blessings (1:17–19)

In the NIV, verse 17 is a new sentence beginning with "I keep asking that." In the original, verse 17 is a continuation of the sentence that began with verse 15. Paul has not stopped giving thanks for the recipients of his letter, remembering them in his prayers, "[that] the God of our Lord Jesus Christ, the glorious Father, may give . . ." (1:17).

This identification of God is reminiscent of 1:3, "Praise be to the God and Father of our Lord Jesus Christ," though it adds a new element, "glorious." "Glorious Father" faithfully captures the meaning of the literal construction, "the father of glory." Glory has already figured prominently in Ephesians: "to the praise of [God's] glorious grace" (1:6); and "the praise of his glory" (1:12, 14). Even though Paul has moved from praise to supplication, an undercurrent of worship still pervades his requests.

The Spirit of wisdom and revelation (1:17). In 1:17–19 Paul asks God to help the readers of Ephesians grow in knowledge of God and his blessings. In the NIV he asks God to give "the Spirit of wisdom and revelation, so that you may know him better" (1:17). The Greek behind this translation reads more precisely "a spirit [*pneuma*, without the definite article] of wisdom and revelation." This opens the possibility that Paul is referring not to the Holy Spirit but to some human "spirit" or capacity for knowing. Several English translations lean in this direction: both the CEB and the NRSV prefer "give you a spirit of wisdom and revelation." Similarly, Ephesians 4:23 says we are "to be made new in the attitude [*pneuma*] of [our] minds." It's possible that this is the sense of "spirit" in 1:17. Yet if a "spirit of wisdom" might be possible in 1:17, a spirit "of revelation" seems "virtually unintelligible."[1] Moreover, in Ephesians 3 the Spirit is identified as the divine source of revelation (3:4–5; see also 1 Cor 2:10; 12:8). Ephesians 1:17 echoes Isaiah 11:1–2, where "the Spirit of wisdom and of understanding" will rest on the "shoot" from the stump of Jesse.[2] So the NIV rightly takes Paul as asking God to give "the [Holy] Spirit of wisdom and revelation."

So that you may know him better (1:17). The Greek of this phrase reads "in knowledge of him [*en epignōsei autou*]." Given that Paul is writing to believers who already know God through Christ, the NIV rightly renders it as "know him better." This knowledge will include theological content, to be sure. But in Scripture, knowing God is never just a matter of intellectual understanding. It is also deeply personal, relational, and experienced by a community. It includes experience, emotions, and intimate communication as well as right thinking. (As an illustration of how personal and intimate is this knowing, the Hebrew verb "to know" is even capable of being a euphemism for sexual intercourse.[3]) Throughout Ephesians, knowledge is an essential element of the Christian life, without which we cannot be the people God intends us to be.

I pray that the eyes of your heart may be enlightened (1:18). In addition to praying that the readers of Ephesians might know God better, Paul asks that they might know more of God's blessings. The Greek uses a perfect participle ("having been enlightened," *pephōtismenous*), which may indicate an additional request (as in the NIV) or alternatively something that has already occurred or is occurring (as in the ESV, "having the eyes of your hearts enlightened"). Either way, having the "eyes" of our inner being enlightened allows us to know God's blessings more deeply, namely: "the hope to which he has called you," "the riches of his glorious inheritance in his holy people," and "his incomparably great power for us who believe" (1:18–19). These blessings constitute the specific content of the knowledge for which Paul prays in this passage.

The hope to which he has called you (1:18). The first two blessings for which Paul prays have to do with the future: hope and glorious inheritance. The Greek is more precise: that you may know "the hope of his calling" (1:18). "Calling" echoes earlier affirmations in Ephesians 1: God chose us (1:4), predestined us (1:5), revealed his plan for the cosmos to us (1:9–10), and determined that we should exist for "the praise of his glory" (1:12, 14). These echoes indicate that the calling in verse 18 is "his" calling of Christians to believe and to participate in his work of uniting all things in Christ. Later in 4:4 this calling will be seen from a human perspective as our calling.

---

1. Thielman, *Ephesians*, 96.
2. Yoder Neufeld, *Ephesians*, 70.
3. BDB 393–95 (*yada*).

Though Ephesians often focuses on the present experience of believers, God's plan points to the future, when all things will be brought together in Christ. This is the center of our hope according to Ephesians. When English speakers use the word "hope," we imply that the state of affairs we desire is somehow uncertain. We may hope that tomorrow's weather will be delightful. On the other hand, we would not say that we hope tomorrow's date will be different than today's. This second usage is in play here: when Paul speaks of hope, he is not implying a lack confidence about the future. Rather, hope is the future reality about which we may be fully assured right now. This assurance is based on God's actions in history, most of all in Christ, as well as the work of the Holy Spirit in us (Rom 5:5; 15:13).

The riches of his glorious inheritance in his holy people (1:18). This phrase presents a challenge not unlike the one found in verses 11 and 14, which could mean either that God has inherited us or that we have received an inheritance from God. Similarly in verse 18, the "glorious inheritance" could be God's inheriting his holy people or his holy people inheriting good things from God. Though arguments can be made for both interpretations, the fact that the text refers to "God's inheritance [*tēs klēronomias autou*]" suggests that God is the one doing the inheriting. (Grammatically, the genitive "of him" could mean that God is the source of the inheritance, however.) Moreover, the main storyline of Ephesians 1 emphasizes God's choice of us to belong to him as his holy people and beloved children. Thus, the fact that God will fully inherit us in the future fits beautifully in the story. Yes, we will inherit many blessings in the future, but this is not the main point of Ephesians 1:18.

Incomparably great power for us who believe (1:19). In this, the third petition, Paul accentuates the greatness of God's power by stacking words upon words: *to huperballon megethos tēs dunameōs autou*—literally, "immeasurable greatness of his power"; and then *kata tēn energeian tou kratous tēs ischuos autou*—"according to the energy of the might of his strength." Yet words are hardly necessary, because God's power is seen most dramatically "when he raised Christ from the dead" (1:20). The power of the resurrection is "for us who believe" (1:19). The Greek preposition *eis*, translated here as "for," does not mean that God's power is *in us* (though this is true through the Spirit). Rather, *eis* emphasizes the fact that God's power is *for us*, for our benefit.

To be sure, this power is something we each experience individually. But the plural "for us" suggests that God's power is for God's people together. Similarly, God's inheritance of "his holy people" underscores the corporate dimension of Paul's prayers. In Ephesians the emphasis is upon the people of God together being claimed as God's own.

The Sovereignty of Christ and the Introduction
of the Church (1:19–23)

In Greek, the sentence in the middle of verse 19 that begins "That power is the same" is part of the single-sentence prayer report that extends from verse 15 through verse 23. Yet the passage beginning in the middle of verse 19 is less a part of Paul's prayerful request and more a celebration of Christ's sovereignty. In the midst of this celebration, Paul introduces the church in a most perplexing way.

Seated him at his right hand in the heavenly realms (1:20). If God's power is seen most clearly in the resurrection of Christ (1:20), it is also glimpsed when God then "seated him at his right hand in the heavenly realms." In our earlier examination of 1:3 we showed that "the heavenly realms" (in Greek, "the heavenlies") are the domain of supernatural beings, including God, angels, and all sorts of evil powers. And what happens in the heavenly realms affects life on earth.

God dwells in the highest level of the heavenlies and that's where he has enthroned the exalted Christ. In the ancient world, to be seated at the right hand of a sovereign was to be in a place of honor, power, and glory. This means that Christ shares in God's authority and even in his worship. This is made clear in Philippians 2, where God exalted Christ "to the highest place and gave him the name that is above every name, that at the name of Jesus every knee should bow, in heaven and on earth and under the earth, and every tongue acknowledge that Jesus Christ is Lord, to the glory of God the Father" (Phil 2:9–11).

Far above all rule and authority (1:21). If Christ has been enthroned alongside God, then, by very definition, he has been exalted "far above all rule and authority, power and dominion, and every name that is invoked, not only in the present age but also in the one to come" (1:21). The entities identified here figure prominently in Ephesians. In *The Drama of Ephesians*, Timothy Gombis devotes a chapter to what he calls, "Some Mysterious Actors on the Stage."[4] These actors are the "powers and authorities" who "have a long history in the Scriptures and in Jewish tradition."[5] According to this tradition, God created supernatural beings to help rule the cosmos. When these beings rebelled against God's authority, they assumed a malevolent influence over the earth. In 1 Corinthians 2:6–8 for example, Paul refers to the "rulers of this age" who participated in Christ's crucifixion. Contrary to some interpretations of this text, the rulers in 1 Corinthians 2 are not merely human leaders,

4. Timothy G. Gombis, *The Drama of Ephesians: Participating in the Triumph of God* (Downers Grove: IVP Academic, 2010), 35–58. See also D. G. Reid, "Principalities and Powers," *DPL* 746–52.
5. Gombis, *Drama*, 36.

institutions, or social forces.[6] Rather, they are supernatural beings who exist and operate in the heavenly realms and from there have an earthly impact.

In Ephesians, these powers appear in four additional passages. According to 2:2, before we were saved, we "followed the ways of this world and of the ruler of the kingdom of the air, the spirit who is now at work in those who are disobedient." In 3:10, the "manifold wisdom of God" will be revealed "to the rulers and authorities in the heavenly realms." In 4:26–27, we are told not to let our anger "give the devil a foothold." Finally, in the most detailed treatment of the powers in Ephesians, 6:12 states, "For our struggle is not against flesh and blood, but against the rulers, against the authorities, against the powers of this dark world and against the spiritual forces of evil in the heavenly realms." Not only are there abundant and diverse evil powers in the heavens, but these powers are our opponents. This would be frightening news, except for the fact that Christ reigns over all powers. There is no name invoked at any time that is not subordinate to the authority of Christ: neither Satan, nor the Greek god Zeus, nor even Artemis, whose spectacular temple in Ephesus would have been a regular sight for some of the recipients of Paul's letter.

And God placed all things under his feet (1:22). This additional claim underscores the authority of Christ, using biblical psalms that early Christians applied to him. Psalm 8:6 says to the Lord, "You have made [human beings] rulers over the works of your hands; you put everything under their feet." But this psalm is now applied to Christ through the influence of Psalm 110:1, which the early church took as a messianic prophecy: "The LORD says to my lord: 'Sit at my right hand until I make your enemies a footstool for your feet.'" If one combines Psalm 110:1 with Psalm 8:6, as Paul did, it results in the sort of statement made in Ephesians 1:22: "God placed all things under [Christ's] feet." The stories of God's work in the Old Testament are picked up, interwoven, and applied to Christ in a story both old and new.

Appointed him to be head over everything for the church (1:22). In the final words of chapter 1, Paul introduces one of the central "characters" in Ephesians: the church. This introduction reveals essential qualities of the church, even as it raises puzzling issues. In 1:22, not only did God place everything under Christ's feet, but also he "appointed him to be head over everything for the church." The verb rendered as "appointed" could be translated more literally as God "gave" (*edōken*). God gave Christ as head over everything for the church's benefit or advantage. Curiously, Christ is not identified here as the head over the church or of the church, but rather the head over all things

---

6. Walter Wink shows how the language of powers has sociological implications, but he goes too far when he denies the supernatural reality of the powers. See *Naming the Powers: The Language of Power in the New Testament* (Philadelphia: Fortress, 1984).

for the church. If we remember that the church's opponents are the evil powers in the heavenlies, and if we recognize that they are included among the "all things" over which Christ rules, then what Paul says here would surely have encouraged his readers. Christ's authority over the powers means that the church, however powerless it may feel in the moment, shares in Christ's victory. The power that is for us is superior in every way to the evil powers that oppose us. This truth would be especially encouraging to the first recipients of Ephesians, an insignificant minority in the Greco-Roman world surrounded by prominent "gods" and their influential adherents. But if God put all the powers under Christ's authority, then his followers could feel confident and hopeful no matter how challenging their earthly life might be.

Much needs to be said about the church, but I'll hold part of the discussion for later (see especially commentary on 2:11–22; 3:8–12; 4:1–6, 7–16). At this point, it's worth noting that the Greek word for church, *ekklēsia*, in other contexts means a regular "legislative body" or informal "gathering."[7] Yet Paul's use of *ekklēsia* was influenced strongly by the Jewish use of the Hebrew word *qahal*, translated as *ekklēsia* in the Greek Old Testament (Septuagint), where it refers to the congregation of God's people. In many of his letters, Paul uses *ekklēsia* to refer to actual gatherings of believers. In Ephesians, however, *ekklēsia* takes on a much wider, less local sense. It refers, perhaps, to the universal collection of all Christians or to all believers as if they were gathered together in the heavenly realms in Christ. No matter how we understand *ekklēsia* at this point in our reading of Ephesians, its appearance in 1:23 highlights the corporate dimension of Paul's prayer report.

Which is his body, the fullness of him who fills everything in every way (1:23). Paul concludes his prayer report: Christ is the head, and the church is the body. But Paul does not stop with the conclusion that Christ is the head of the church. Rather, the church is also "the fullness of him who fills everything in every way" (1:23), a phrase that is disputed among the commentators.[8] The main questions include: Does "fullness" refer to the body/church or to Christ? What is the meaning of "fullness"? What is the meaning of "who fills everything in every way"? The best rendering of the original is the one taken by the NIV (and many others, see ESV, CEB, NRSV, KJV): "fullness" is in apposition to "body" (the body which is the fullness) not Christ who is the fullness.

Next we must examine the sense of "fullness"; it translates the Greek word *plērōma*, which appears four times in Ephesians. In 1:10 it is used in the phrase "when the times reach their *fulfillment*." In 3:19 Paul prays that the recipients of his letter "may be filled to the measure of all the *fullness* of God."

---

7. BDAG 303–4.

8. See, for example, Lincoln, *Ephesians*, 72–78; Arnold, *Ephesians*, 116–20.

According to 4:13 the church is to grow in unity and stature until it attains "to the whole measure of the *fullness* of Christ" (in all cases, emphasis added). In 1:23, the church is already the fullness of Christ. In 4:13, the church is growing into Christ's fullness. Thus when it comes to fullness, the church is to become more completely what it already is in Christ.

The language of fullness, though it might have been familiar to the first recipients of Ephesians because of its use in philosophical and religious circles, seems strange to our ears. In our effort to understand this language, we get help from *The Message*, which interprets 1:23 in this way: "The church is Christ's body, in which he speaks and acts, by which he fills everything with his presence." The language of presence may help us grasp the elusive sense of fullness. The church is the fullness of Christ in that Christ is truly present in the church. He will fill the universe with his presence through the church.

The claim that Christ "is filling everything in every way" is another way of expressing God's plan in Ephesians 1:10, to bring "unity to all things in heaven and on earth under Christ." The Greek phrase translated as "all things" in 1:10 is *ta panta*; likewise in 1:23, Christ is filling "everything," *ta panta*, in every way. So 1:10 envisions all things summed up and rightly ordered under Christ, while 1:23 envisions all things filled by Christ's presence. These are different but compatible visions of the cosmos as God intends the whole creation to be perfectly arranged by and completely filled by Christ.

The church as the body of Christ, as his fullness or presence, plays a central role in God's drama of restoring the cosmos. Later in Ephesians, Paul will spell out in greater detail how the church can benefit from and participate in God's work of uniting all things in Christ, which is to say, filling all things with Christ's presence.

LIVE the Story

Paul reports on his prayer for the recipients of Ephesians not only because such descriptions of prayer were conventional in letters and not merely because he wanted the recipients to know how he prayed. Rather, the prayer report in 1:15–23 adds to the story of God's plan for the cosmos found in 1:3–14, thus encouraging all readers of Ephesians. Paul's example also invites us to enlarge and enrich our prayers by shaping them in light of God's story.

Prayers Enlarged and Enriched by the Story of God

Now that we've examined Paul's prayer report in 1:15–23, I want to ask: Do you pray this way? If you are a pastor or church leader, do you pray like this for the people God has entrusted to you? If you are a parent, do you pray like this for your children? No matter the context in which you find yourself, do your prayers sound anything like this prayer?

I know a few people who could honestly answer "yes" to these questions. Years ago, I served on the staff of Hollywood Presbyterian Church under the leadership of Dr. Lloyd Ogilvie. In staff meetings as we interceded for our congregation, Lloyd's prayers often sounded like Paul's prayer in Ephesians 1. Lloyd wouldn't pray only about the immediate needs and concerns of our church family. He'd also ask the Lord to do things like help our members know the hope of God's calling, the riches of his glorious inheritance, and his incomparably great power for us as a church. Lloyd had steeped his mind so deeply in Scripture that prayers of this sort came naturally to him.

Most of us don't pray like this. We tend to pray for immediate needs, for things like financial help and daily guidance. Many of us are particularly adept at praying for healing for others when they are not present. I've been in many Christian groups who spend most of the time praying for "Jim's cousin's neighbor's friend." I am not suggesting that there is anything wrong with such specific prayers or that God doesn't care about the smallest things in life. Our problem isn't that we pray for too many tiny needs; it's that we don't pray for enough big ones. One main reason we don't pray with broad vision is that our prayers are not shaped and stretched by the biblical story of God.

Paul's prayers for the readers of Ephesians, as reported in 1:15–23, reflect his understanding of God's story. He asks God to grant "the Spirit of wisdom and revelation" because he knows that God has poured out his Spirit on all flesh and continues to gift his people through the Spirit. Paul asks God that we might "know him better" because Paul is well aware of stories throughout Scripture in which God reveals himself to his people. Paul asks God to help us know "the hope to which he has called us" because Paul knows where the story of God is heading. When Paul asks that we know God's power, he remembers the resurrection of Jesus. Paul's prayer includes an inspired narration of the exaltation of Christ.

We can find many other examples in Scripture of prayers sculpted by a deep grasp of God's story. In Nehemiah 1:5–11, for example, Nehemiah asks God to give him success as he brings a special request to the king. Almost half of his prayer focuses on what God has done in the past: keeping his covenant, instructing his people, and promising to gather them together again if they repent (Neh 1:5, 8–9). In Acts 4, when the first Christians were commanded by the Sanhedrin to stop talking about Jesus, they gathered to pray for God's help (Acts 4:24–30). Their request for boldness and miraculous power fills the final two verses of their prayer, but the first five verses recount what God has said and done. Many of the biblical psalms narrate in detail the story of

God's relationship with Israel. Psalm 106, for example, ends with a request to be saved and gathered from the nations (106:47). The first forty-six verses of this psalm tell the story of God's mercy in spite of Israel's sin. Next, Psalm 107 calls us to thanksgiving by reminding us in forty-three verses of God's unfailing love revealed through his many acts of mercy.

If you're not used to praying the story of God, it can seem strange to do so. You might wonder why God needs to hear the story he authored and in which he is featured. I expect that reciting God's story in prayer is less for God's benefit and more for ours. I learned this lesson from Howard E. Butt, Jr., the founder of Laity Lodge and my mentor during the years I worked there. Howard prays the story of God as a regular spiritual discipline. He explains:

> In my morning quiet time, I start by being thankful for the trustworthiness of God. Eventually, I ask for spiritual guidance in the dilemmas of the moment, but first I concentrate on God's character and His action in history. Beginning with praise and thanksgiving pulls me out of my subjective hullabaloo and turns my thoughts to God's reliability, which He has proven again and again. Trusting God is first of all a matter of remembering who He is and what He has done for us.[9]

In his book *Who Can You Trust?* Howard writes, "When I'm in a really bad place, I make it a habit to mentally review before God—daily if necessary—my own private history. I deliberately go back and plug it into God's Holy History: Creation, biblical Israel, Jesus and the Incarnation, his Cross and Resurrection, his Ascension and outpoured Spirit, the Church." Then, Howard remembers before God some of the momentous events of church history, his family's history, and his personal experience of God's faithfulness. What is the result of this recital of God's actions? "Inevitably," Howard says, "such a review overwhelms me with God's faithfulness, and makes my current bad patch no huge problem—at all—for Him."[10]

Yet Howard does not pray the story of God only in his private devotions. He does this also with others. On many occasions when I was with Howard, either in private mentoring sessions or in leadership meetings, he'd open with a prayer that spent several minutes reviewing God's mighty deeds, beginning with creation, the call of Abraham, the exodus, and so forth. He'd always end up focusing on what God did in Christ and what God will do in the future. Then, with his expectations formed by the recital of God's story, Howard

---

9. Howard E. Butt, Jr., "How to Pray About Your Work," http://www.thehighcalling.org/family/how-pray-about-your-work.

10. Howard E. Butt, Jr., *Who Can You Trust? Overcoming Betrayal and Fear* (Amazon digital, 2009), Kindle edition, 2764, 2787.

would pray for the needs of the moment, but not in the way we Christians commonly do. Rather, he'd pray expansively, asking a great God for great things.

I confess that I have a long way to go when it comes to praying God's story. I haven't yet developed the mature discipline of people like Howard Butt. Yet I have been encouraged by his example, not to mention the example of Paul in Ephesians, to include in my daily prayers a short recapitulation of some part of God's story. Usually this is based on whatever biblical text I am using for my personal devotions. There is nothing complicated about this practice. Basically, I let the text of Scripture become the content of my prayers. For example, if I were praying on the basis of Ephesians 1:15–23, I might say something like this:

> God of our Lord Jesus Christ, the glorious Father, thank you for your Spirit, who reveals to us who you are. Thank you for the hope of your calling and for the fact that we are your glorious inheritance. Thank you for your great power that is for our good and for making this power known to us through the resurrection of Christ. Thank you for enthroning Christ above all other powers in the whole cosmos and for placing all things under his feet for the church. Thank you for being fully present in the church and for making your presence known through the church to the universe. Help me, I pray, to know you better and to know the blessings you bestow on your people. May I have confident hope in you. May I rejoice that I am numbered among your glorious inheritance. May I experience your power that is for your people. May I live each day with the confidence that Christ reigns above all powers. May your church live truly as your body, full of your presence, making your presence more fully known throughout the world. All praise and glory be to you, O God. Amen.

Knowing God

In his prayer, Paul focuses on the knowledge of God. He prays that God would give us "the Spirit of wisdom and revelation, so that [we] may know him better" (1:17). He asks that "the eyes of [our] heart may be enlightened in order that [we] may know" the hope of God's calling, his glorious inheritance, and his great power (1:18–19).

The importance of "knowing" pervades Ephesians. Consider how the following words and phrases show up throughout the letter: "with all wisdom and understanding" (1:8); "wisdom and revelation" (1:17); "you may know" (1:18); "mystery made known" (3:3); "understand my insight" (3:4); "be made known" (3:10); "to know this love" (3:19); "knowledge of the Son of God" (4:13); "understanding" (4:18); "your minds" (4:23); "not as unwise but as wise" (5:15); "understand" (5:17); "make known the mystery" (6:19).

Ephesians is most concerned, of course, about a particular kind of knowledge, the knowledge of God and his ways. Paul writes this letter so that those who read it might know God better (1:17). Paul wants us to know the plan of God to unite all things in Christ (1:9–10). He wants us to know the love of Christ "that surpasses knowledge" (3:19). He writes so that the church might "reach unity in the faith and in the knowledge of the Son of God" (4:13).

Ephesians tells a distinctive story about how we come to know God and his truth. In our life before Christ, we were trapped in the "futility of [our] thinking" and were "darkened in [our] understanding" (4:17–18). Worse still, we were "separated from the life of God because of the ignorance" that was in us (4:18). Yet by grace, God made known to us the mystery of his will "with all wisdom and understanding" (1:8). We were "made new in the attitude of [our] minds" (4:23). We learned the way of Christ and "were taught in him in accordance with the truth that is in Jesus" (4:21). When we know this truth and speak it in love, then we will grow up as the body of Christ (4:15–16). We will "reach unity in the faith and in the knowledge of the Son of God and become mature, attaining to the whole measure of the fullness of Christ" (4:13).

Paul's desire for us to grow in the knowledge of God and his ways can be seen not only in the things he says about the centrality of knowledge but also in the fact that this epistle exists at all. The main point of this letter is Paul's passing on the story of God's work, including his plan for the cosmos. When we know this story, we will be inspired, empowered, and, yes, obliged to live our whole life for God's glory.

Even in today's increasingly secular world, millions upon millions of people want to know God. In Western culture, for example, we are stirred by the metanarrative (the story that controls all our stories) of the religious seeker, the one who sets aside traditional religion and doctrinal clarity in order to search for God. This search might take us to all sorts of exotic religious and philosophical destinations. Along the way, we are free to pick and choose the elements of our own belief system. The God we end up knowing is the "God" we have pieced together from all that we have collected along the way.

An example of this kind of religious search and its results is found in the landmark study of American culture, *Habits of the Heart*, by Robert Bellah and his team. They describe the religion of a person they call Sheila Larson who told them: "I believe in God. I'm not a religious fanatic. I can't remember the last time I went to church. My faith has carried me a long way. It's Sheilaism. Just my own little voice." The core of her own "Sheilaism" could be put this way: "It's just try to love yourself and be gentle with yourself. You know, I guess, take care of each other. I think He would want us to take care of each other."[11] Though Sheila is an extreme case of the democratic, individualistic American spirit, nevertheless, for many it rings true that we can and should know God on our own terms.

This is not the biblical story of knowing God, however. Rather, according to Scripture, we know God only because God makes himself known to us. We know God through revelation. Though certain truths about God can be discerned through God's self-revelation in nature (see Ps 8; Rom 1:18–23), deep knowledge of God comes only through what is called "special revelation." In the story of Moses, for example, God makes himself known to Moses at the burning bush (Exod 3:1–15). God reveals his power through ten plagues (Exod 7–12). God makes himself and his plans known to the Israelites by demonstrating his holiness to them at Mt. Sinai, entering into a covenant relationship with them, and giving them his law (Exod 19–20). Throughout the Old Testament God acts and speaks, thus revealing his identity, character, and will.

God's supreme revelation comes not merely in words or deeds but most of all in the incarnation of the divine Word. According to John 1, this Word was present with God in creation and is, in fact, God (John 1:1). At a point of time, "The Word became flesh and made his dwelling among us. We have seen his glory, the glory of the one and only Son, who came from the Father, full of grace and truth" (John 1:14). John adds, "No one has ever seen God, but the one and only Son, who is himself God and is in closest relationship with the Father, has made him known" (John 1:18). Similarly in language reminiscent of Ephesians 1, Paul's letter to the Colossians affirms the unique presence of God in Christ: "For God was pleased to have all his fullness dwell in him, and through him to reconcile to himself all things" (Col 1:19–20).

Though God has revealed himself fully in Jesus Christ, the Word made flesh, we will know Christ truly only in the context of God's story. The one we call Christ is the Messiah of Israel, a role that makes sense only in terms of the wider narrative of God's relationship with the Israelites. The Lord Jesus must also be understood in light of the story of his incarnation, proclamation, demonstration, humiliation, crucifixion, resurrection, and exaltation (for example, Phil 2:5–11). We will know what it means for Christ to be our Savior when we remember how God saved the Israelites from slavery in Egypt. We will know Christ as our Redeemer when we see him in the story that begins with creation and ends with the new creation.

Knowing God, therefore, isn't something fixed and static, some list of facts that we master and then move on to other things. Rather, it is a lifelong

11. Robert N. Bellah, Richard Madsen, William M. Sullivan, Ann Swidler, and Steven M. Tipton, *Habits of the Heart: Individualism and Commitment in American Life* (Berkley: University of California Press, 1985), 221.

growing in our understanding and experience of God. The prayer in Ephesians 1:15–23 reminds us that no matter how well we think we know God, there is always more to be known.

When I was a freshman in college, I went through a difficult season of doubt. Though I had been a Christian for years, I wasn't sure I believed anymore. I worried that I would never be able to have faith in God, let alone know God. Yet God through his grace did indeed give me the Spirit of wisdom and revelation so that I might believe in him and know him. I renewed my faith in God and committed myself to knowing him better.

A friend then suggested that I might be helped by a recently published book. So I trekked down to the Logos Bookstore in Harvard Square to see if I could find it. Sure enough, there on the shelves were many copies of *Knowing God* by J. I. Packer.[12] I eagerly bought a copy, thus claiming my very first book of theology.

From Packer I learned that "one can know a great deal about God without much knowledge of him."[13] As he explains, "Interest in theology, and knowledge about God, and the capacity to think clearly and talk well on Christian themes, is not at all the same thing as knowing him."[14] Knowing God, according to Packer, is first of all "a matter of personal dealing, as is all direct acquaintance with personal beings."[15] Second, it is "a matter of personal involvement—mind, will and feeling."[16] Third, "knowing God is a matter of grace. It is a relationship in which the initiative throughout is with God."[17]

When we speak of knowing God as something personal, those of us who are influenced by the individualism of American culture and religion might naturally assume that one's personal knowledge of God is one's private business. We assume that God reveals his truth to us individually and that we ought to make sense of it on our own. We end up practicing a Christian version of Sheilaism.

From a biblical perspective, however, knowing God is deeply personal but also profoundly corporate. It is shared knowledge of God, knowledge shaped not just by personal discoveries but also by the shared beliefs and practices of the people of God. Paul does not state this explicitly in Ephesians, but it is an assumption that pervades his prayer report in chapter 1 as well as the whole letter. Plus it is a clear implication of his teaching about the church. As we'll see later, we will grow in our personal faith when we are part of a

12. J. I. Packer, *Knowing God* (Downers Grove, IL: InterVarsity Press, 1975).
13. Packer, *Knowing God*, 21.
14. Packer, *Knowing God*, 22.
15. Packer, *Knowing God*, 34.
16. Packer, *Knowing God*, 35.
17. Packer, *Knowing God*, 36.

growing Christian community where all members speak the truth in love to one another.

The story of God is an essential element of this truth. If we want to know God personally, we would do well to listen to his story in Scripture. This story prepares us to know God through his incomparable revelation in Jesus Christ, the Word incarnate. This story is something we tell, celebrate, enact, embody, and pass on when we come together as the people of God. Moreover, because we recognize that knowing God is more than knowing about God, and that it is a gift of God's grace, we echo Paul's prayers in Ephesians 1, both for ourselves and for others, asking that "the God of our Lord Jesus Christ, the glorious Father, may give [us] the Spirit of wisdom and revelation, so that [we] may know him better."

CHAPTER 4

Ephesians 2:1–10

📖 LISTEN to the Story

¹As for you, you were dead in your transgressions and sins, ²in which you used to live when you followed the ways of this world and of the ruler of the kingdom of the air, the spirit who is now at work in those who are disobedient. ³All of us also lived among them at one time, gratifying the cravings of our flesh and following its desires and thoughts. Like the rest, we were by nature deserving of wrath. ⁴But because of his great love for us, God, who is rich in mercy, ⁵made us alive with Christ even when we were dead in transgressions—it is by grace you have been saved. ⁶And God raised us up with Christ and seated us with him in the heavenly realms in Christ Jesus, ⁷in order that in the coming ages he might show the incomparable riches of his grace, expressed in his kindness to us in Christ Jesus. ⁸For it is by grace you have been saved, through faith—and this is not from yourselves, it is the gift of God—⁹not by works, so that no one can boast. ¹⁰For we are God's handiwork, created in Christ Jesus to do good works, which God prepared in advance for us to do.

Listening to the text in the Story: Psalms 1; 30:1–3; 88; Ezekiel 37; John 3:16; Romans 3:1–26; 6:1–14; 8:1–17; 1 Corinthians 15; 2 Corinthians 5:16–21; Colossians 2:12–14; 2 Timothy 1:9–10.

The final two verses of Ephesians 1 introduced the church as Christ's "body, the fullness of him who fills everything in every way" (1:23). We might therefore expect Ephesians 2 to say more about the church. It does, but not right away. Before showing how the death of Christ brings the church into existence, Ephesians 2 begins by telling the story of how human beings have been saved by God's grace.

Ephesians 2 is divided into two roughly equal parts. The first half (2:1–10) focuses on the salvation of all believers, using the language of death and resurrection in a surprising way. This passage contains one of the most familiar and influential sentences in Scripture: "For it is by grace you have been saved, through faith" (2:8). The second half of the chapter (2:11–22) reveals that the cross of Christ accomplishes not just individual salvation but also the reconciliation of alienated communities of people, represented by the mending of the breach between Jews and Gentiles. Both halves of Ephesians 2 begin with a strong statement of bad news, the problem of our godless existence, which sets up the solution, the good news of God's work through Christ and its multifaceted consequences.

EXPLAIN the Story

Summary of Ephesians 2:1–10

Ephesians 2:1–10 begins with a problem: the dire condition of human beings apart from Christ (2:1–3). We were dead, following worldly, evil powers, not to mention our own sinful cravings. Yet our sad story takes a stunning turn for the better because of God's amazing grace, which offers a solution to our problem. God made us alive with Christ, even raising us from the dead and enthroning us with him (2:4–6). We have been saved by God's grace, which we receive in faith (2:8). Consequently, we are God's handiwork, newly created in Christ for a life of good works (2:10).

Ephesians 2:1–10 tells the story of our salvation, showing what we are saved from, what enables us to be saved, how we are saved, and for what purposes we are saved.

The Problem: Deathly Living Before Christ (2:1–3)

Ephesians 2:1–10 begins with news that is about as bad as it gets: "As for you, you were dead in your transgressions and sins." "You" picks up the second person plural from chapter 1, where "you" addresses the recipients of the letter (1:15–16). These are mainly if not exclusively Gentile Christians (see 2:11, 3:1).

As for you (2:1). There is a curious interplay of "you" and "we" in Ephesians 2:1–10:

"*you* were dead" (2:1–2)
"all of *us* also lived" (2:3)
"God made *us* alive" (2:4–5)
"by grace *you* have been saved" (2:5)
"God raised *us*" (2:6)
"by grace *you* have been saved" (2:8)
"*we* are God's handiwork" (2:10)

The movement back and forth between first person and second person plural may reflect Paul's effort to emphasize the fact that those who are reading the letter were once dead but now have been saved by grace. Or Paul may be using "you" in the sense of "you Gentiles," emphasizing the deadness of Gentile life before Christ and the good news that God has saved even the Gentiles by grace. But the story in 2:1–10 underscores the fact that "all of us," Gentiles and Jews alike, were "dead" apart from Christ and were brought into new life by God's grace. Thus the distinction between "you" and "us" should not be overstressed.

You were dead in your transgressions and sins (2:1). "You were dead" (2:1) is not to be taken as literal, biological death; it is a dramatic metaphor for human existence apart from God. This metaphorical use of death first appeared in the biblical story in Genesis 2:17, when the Lord told Adam that if he ate from the tree of the knowledge of good and evil, he would "certainly die." In chapter 3, the man does eat the forbidden fruit but does not instantly die physically. Rather, he begins to live apart from God in a death-saturated existence. In the Psalms, the psalm writers can speak of life filled with troubles in terms of death. For example, "I am overwhelmed with troubles, and my life draws near to death. . . . I am set apart with the dead" (Ps 88:3, 5). The deathly state of the psalmist includes the sentence of God's "wrath" (88:7), even as the Lord is identified "the God who saves me" (88:1).[1]

Sin leads to death in various senses, including the physical (see Rom 6:23). Because of the trespass of Adam, "death reigned through that one man" (Rom 5:17). Through our solidarity with Adam, we participate in death even while we are still physically alive. Ordinarily, however, we think of ourselves as being alive now, with our physical death off somewhere in the future. Ephesians 2 gets our attention by delivering the bad news that we are dead now if we are cut off from the God of life because of our "transgressions and sins" (2:1; these two words have virtually the same meaning).[2]

In which you used to live (2:2). "To live" translates the Greek verb *peripateō*, which can mean literally "to walk." This same verb figures prominently in Ephesians, where it is used as a dramatic way of talking about how we live (2:10; 4:1, 17; 5:2, 8). The Greek Old Testament, the Septuagint, occasionally uses *peripateō* to translate the Hebrew verb *halak*, "to walk," and was commonly used among Jews as a metaphor for "to live" (for example, 2 Kgs 20:3; also John 8:12). Apart from Christ, transgression and sin characterized our way of walking/living.

When you followed the ways of this world (2:2). The Greek reads more literally, "When you walked according to the aeon [*aiōna*] of this world" (2:2).

---

1. Paul may have been influenced by Jesus's reference to those who live apart from the kingdom as "the dead" (for example the saying in Matt 8:22, "Let the dead bury their own dead").

2. The Greek word translated here as "transgressions" (*paraptōma*) appears in Eph 1:7 in the phrase rendered by the NIV as "the forgiveness of sins [*paraptōmaton*]."

The word *aiōn* in Greek often means "a long period of time." It has this sense in 1:21 and 2:7 ("the present age," "the coming ages"). In Hellenistic culture, *aiōn* might also mean a supernatural being. This has led some interpreters to understand "the aeon of this world" as a reference to Satan, parallel to "ruler" and "spirit." Nevertheless, the normal New Testament usage of *aiōn* does not support this interpretation in 2:2. In the end, the word is best translated as "ways" (NIV) or its synonym "course" (ESV, NRSV). The *aiōn* way in which we lived is dominated by demonic powers.[3]

And of the ruler of the kingdom of the air, the spirit who is now at work in those who are disobedient (2:2). Outside of Christ, we live not only according to the fallen ways of this world but also under the power of Satan, who is identified here as "the ruler of the kingdom of the air" and "the spirit who is now at work in those who are disobedient" (2:2). Hellenistic people considered the air to be the abode of demonic powers. The fact that these powers lived near the earth enabled them to be "at work" among human beings. Thus when we were dead because of our own sins, we were also in bondage to the spiritual power of evil (see 6:11–12).

"Those who are disobedient" (2:2) in the NIV translates the Greek phrase *tois huiois tēs apeitheias*, which more literally is "the sons of disobedience." This use of "sons" suggests a contrast between these disobedient children and those whom, in Ephesians 1:5, God predestined "for adoption to sonship." It also anticipates the use of the phrase "children of wrath" at the end of 2:3 (obscured in the NIV translation, which makes it "deserving of wrath").

All of us also lived among them at one time (2:3) Though the first two verses of Ephesians 2 address the Gentile recipients of the letter specifically, their terminal diagnosis applies to everyone, including Paul and the Jewish people. In Greek, the masculine plural form of "among them" points back to "those who are disobedient." Nobody lived apart from the community of human beings who were caught in sin and its consequences.

Gratifying the cravings of our flesh and following its desires and thoughts (2:3). The word "flesh" (*sarx* in Greek) can refer to actual human flesh (as in John 1:14, "The Word became flesh"). But in Ephesians 2:3 and many other New Testament passages (e.g., Rom 8:4–9), it represents human sinfulness. Notice that sin infects not just the body and its desires but also our thoughts. Apart from Christ, even our thinking is tainted by sin and in bondage to the spirit of this age.

Like the rest, we were by nature deserving of wrath (2:3). Given that "we" were "like the rest" means that no distinction can be made between the letter recipients and the letter writer, or between Gentiles and Jews, when it comes

---

3. Yoder Neufeld, *Ephesians*, 93.

to the presence and penalty of sin. All human beings are "by nature deserving of wrath." The Greek actually calls us "children … of wrath" (*tekna … orgēs*), using a Semitic expression.[4] The phrase "by nature" probably means "from our birth."[5] Paul does not develop any particular doctrine of original sin here; his point is simply that we all are naturally sinful and cannot escape our fate.

"Wrath" refers not just to God's anger but also to his righteous judgment of sin (see Rom 3:5–7). Thus to the Romans Paul wrote, "The wrath of God is being revealed from heaven against all the godlessness and wickedness of people" (Rom 1:18). As it says in Psalm 7:11, "God is a righteous judge, a God who displays his wrath every day."

Thus ends the bad news. In our former life, we were spiritually dead, following the corrupted spirit of this age as well as the demonic spirit at work among human beings. All of us were once in this state, driven to gratify our fleshly cravings and deserving God's judgment.

The Solution: Saved by Grace into Resurrection Living in Christ (2:4–9)

Yet thanks be to God, the news doesn't end there. Rather, the bad news of 2:1–3 is a precursor to the good news revealed in the rest of the passage. In fact, the main verb of the long sentence that begins with verse 1 does not appear until verse 5, "made us alive with."

But … God (2:4). The contrast between the bad news of our deathly life and what follows is accentuated by the Greek phrase that begins verse 4, *ho de theos*, which means "but God." The NIV interjects "because of his great love for us" between "but" and "God," which lessens its rhetorical power. Verses 1–3 demonstrate our dire condition as sinful people, *but God* intervenes. We were dead … but God! We were in bondage … but God! We were under God's judgment … but God! In the story of God, his sudden intervention is a major and recurring theme.

Because of his great love for us (2:4). Why did God reach out to save us when we were lost? "Because of his great love for us" (2:4). In the Old Testament, God's love for his people is central to his identity as revealed through Moses: "The LORD, the LORD, the compassionate and gracious God, slow to anger, abounding in love and faithfulness, maintaining love to thousands, and forgiving wickedness, rebellion and sin" (Exod 34:6–7). In the New Testament, God's love is not just for Israel. Rather, it encompasses the whole world (John 3:16). This love is revealed through God's Son (1 John 4:9–10). Ephesians 2:4 describes God's love as being "great," and in the next chapter

---

4. For example, Cain is called a "son of wrath" in *Apoc. Mos.* 3:2 (*APOT*).
5. See, for example, Gal 2:15.

God's love will be depicted as extraordinarily large and beyond our capacity of understanding (3:18–19). God's great love begins to explain why he has saved us.

Rich in mercy (2:4). Along with his love, God saved us because he is "rich in mercy." The Greek word translated as "mercy" appears in the Septuagint version of the passage from Exodus 34, which Paul quoted in the previous paragraph. There, God is "gracious" (34:6; *eleēmōn*, related to *eleos*) and "making mercy to thousands" (34:7, *eleos*). In the Hebrew context, God's mercy is often associated with his care for his covenant people. In Ephesians 2, God's mercy extends to all people.

Notice that God is "rich" in mercy (Greek *plousios*). We have already heard of God's wealth in Ephesians 1:7, "the riches of God's grace," and 1:18, "the riches of his glorious inheritance"; later on Paul speaks of the "incomparable riches of his grace" (2:7), "boundless riches of Christ" (3:8), and "glorious riches" (3:16). In fact, *plousios* occurs with far greater frequency in Ephesians than in any other book of the New Testament. Since God is "rich in mercy" and full of love, he saves us even when we are undeserving. God's mercy is an outflow and an expression of his great love for us.

Made us alive with Christ even when we were dead in transgressions (2:5). Finally, we come to the main verb of the sentence that begins in verse 1 and extends through verse 7: "made us alive with." In Greek, this verb is *suzōopoieō*, made from the base verb *zōopoieō* ("to make alive"), with *su-* as a prefix (a shortened form of *sun*, "with"). This is the first of three verbs of this form in the Greek: "made alive with" (*suzōopoieō*; 2:6), "raised with" (*sunegeirō*; 2:6), and "seated with" (*sugkathizō*).

Again we find a surprising use of language, though one that corresponds with the bad news of 2:1–3. If, indeed, "we were dead in transgressions" (2:5), then salvation would have to include being made alive. Christ was made alive at his resurrection, as the next "with" verb in 2:6 will demonstrate.

It is by grace you have been saved (2:5). This phrase might strike the reader as awkward: Paul interrupts the chain of "with" verbs; he suddenly addresses the readers as "you" rather than "we"; he uses a perfect verb form rather than the past (aorist) tense of the verbs; and finally he uses a phrase that will be repeated verbatim in verse 8. It seems as if Paul simply cannot contain himself with the good news that his readers have been saved by God's grace. Just as Paul loved to share the good news of salvation with those who had not heard it before, so he also loved to remind believers of this news: you have been saved by grace.

And God raised us up with Christ and seated us with him in the heavenly realms in Christ Jesus (2:6). When God brought Christ back to life through his resurrection, this was not just Christ's personal experience of defeating death and returning to life. Rather, because we are in Christ, in a sense we participated with him in his resurrection. This is a different perspective on resurrection than the one that is common in the New Testament, in which Christ rose as "the firstfruits of those who have fallen asleep," meaning that his resurrection in the past signals our resurrection in the future (1 Cor 15:20, 23). Ephesians uses the familiar language of resurrection in a new way, stressing our present experience of resurrection without denying a future experience that is yet to come.

Perhaps even more startling is the claim that God also "seated us with him in the heavenly realms in Christ Jesus" (2:6). (For a discussion of "the heavenly places," see the commentary on 1:3, 20.) The bad news of our death might have required the good news of our being made alive and being raised up with Christ, but our being seated with him is an extra bonus.

Since we are not physically "up there" in the highest of the heavenly places, in what sense are we seated with Christ now? If we look back at Ephesians 1:20, we see the close connection between the resurrection and the enthronement of Christ. In one mighty act, God "raised Christ from the dead and seated him at his right hand in the heavenly places." Thus if we share in Christ's resurrection, we also share in his enthronement as part of the same act of God. Moreover, 2:6 seems almost redundant when it says God "seated us *with him* in the heavenly realms *in Christ Jesus*" (emphasis added). But the additional "in Christ Jesus" shows that we are seated in the heavenlies now, not because we are physically present there but because Christ is there and we are in Christ.

In order that in the coming ages he might show the incomparable riches of his grace, expressed in his kindness to us in Christ Jesus (2:7). Earlier we identified two reasons why God saved us from death into life: love and mercy (2:4). Verse 7 offers a third reason: God saved us so that "he might show the incomparable riches of his grace." This statement raises some curious questions. To whom is God wanting to show the riches of his grace? When? And why?

There seems little doubt that God wants to show his grace to human beings. But if we look further ahead in Ephesians, we learn that God also intends to make known to "the rulers and authorities in the heavenly realms" his "manifold wisdom," his "eternal purpose that he accomplished in Christ Jesus our Lord" (3:10–11). Thus, it is likely that God wants to "show the incomparable riches of his grace" not only to human beings but also to all beings throughout the cosmos, including angelic beings, including even the dark powers that oppose God.

When will God demonstrate his grace? Verse 7 answers, "in the coming ages," using the plural of the word *aiōn*. Back in Ephesians 1:21 is a reference to "not only in the present age but also in the one to come." It's likely that "in the coming ages" has a similar meaning, referring not just to the final future age but also to however many ages there will be between the resurrection of Christ and the uniting of all things in him. Thus, God wants to show the riches of his grace beginning in the past and extending into eternity.

Why does God want to show the incomparable riches of his grace? Perhaps the most obvious answer is that by showing his grace, God enables people to respond to it. Moreover, when we see God's grace, we are called to worship him, to live "for the praise of his glory" in everything we do (1:12).

Expressed in his kindness to us in Christ Jesus (2:7) The word "kindness" adds yet another nuance to God's relationship with us in addition to his love, mercy, and grace. The last part of verse 7 repeats the fact that God's goodness comes to us "in Christ Jesus." This could mean, on the one hand, that God's kindness comes to us by means of Jesus Christ. On the other hand, it might suggest that when we are in Christ Jesus, we receive God's kindness again and again. However we parse the nuances of the phrase, the point is clear: God's kindness for us is *in Christ.*

For it is by grace you have been saved (2:8). The Greek word translated as "grace" is *charis*, which has a range of meaning including: "graciousness, charm, favor, goodwill, grace, gift."[6] In the Greek Septuagint, *charis* often translates the Hebrew word *khen*, which means "favor" and "denotes the stronger coming to the help of the weaker."[7] We are saved by grace because we cannot help ourselves. Only God has the ability to save us, and this salvation does not depend on our worthiness or effort. Grace is God's unmerited favor, his undeserved kindness. As 2:8–9 makes abundantly clear, we do not earn our salvation because it is by grace alone. In a recent study, John M. G. Barclay shows that grace in Paul is best understood as "gift." This gift, though given freely, draws us into a reciprocal relationship with God and, as we'll see in the latter part of Ephesians 2, with each other as well. Grace doesn't leave us untouched: it leads to new creation, new community, and a whole new way of living (2:10).[8]

The verb "you have been saved" is a perfect passive participle in Greek, indicating that something has happened in the past that has a continuing effect in the present. In Paul's letters, depending on the context, salvation can be past, present, or future.[9] The perfect combines these senses, indicating that our salvation

---

6. BDAG 1079–81.
7. *NIDNTT* 2:116.
8. Thanks to Scot McKnight for the reference to John M. G. Barclay, *Paul and the Gift* (Grand Rapids: Eerdmans, 2015), in http://www.patheos.com/blogs/jesuscreed/2015/7/7/the-next-big-paul-book-is-imminent/.
9. Leon Morris, "Salvation," *DPL* 858–62.

has been accomplished and continues to be experienced in our lives. The passive voice of "you have been saved" reveals that our salvation is not something we do for ourselves but rather is something given to us. Grammatically speaking, the agent of salvation in this sentence is grace. But, of course, it is God's grace that saves us, and therefore God is the real agent of the verb "have been saved."

Through faith (2:8). The phrase "by grace you have been saved" was introduced in verse 5 and repeated in verse 8. In the latter instance there is an addition: "through faith" (2:8). This phrase has been traditionally understood as referring to our faith through which we accept the gift of salvation. This fits what we have seen elsewhere in Ephesians. The introduction identified the recipients of the letter as "the faithful in Christ Jesus" (1:1). Similarly, 1:15 referred to the readers' "faith in the Lord Jesus." Given that believing the gospel (see especially Rom 1:16; 10:9) and putting our trust in Christ is central to salvation, it would seem obvious that "through faith" means" "through your faith."

However, the Greek word *pistis*, translated here as "faith," can also mean "faithfulness." This has led some interpreters to understand "through faith" as meaning "through the faithfulness [of God]." This reading is consistent with the overall story of Ephesians in which God's faithfulness lies behind all of our blessings. But given the use of the verb "to believe" in Ephesians 1 ("When you believed," 1:13; "power for us who believe," 1:19), it seems likely that "through faith" refers to our faith rather than the faithfulness of God. Yet if this is true, it is essential that we do not turn faith into some kind of act that merits salvation. Moreover we should remember that faith in the biblical perspective includes more than just believing certain truths. We have faith in Christ not just when we believe that the gospel is true but also when we put our trust in Christ to save us. Given the penchant in contemporary English for "have faith in God" to mean "believe that God exists," we may be better off rendering *pistis* as "trust": we are saved by grace when we put our trust in God to save us in Christ.

Christians who are particularly fond of the language of "justification," such as that found in Romans and Galatians, are sometimes perplexed that this set of terms does not appear in Ephesians. Here Paul prefers to speak of salvation, which conveys much the same reality as justification, though with broader implications.[10] From what are we saved, according to Ephesians 2? Not only from the righteous judgment of God but also from all that was mentioned in the opening verses of the chapter: death, transgressions and sins, bondage to spiritual powers, bondage to sensual gratification, and God's righteous wrath.

And this is not from yourselves, it is the gift of God (2:8). In English, "this" looks like it might refer back to the most recent noun, namely "faith." But the

---

10. Cohick, *Ephesians*, 66–67.

Greek "this" is in the neuter form (*touto*), of which the feminine "faith" (*pistis*) could not be the grammatical antecedent. "Grace" is also feminine in Greek. Thus, "this" refers not to any single element of the previous sentence but rather to the whole process of salvation. Being saved by God's grace received in faith—all of this is God's gift. The word translated as "gift" is *dōron*, which appears only here in all of the Pauline corpus, though elsewhere Paul does use the related noun *dōrea* to identify gifts from God.[11] *Dōron* underscores the graciousness of God in saving us.[12]

Not by works, so that no one can boast (2:9). Usually, Paul refers to works when he is speaking of "works of the [Jewish] law" (for example, Rom 3:20). Yet the readers of Ephesians are, for the most part, Gentiles. So the works to which Paul is referring here must be any human works which seek to earn salvation. The Greco-Roman world was filled with religions that required humans to do certain things in order to receive blessings from the gods. So for example if you needed healing, you could go to the temple of Asclepius and offer sacrifices in order to try to get healed. Healing was then given by the god in response to human effort. Yet according to 2:9, our works will not save us. Our hope is not based on wishful thinking or our worthiness but on God's gracious work in Jesus Christ. One result of this is that we can never boast in our salvation, as if we had somehow earned it.

The Consequences: We Are God's Handiwork (2:10)

Ephesians 2:8 is one of the most familiar and influential verses in the Bible. Ephesians 2:10, on the contrary, is one of the most unfamiliar verses of the Bible. Yet once it is known and taken seriously, it becomes one of the most important verses.

For we are God's handiwork, created in Christ Jesus (2:10). The word "for" connects verse 10 with what precedes it, especially the fact that we have been saved by grace. Salvation is not only deliverance from death into life. It also involves being newly created in Christ. The verb translated here as "created" is *ktizō*. In the New Testament it is used exclusively to denote creating done by God. The related noun, *ktisis*, appears in 2 Corinthians 5:17: "Therefore, if anyone is in Christ, the new creation [*ktisis*] has come." Similarly in Ephesians 2, when we receive God's salvation by trusting him, we participate in the new creation, his "handiwork" (2:10).

The word translated as "handiwork" is *poiēma*, which is related etymologically to our word *poem*. Contrary to what we sometimes hear in sermons, the word *poiēma* does not really mean "poem." Rather it means "something

---

11. For example, Rom 5:15, 17; also Eph 3:7; 4:7.
12. Cohick, *Ephesians*, 65–66.

made by someone," a "work" of someone's hands. The ESV goes with "workmanship." The NRSV has "we are what he has made us." The NLT perhaps overtranslates the Greek word in its rendering "we are God's masterpiece."

Created in Christ Jesus to do good works, which God prepared in advance for us to do (2:10). The fact that "good works" show up so positively in this passage can shock those of us who know Ephesians 2:8–9 and its clear statement that salvation does not come by works. But we miss the full implications of salvation if we stop reading in verse 9. No, our works do not earn our salvation. But our salvation should indeed lead us to a life of good works, works God has prepared "for us to do." Yes, we are saved by God's grace. But receiving this gift means living with and for God in a new way. The Greek reads, "in order that we might walk in them," thus ending 2:1–10 as it began, with a description of how we walk/live (see 2:2). The first three verses of this passage chronicle the sorry state of living apart from God's grace. But when we receive this grace, we aren't merely delivered from a bad way of living into some kind of neutral existence. Rather, we are created anew in Christ for a new way of living, a way embodied in good works.

The truth that God has good works for us to do is fully consistent with what we have seen earlier in Ephesians. God chose us to be holy so that we might belong to him and be devoted to his purposes (1:3). God determined that we should exist "for the praise of his glory" (1:12, 14). In the latter chapters of Ephesians, we'll learn much more about the nature of these good works that glorify God.

One thing we will learn as we continue on in Ephesians is that our good works are an expression of a Christian community. We can easily miss this through an individualistic reading of 2:10. Yes, you are individually God's handiwork. And, yes, God has good works for you yourself to do. But that's not the whole story. As will become clear in the next part of Ephesians 2, God has good works for the community of the faithful to do together. In fact, you and I cannot walk in the good works God has for us apart from intentional fellowship with other members of Christ's body (see 4:16, for example).

LIVE the Story

Ephesians 2:1–10 invites us into God's story by telling it in an unexpected way. We start out as the "walking dead" and end up "walking in good works" as God's new creation.

Hope for the Walking Dead

If Paul were writing Ephesians today, I have a hunch he'd mention zombies. Now, zombies are not ordinarily the stuff of theology, but they are familiar to anyone who pays attention to pop culture. When I was young, zombies were rarely talked about outside of Haitian culture and religion. But in 1968 George Romero spent $114,000 to film a frightening thriller called *Night of the Living Dead.* When fans associated the walking dead in his film with zombies, a new genre was born. This genre grew slowly but steadily, capped in 2010 by the wildly popular and critically acclaimed television series, *The Walking Dead.*

Cultural experts offer their reasons for the popularity of zombies in our day, but I have my own hunch. I agree with those who believe zombies embody our fears about a world run amuck with apocalyptic dangers. But I think many people are drawn to zombies because they themselves feel like zombies much of the time. Zombies experience no pleasure in life, but still they keep trudging on in search of something that will never satisfy them. They are driven, insatiable, unhappy, helpless, and barely conscious, just like many people in today's world.

For sixteen years I was the pastor of a church in suburban Southern California. Most of my members appeared to have it made. They lived in elegant homes, drove the latest cars, raised highly successful children, and participated regularly in church. Some of these people were truly happy. But over the years, many shared their angst with me. They had allowed their drive to squeeze the joy out of their lives. They kept striving, however, because that's what they were wired to do. Though many were highly paid, they did not value their work but felt trapped in their careers because of how much money it took to pay for their homes and cars and to fund the appetites and activities of their children. Some even felt strapped financially because of their support for the church. Many of the people I served fell into addictions that damaged their families, friendships, and professional lives. Others let their fleshly desires lead to momentary euphoria but long-term despair.

Those I have just described felt dead inside. There were not the zombies of cinema, but they lived rather like them. Thus they might feel drawn to zombies portrayed in movies and television because the walking dead seem familiar, like old friends.

Ephesians 2 speaks to the walking dead among us. It resonates with those who, though physically alive, are missing real life. In language that is both foreign yet strangely familiar, Ephesians 2:1–3 describes the deadly life that many of us know all too well. Even if, because we are Christians, we are no longer completely dead in our sins, we still walk according to the lethal ways of this world. We still feel demonic power drawing us into toxic behaviors. We choose what we know to be harmful in order to gratify our desires.

But Ephesians 2 doesn't leave us with the depressing diagnosis of a living death. Rather, it offers the good news of what God has done in Christ and the hope of a different way of living. At the center of this good news is the truth that we have been saved by grace. Though we cannot save ourselves, God can and does save us through Christ.

This gospel can sound hollow to many of us, since the gospel we have heard is mostly about a great life after death. Our life in this world is relatively unaffected, except for the fine print that came along with it: a long list of regulations to rule our life. Most of us have never heard that we have been made alive with Christ, raised with Christ, and enthroned with Christ. We do not realize that when we trusted God for salvation, we became his handiwork, newly created in Christ for good works that God had planned for us.

When we understand what God's salvation really entails in this life, we begin to realize that we are not sentenced to a zombie-like existence. We don't have to settle for a driven, empty, unhappy life. Rather, we can begin to live now in Christ and with Christ. We can begin now to experience the power of the resurrection that is for us because we have been raised with Christ. We can begin now to live as God's workmanship, contributing to God's work in the world and, therefore, knowing that our lives really matter.

As I write these words, there is something in me that demands, "Okay, so what should I do?" But Ephesians 2:1–10 tells me this is the wrong starting point. I should not begin with my efforts. Rather, I should begin by listening deeply to the story of God's gracious salvation in Christ. I begin by seeing myself in this story. I begin by leaning back into God's great love, wealthy mercy, and incomparably rich grace. I let the truth that God has saved me by grace be the foundation of my life. I start to see myself as God's handiwork, letting this inspired vision transform my sense of identity and purpose. Only then may I take the time to consider what I might do as God's handiwork, since there are good works God has prepared for me to do. But if you're the sort of person who wants to run your own life, and if, like me, you rush to the question of what you must do, then you need to take time to let the story of God's grace in Ephesians 2:1–10 sink in. Grace changes us. It changes our stories. Let grace rewrite your story.

Another Story Must Begin

I'm reminded of a scene from Victor Hugo's masterpiece, *Les Misérables*. Jean Valjean, a recently released convict, cannot find a place to sleep or a morsel to eat. Finally, he ends up at the house of the Bishop of Digne, a man of deep Christian faith and character. The bishop welcomes Valjean and treats him with uncommon decency and kindness. But in his desperation, Valjean steals the bishop's silver and escapes. When he is caught by the *gendarmes*, Valjean is dragged back to the bishop's house, where he expects his thievery to be confirmed by the bishop and his future to be lost by more decades in prison. Yet much to his amazement, Valjean hears the priest confirm Valjean's trumped-up story that the silver had been a gift. When the *gendarmes* depart, the bishop tells Valjean to use the silver to become an honest man. "Jean Valjean, my brother: you belong no longer to evil, but to good. It is your soul that I am buying for you. I withdraw it from dark thoughts and from the spirit of perdition, and I give it to God!"[13]

When Jean Valjean leaves the bishop's presence, he is disturbed. He does not know what to make of grace, because he has never before encountered it. Yet as he considers his options, he decides to leave his old life for something altogether new. The light the bishop had shown him "filled the whole soul of this wretched man with a magnificent radiance."[14] Thus, in the musical version of *Les Misérables*, Valjean sings:

> I'll escape now from that world,
> From the world of Jean Valjean.
> Jean Valjean is nothing now.
> Another story must begin![15]

Another story must begin, a new story of life in place of death, a story birthed by grace.

Resurrection in the Life of Ben

Yet the story of Jean Valjean's encounter with grace leaves us with a question: Do things like this happen in real life? Does God's grace transform the stories of actual human beings, or just fictional characters?

You can probably come up with some notable real-life examples of transforming grace. For example, there is the story of John Newton, the slave trader whose encounter with grace ultimately led him to become an abolitionist, not to mention the writer of "Amazing Grace." Or you might think of the story of Chuck Colson, who left behind Machiavellian power games in order to devote himself to serving prison inmates in the name of Christ. These are true, wonderful stories. But they might still leave us wondering if ordinary people ever live out the story of Ephesians 2:1–10.

I once knew an apparently ordinary man who was a surprising example of the transforming power of grace. "Ben" was a lay leader in a church I once pastored. He served as a church elder, where he exercised quiet, solid wisdom.

---

13. Victor Hugo, *Les Misérables* (New York: Random House, 1992), 92.

14. Hugo, *Les Misérables*, 98.

15. Claude-Michel Schonberg, Alain Boublil, and Herbert Kretzmer, "What Have I Done (Valjean's Soliloquy)," in *Les Misérables: The Complete Symphonic Recording* (First Night Records, 1989). The musical is based on the book by Victor Hugo.

He always seemed willing to pitch in and help when there was a need. Ben was especially devoted to caring for the "down and outers." I didn't know much about Ben's personal life other than that he was a faithful husband and a manager of a small business.

But one evening I heard Ben tell the story of his life. After that, I never saw him in the same way again. As a young man, he had shown great potential in business. His keenness in brokering deals led to worldly success. Along the way, Ben began to abuse alcohol. After a while, his drinking affected his work. Before long, Ben lost his job, his friends, and his self-esteem. For solace, he immersed himself more deeply in drinking. When his money ran out, he was evicted from his home and found himself living on the street. In Ben's own words, he "became a bum on Skid Row, sleeping on the streets and in the alleys."

Ben never had much interest in God, and he spurned the street evangelists who sought to reach the walking dead of the Skid Row section of Los Angeles. But one night, as Ben tripped along in a drunken cloud, he heard a preacher sounding forth in one of the rescue missions in the area. Ben wasn't particularly interested in God, but he did want a clean, safe place to sit, maybe even a free meal. So Ben wandered into the meeting and plopped down.

As he listened to the preacher, Ben, even in his inebriated state, heard the truth of his own life. I don't know if that preacher was using Ephesians 2:1–10, but his message was the one writ large in this passage. For the first time in his life, Ben saw himself as he was, a man who was lost and needed to be found, one who was dead and needed to be made alive. When the preacher ended his sermon with an invitation for people to receive Christ, Ben went forward and, like Jean Valjean, was forever changed by grace.

Ben faced many challenges from that moment on. Yet as he began to live as a new creation in Christ, he experienced life as he had not known it before. He found a job and started to rebuild his professional life. He never achieved the success that he had once had, but he lived with gratitude for the life God had given him. In time, he met the woman who became his wife, and they shared a long, good life together.

As Ben told his story, I was shocked. The Ben I knew seemed like the last person in the world whose story might actually be such an apt picture of resurrection from death to life. I glimpsed God's amazing grace in a new way that night. In Ben's life I could see clearly how God had created him anew in Christ, and how faithful Ben had been to walk in the good works God had planned for him.

What Are the Good Works God Has Prepared for Us?

When I first heard Ben's story many years ago, if you had asked me about the good works God had prepared for him, I could have told you many of them.

I might have said, "Ben is an outstanding church leader. He is an exemplary church elder. He serves in many ways around the church as an usher, a class leader, and a volunteer in the church's outreach mission. Ben is kind and loving to people. He faithfully bears witness to Christ."

Today, I look back on that answer as being correct but inadequate. There is no doubt in my mind that Ben's church-related and evangelistic activities were among the good works God had planned for Ben. But the good works of Ben's life extended far beyond his actions in church and obvious "ministry." I know relatively little about these other good works. I know that Ben was a well-regarded manager in a modest business, and I know that he was a loving husband. In his professional and personal life, Ben lived out the good news of grace. I expect he was the kind of boss who valued people and treated them with respect. I know he was that kind of husband. So in his daily life, too, Ben faithfully engaged in the good works of God.

Why am I convinced that the good works of God include things like managing people in a secular business or loving one's spouse well? Partly I'm sure of this because of what comes later in Ephesians, where we'll see that work and family are prime contexts for living out the story of God (see 4:28; 5:21–6:9). But I'm also remembering God's plan in Ephesians 1:10, "to bring unity to all things in heaven and on earth under Christ." As you may recall, "all things" includes *all things*, things such as work, marriage, etc. God's plan is to mend the brokenness in creation that comes from sin. Quite specifically, Genesis 3 reveals that this brokenness affects marriage and work, and so our good works will appear in those areas, too.

By all means, join the church, do mission projects, share the gospel with your colleagues at work, and so forth. I don't want to remove anything from that list of potential good works; rather I want us to add things we might easily neglect.

The Good Works of Jean Valjean

This brings us back to Jean Valjean. If you're unfamiliar with Victor Hugo's original novel *Les Misérables*, you may wonder whatever happened to Valjean. How did the bishop's grace change the story of Valjean's life? If you are familiar with this narrative through the musical or movie, you have some idea of the answer but may not be fully aware of the details of the good works of Jean Valjean.

After his encounter with the bishop, Valjean created for himself a new identity, "Monsieur Madeleine." He moved to a city in France that was famous for producing a unique kind of jewelry, and he invented a more cost-effective way to produce it, which revolutionized the business. As a result, Valjean became a rich businessman, using his new resources to build a new factory that added to his wealth. Yet this factory was designed by Valjean with the specific aim of showing respect to its workers. As Hugo observes, "It seemed that he thought much for others and little for himself."[16] He paid his laborers well, offering good work to anyone who was willing to labor faithfully and live honestly. According to Hugo, "Before the arrival of Father Madeleine, the whole region was languishing; now it was all alive with the healthy strength of labour."[17]

The main focus of Valjean's good works for his city was his business. But he also gave substantial sums to the city, adding to the hospital, improving the school, and building a place of refuge for "old and infirm workers."[18] His efforts on behalf of the people of his city became so well known that, in time, the king of France named Valjean as mayor. He was also faithful in his Christian disciplines, attending mass regularly and giving alms. He was beloved by the people of the city, especially the poor, so much so that they called him "Father Madeleine."

Jean Valjean engaged in the sort of activities that we readily identify as good works: going to church, caring for the poor and the infirm, loving the downtrodden. But Valjean's good works also included his technological innovations, his construction of a factory that dignified workers, and his excellent management of a business that improved the lives of all.

We'll return to considering the nature of our good works later in Ephesians, especially as we examine portions of chapters 4 and 5. For now, the story of Jean Valjean reminds us not only that God's grace rewrites our stories but also that our new story features a life of good works broadly envisioned, the kind of good works God intended for human beings in creation, as well as those good works that contribute directly to the mission, growth, and health of the body of Christ.

---

16. Hugo, *Les Misérables*, 140.
17. Hugo, *Les Misérables*, 139.
18. Hugo, *Les Misérables*, 140.

Ephesians 2:11–22

📖 LISTEN to the Story

¹¹Therefore, remember that formerly you who are Gentiles by birth and called "uncircumcised" by those who call themselves "the circumcision" (which is done in the body by human hands)—¹²remember that at that time you were separate from Christ, excluded from citizenship in Israel and foreigners to the covenants of the promise, without hope and without God in the world. ¹³But now in Christ Jesus you who once were far away have been brought near by the blood of Christ.

¹⁴For he himself is our peace, who has made the two groups one and has destroyed the barrier, the dividing wall of hostility, ¹⁵by setting aside in his flesh the law with its commands and regulations. His purpose was to create in himself one new humanity out of the two, thus making peace, ¹⁶and in one body to reconcile both of them to God through the cross, by which he put to death their hostility. ¹⁷He came and preached peace to you who were far away and peace to those who were near. ¹⁸For through him we both have access to the Father by one Spirit.

¹⁹Consequently, you are no longer foreigners and strangers, but fellow citizens with God's people and also members of his household, ²⁰built on the foundation of the apostles and prophets, with Christ Jesus himself as the chief cornerstone. ²¹In him the whole building is joined together and rises to become a holy temple in the Lord. ²²And in him you too are being built together to become a dwelling in which God lives by his Spirit.

Listening to the text in the Story: Genesis 1–3; 12:1–3; Isaiah 9:2–7; 52:7–10; 53:3–5; 57:15–19; Matthew 5:9; John 17; Acts 1–2; 1 Corinthians 3:16–17; 6:19–20; 2 Corinthians 5:16–21; Galatians 3:26–28; Colossians 3:9–17; Revelation 21–22.

Ephesians 2 overflows with the good news of what God has done in Jesus Christ. Unfortunately, many of us hear only half of this good news. We are rightly astounded by the fact that "by grace [we] have been saved, through faith" (2:8). But some of us stop there, rarely moving on to the truth that we are also "God's handiwork, created in Christ Jesus to do good works" that God has prepared for us (2:10). And even if we appreciate 2:10, we might miss the stunning news in the second half of the chapter or fail to connect its good news with what has gone before. We see it as something additional, as evangelical extra credit, rather than as an essential and glorious element of the good news of God's saving work in Christ. Surely the second half of Ephesians 2 deserves our full attention, especially in a day when its truth is sorely needed both in the church and in the world.

Ephesians 2:11–22 reveals more of the consequences of the cross of Christ. Its message can be quite surprising if you're familiar with the good news of personal salvation by grace but not as familiar with the corporate dimensions of this salvation. By paying close attention to the second half of Ephesians 2, we'll discover more details about the story of God, and we'll be drawn to live more fully for his cosmic purposes.

EXPLAIN the Story

Summary of Ephesians 2:11–22

The basic form of 2:11–22 is similar to 2:1–10. Both passages begin with bad news, the problem of our condition apart from God (2:1–3, 11–12). A summary of this problem is followed by a heartening introduction to the solution: "But God" (2:4, 13). What follows is the good news of how God, in Christ, has solved the problem of our godless condition (2:4–7, 14–18). Then, the consequences of this solution are spelled out in terms of who we are in Christ (2:8–10, 19–22). The formal similarities between 2:1–10 and 2:11–22 underscore the point that both halves of chapter 2 proclaim the good news of how God has saved us by his grace from death and division.

The Problem: Gentiles Excluded (2:11–12)

According to 2:11–12, the recipients of Ephesians, who were Gentiles before they encountered God's grace, suffered a fivefold plight: they were separated from Christ, excluded from Israel, strangers to God's promises, hopeless, and godless. This unhappy picture of Gentile life, which adds to the woes spelled out in 2:1–3, prepares us for the contrast that comes in verse 13 and beyond.

Therefore (2:11). The word "therefore [*dio*]" makes a strong connection between the first half of Ephesians 2 and the second half. Thus what follows in 2:11–22 reveals an essential dimension of God's salvation in Christ.

Formerly you who are Gentiles by birth (2:11). This is the first appearance of the word "Gentiles" in Ephesians. Its use here and in 3:1 shows that the recipients of Ephesians are primarily (if not exclusively) Gentile believers. The Greek word translated as "Gentiles," *ethnē*, can refer to nations or people groups and was used by Jews as a label for non-Jews.[1] Notice that the recipients of the letter *were* (so the CEB, not the NIV) Gentiles "by birth" (literally, "in flesh," *en sarki*). They did not become Jewish when they received God's grace through Christ. Rather, Christ made them into something different from ordinary Gentiles and Jews. The early Christian writing known as the Epistle to Diognetus expresses this same point when it calls Christians a "new race," neither Jewish nor Gentile.[2]

Called "uncircumcised" by those who call themselves "the circumcision" (which is done in the body by human hands) (2:11). "In the body" translates the Greek expression *en sarki*, which means "in the flesh." The label "uncircumcised" is a literal description of Gentile males, since, at that time, Jewish men were known as having been circumcised. This physical characteristic distinguished Jews from Gentiles and identified Jews as God's chosen people. Jews used "uncircumcised" derogatively. Their perspective on the Gentiles is spelled out in 2:12.

Remember that at that time you were (2:12). This phrase introduces a list of five ways in which the letter recipients, as Gentiles, were excluded from the blessings of God's people. "At that time" suggests that a new time has come, the "now" of 2:13.

Separate from Christ (2:12). In this verse, *Christos* might be translated as "a messiah," given that Paul is speaking from within a Jewish context. Gentiles were "without a messiah [*chōris Christou*]" because they were cut off from those to whom the Messiah had been promised.

Excluded from citizenship in Israel (2:12). The Greek word translated here as "citizenship" (*politeia*) appears elsewhere in the New Testament only in Acts 22:28, where it refers to Roman citizenship. (Philippians 3:20 uses a related word, *politeuma*, for our heavenly citizenship.) In 2:12, *politeia* could also mean "commonwealth."[3] Israel is, in principle, the official community of God's people, even if it was under Roman rule when Paul was writing. In the first century, citizenship was not about the right to vote; it was a matter of community, privilege, and honor.

Foreigners to the covenants of the promise (2:12). The Gentiles are "foreigners." The Greek is *xenoi*, which also means "strangers or aliens."[4] In Ephesians 2:12 we find a phrase unique in Scripture, "the covenants of the promise." The major covenants between God and Israel in the Old Testament related

---

1. BDAG 276–77.
2. Diogn. 1 (http://www.ccel.org/ccel/richardson/fathers.x.i.ii.html).
3. So the NRSV; ESV. See Lincoln, *Ephesians*, 137.
4. BDAG 684.

to a chosen leader are: Abraham (Gen 12:1–3; 15:18; 17:1–14); Jacob (Gen 28:13–15); Moses (Exod 19:3–6); and David (2 Sam 7:11b–16). Paul might also be thinking of the promised new covenant (Jer 31:31–34; 32:38–40; Ezek 36:24–36). Two Old Testament covenants include the Gentiles (Gen 9:8–17; 12:1–3; 28:13–15), but the Gentiles would not have known these covenants and thus would have been "foreigners" to their promises. In Romans 9:4 Paul refers to the blessings of the people of Israel, including "the covenants, the receiving of the law, the temple worship and the promises," though without linking covenants and promises explicitly.

Without hope (2:12). Hope, as we saw in the commentary on 1:18, is not an optimistic yearning but confidence in a future reality.

Without God in the world (2:12). The Greek uses the word *atheoi*, plural of *atheos* ("without God"), from which we get "atheist." It does not mean that Gentiles do not believe in God or gods so much as that their lives are godless because they are separated from the true God.

The Solution Summarized: Gentiles Brought Near in Christ (2:13)

But now (2:13). "But now" sets up a contrast between the recipients' former existence as Gentiles and their new existence "in Christ Jesus." This language parallels a similar contrast made in 2:4, where God is also the main actor ("But God"). Here, God's activity is implied, with "the blood of Christ" identified as that which brought the Gentiles near.

Far . . . near (2:13, 17). The language of "far" and "near" describes the state of Gentiles before and after their experience of "the blood of Christ." This language is reminiscent of Isaiah 57:19, where "far" and "near" are used with reference to Jews who are "far" (in exile) and "near" (within the territory of Israel). It's possible that Paul's use of "far" and "near" in this passage was influenced by Jewish descriptions of proselytes who were once far but became near when they converted to Judaism.[5] Yet in 2:13 Gentiles are now brought near, not through conversion to Judaism but through Christ's saving activity.

By the blood of Christ (2:13). Paul uses the phrase "by the blood of Christ" to designate Christ's saving activity. This echoes 1:7, where Paul wrote, "In [Christ] we have redemption through his blood, the forgiveness of sins." The sacrifice of Christ on the cross, which involved the shedding of his blood, not only redeemed us for relationship with God but also brought us near to God and his people.

Ephesians 2:13 summarizes the main storyline of 2:11–22. Once the Gentiles were far away from God and his blessings. "But now" they have been "brought near" by God through Christ's death on the cross.

---

5. See Lincoln, *Ephesians*, 138–39.

The Solution Explained: The Peace of Christ (2:14–18)

Though Paul could have skipped immediately from 2:13 to the consequences of this saving action (2:19–22), instead he devotes five densely worded verses to explaining what being brought near involves and how Christ accomplished it.

For he himself is our peace. . . . making peace. . . . preached peace . . . and peace (2:14, 15, 17). How did Christ bring the Gentiles near? The answer in 2:14–18 is centered in peace. Christ "is our peace" (2:14). He was "making peace" (2:15). He "came and preached peace" to the Gentiles who "were far away" and "peace" to the Jews who were near (2:17). The Greek word for peace, *eirēnē*, usually means "the absence of war," though it can also refer to "peaceful conduct."[6] The New Testament usage of *eirēnē* is strongly influenced by the Hebrew *shalom*, which can refer to the absence of war but also means "peace, friendship, happiness, well-being, prosperity, health, luck, kindness, salvation."[7] This robust notion of peace is found for example in Isaiah 32:16–18: "The LORD's justice will dwell in the desert, his righteousness live in the fertile field. The fruit of that righteousness will be peace; its effect will be quietness and confidence forever. My people will live in peaceful dwelling places, in secure homes, in undisturbed places of rest."[8]

In Ephesians 2:14–18 Christ makes peace in that he eradicates the "hostility" between Jews and Gentiles (2:14, 17). Yet the peace Christ forges is more than the end of enmity. It involves making Jews and Gentiles "one" (2:14), creating "one new humanity out of the two" (2:15), and reconciling "both of them to God" (2:16). So essential is Christ to this peacemaking effort that he is called, simply, "our peace" (2:14), that is, the peace *of both Jews and Gentiles.*

Christ's making peace in 2:14–18 expresses and exemplifies God's cosmic purpose as revealed in 1:10: "to bring unity to all things in heaven and on earth under Christ." Paul could just as well have said in chapter 1 that God's purpose is "to make peace among all things in heaven and on earth under Christ." Thus, the peace that exists between Jews and Gentiles is one essential aspect of the uniting of all things in Christ.[9]

According to Ephesians 2:17, Christ "came and preached peace to you who were far away and peace to those who were near." To what does "preaching peace" refer? In the Gospel of John, Jesus spoke of peace with his disciples and offered peace to them after his resurrection (John 14:27; 20:19). Yet Jesus also said that he came not to bring peace (Matt 10:34), so it's unlikely that "preaching peace" refers mainly to the teaching of Jesus. Rather, Ephesians

6. *NIDNTT* 2:776–77.
7. *NIDOTTE* 4:130.
8. See also Ps 85:8–10.
9. See Col 1:20, where the connection between all things, reconciliation, and Christ's blood is explicit.

2:17 employs the language of Isaiah 52:7–10, where the messenger of God brings "good news" and "proclaim[s] peace." Here, peace is the salvation that comes when God reigns on earth. This prophecy of Isaiah ends with the promise that "all the ends of the earth will see the salvation of our God." Thus, in Ephesians Christ "preached peace" through the whole of his messianic, saving mission, including his proclamation of the kingdom of God and his enactment of this message in his death and resurrection.

The language of Ephesians 2:17 was also influenced by Isaiah 57:19, where the Lord himself speaks "Peace, peace, to those far and near." Yet now the peace proclaimed encapsulates the whole mission of Christ and is delivered not just to Jews far and near but to all people, including the Gentiles.[10]

Who has made the two groups one (2:14). As "our peace," Christ not only brought an end to conflict between Jews and Gentiles. He also "made the two groups one," a claim reminiscent of the vision of unity in 1:10. The particulars of Christ's peacemaking, unifying effort are spelled out in 2:14–18, with special attention given to how Christ took away that which separated Jews from Gentiles and fostered hostility between them.

Has destroyed the barrier, the dividing wall of hostility, by setting aside in his flesh the law with its commands and regulations (2:14–15). The NIV rendering of this phrase partly solves and partly obscures problems in the original Greek, which could be translated literally as "having destroyed the dividing wall of the fence, the hostility in his flesh, having set aside the law of commands in regulations." Several questions arise: What is "the dividing wall of the fence"? How was it destroyed? What is "the hostility"? What is the "law of commands in regulations," and how was it set aside?

Paul in Ephesians often heaps words upon words, and this may be what is happening with the phrase "the dividing wall of the fence." Many interpreters suggest this was the actual wall that existed in the courts of the Jewish temple in Jerusalem. This fence separated the court of the Gentiles from the court of the Israelites, thus keeping Gentiles away from the holier sections of the temple. A sign on the fence warned that Gentiles who crossed the barrier would be put to death. This interpretation is supported by the fact that, a few verses later, Paul will speak of building the new temple of God's people (2:21–22).

Though Paul may have pictured the dividing wall in Jerusalem as he wrote, the text and its cultural context suggest another, metaphorical meaning for this barrier. In 2:14–15, destroying the wall is linked with setting aside "the law of commands in regulations." The Jewish law included many commands that distinguished Jews from Gentiles (circumcision, Sabbath, kosher, etc.).

---

10. See Lincoln's extensive discussion of 2:17 in *Ephesians*, 146–49.

Thus the law could be seen as a wall dividing Jews from Gentiles. This imagery appears in a document known as the Letter of Aristeas, written by a Jewish author in the mid-second-century BC.

> Now our Lawgiver being a wise man . . . fenced us round with impregnable ramparts and walls of iron, that we might not mingle at all with any of the other nations, but remain pure in body and soul. . . . Therefore lest we should be corrupted by any abomination, or our lives be perverted by evil communications, he hedged us round on all sides by rules of purity, affecting alike what we eat, or drink, or touch, or hear, or see.[11]

Paul sees the Jewish law along these lines, especially those elements that divided Jews from Gentiles. For Paul, the law is a wall of separation not unlike the physical wall in the temple. Not only did the barrier of the law keep Jews distinct from Gentiles, but also it fostered hostility between Jews and Gentiles in the Roman world. Jews looked down on unclean Gentiles for their failure to live according to God's standards, and Gentiles despised Jews for their peculiar practices that kept them separate from common society. Thus the law could function as a "dividing wall" and could even be thought of as "hostility" since it was a source of enmity between Jews and Gentiles.

In Ephesians 2:14–18, Christ made peace between Jews and Gentiles by "setting aside . . . the law" (2:15). He did this "in his flesh," which is a reference to his death on the cross (see 2:13). Furthermore in verse 16, Christ sought "to reconcile both of them to God through the cross, by which he put to death their hostility." The irony in this phrase is striking. Literally, Christ was put to death on the cross. Yet at the same time, he was putting to death the hostility between Jews and Greeks through the cross.

Some interpreters limit "the law of commands in regulations" to only the ceremonial portions of the Torah. They bolster this case by pointing to the positive use of the law in Ephesians 6:2. Evidently, Paul does not believe that the law has no relevance to those who are in Christ. Yet in 2:15, the law that Christ sets aside is not limited to the ceremonial law.[12] The whole law is composed of "commands and regulations." In some way, this whole law has been set aside through the death of Christ. Without wading into the treacherous waters of controversy concerning Paul's view of the law,[13] we see in Ephesians that the law is not that which redeems us, saves us, or gives us life. The death of Christ has supplanted the law, and therefore all people can belong to God through faith because of his grace in Christ.

---

11. Let. Aris. 139, 142 (APOT).
12. Arnold, Ephesians, 162–64.
13. See an overview in F. Thielman, "Law," DPL 529–42.

His purpose was to create in himself one new humanity out of the two, thus making peace (2:15). The verb "to create [*ktizō*]" is used in Ephesians, as in the rest of the New Testament, only in reference to God's creative activity (see 2:10). In 2:15, the new creation is of "one new humanity," in Greek "one new human being [*kainon anthrōpon*]." This language is reminiscent of 2 Corinthians 5:17: "Therefore, if anyone is in Christ, the new creation [*kainē ktisis*] has come." Part of this new creation is the unity of Jews and Gentiles, a result of Christ's "making peace." When we are saved by God's grace (Eph 2:8), we become God's handiwork created for good works (2:10) and become part of the one new humanity in Christ in which the division between Jew and Gentile has been torn down (2:15). New creation and new community are part and parcel of the salvation we have by grace.

And in one body to reconcile both of them to God through the cross (2:16). The phrase "one body" in verse 16 points both to the literal body of Christ, the sacrifice that brought reconciliation, and the metaphorical body of Christ, namely, the church (1:22). The unexpected order of reconciliation in this verse is striking. Ordinarily we would think of Christ as reconciling us first to God and then to each other, with the main emphasis on the vertical divine-human reconciliation (see 2 Cor 5:16–21). In Ephesians 2, however, the horizontal reconciliation between humans comes to the fore. Thus, in 2:16 the picture is of Christ forming Jews and Gentiles into one body and then reconciling this united body to God. There is no contradiction here between Ephesians and 2 Corinthians. The differing emphases point out that both vertical and horizontal reconciliation matter to God. Both are essential to God's plan for bringing all things together in Christ (see 1:10; also Col 1:20–22).

For through him we both have access to the Father by one Spirit (2:18). In 2:17 Christ preached peace to "you" far away Gentiles and the nearby Jews. Verse 18 changes to the first person "we," emphasized further by "both." Both Jews and Gentiles "have access to the Father" in the same manner, not through the law, but "through [Christ]" and "by one Spirit." The word translated as "access" (*prosagōgē*) also appears in 3:12, where we have *prosagōgē* in Christ, that is, access to God the Father in Christ.[14] This noun *prosagōgē* does not appear in the Greek Septuagint, but the related verb, *prosagō*, is used for presenting offerings to God, which opens access to him.[15] Given the sacrificial and temple imagery in 2:11–22, not to mention the addition of "to the Father" in verse 18, it's clear that all people can have access to God the Father through Christ and "by one Spirit." The sacrifice of Christ opens up the way to the Father. The Trinitarian scent of this verse cannot be missed.

---

14. See also Rom 5:1–2, where "access" is associated with peace, as in Eph 2:17–18.
15. For example, Lev 1:2–3 in the LXX.

Though the details of 2:14–18 can be perplexing, the main storyline is clear. Christ forged peace between Gentiles and Jews through his death on the cross, by which he took away the barrier of the law that had divided Gentiles and Jews. The peace of Christ is not just the absence of hostility but also the unifying of the two groups, creating one new humanity out of the two and reconciling this unified humanity to God. Now, all people receive peace through Christ as well as access to God the Father through him and by the Spirit.

The Consequences: Gentiles Included (2:19–22)

The last four verses of 2:11–22 spell out the consequences of Christ's peacemaking work for those who were Gentiles. These consequences are represented with three parallel metaphors: "you are no longer foreigners and strangers, but fellow citizens with God's people"; you are "members of God's household"; and you are stones in God's temple.

Consequently, you are no longer foreigners and strangers, but fellow citizens with God's people (2:19). These "foreigners and strangers" are by implication Gentiles "excluded from citizenship [*politeias*] in Israel" (2:12). Now the former Gentiles are "fellow citizens [*sumpolitai*] with God's people." "God's people" renders the Greek *tōn hagiōn*, namely, all who belong to God, both Jews and Gentiles. The former Gentiles now are included as citizens not in the actual nation of Israel but among those who live in God's kingdom.

Members of his household (2:19). Paul's addressees are "also members of [God's] household" (2:19). The underlying Greek word for "members," *oikeioi*, has the root *oikos*, or "house"; this is also the root of the word *paroikoi*, which is used earlier in verse 19 and translated as "strangers." To be members of God's household or family is an even more intimate relationship than being a citizen in God's kingdom.

Built on the foundation of the apostles and prophets, with Christ Jesus himself as the chief cornerstone (2:20). Verse 20 moves from a family metaphor to a building metaphor. This building has a foundation, "the apostles and prophets," and a cornerstone, "Christ Jesus." For those familiar with 1 Corinthians, this use of foundation language can be surprising. In his earlier letter Paul wrote, "For no one can lay any foundation [for the church] other than the one already laid, which is Christ Jesus" (1 Cor 3:11). Now we find a different foundation, the apostles and prophets, with Christ relegated to the cornerstone. For some interpreters, this is a contradiction that either counts against Pauline authorship of Ephesians or points out Paul's inconsistent theology. But this is a rigid manner of judging Paul. Surely Paul is entitled to use his metaphors freely, shaping them to fit the particular context of his writing. Thus as he writes Ephesians, he looks at the church from a different perspective than is found in his earlier letter to the Corinthians. He still emphasizes the fundamental, initiatory, essential role of Christ in the church. But he also wants to underscore the importance of those human beings who played a founding role in the church. (Apostles and prophets will appear again in Ephesians 3:5 and 4:11.) Indeed, as we'll see in Ephesians 4, the growth of the church comes from Christ yet also depends on the work of each and every member.

Most English translations of 2:20 use the word "cornerstone" for the Greek *akrogōniaios*. Yet among recent commentators, a substantial number argue for "capstone" or "keystone" instead.[16] This would make Christ a keystone of an arch, the final stone put in place as the crown of the edifice. While this translation is possible, it does not give enough weight to the use of *akrogōniaios* in the Septuagint version of Isaiah 28:16, "See, I lay a stone in Zion, a tested stone, a precious cornerstone [*akrogōniaion*] for a sure foundation." There, the cornerstone is part of the foundation, the first stone to be laid, which determines the location of the structure. Given the foundational role of Christ in the formation of the church and the use of the foundation metaphor in 1 Corinthians 3:11 and Isaiah 28:16, it seems best to translate *akrogōniaios* in 2:20 along with the NIV and most other English translations as that part of the foundation known as the "cornerstone." Christ is the stone that determines the placement of every other stone.

In him the whole building is joined together and rises to become a holy temple in the Lord (2:21). The building in which God's people are stones is not yet complete, as indicated by the present tense of "rises." Rather, it is in process as it grows to become more fully "a holy temple in the Lord." This image of the church being built anticipates Ephesians 4:11–16, where the church is described as a body that is being built up in love. In that passage, the body is said to be "joined . . . together [*sunarmologoumenon*]" (4:16). Similarly in 2:21, "the whole building is joined together [*sunarmologoumenē*]." This underscores the importance of the unity of all of the "blocks of stone" in God's temple, including, of course, the unity between Jews and Gentiles.

The people of God are not just parts of any building, however. They are stones in the growing "holy temple in the Lord" (2:21). In an earlier letter to the Corinthians, Paul used similar language, though without the aspect of growth: "Don't you know that you yourselves are God's temple and that God's Spirit dwells in your midst?" (1 Cor 3:16). The temple is the local community of believers in Corinth (in contrast with 1 Cor 6:19, where the individual human body is said to be a temple of the Spirit).

This portrayal of the Christian community as a temple is striking for two reasons. First, it sets Christianity apart from virtually every other religion in

---

16. See, for example, Barth, *Ephesians*, 1:317–19.

the Roman world, which featured temples, holy buildings where adherents worshiped their gods. The implicit claim of 2:21 is that God is to be encountered not in special places but in a special people. Second, the Gospels reveal that Jesus fashioned himself as a replacement for the temple. For example, forgiveness of sins could be found in him, not in the temple and its sacrifices (Mark 2:1–12). Thus, for Paul to speak of the Christian community as a temple was to associate the church with Jesus and his mission in a stunning way.[17]

And in him you too are being built together to become a dwelling in which God lives by his Spirit (2:22). "You too" highlights the inclusion of the former Gentiles in the building of God, while assuming that Jews are also part of this building (2:22). This is true for all stones that are "in [Christ]." The passive "are being built together" suggests that God is doing the building, something that will be expanded upon in Ephesians 4. "A dwelling in which God lives" is another way of describing the temple of God. The Greek word translated here as "dwelling," *katoikētērion*, is used in the Septuagint for God's dwelling place in heaven (for example, 1 Kgs 8:39) as well as the temple in Jerusalem (Ps 76:2; LXX 75:3). God is present in the community of Christians "by his Spirit" (also 1 Cor 3:16).

As we come to the close of Ephesians 2, we hear the story of God's grace in a new way. Not only has God raised us from death to life, not only has God saved us by grace through faith, not only has God created us anew for good works, but God has also united formerly divided people groups, namely Jews and Gentiles, bringing near those who once were far away and joining all in his kingdom, his family, and his temple. Where we Gentiles were once excluded from God, his people, and his blessings, now we are included in Christ. Where we once were without God, now we are not only reconciled to God but are also joined together with the rest of God's people as a temple, the dwelling of God on earth. The unifying of Jew and Gentile, far from being something extra in God's plan, is a powerful symbol of the uniting of all things in Christ and a central element in God's saving work.

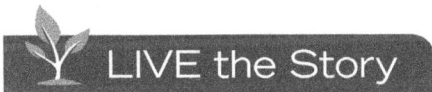

LIVE the Story

The Broken Wall

Many years ago, my friend Steven traveled to Berlin, Germany, on a mission to secure a piece of the Berlin Wall. That wall, emblematic of one of the most menacing divisions in the world in the twentieth century, had recently fallen.

---

17. See N. T. Wright, *Jesus and the Victory of God* (Minneapolis, MN: Fortress, 1996); and his "Jesus' Self-Understanding," in *The Incarnation*, ed. S. T. Davis, D. Kendall, and G. O'Collins (Oxford: Oxford University Press, 2002), 47–61.

People from around the world went to help tear it down and to collect a piece of history.

After he arrived in Berlin, Steven searched for a portion of the wall from which to retrieve a chunk. The most familiar sections of the wall had already been torn down, so he headed to a residential neighborhood where the wall was accessible. Seeing an exposed portion of the wall, Steven took out his tools and began to chip away at the concrete. Promptly, a resident of the neighborhood emerged from his home and yelled angrily, "Dat is not de vall! Dat is an apartment haus." Embarrassed, Steven stopped damaging this innocent building and went to find the actual wall.

Why would my friend and so many others like him go to such trouble to chip away at a wall? Some folks may have wanted an unusual souvenir. But Steven and thousands of others wanted more than a hunk of history: they sought a personal connection to one of the most compelling stories of our time.

East Germany began the Berlin Wall in 1961 as a wire fence dividing the city into east and west. It separated people from their jobs and families. Later, the original fence was replaced by a twelve-foot high concrete barrier. This wall not only split Berlin but also represented the fearsome division between the Eastern Bloc countries with their repressive socialism and the democratic West. For decades the Berlin Wall symbolized the hostility between East and West that threatened nuclear annihilation. It was an emblem of oppression and fear.

On November 9, 1989, as an international movement was ending the division of Europe, the East German government decided to allow its citizens to pass freely through the Berlin Wall, effectively initiating its fall. That was a moment of great celebration both in Germany and throughout the world. Berliners instantly began demolishing sections of the wall, chiseling off small pieces. A year later, the East German army began to take down the wall officially. During this time, people from around the world made pilgrimages to Berlin in order to contribute to the demolition of the wall and to save pieces of it. In this way, they could celebrate the reunification of a nation and the hope for a more peaceful world. Moreover, they could participate in the story of the destruction of a real dividing wall of hostility.

According to Ephesians 2:11–22, we can participate in a similar story. Christ has broken down the wall of hostility between Jews and Gentiles. Thus if we are in Christ, we step into this story. We experience life without the dividing wall as we join the unified people of God.

Like the case of Berliners and their wall, we do not bring about the fall of the wall. The Berlin Wall was essentially destroyed when the East German government chose to open it. The wall dividing Jews from Gentiles was essentially destroyed when Christ died on the cross. Yet like the Berliners with their hammers and chisels, we can participate in the story of the wall's destruction and, in a practical way, even contribute to that destruction. We, along with all other believers, can live in the unity created in Christ as citizens in the one kingdom of God. Plus, we can live as blocks of stone in a new building, the unified temple of the living God composed of all who are in Christ.

Like those who once chipped away at the Berlin Wall, we care deeply about the demolishing of hostility between and the establishment of unity among once divided people. So does God, according to Ephesians 2:11–22. This passage reveals that God cares enough about unity for Christ to sacrifice his life on the cross so as to break down enmity between Jews and Gentiles, thus creating one new humanity. Christ's peacemaking work is not incidental to the story of salvation; it is an essential element.

A Bigger Story of Reconciliation

Given the truth of Ephesians 2:11–22, one might expect that Christians today would put a premium on making peace between alienated people. The fact that they do not may be because Paul's specific topic addresses one particular social division, the enmity between Jews and Gentiles. For Paul and the early Christians, this division was as significant as the division between East and West in the late twentieth century. But for many of us, this particular disunity is not on center stage. We worry more about the divisions that trouble our lives today: alienation in families, strife in cities, discord between races, socioeconomic gaps, schisms in churches and denominations, and conflict between ethnic and religious groups. Thus we may wonder if Ephesians 2:11–22 has anything to say to us and our contemporary struggles. But if Christ's death pushed aside the barrier that separated Jews and Gentiles, then by analogy we can conclude that God seeks to remove barriers and enmity wherever people are divided. The peacemaking and unifying work of God, illustrated in the reconciliation of Jews and Gentiles, touches all of life.

Yet analogy alone may not be enough to stimulate God's people to live the story of broken walls and unified humanity. We need a stronger theological rationale if we are going to see the second half of Ephesians 2 as equally important as the first half. We need a bigger story if we are going to be convinced that Ephesians 2 is as relevant to our lives today as it was in the first century. We need the biblical story of God.

That God's story is bigger than reconciliation between Jews and Gentiles is suggested by several elements of 2:11–22. If *all* Christians have been brought near through Christ, should not *all* hostilities among us be destroyed as well (2:13)? If Christ is indeed "our peace" (2:14), would not his peacemaking work touch all places of enmity in the world? If Christ's purpose is to create one new humanity, wouldn't this include all peoples delivered from all divisions (2:15)?

The larger story of God in Ephesians answers these questions in the affirmative. God's grand plan is "to bring unity to all things in heaven and on earth under Christ" (1:10). The unifying of Jews and Gentiles is a central aspect of this cosmic unity. It reveals in one, crucial setting what unity looks like and how it occurs. But if God is unifying *all things*, then surely he seeks to end *all divisions* among people.

A passage in Colossians strengthens this conviction: "[You] have put on the new self, which is being renewed in knowledge in the image of its Creator. Here there is no Gentile or Jew, circumcised or uncircumcised, barbarian, Scythian, slave or free, but Christ is all, and is in all" (Col 3:10–11). In Christ the disunity between Gentile and Jew is abolished, but so are other kinds of disunity, including ethnic (barbarian, Scythian) and economic divisions (slave, free).

The entire biblical story confirms that God through Christ is in the global reconciliation business. In Genesis, human beings at first experienced unfettered intimacy with each other (Gen 2:25). Yet when they sinned, the initial result was the shattering this intimacy as the man and woman hid from each other (Gen 3:7). Thus began the saga of separation between human beings, which is epitomized in the enmity between Jews and Gentiles. Jesus, through his death on the cross, not only takes away the law as a barrier between Jews and Gentiles but also addresses the deeper problem of human sin, the source of all human dissension. Thus the cross brings reconciliation not only between Jews and Gentiles but also between all peoples who experience division and enmity rooted in sin. Just as sin against God led to brokenness in relationship among people, so reconciliation to God leads to reconciliation among people. This vision of unity among all peoples is highlighted at the end of the biblical story. In Revelation 21:24–26, all nations (again, *ethnē*) walk in the light of God, and the inclusive people of God share together in the peace of the age to come. Social divisions and injustice disappear when God unifies all things in Christ (Eph 1:10).

Ephesians 2:11–22 is not a distraction from the reconciliation that we, as individuals, have with God through Christ. Rather, this passage enlarges our vision of God's work. It shows that reconciliation between divided peoples, far from being a minor tangent in God's story, is a glorious and major theme. If we are going to live fully in the grace of God in Christ and participate in his cosmic work, then we must live out the story of reconciliation both as reconciled people and as agents of reconciliation. Even as Christ, our peace, made peace through the cross, so we are to be peacemakers in every dimension of life: in our relationships and families, in our neighborhoods and workplaces, in our churches and denominations, and in our cities and nations.

Living the Story of Reconciliation

We have a great need for the peace of Christ in our world today. All around us we see strife and division, conflict and injustice. Digital social media has increased our awareness of the disunity of human society, even as it has spawned greater meanness and intolerance that exacerbate this disunity. Racial tensions in our society are growing, spurred by economic disparities and alarming stories of cultural bias. Ethnic hatred breeds oppression and terrorism across the world.

Given the widespread divisions in our world, we can feel overwhelmed. We may ask: How can I hope to bring reconciliation to this world? We need to remember the truth of Ephesians 2. The multiple wounds of the world will only be mended by God's grace. We cannot begin to make a lasting difference except inasmuch as we are in Christ. Moreover, because we are in Christ, we are no longer one person trying to make a difference. Rather, we are now part of God's kingdom, God's family, God's temple. God, through the Spirit at work in the community of his people, will extend the peace of Christ into the world.

Often God begins with us, helping us see the walls that we erect or to which we contribute. These walls might be obvious ones, like racial prejudice, ethnic hatred, greed, or unbridled nationalism. Yet the walls that keep us from experiencing reconciliation may be more hidden, such as physical and relational distance from people who are different from us, habits of self-centeredness, traditions that foster separatism, or just plain ignorance that breeds insensitivity.

I can illustrate that last point, although the story is embarrassing. I grew up in a community that was more than 95 percent Anglo. I was not raised with obvious racism, but I never really thought about how my behavior might build walls between me and others. In college, my blindness to my own bias began to be revealed as I got to know people from different races, ethnicities, and life experiences.

Once I was hanging out with one of the leaders of my InterVarsity chapter. Jeanette and I were talking about the crazy things I had done while in high school when I mentioned something about a "Chinese fire drill." Jeanette—a Chinese-American—bristled just a bit when I used that phrase. In a kind but firm voice, she said, "Mark, many of us who are Chinese don't really appreciate that expression. It makes fun of us, and it can be hurtful." I felt immediately ashamed. Of course what I said was insensitive. The fact that I had said it to a Chinese person whom I greatly admired revealed the extent of my ignorance. I quickly apologized, and Jeanette quickly forgave me. But the memory of what I had done stayed with me. I wondered how many more things in my life were inherently racist. Since that time, I have found quite a few. No doubt there still are more to be identified, confessed, and discarded.

My former InterVarsity leader Jeanette is now a pastor on the staff of a church that is committed to living the biblical story of reconciliation. When in 1980 I visited Grace Chapel in Lexington, Massachusetts, it was as Caucasian as the population of the town it served. But over the years Lexington became more ethnically diverse. Grace Chapel saw its mission as extending throughout the Boston area, a region that was becoming thoroughly multicultural. In the 1990s visionary members of this church, inspired by the biblical story of God's unified people, began a ministry for members from a variety of cultural backgrounds. The church began to offer English classes for those who spoke other languages and to sponsor a Cultural Awareness Weekend. Worship services were translated into Korean, Spanish, and Mandarin. Later, in 2005 church leaders began to ask themselves, "How should Grace Chapel respond to the changing demographics in our church and the region in a biblical way?" This led to the formation of a Multicultural Leadership/Learning Team to expand the perspectives of the church. Since then, the church has intentionally sought to bring cultural diversity to its leadership. It hired a pastor to oversee its multicultural ministries. In fact, Grace Chapel called my friend Jeanette, the first American-born Asian American member of the staff, as Pastor of Global and Regional Outreach. Today, 30 percent of the membership of Grace Chapel comes from cultures other than Euro-American. The church also partners with non-Anglo churches in the Boston area and throughout the world.

This is just one story of one church that is seeking to live the story of reconciliation through Christ. I tell this story partly because I know it and partly because it can serve as a model for other churches. Grace Chapel did not begin with big declarations or big programs. Rather, it began its growth in multicultural ministry through relationships, including plenty of listening. Dana Baker, the pastor of Multicultural Ministries at Grace Chapel, wrote about the importance of listening in the book *Ethnic Blends: Mixing Diversity into Your Local Church*: "As we transitioned from being an almost entirely monocultural church of people of western European descent, fifteen years ago, to a congregation now approaching 30 percent non-Anglo ethnicity, we have learned how important it is to listen to the voices of the people whom God has brought to our church and not, as leaders from the majority culture, try to figure it out for ourselves."[18]

---

18. Mark DeYmaz and Harry Li, *Ethnic Blends: Mixing Diversity into Your Local Church* (Grand Rapids: Zondervan, 2010), 155.

In 1968, while preaching at the National Cathedral in Washington, D.C., Martin Luther King, Jr., famously said, "We must face the sad fact that at eleven o'clock on Sunday morning when we stand to sing 'In Christ there is no East or West,' we stand in the most segregated hour of America."[19] This still may be true today, but with the model of churches like Grace Chapel, things are changing. A recent column in the *Huffington Post* bore the title, "Racial Diversity Increasing in U.S. Congregations." Sociologist Scott Thumma sums up recent research that finds among U.S. churches "a major shift toward desegregation." According to Thumma, the percentage of multiracial congregations "had nearly doubled in the past decade to 13.7%."[20]

The Challenge and Reward of Living as People Reconciled in Christ

When I last checked, 13.7 percent is not an "A" grade, though it's better than the 7.5 percent that was the score from 1998. If we are going to live the story of reconciliation through Christ, we must acknowledge that we have a long way to go. We will make progress not merely through our good intentions and hard work but mainly as we live out who we are in Christ. Christ can do in and through us what nothing or nobody else can do.

A couple of years after my gaffe with Jeanette, I found myself in the most uncomfortable cross-cultural experience of my young life. I was leading a team of Anglo-American Christians from Harvard who spent a weekend with members from Deliverance Tabernacle, an African-American Pentecostal church in Bridgeport, Connecticut. We slept on their sofas, ate at their tables, and worshiped with them on Sunday morning. That service, which lasted three hours, was the longest worship service of my life. (The pastor told me afterwards that they had shortened it up a bit "for you white kids.") But it wasn't just the length of the service that stretched me. I was used to a well-ordered Presbyterian form of worship, with some forays into charismatic praise. The service at Deliverance Tabernacle included more than a few praise songs, however. The singing seemed to be endless. Plus the service featured clapping, dancing, several enthusiastic testimonies, speaking in tongues, crying, shouting, and skipping around the sanctuary. (You really don't want to see me skip in a worship service.)

But the most awkward moment of all came in the middle of the pastor's lengthy sermon, which had been continuously interrupted by cries from the

---

19. Martin Luther King, Jr., "Remaining Awake through a Great Revolution," March 31, 1968, http://mlk-kpp01.stanford.edu/index.php/encyclopedia/documentsentry/doc_remaining_awake_through_a_great_revolution/.

20. Scott Thumma, "Racial Diversity Increasing in U.S. Congregations," *Huffington Post*, March 24, 2013, http://www.huffingtonpost.com/scott-thumma-phd/racial-diversity-increasing-in-us-congregations_b_2944470.html.

congregation ("Yes, Lord," "Amen," and "Preach it, pastor") and accompanied by regular drum and organ music. For some reason, the pastor felt inspired to call me up: "Mark, you're the leader of this group from Harvard. Why don't you bring the Word to us." He pointed to the pulpit, and I trudged forward reluctantly.

I tried to be energetic. I tried to be enthusiastic. But mostly I felt like the most lifeless white guy who ever lived. After a while, the congregation had pity on me. Instead of shouting, "Amen," they called out things like, "Help him, Lord." Finally, after ten minutes of humiliating misery, the Lord did help me—back to my seat, that is.

Once more I felt keenly aware of my narrow life experience. I felt embarrassed by who I was and how poorly I had brought the gospel to these people. I wished I could just disappear. Yet after the service, the members of Deliverance Tabernacle were gracious and encouraging. I felt loved in spite of my stilted Anglo ways. As church members embraced me warmly, I sensed that we were, indeed, one in Christ. Though there were still many cultural walls between us, in Christ we were fellow citizens, members of the same family, and building blocks in the amazingly diverse temple of the Lord. I experienced for the first time in my life the joy of being one new humanity with people I would never even have met outside of Christ.

CHAPTER 6

Ephesians 3:1-13

📖 LISTEN to the Story

¹For this reason I, Paul, the prisoner of Christ Jesus for the sake of you Gentiles—

²Surely you have heard about the administration of God's grace that was given to me for you, ³that is, the mystery made known to me by revelation, as I have already written briefly. ⁴In reading this, then, you will be able to understand my insight into the mystery of Christ, ⁵which was not made known to people in other generations as it has now been revealed by the Spirit to God's holy apostles and prophets. ⁶This mystery is that through the gospel the Gentiles are heirs together with Israel, members together of one body, and sharers together in the promise in Christ Jesus.

⁷I became a servant of this gospel by the gift of God's grace given me through the working of his power. ⁸Although I am less than the least of all the Lord's people, this grace was given me: to preach to the Gentiles the boundless riches of Christ, ⁹and to make plain to everyone the administration of this mystery, which for ages past was kept hidden in God, who created all things. ¹⁰His intent was that now, through the church, the manifold wisdom of God should be made known to the rulers and authorities in the heavenly realms, ¹¹according to his eternal purpose that he accomplished in Christ Jesus our Lord. ¹²In him and through faith in him we may approach God with freedom and confidence. ¹³I ask you, therefore, not to be discouraged because of my sufferings for you, which are your glory.

Listening to the text in the Story: Acts 22:27–29; 28:19–23; Romans 15:14–29; 1 Corinthians 15:8–11; Galatians 1:11–12; Colossians 1:21–29; 1 Thessalonians 1:1–10.

The first two chapters of Ephesians tell the story God's saving work in Jesus Christ. Human beings figure in the story not primarily as actors but as recipients of God's gracious action. In 1:15–18 there is a brief interruption as Paul shares with the letter recipients his thanks for them. But this interlude quickly becomes a celebration of what God has done in raising and enthroning Christ. In 2:1–3 and 11–12 human beings briefly take center stage as Paul spells out our misery apart from Christ. Both of these short sections introduce longer narratives of God's gracious activity. Indeed, throughout Ephesians 1–2 God, who is portrayed as Father, Son, and Spirit, plays the starring role.

Thus the beginning of chapter 3 can feel jarring with its focus on "I, Paul." The first part of this chapter explores Paul's participation in the story of God's salvation, though God remains the primary actor. If we remove 3:2–13, the flow from 3:1 into the prayer beginning in 3:14 is relatively seamless. Thus we wonder why does Paul include this "excursus" about himself and his role in the divine drama? As we work through 3:1–13, we'll discover that this section too contributes significantly to the story of God's saving work.

EXPLAIN the Story

Summary of Ephesians 3:1–13
After Paul's self-reference in 3:1, the next Greek sentence (3:2–7) describes how God revealed to Paul the "mystery of Christ" (3:4) and gave him stewardship of this mystery (3:2). The following Greek sentence (3:8–12) moves from how God involved Paul in his work to the vital role of the church in God's cosmic plan (3:10–11). Verse 13 concludes the opening section of chapter 3 with encouragement for the letter recipients as they are related to Paul's sufferings.

Paul as Steward by Grace of the Mystery (3:1–7)
For this reason I, Paul, the prisoner of Christ Jesus for the sake of you Gentiles (3:1). "For this reason" points back to what chapter 2 revealed about the inclusion of the Gentiles among God's people (perhaps to all of Ephesians 1–2). For the first time in the letter, in 3:1 Paul refers to his imprisonment (mentioned also in 4:1 and 6:20). Paul was literally imprisoned when he wrote Ephesians (see Introduction; cf. Acts 22:28–29; 28:19–23), yet he refers to himself as a "prisoner of Christ" (*desmios tou Christou*; see Phlm 9). He is bound to Christ because Christ called him to preach the gospel to the Gentiles, a calling that led to Paul's physical imprisonment. Yet Paul sees himself not in terms of his earthly condition so much as his heavenly calling. The meaning of "for the sake of you Gentiles" will be spelled out in the following verses.

Surely you have heard about the administration of God's grace that was given to me for you (3:2). "Surely you have heard" suggests that at least some of the readers of this letter do not know Paul personally. If, as proposed in the Introduction, Paul wrote this letter himself, then given the fact that the Ephesians

knew Paul personally (Acts 19), "surely you have heard" underscores the likelihood that this letter was intended to be read beyond Ephesus.

The readers of this letter have heard "about the administration of God's
grace that was given to me" (3:2). "Administration" renders the Greek word
oikonomia, which can mean "plan" (1:10), but here speaks of the "administration, stewardship, or responsibility" that God gave Paul to be a steward of
God's grace for the Gentiles.[1]

*That is, the mystery made known to me by revelation, as I have already written
briefly* (3:3). The grace entrusted to Paul is the "mystery" revealed to him "by
revelation" (see also 1:8–9). As we saw in the commentary on 1:9, "mystery"
does not suggest something hidden but rather a secret that is now revealed.
In 1:10, that mystery is God's plan "to bring unity to all things in heaven and
on earth under Christ." In chapters 2 and 3, this mystery is centered in the
inclusion of the Gentiles among the people of God (3:6). "As I have written
briefly" refers to the concise statement of the mystery in 1:10, along with its
exposition in Ephesians 1–2, especially in 2:11–22.

*In reading this, then, you will be able to understand my insight into the
mystery of Christ* (3:4). Ephesians discloses Paul's particular "insight into" or
expression of the mystery. The following verse shows that others, in addition
to Paul, have received the same basic revelation.

*Which was not made known to people in other generations as it has now been
revealed by the Spirit to God's holy apostles and prophets* (3:5). Though God
foreshadowed his mystery in the past, "now" he speaks by the Spirit through
the early Christian prophets and apostles. The phrase "God's holy" could
modify either apostles alone or apostles and prophets together; either reading
is grammatically and theologically possible.[2]

The use of "holy apostles" in this phrase suggests to some commentators
that the writer of Ephesians lived years after the time of the first apostles,
including Paul. Yet, given the fact that all of God's people are holy (*hagios* in
Greek; 1:15, 18; 2:19), it is not necessary to understand "holy" in the phrase
"holy apostles" as something Paul could not have written; it simply underscores the special role of these others in God's work.

The terms "apostle" and "prophet" in the New Testament have given birth
to many scholarly conversations.[3] In Ephesians these terms appear without

---

1. BDAG 697–98.
2. The placement of "God's" (Greek *autou*) could support the reading "God's holy apostles
and prophets," the word "prophets" being unmodified (Lincoln, *Ephesians*, 178). Yet the linking of
"apostles and prophets" in 2:20 supports "God's holy apostles and God's holy prophets" (Arnold,
Ephesians, 190–91).
3. For helpful summaries, see P. W. Barnett, "Apostle," *DPL* 45–51; C. A. Evans, "Prophet,
Paul as," *DPL* 762–65; and C. M. Robeck Jr., "Prophesy, Prophesying," *DPL* 755–62. Also Hans

explanation because both Paul and his readers would have already under-stood them. The word *apostolos* in secular Greek means "messenger or envoy."[4] Among the first Christians, apostles were authorized and sent as messengers of the gospel. They also planted, nurtured, and oversaw churches. The prophet, *prophētēs* in Greek, proclaimed God's will by divine revelation. Sometimes, though not always, this revelation would foretell the future (see Rev 1:1). In the church, prophets spoke "to people for their strengthening, encouraging, and comfort" (1 Cor 14:3). The work of apostles and prophets was inspired by the Holy Spirit (Acts 2:17; 1 Cor 12:28; 14:1) and centered in the com-munication of God's word.

Paul has a distinctive take on the mystery of Christ (3:4). However, it was not revealed only to him but also to other "holy apostles and prophets." Because his letter was going to churches that others had founded, it is possible that Paul wanted to acknowledge them and their work as well as the divine mystery they shared in common.

This mystery is that through the gospel the Gentiles are heirs together with Israel, members together of one body, and sharers together in the promise in Christ Jesus (3:6). Verse 6 summarizes 2:11–22 by featuring three distinctive nouns all beginning with the Greek *sun-* (as *sug-, sum-,* or *sus-*), meaning "with." The Gentiles are coinheritors (*sug-klēronoma*), co-body members (*sus-sōma*), and copartakers (*sum-metocha*) of the promise with Israel. The word *sussōma* does not appear in Greek literature before this instance and may have been coined by Paul to convey the fact that Gentiles and Jews are equally members of the body of Christ. The promise in which Gentiles and Jews share together is the hope of participating in the cosmos made right when it is unified in Christ (1:10).

I became a servant of this gospel by the gift of God's grace given me through the working of his power (3:7). Verse 7 begins a new paragraph in the NIV, though it is the last part of the Greek sentence that starts in verse 2. It serves as a bridge between what goes before and what comes after.

Paul is "a servant [*diakonos*] of this gospel" (3:7). "Servant" is a humble term that emphasizes the superiority of the gospel and prepares the way for Paul to say that he is "less than the least of all the Lord's people" (3:8). As has been made clear above, Paul did not earn his ministry. Rather, it came "by [*kata*] the gift of God's grace," a phrase that shows again the pil-ing up of words in Ephesians ("gift" and "grace"). Parallel to "by the gift of God's grace" is "through [*kata*] the working of his power." God's power,

---

Dieter Betz, "Apostle," *ABD* 1:309–11; and M. Eugene Boring, "Prophecy (Early Christian)," *ABD* 5:495–502.

4. BDAG 122.

demonstrated in the resurrection (1:19–20) and experienced through the Spirit (see Rom 15:13, 19), gave Paul his ministry (perhaps a reference to his conversion in Acts 9).[5]

The Church Makes Known God's Wisdom (3:8–12)

Although I am less than the least of all the Lord's people (3:8). "The Lord's people" translates *hagioi.* In 1 Corinthians 15:9, Paul describes himself as "the least of the apostles" who does not "even deserve to be called an apostle" because he persecuted the church of God. In Ephesians 3, being "the least of all the Lord's people" means that only by God's grace has Paul been able to preach the gospel. Moreover, it sets up the importance of the church, the rest of the Lord's people, in the cosmic plan of God (3:10).

This grace was given me: to preach to the Gentiles the boundless riches of Christ (3:8). Again, Paul received his ministry by grace (3:2, 7; also 1 Cor 15:10). "The boundless riches of Christ" echoes earlier language in Ephesians: "the riches of God's grace" (1:7); God is "rich in mercy" (2:4); and "the incomparable riches of his grace" (2:7). The word translated as "boundless" suggests that there is no end to the riches found in Christ. "To preach" in Greek is *euangelisasthai,* which means "to communicate good news."

And to make plain to everyone the administration of this mystery, which for ages past was kept hidden in God, who created all things (3:9). "To make plain" (3:9) could also be "to shed light on" (*phōtisai*). Here the Greek word *oikonomia,* which is used in 3:2 in reference to the "administration" of grace given to Paul, points to God's own management of the mystery of Christ. This is what Paul is to shed light on. The use of *oikonomia* here is similar to that in 1:9–10, where God's mystery is worked out in his *oikonomia.* The description of God as the one "who created all things [*ta panta*]" echoes 1:4, where God's saving activity began "before the creation of the world," and 1:10, where God is bringing "unity to all things [*ta panta*]." The timing of God's revelation was all part of his plan from the very beginning.

His intent was that now, through the church, the manifold wisdom of God should be made known to the rulers and authorities in the heavenly realms (3:10). After an extended depiction of Paul's own ministry, all of a sudden Ephesians 3 takes an unexpected turn. Now, the task of making known God's wisdom does not belong just to Paul or to the apostles and prophets. Rather, the whole church is the channel through which God will make known his manifold wisdom "to the rulers and authorities in the heavenly realms" (3:10).

---

5. For a recent Christian discussion of power, see Andy Crouch, *Playing God: Redeeming the Gift of Power* (Downers Grove, IL: InterVarsity Press, 2013).

God is the unexpressed agent of the verb "should be made known." Yet God does this revealing "through the church." Thus, the church plays an essential role in this work of God (see 4:11–16).

"The manifold wisdom of God" is to be made known through the church. This wisdom, centered in Christ, is not simply Christ as personified divine wisdom. Rather, the wisdom of God is seen in the mystery of God's saving work in Christ. In 1 Corinthians 2:7, Paul equates "God's wisdom" with "a mystery that has been hidden." In Ephesians, God's wisdom is seen in his plan to unite all things in Christ. It is also seen in God's unifying of Jews and Gentiles through the cross, as well as in everything we have read in Ephesians 1–3. *Polupoikilos*, which appears only here in the New Testament, means something like "multiply-multicolored." It conveys the sense that God's wisdom takes on varied, glorious, brilliant forms.

God's kaleidoscopic wisdom will be made known "to the rulers and authorities in the heavenly realms." A similar image appears in 1:20–21, where Christ is enthroned above all heavenly powers. In 6:12, these powers are identified as hostile, those against whom we are struggling. As the commentary on 1:20–21 makes clear, the rulers and authorities are spiritual forces of evil who dwell in "the heavenlies," but which, nevertheless, affect earthly reality and thus are the true enemies of the church. These cosmic powers are closely associated with and, in some way, work through human institutions.[6]

The text does not explain how the church will make God's polychromatic wisdom known to the supernatural powers. Some commentators focus on the work of the church in declaring the good news.[7] This is part of the meaning, but not all. Lincoln's vision is more expansive: "The writer's thought is, therefore, best understood as being that *by her very existence as a new humanity*, in which the major division of the first-century world has been overcome, the Church reveals God's secret in action and heralds to the hostile heavenly powers the overcoming of cosmic divisions with their defeat."[8] As the church proclaims the good news of God's salvation in Christ, and as the church lives out this good news in a unified community, all of heaven and earth will grasp the wonder and truth of God's plan for the cosmos.

According to his eternal purpose that he accomplished in Christ Jesus our Lord (3:11). God's plan, including the unifying work of Christ, the revelation to Paul and other apostles and prophets, and the role of the church in demonstrating God's work to the cosmic powers, is "according to his eternal purpose" (3:11). This purpose was both formed and fulfilled "in Christ Jesus our Lord."

6. See Gombis, *Drama*, 35–58.
7. Francis Foulkes, *Ephesians*, TNTC (Downers Grove, IL: InterVarsity Press, 1978), 98.
8. Lincoln, *Ephesians*, 187 (emphasis added).

In him and through faith in him we may approach God with freedom and confidence (3:12). The Greek reads more literally that in Christ and through faith in him we have "freedom of speech" (*parrēsia*) and "freedom of access" (*prosagōgē*). God is not mentioned explicitly but is surely the one to whom we can speak openly and into whose presence we are welcome, as in 2:18.[9] The first person plural "we" highlights the fact that all people, Gentiles and Jews, have relationship with God through Christ.

Suffering and Glory (3:13)

I ask you, therefore, not to be discouraged because of my sufferings for you, which are your glory (3:13). Verse 13 circles back to a theme introduced in 3:1, Paul's hardships "for the sake of you Gentiles." He does not want the recipients of his letter to be distressed by the news of his imprisonment.

Paul adds an intriguing comment about his sufferings: they "are your glory." In Romans 8:17, sharing in Christ's sufferings is a prelude to sharing in his glory. Yet in Romans those who suffer are the ones who are glorified. In Ephesians 3:13 Paul's suffering is the glory of his readers. A clue to this odd equation may be found in 2 Corinthians 1:6: "If we are distressed, it is for your comfort and salvation." If Paul's afflictions lead to the Corinthians' salvation, and if their salvation leads to their glorification, then it might be said that his afflictions are for their ultimate glory. It is a small rhetorical step from this insight to the claim that Paul's sufferings for the readers are their glory.

LIVE the Story

Ephesians 3:1–13 focuses mainly on Paul and the stewardship of grace he received from God to share with the Gentiles the mystery of their inclusion among the people of God. This episode in God's story might inspire us to be good stewards of the grace given to us and to share with others the good news of Christ. But beyond this, embedded in Paul's account of his ministry is something that propels us into the larger story of God.

The Unique and Invaluable Mission of the Church

God's intent was "that now, through the church, the manifold wisdom of God should be made known to the rulers and authorities in the heavenly realms" (3:10). It is not Paul or the other apostles or prophets who announce the mystery of Christ to the heavenly powers. Rather, the crucial task of making known God's wisdom to the powers now belongs to the church, to the people of God together.

---

9. See for example Heb 4:14–16.

If you were to ask a hundred Christians, "Why does the church exist?" you'd hear about worship and witness, community and caring, discipleship and doing justice. But I doubt you'd hear one person say, "The church exists to make God's manifold wisdom known to the rulers and authorities in the heavenly places." Yet according to Paul, this is central to the church's calling and God's eternal purpose.

Of course worship, witness, community, caring, discipleship, and doing justice are essential elements of church life. But from the perspective of Ephesians 3, these are part of something truly cosmic. The church participates in the grand plan of God to unite all things in Christ by making known this plan to the heavenly powers.

Paul does not say in this chapter how the church influences cosmic powers. From other things Paul writes, however, we can see why making God's wisdom known to them matters so much. For one thing, these powers have actual influence not just up in heaven but also on earth. They were intimately involved in the death of Christ (1 Cor 2:8). They influence human affairs through institutions in addition to individuals. They dominate human life outside of Christ (Eph 2:1–3) and hinder our effort to live the gospel faithfully (6:11–12). Moreover, we already live "in the heavenly realms in Christ Jesus" (2:6). Thus we cannot ignore our cosmic neighbors or minimize their impact on our lives.

We can only speculate about why God deems it essential for the heavenly powers to know his manifold wisdom. Some suppose that God seeks to redeem the powers as a part of unifying all things in Christ. Others believe that if the powers see what God has done in Christ, somehow their influence will decrease. They will see that their efforts to shatter God's creation are doomed to fail. It's hard to fight a battle when you know for sure you're going to lose.

The role of the church in the cosmic arena may be rather like that of Jesse Owens, an African-American athlete from the United States, in the 1936 Summer Olympics in Germany. At first Germany would not allow blacks to compete. But facing worldwide pressure, Germany relented. Adolf Hitler, the German chancellor, thought he would have his chance to demonstrate to the world the superiority of white, "Aryan" people.

Hitler's plan failed dismally. In fact, the strongest message of the 1936 Olympics was made by Jesse Owens, not through his words but through his extraordinary athleticism. Owens put on one of the greatest shows in the history of sport, winning four gold medals: in the 100 meters, the 200 meters, the 4x100 meter relay, and the long jump. We can only imagine the devastation of Hitler and his fellow Nazis as their plan to proclaim Aryan superiority to the world was dashed by the exploits of a black man who was clearly a superior athlete.

Similarly, as the church lives out its identity in Christ, especially as it demonstrates the unity between formerly hostile peoples such as Jews and Gentiles, the cosmic powers will see that God is indeed uniting all things in Christ. God's plan is working and will prevail. The powers will be defeated in their efforts to ruin God's creation for good. The church proves it.

The Example of the Church

Cosmic powers infiltrate and infect human life in multiple dimensions. What happens in the heavens matters to life on earth. Though Paul did not say so in Ephesians 3, he certainly believed that the church's demonstration to the heavenly powers also influences human life. We will see clearly Paul's concern for our outreach to human beings when we get to Ephesians 5:8–17. This passage states that we are to "live as children of light" (5:8). Paul writes, "Have nothing to do with the fruitless deeds of darkness, but rather expose them" (5:11). When we shine the light of Christ into the darkness, we invite those who sleep in the darkness to wake up (5:14). We make it possible for the darkness of this world to become light (5:13).

Therefore, as the church makes known God's wisdom to the heavenly powers, the church also demonstrates this wisdom to earthly powers and peoples by word and by deed. If a skeptic were to have asked Paul, "How can I know that your gospel is true?" Paul would point to the church and say, "Look, here Jews and Gentiles who once were enemies are living together in peace."

Could we say something like this today? If someone were to ask us how we know that the gospel is true, could we point to the church? It's common today for Christians to bemoan the failures of the church, but I have also seen examples of God's people living God's story in such a way that people are drawn to Christ.

I remember, for example, a woman named Carol. She made an appointment to meet with me when I was senior pastor of Irvine Presbyterian Church, saying she was looking into becoming a Christian. When we met, Carol introduced herself as a Jewish woman, a doctoral student in physics, and someone who had carefully investigated many religions. She had questions about Christianity that she wanted to ask me. Knowing that she was Jewish and a graduate student in science at a secular university, and seeing that her list of questions covered at least two pages, I confess I felt discouraged. No matter how well I answered her questions, I worried that she would never, ever believe the gospel.

I invited Carol to ask her questions, and she began. A few of them were softballs pitched down the middle of the plate. But most were challenging. Carol wondered about the problem of evil, the scandal of Christian exclusivism, the reliability of the Gospels, and so on. We talked for at least ninety minutes, which still left many of her questions for our next meeting.

As we drew near the end of our conversation, I said, "I have one question for you. You are Jewish, and Jews don't often consider conversion to Christianity. You are a scientist, and most scientists are atheists or agnostics. You have studied most major religions. So why in the world are you thinking about becoming a Christian?"

Carol's answer was simple. "It's because of the Christians I have known. They lived so differently than others. They loved each other and even me in ways I had not experienced before. What I saw in them intrigued me, and it still does."

A year later I had the privilege of baptizing Carol as she confessed her faith in Jesus Christ.

We know that there are countless stories that don't end like this. Many who consider Christianity because of the example of a Christian community do not in the end come to faith. And many others are chased away from Christ because of the selfish, divisive, and hateful actions of confessed Christians. But if you've been a Christian for a while, I expect you know a story like Carol's. You have seen how living the gospel can draw people to the Lord.

Sometimes the witness of Christians has an influence not just over individuals but over a whole society. Consider the case of the church of the early centuries. It surely had its share of problems, failures, and schisms. But in spite of these issues, the church grew in stature and influence in the Roman world. One reason is the way Christians lived out the gospel in their relationships.

About two hundred years after Christ, a North African Christian known as Tertullian wrote a defense of Christianity. In that *Apology*, he wrote that Christian love was famous (or infamous) among critics of Christianity who said, "Look . . . how they love one another."[10] This love was evidence for the truth of Christianity.

Years later, the love of Christians for one another and for others was so well known that the Roman Emperor Julian, a virulent opponent of Christianity, wrote to one of his pagan high priests: "For it is disgraceful that, when no Jew ever has to beg, and the impious Galileans [Christians] support not only their own poor but ours as well, all men see that our people lack aid from us."[11]

---

10. Tertullian, *Apology* 39:7, Tertullian, *Apology. De Spectaculis*; Minucius Felix: *Octavius*, trans. T. R. Glover and G. H. Rendall, LCL 250 (Cambridge: Harvard, 1931), 177.

11. Julian, "22. To Arsacius," in *Letters. Epigrams. Against the Galilaeans. Fragments*, trans. W. C. Wright, LCL 157 (Cambridge: Harvard, 1923), 71.

According to sociologist Rodney Stark in his book *The Triumph of Christianity*, one of the reasons the Christian movement grew during its first centuries was its demonstration of mercy to those in need, both Christians and others. "In the midst of the squalor, misery, illness, and anonymity of ancient cities," Stark writes, "Christianity provided an island of mercy and security."[12] Christians generously supported the poor, cared for destitute children and the elderly, and ministered to prisoners. Stark observes, "These charitable activities were possible only because Christianity generated congregations, a true community of believers who built their lives around their religious affiliation."[13]

What made possible the acts of love that touched so many lives, bore witness to the gospel, and ultimately transformed an empire? Stark answers, "Congregations, a true community of believers who built their lives around their religious affiliation." Paul might have said it this way: "The church, the body of Christ, the true community of believers made one in Christ, through whom God makes known his manifold wisdom."

---

12. Rodney Stark, *The Triumph of Christianity: How the Jesus Movement Became the World's Largest Religion* (New York: HarperCollins, 2011), 112.

13. Stark, *Triumph*, 113.

CHAPTER 7

Ephesians 3:14–21

📖 LISTEN to the Story

¹⁴For this reason I kneel before the Father, ¹⁵from whom every family in heaven and on earth derives its name. ¹⁶I pray that out of his glorious riches he may strengthen you with power through his Spirit in your inner being, ¹⁷so that Christ may dwell in your hearts through faith. And I pray that you, being rooted and established in love, ¹⁸may have power, together with all the Lord's holy people, to grasp how wide and long and high and deep is the love of Christ, ¹⁹and to know this love that surpasses knowledge—that you may be filled to the measure of all the fullness of God.

²⁰Now to him who is able to do immeasurably more than all we ask or imagine, according to his power that is at work within us, ²¹to him be glory in the church and in Christ Jesus throughout all generations, for ever and ever! Amen.

Listening to the text in the Story: Job 11:5–9; John 15:1–12; 17; Acts 9:40; 21:5; Romans 8:35–39; 11:36; 16:25–27; Colossians 1:9–12; 1 Timothy 1:17; Jude 24–25.

After concluding his personal digression in 3:1–13, Paul turns to prayer. In 3:14–19 he reports on his intercession for the recipients of Ephesians, and 3:20–21 features a doxology, a statement glorifying God. These two prayerful activities draw to a close the theological reflections of Ephesians 1–3 and lay the groundwork for the ethical exhortations of Ephesians 4–6.

Ephesians 3:14–21 challenges us to expand our own prayers in light of Paul's example and the sweeping narrative of Ephesians 1–3. This passage encourages us to seek a deeper knowledge and experience of God's power, love, and presence. It opens our eyes to the untapped potential of God's power in us, inspiring us to live for the praise of God's glory in new and bold ways.

EXPLAIN the Story

Summary of Ephesians 3:14–21

The first two verses of this section (3:14–15) set up the prayer report that follows (3:16–19). This report contains three major requests of Paul for the readers of Ephesians: 1) that God would give them power both through his Spirit and also through the indwelling of Christ; 2) that God would strengthen them to grasp the magnitude of Christ's love; and 3) that they would be filled to the measure of God's own fullness. This structure cannot be seen in English translations but is obvious in the Greek original: "I kneel before the Father (to pray): *that* (*hina*) he might give you to be strengthened (3:16); *that* (*hina*) you may have power to grasp (3:18); *that* (*hina*) you may be filled" (3:19). Paul reports on what could be called "expansive intercession" because his requests are comprehensive and because they expand our vision of what life in Christ is all about.

The closing doxology, offered to God though addressed to the readers ("Now to him"), begins by identifying God as the one who is "able to do immeasurably more than all we ask or imagine" (3:20). The final verse gives glory to God "in the church and in Christ Jesus" (3:21), thus underscoring the centrality of the church, a theme found in chapters 1–3 as well as in what is yet to come in chapters 4–6. This doxology is expansive because it enlarges our vision of what God can do through us and augments our understanding of the cosmic significance of the church, even as it lifts our hearts in praise to God.

The content of Paul's intercession in 3:16–19 is similar to his earlier prayer in 1:17–19. In both places, prayer is directed to God the Father (1:17; 3:14). Both prayers, with slightly different language, ask God to give the readers knowledge and power. In both passages, the Spirit is featured (1:17; 3:16). Differences between the two prayers include the future focus in chapter 1 ("hope," "inheritance," v. 18) and the centrality of love in chapter 3 (vv. 17–19). Both prayers are steeped in the language and story of Ephesians 1–3.

Expansive Intercession (3:14–19)

For this reason I kneel before the Father (3:14). Through this phrase in 3:14, Paul indicates that he is praying. The verb "I pray" in 3:16 NIV is inferred from Paul's posture. Standing, rather than kneeling, was the typical posture for Jewish prayer, though sometimes Jews did kneel in prayer (see 1 Kgs 8:54; Ps 95:6; Dan 6:10). The use of "I bow my knees," a more literal translation of the Greek, might indicate a sense of reverent urgency, or perhaps it underscores the sovereignty of God (see Phil 2:5–11). It is also profoundly worshipful, part of what it means to exist for the praise of God's glory (Eph 1:12). In

1:17 Paul's prayers were directed to God "the glorious Father," and the use of "Father" in 3:14 sets up the unusual statement in 3:15.

From whom every family in heaven and on earth derives its name (3:15). Without the footnote in the NIV, English readers would not catch the parallel between "Father" in verse 14 and "family" in verse 15 (in Greek, *patēr* and *patria*). The word *patria* can mean "family," though it also signifies clan, relationship, people, or nation.[1] The 1984 version of the NIV translated this verse, "from whom his whole family in heaven and on earth derives its name." This large, singular family fits neatly with the theological vision of Ephesians, but it is not supported by the grammar of the verse.[2] The breadth of meaning of *patria* plus the unexpected inclusion of "every family in heaven" indicate that *patria* refers not just to households of related people but also to various groupings of beings, both earthly and heavenly.

Why does Paul make this connection between God the *patēr* and every *patria* of heaven and earth? A clue comes in the phrase "derives its name." In the ancient world, the one who named something claimed authority over it. So if every grouping of created beings acquires its name from God the Father, then he is implicitly sovereign over all beings. Moreover, the linguistic connection between *patēr* and *patria* is another way of conveying the connection between God and creation. The one who created all things seeks to unite all things in Christ. Everything in the cosmos, including all groupings of people and heavenly powers, comes from God, exists under his sovereignty, and figures in his plan for the fullness of time. A similar connection between God and all things comes later in 4:6, which refers to "one God and Father of all, who is over all and through all and in all."

I pray that . . . he may strengthen you with power through his Spirit (3:16). Verse 16 is the first of three main requests in Paul's prayer. Literally, he asks that God might "give" his readers "to be strengthened with power through his Spirit." God's power appeared in the prayer in chapter 1, where Paul asked that we might know God's "incomparably great power for us who believe" (1:19). There, God's power is associated with the resurrection but not explicitly with the Holy Spirit. At the end of chapter 3, Paul highlights God's "power that is at work within us" (3:20), yet without mentioning the Spirit. Ephesians 2 states that the Spirit of God helps us have access to God (2:18) and is the means by which God dwells in his people (2:22). Elsewhere in his writings Paul frequently associates the Holy Spirit with power (Rom 15:13, 19; 1 Cor 2:4; 1 Thess 1:5). Thus through the Spirit God acts in and among us, strengthening us to live for his glory.

In your inner being (3:16). In Greek this is "in the inner human being" (*eis ton esō anthrōpon*). This does not mean that the Spirit's energy is only internal or that the Spirit works only in the hearts of individuals and nowhere else. In

---

1. BDAG 788.
2. Lincoln, *Ephesians*, 202.

Ephesians 2:15 Paul described not an individual but a group as the "one new humanity" comprising both Jews and Gentiles (2:15). In 4:3 the Spirit is said to forge unity among believers. In 5:18–19 the Spirit inspires songs of worship that are shared in community. In 6:17 the Spirit supplies a sword with which the Christian community engages in heavenly warfare. In each of these passages, the inner power of the Spirit is expressed externally. In 1 Corinthians 12–14 the Spirit empowers Christians to serve others in multiple ways, including speaking God's truth, teaching, and healing (1 Cor 12:7–11). Thus the Spirit empowers us inwardly for external actions.

Out of his glorious riches (3:16). In making his request for the Spirit's power, Paul asks that God might give, literally, "according to the riches of his glory [*kata to ploutos tēs doxēs autou*]." This echoes earlier phrases in Ephesians, most obviously a passage from the prayer in 1:18, "in order that you may know … the riches of his glorious [*ploutos tēs doxēs*] inheritance in his holy people." Elsewhere we read of "the riches [*ploutos*] God's grace" (1:7), "the incomparable riches [*ploutos*] of his grace" (2:7), and "the boundless riches [*ploutos*] of Christ" (3:8). Here, as in other letters, Paul sees God's glory as a source of divine power (Rom 6:4; Col 1:11). God meets human needs "according to the riches of his glory in Christ Jesus" (Phil 4:19). In the Old Testament, when God's glory settled on Mt. Sinai, it looked to the Israelites "like a consuming fire on top of the mountain" (Exod 24:17), a vision of awesome power. Other passages in the Hebrew Scriptures associate God's power with his glory (e.g., Ps 63:2; Dan 7:14). Moreover, since God's glory is seen in his mighty works (Exod 15:11), it makes sense to envision power connected with his glory. Of course, all of this must be understood in light of the ironic, countercultural glory of the cross, where God's power is expressed through the ultimate act of servanthood.

So that Christ may dwell in your hearts through faith (3:17). The NIV supplies "so that" in order to make sense of a complicated sentence. The Greek infinitive "to dwell in" is parallel to "to be strengthened" in 3:16. Christ dwelling in our hearts in verse 17 represents virtually the same experience as the Spirit present in our inner being in verse 16. This is not to say that Christ and the Spirit are the same person. Rather, in their work in us and in our experience of them, Christ and the Spirit are inseparable (see Rom 8:9–10; 2 Cor 3:17; Gal 4:6). As John Calvin wrote in his commentary on Ephesians, "It is a mistake to imagine that the Spirit can be obtained without obtaining Christ; and it is equally foolish and absurd to dream that we can receive Christ without the Spirit."[3] Andrew Lincoln agrees: "Believers do not experience Christ except as Spirit and do not experience the Spirit except as Christ."[4]

---

3. John Calvin, *Commentary on Galatians and Ephesians*, Kindle edition, 4045–46.
4. Lincoln, *Ephesians*, 206.

In the rest of Ephesians, as in Paul's other writings, the emphasis is on believers being "in Christ." This is the only place where Paul (or the New Testament writers in general) speaks of Christ being in our heart. In Colossians 1:27 the "glorious riches" of God's mystery is, Paul writes, "Christ in you, the hope of glory." In the Gospel of John Jesus talks about being in his followers and his followers being in him (John 14:20; 15:5; 17:21). All of this language of being "in" is, of course, metaphorical. It's an effort to express in the language of space and time the nonphysical, spiritual reality of our deep connection to and experience of the Triune God.

And I pray that you, being rooted and established in love (3:17). The NIV cleans up a phrase that is unusually complicated in Greek. It could be translated strictly, "in love having been rooted and grounded." The main problem with this phrase is its peculiar grammar, which makes it unclear where and how the phrase connects to the rest of the sentence. For example, this phrase could be a parenthetical statement, "(you have been rooted and established in love)." Or it could be a prayer, "May you be rooted and grounded in love." Or it could be a prelude to the following request, as in the NIV. In his commentary, Clinton Arnold lists five distinct options, concerning which there is considerable scholarly disagreement.[5]

Since grammar will not determine the best meaning here, we should consider how this phrase fits the story of Ephesians. Back in chapter 1 Paul writes that God chose us "in love" before the creation of the world (1:4). In chapter 2 we were made alive in Christ "because of [God's] great love for us" (2:4). Moreover, Jews and Gentiles together form a temple for God, "built on the foundation of the apostles and prophets" (2:20). (The perfect participle in 3:17, *tethemeliōmenoi*, translated as "grounded," has as its root the word *themelios*, "foundation," which is found in 2:20.) Thus, the recipients of Ephesians had been, in fact, rooted and established in love before Paul prayed for them in the way of 3:14–19. It would be odd if he were asking for something that had already happened. The NIV's translation, therefore, seems to capture the sense of Paul's complex Greek phrasing. On the basis of the fact that his readers have already been rooted and established in love, Paul prays in 3:18–19 that their knowledge of God's love may increase.

May have power . . . to grasp how wide and long and high and deep is the love of Christ (3:18). This is the second major request in Paul's prayer, introduced by *hina* in Greek. Once again, this translation might obscure one of the problematic puzzles of Ephesians, since the Greek lacks the phrase "is the love of Christ." It simply reads, "May have the power to grasp . . . what is the width and length and height and depth." The ambiguity of this multidimensional

---

5. Arnold, *Ephesians*, 212.

phrase has spawned a wide array of scholarly interpretations; Arnold outlines seven of them.[6] The NIV may be right that the phrase refers to Christ's love. Another possibility is that the phrase refers to God's wisdom. In Job 11:5–9 God's wisdom is portrayed as mysteries that are "higher than the heavens," "deeper than the depths," "longer than the earth and wider than the sea." A few verses earlier, in Ephesians 3:10, Paul refers to "the manifold wisdom of God," and perhaps that verse harks back to Job as well.

But such a reference to Job would be an unusually obscure figure of speech. I am convinced that the particular context of Ephesians 3 elucidates the most likely meaning of width, length, height, and depth. Right before this phrase, Paul mentions "being rooted and established in love" (3:17). Right afterwards he asks that his readers might "know this love that surpasses knowledge" (3:19). Thus the context on either side of the multidimensional phrase is love. Moreover, this love is so vast that it cannot be fully comprehended: wider than wide, longer than long, higher than high, and deeper than deep. So the NIV's addition "is the love of Christ" seems to capture the meaning.

With all the Lord's holy people (3:18). The Greek reads more simply "with all the saints [*hagiois*]" (3:18). Christian knowledge of God's love is shared knowledge. God makes himself known to us and helps us grow in our understanding of him in the community of his people. We must not read Paul's prayer as if it were meant just for individual Christians, but rather for God's people together.

And to know this love that surpasses knowledge (3:19). The love of Christ can be known, but never completely. There is always more of his love to be discovered. In verse 19, as is true elsewhere in Scripture, the verb "to know" suggests both intellectual understanding and personal experience. Paul does not want his readers simply to know more about God's love. He wants them to be intimately familiar with it, to be embraced by it, and to embrace it in return.

That you may be filled to the measure of all the fullness of God (3:19). This is the third major request in Paul's prayer. Like the others, it is introduced by *hina* followed by a passive verb: "may be filled." "To the measure" renders the Greek preposition *eis*, which generally means "into" but can sometimes mean "with."[7] The word "fullness," *plērōma* in Greek, appears in 1:23 in the phrase that depicts the church as "the fullness of him who fills everything in every way." God's fullness includes all of the goodness of God, his grace, mercy, truth, wisdom, power, love, and a whole lot more. Paul prays that we might be filled to the brim with these gifts, and a whole lot more.

This third request stretches our imaginations. How could we, as mortal, limited beings, ever be filled to the measure of God's own fullness? The

---

6. Arnold, *Ephesians*, 215–17.
7. BDAG 291.

seeming impossibility of this intercession is part of the point. It prepares us for what follows in verse 20, namely, the revelation that God "is able to do immeasurably more than all we can ask or imagine, according to his power that is at work with us." The juxtaposition of the prayer for fullness and the profession that God can do amazing things through us reminds us that we experience the fullness of God not mainly for our own benefit but for the benefit of others whom we serve.

Expansive Doxology (3:20–21)

Following the prayer of 3:14–19 is a two-verse doxology, an offering of glory (*doxa* in Greek) to God. The verb of this sentence is an implied "be," to him be glory.

Now to him who is able to do immeasurably more than all we ask or imagine, according to his power that is at work within us (3:20). This follows nicely on the heels of verse 19, which asks that we "be filled to the measure of all the fullness of God." Verse 20 helps to explain why Paul was able to pray so expansively in verses 14–19: he believes there is no limit to what God can do in and through us.

It's hard to capture the sense of the Greek phrase translated here as "to do immeasurably more." A literal rendering of the Greek might be, "to do beyond everything quite exceedingly beyond measure." Paul stacks up words to convey the extreme immeasurability of what God is able to do through us. We cannot ask for more than God can do. We cannot even imagine it.

Moreover, God is able to do the incomprehensible "according to his power that is at work within us" This echoes the description of God's "incomparably great power for us who believe" in 1:19. Yet in 3:20 God's power is not just for us but in us. No doubt this refers to the indwelling presence of God's Spirit.

To him be glory in the church and in Christ Jesus throughout all generations, for ever and ever! Amen (3:21). Paul may have been inspired by Psalm 79:13, "Then we your people, the sheep of your pasture, will praise you forever; from generation to generation we will proclaim your praise."[8]

That God should be glorified "in Christ Jesus" is theologically profound, but not especially surprising. In Ephesians 1:6 God's "glorious grace" is given in Christ. In 2 Corinthians 4:6 God's glory is "displayed in the face of Christ." Since Christ reveals God's glory, it follows that God will be glorified in Christ.

The inclusion of "the church" in Ephesians 3:21 is theologically profound and, at first, quite surprising. As we consider the story of God in Ephesians

---

8. The same Greek words translated "forever" and "generation" appear in the Septuagint version of Ps 79:13 (in the LXX numbering, 78:12) and in Eph 3:21.

1–3, however, it makes perfect sense to think of God being glorified in the church. All Christians, those who make up the church, exist for "the praise of his glory" (1:12, 14). The church makes known to the heavenly powers the manifold wisdom of God (3:10), thus demonstrating God's glorious grace by word and by deed.

The doxology of 3:20–21 connects what has gone before in Ephesians with what follows. By grace God has saved us and created us anew for good works (2:10). When we do these works as a response to grace, we fulfill our purpose, which is to be for "the praise of his glory" (1:12, 14). The "we" who do these works is not a collection of isolated individuals, however, but the unified body of Christ, the church as we live faithfully as God's people together to the praise of his glory. This does not mean that we spend all of our time singing praises to God in what we refer to as worship services, though there is a time and place for such intentional praise (5:18–20). Rather, we live for the praise of God's glory—which is another way of saying that God receives glory in the church when everything we do is a response to God's grace and shaped by God's story. Therefore, the doxology that finishes the first half of Ephesians prepares the ground for the ethical teachings in the second half of the letter.

LIVE the Story

Perhaps one of the most obvious ways we might live the story of Ephesians 3:14–21 is by praying and praising God expansively. In the commentary on 1:15–23, I explored how our prayers might be enlarged and enriched by the story of God. Ephesians 3:14–21 adds even more encouragement to what we gleaned from 1:15–23. But the prayer report at the end of chapter 3 also opens us to a deeper experience of God and invites us to live beyond our expectations as we devote ourselves to God's glory.

Knowing and Experiencing Far More of God
The Christians who first read Paul's letter had not known God. As Gentiles, they had been "without God in the world" (2:12). But through the apostles and prophets who delivered the good news of God's grace in Christ, these former Gentiles were saved, renewed, and adopted into the family of God. Thus, they knew God through Christ with a knowledge that was both intellectual and personal.

Yet as wonderful as it was for these early Christians to know God and to be able to approach him freely (3:12), Paul knew that their knowledge of God was still incomplete. Yes, they had experienced God's power, but there was more power available to them. Yes, they had encountered God's love for them in Christ, but there was infinitely more love waiting for them. Thus Paul prayed for his readers to know and to experience far more of God.

When I speak of experiencing God in today's world, I am aware of the danger of turning Christianity into something *merely* experiential, thus neglecting the doctrinal and ethical dimensions of the Christian life. Some Christians want to feel more of Jesus, and that's about it. Yet at the same time, many of us have settled for knowledge of God that falls far short of what is offered to us. Most of us, I expect, don't imitate Paul's example by asking regularly for more of God, both for ourselves and for others. When was the last time you prayed to know the love of Christ that surpasses knowledge? When did you last ask to be filled to the measure of all the fullness of God?

Throughout church history, believers in Christ have had transformational experiences of God's presence and power, and these experiences have strengthened them to live for the praise of God's glory. Consider the story of the nineteenth-century evangelist Dwight L. Moody. By 1871 he had successfully built a large church through his preaching. But some in his flock believed he needed greater empowerment for ministry, and so they prayed for him. After three months of their intercession, Moody had a life-changing experience of God's presence. He describes it in this way:

> *The blessing came upon me suddenly like a flash of lightning.* For months I had been hungering and thirsting for power in service. . . . I remember I was walking the streets of New York. . . . Right there, on the street, the power of God seemed to come upon me so wonderfully that *I had to ask God to stay his hand. I was filled with a sense of God's goodness, and felt as though I could take the whole world to my heart.*[9]

In another place, Moody describes this experience thus:

> Well, one day, in the city of New York—oh, what a day!—I cannot describe it, I seldom refer to it; it is almost too sacred an experience to name . . . I can only say that God revealed Himself to me, and I had such an experience of His love that I had to ask Him to stay His hand. I went to preaching again. The sermons were not different; I did not present any new truths, and yet hundreds were converted.[10]

If we were to use the language of Paul's prayer in Ephesians 3, we might say that Moody was *strengthened with power through the Spirit in his inner being, that he received new power to grasp the love of Christ that surpasses knowledge,*

---

9. Quoted in John Rives Brooks, *Scriptural Sanctification: An Attempted Solution of the Holiness Problem* (Nashville: The M. E. Church, South, 1902), 148 (emphasis in the original).

10. Quoted in William R. Moody, *The Life of Dwight L. Moody by his Son* (Old Tappan, NJ: Fleming H. Revell, 1900), 149.

and that he was filled to the measure of all the fullness of God. Moody's second description of his divine encounter emphasizes the connection between his experience and his greater empowerment for ministry.

Such stories encourage us to seek more of God, not simply for ourselves but also so that we might be empowered to do the good works God has prepared for us. Yet we must not limit the possibilities of experiencing God more deeply to one watershed event, no matter how wonderful it might be. There will never come a time in this life when we can say that we have all of God we need, when we know God's love completely, and when we can stop praying like Paul both for ourselves and the church.

Remember, too, that although Moody experienced God's love when he was alone, this experience was the result of his participation in a Christian community where people were faithfully praying for him. Moreover, he did not take his experience and hide it away for just himself. Rather, he offered himself more fully to the work of sharing the gospel and building up the church. God gave Moody a deeper knowledge of his love, "together with all the Lord's holy people" (3:18).

Experiencing More Than All We Ask or Imagine

The closing doxology of Ephesians 3 not only glorifies God but also invites us to experience more of God's power at work through us. This experience comes, in part, when we take seriously the claim of verse 20 and believe that God "is able to do immeasurably more than all we ask or imagine, according to his power that is at work within us." What would happen in our lives and our churches if we really believed this and began to live as if it were true?

Yet we must avoid getting so caught up in our own experience that we forget the real point. Simply stated, it's not about us. It's about God. We are to live for the praise of God's glory, not our own glory, the glory of our church, the glory of our family, or the glory of our business. This is easy to say but sometimes hard to do because we naturally focus on ourselves first.

For example, in 1991 I was a candidate to become senior pastor of Irvine Presbyterian Church. The final step in a long discernment process involved my preaching at the church in a worship service, after which the congregation would vote on the recommendation to call me.

As the big day approached, I was both excited and nervous. The night before my candidating sermon, I couldn't sleep. I left my hotel and went over to the church grounds to pray. I circled the campus again and again, praying as I did. At first my prayers focused on me: "God, help *me* do a good job tomorrow. Help them to like *me*. Help them to vote for *me*." But as I walked and prayed, I found my desires and prayers changing. They became less about me and more about the church and its flourishing. After a while I found myself praying for *God's* glory: "Whatever happens tomorrow, Lord, may you be glorified. As I preach, may you get the glory. If I am called to pastor this church, may it be for your glory." The more I walked and prayed, the more I desired God's glory beyond all else.

The next day I preached, and the congregation did vote to call me as their pastor. Three months later, I delivered my first sermon as the new pastor of Irvine Presbyterian Church. What was my text for that Sunday? Ephesians 3:20–21. I talked about the fact that God is able to do so much more than all we can ask or think. I shared my vision of our church as existing for God's glory. Thus began sixteen years of fruitful ministry.

If I had the space, I could tell dozens of stories of how God in fact did far more than what we had asked or imagined. I can share only one here. A couple of years into my pastorate, the church leaders voted to begin a capital campaign to build a sanctuary. Before we started building, we needed to collect pledges for what was for us a large amount of money. Moreover, a few years previously the church had attempted such a campaign with disappointing results. For this reason, many church members did not support the building program and weren't persuaded that God was behind it.

The theme passage we chose for our capital campaign was Ephesians 3:20–21. We spent months thinking about, being inspired by, and praying based on this inspired doxology. We needed God to do far more than all we could ask or imagine by his power in us. We sought to offer our church to God so that he might be glorified in us.

As the capital campaign came to a close, the building committee figured out exactly how much money we needed to raise in pledges if we were to even begin the project: $1,353,000—an intimidating figure.

When the time came for people to submit their pledges to the campaign, I was too nervous to ask how we were progressing. I waited until all the pledges came in, shortly before I was to announce the results to the congregation. Late on Friday afternoon I stopped by the financial office. "How did we come out?" I asked, both hopeful and fearful.

Our financial officer smiled and said, "The pledges totaled $1,353,000."

"No," I responded, "I already know that number. That's the goal. I want to know the pledge figure."

"I know," she said, "I gave you the amount *pledged*. It is $1,353,000. Yes, that is *exactly* what we need."

Now I realize this probably sounds like one of those pastor stories that stretch the truth. But I've told it straight. The total pledged was exactly what we needed. We could go forward with building, thanks be to God.

At this point, though, you may be thinking, "Wait a minute! God gave you exactly what you needed. Ephesians says God is able to do *far more* than all we can ask or imagine. How does your story fit with what we read in Ephesians?"

First, let me be clear. What God provided was abundant, almost double what the previous capital campaign had produced when the church was larger. Moreover, the fact that the pledged amount perfectly equaled the required amount had a powerful impact on the congregation, including those who had been skeptical about the whole building program. They just couldn't deny that God's power was at work among us.

Of course God could have given us way more than we needed, and part of me would have preferred this. We wouldn't have needed another capital campaign to pay off the sanctuary. We would have been able to give even more to our mission partners. But by providing exactly what we needed, God did give us far more than we had imagined. He gave profound reassurance that we had wisely discerned his will when it came to our building. He gave greater unity in the congregation. And, crucially, he gave us the gift of needing to trust him all the way along. Without any financial surplus, we couldn't rely on what we had in the bank to carry us through the project. We had to rely on God.

Thus, we did indeed receive from the Lord far more than what we had asked or imagined. We received unexpected, invaluable gifts that built our community, not just our sanctuary, and strengthened our shared faith. We were reminded that God's power is not given to us so that we can control it. Rather, God is the one who, according to his power in us, can do immeasurably more than all we can ask or imagine.

Throughout my sixteen years at Irvine Pres, time and again God exceeded our expectations in wonderful ways. Most were not quite as stunning as what happened in our capital campaign, but all encouraged us to live for the praise of God's glory. In 2007, when the time came for me to preach my last sermon at this church I had grown to love, you can probably guess the text I chose. Yes, Ephesians 3:20–21.

CHAPTER 8

Ephesians 4:1–6

📖 LISTEN to the Story

¹As a prisoner for the Lord, then, I urge you to live a life worthy of the calling you have received. ²Be completely humble and gentle; be patient, bearing with one another in love. ³Make every effort to keep the unity of the Spirit through the bond of peace. ⁴There is one body and one Spirit, just as you were called to one hope when you were called; ⁵one Lord, one faith, one baptism; ⁶one God and Father of all, who is over all and through all and in all.

Listening to the text in the Story: Deuteronomy 6:4; Psalm 15:1–2; 119:1–3; John 17:20–23; Acts 2; Romans 12:1–2; 1 Corinthians 8:6; 12:7–26; Galatians 3:27–28; Philippians 2:1–11; Colossians 3:12–17; Philemon; 1 Thessalonians 2:10–12.

The first three chapters of Ephesians tell the story of God's work in Christ. Chapters 1–2 feature a narrative of God's activity, beginning before the creation of the world and centered in Jesus Christ, through whom we experience salvation, new creation, and unification. Chapter 3 focuses on God's revelation to Paul, including the centrality of the church in God's plan for the cosmos. The narrative of chapters 1–3 is punctuated by two lengthy prayers (1:15–23; 3:14–21), both of which reveal more about what God has done and will do in, through, and for us.

The major transition of Ephesians begins in chapter 4 with a move from narrative to exhortation. Though chapters 4–6 contain rich theological content, they emphasize not so much what God has done as what we should do in response to God's actions. These chapters reveal what it means for us to "live a life worthy of the calling [we] have received" (4:1).

In Ephesians 1–3 we listen to the story of God who saves us in Christ. In Ephesians 4–6 we are drawn into the story, not just as people for whom God has acted but also as actors in the divine drama. We discover in detail what it means to exist for the praise of God's glory (1:14) and how we might walk in the good works God has prepared for us (2:10).

EXPLAIN the Story

Summary of Ephesians 4:1–6

This short passage opens with an exhortation that the recipients of the letter "live a life worthy of the calling [they] have received" (4:1). This serves as a topic sentence not just for 4:1–6 but also for the whole second half of the letter.

Following the main exhortation in verse 1, the next two verses provide some initial details about how we are to live in response to God's call. The charge to maintain the "unity of the Spirit" (4:3) leads into a short, seven-part description of the theological basis for Christian unity.

Walk Worthy of Your Calling (4:1–3)

As a prisoner for the Lord, then, I urge you (4:1). The word "then" (*oun*) underscores the connection between what has gone before in Ephesians and the exhortation that follows. The verb translated as "I urge" is the standard Greek term meaning "to exhort, urge,"[1] and it figures regularly in Paul's writings.[2]

The use of "I" in 4:1 draws attention to Paul as the one who issues the exhortation. Many interpreters allege that he is emphasizing his apostolic authority here. Yet it is striking that Paul does not identify himself as an apostle but rather as "the prisoner for [*en*] the Lord." This is similar to his self-reference in 3:1, "the prisoner of Christ Jesus." On a human level, Paul is a prisoner of Rome (see Introduction). But more importantly, his imprisonment falls under the Lord's superintending sovereignty.

To live a life worthy of the calling you have received (4:1). Here is the main exhortation of this passage, indeed, perhaps all of Ephesians. The recipients of the letter are to "live a life" worthy of their calling. "Live a life" paraphrases the Greek verb *peripateō*, which literally means "to walk." This verb has already been used in Ephesians for the sinful behavior of the Gentiles (2:2) and for the good works in which God intends for us to walk (*peripateō*, 2:10). Later in Ephesians the verb "to walk" will be used for our living in a certain way (4:17; 5:2, 8, 15). This use of "to walk" as a metaphor for moral living was part of Paul's Jewish heritage.[3]

---

1. BDAG 764–65 (*parakaleō*).
2. For example, 1 Thess 4:1; 5:14.
3. See Pss 15:1–2; 119:1–3.

What is "the calling you have received" or more literally, "the calling with which you were called" (4:1)? Ephesians 1:18 refers to "the hope to which he has called you," which points back to God's plan to unite all things in Christ (1:10). Similarly, 4:4 says "you were called to one hope when you were called." Thus, in Ephesians the language of calling can have a future orientation. It directs our attention to God's purpose for the cosmos, namely, bringing all things together in Christ.

Though the future colors the meaning of calling in 4:1, the metaphor has a broader scope in this passage. Our calling is that which emerges from the whole narrative of Ephesians 1–3. Through this story God has called us to belong to him, to be part of his holy people, and to join in his cosmic plan. As Mark Labberton writes in *Called: The Crisis and Promise of Following Jesus Today*, "God's primary call is for us to belong to and live for the flourishing of God's purposes in the world."[4]

The first three chapters of Ephesians already begin to sketch out the contours of our response to our calling. We are to live as God's holy people, for the praise of his glory (1:1, 4, 12, 14). Having been saved by grace through faith and created anew in Christ, we are to do the good works God has prepared for us (2:10). As God's people unified in Christ, we are to live as stones in God's own temple (2:19–22). Furthermore, through our words and deeds we are to make known to the cosmic powers the manifold wisdom of God (3:10). These contours help to shape the moral exhortation of Ephesians 4–6, which goes into greater detail on how we are to walk in light of our calling.

In 4:1 the passive verb (literally, "you were called") implies that God is the caller. Our lives are to be lived not according to our personal sovereignty but rather under the sovereignty of the Lord. The plural "you" in 4:1 has a corporate sense. God calls not just solitary individuals but also his people together. We are to live out our individual calling in the context of a community of called people. And we are to live out our communal calling in our individual lives.

Be completely humble and gentle; be patient, bearing with one another in love (4:2). The NIV, as most English translations in verses 2 and 3, adds several additional imperatives to the command "live a life/walk worthy" in verse 1. In the original language, however, these English imperatives are grammatically dependent on the command in verse 1. They spell out explicitly how we begin to live our lives worthy of our calling.

"Be completely humble" renders a Greek phrase that reads "with all humility." The word "humility" (*tapeinophrosunē*) means "lowliness of mind" and

---

4. Mark Labberton, *Called: The Crisis and Promise of Following Jesus Today* (Downers Grove, IL: InterVarsity Press, 2014), 17.

was used in secular Greek with a negative force. Among New Testament writers, however, it is a virtue. It involves seeing yourself as you are, without arrogance or self-aggrandizement. In Philippians, Paul bases a call to humility on Christ's own humbling of himself in his crucifixion ("humility," *tapeinophrosunē*, in Phil 2:3; the verb "to humble" himself, *tapeinoō*, in Phil 2:8). It is striking that the very first way we live out our calling is by doing something Gentiles scorned.

Linked to humility in Ephesians 4:2 is gentleness. The Greek word *prautēs*, close in meaning to humility, appears among the fruit of the Spirit in Galatians 5:23. In 2 Corinthians 10:1 gentleness is a quality of Christ. In Matthew 11:29 Jesus describes himself as "gentle and humble in heart [*praus . . . kai tapeinos tē kardia*]." The KJV renders *prautēs* in Ephesians 4:2 as "meekness," though it should not be thought of as weakness but rather as having the strength to humbly serve others.

"Be patient" translates the Greek phrase "with patience [*meta makrothumias*]." *Makrothumia*, which can also mean "forbearance," is counted among the fruit of the Spirit (Gal 5:22) as well, and it is a quality of God (Rom 2:4). The exhortation to be patient assumes that our fellow Christians need patience from us, even as we need it from them.

The following phrase fleshes out how we show patience. We are patient by "bearing with [*anechō*] one another in love." *Anechō* means "endure, bear with, put up with."[5] Paul uses this verb in 1 Corinthians 4:12 to describe how he endures persecution. Thus the combination of "be patient" and "bearing with one another in love" implies that real life in Christian community is no picnic. Of course, God does not want us to put up with sin: sin needs forgiveness, not endurance (Eph 4:32). But embodying this unity requires hard work, even endurance, as we put up with things in others that bother us, and when they return the favor.

Make every effort to keep the unity of the Spirit through the bond of peace (4:3). In the NIV, verse 3 is an imperative. But in the Greek "make every effort" is a participle, thus linking verse 3 to verses 1 and 2 and expressing another way for us to live out our calling. The verb translated as "make every effort" can mean "hurry, hasten" and has a related sense of "be zealous/eager, make every effort."[6] Unity is not something to be taken for granted but rather is something to be sought eagerly.

We are to strive to "keep" the unity of the Spirit. The Greek verb translated as "keep" can also mean "watch over, guard."[7] Notice that we are not

5. BDAG 78.
6. BDAG 939 (*spoudazō*).
7. BDAG 1002 (*tēreō*).

forging Christian unity on our own. Rather, it is something created by the Holy Spirit. We see a vivid picture of this reality in Acts 2, where the outpouring of the Spirit at Pentecost leads to profound, embodied unity among the followers of Jesus (Acts 2:42–47). A different picture of unity in 1 Corinthians 12 portrays the Spirit as immersing all Christians into the one body of Christ, thus overriding the cultural and economic divisions between us (1 Cor 12:12–13). Though we do not generate unity among Christians, we are to preserve it energetically.

Our unity as believers is held together "through the bond of peace [*en tō sundesmō tēs eirēnēs*]." In Colossians 3:14 love is the bond of perfection [*sundesmos tēs teleiotētos*] that keeps the body of Christ together. Ephesians emphasizes peace beginning in 2:14, where Christ "himself is our peace." Through the cross he created one new humanity, "thus making peace" (2:15). Therefore, the "bond of peace" is a way of speaking about the deep unity among people forged by Christ through his death and made real through the Holy Spirit.[8]

The exhortations of 4:2–3 flow from the injunction to "live a life worthy of the calling you have received" (4:1). This calling, as we noted earlier, echoes the whole story of God in Ephesians 1–3 even as it highlights our future hope. This hope, according to Ephesians 1:10, is centered in God's uniting of all things in Christ. Thus it follows that the first steps in our worthy walk should guard the unity of the God's people. The reconciliation of all things *in the future* is foreshadowed in the reconciliation of believers *in the present*, a demonstration to the cosmos of God's purposes in Christ.

The Theological Basis for Unity (4:4–6)

In 4:3 we are to "make every effort to keep the unity of the Spirit through the bond of peace." The following verses provide a theological basis for our unity. The connection between verse 3 and verses 4–6 is seen more clearly in Greek. The word translated in 4:3 as "unity" is *henotēs*, an unusual word that in the New Testament appears only in Ephesians (4:3, 13). The root of the word *henotēs* is *heis*, the Greek word for "one," which appears repeatedly in verses 4–6 (*henotēs* is based on the genitive form *henos*). So we are to eagerly preserve oneness because our oneness is anchored in the manifold oneness of divine reality. This reality is portrayed through seven—a number representing perfection—"ones" in 4:4–6: one body, one Spirit, one hope, one Lord, one faith, one baptism, one God.

There is one body and one Spirit (4:4). The "one body" mentioned here is the church, the body of Christ (1:22–23), though the word "church" does not appear in this passage. It is the result of Christ's reconciling work on the cross

---

8. Peace is another element of the fruit of the Spirit (Gal 5:22).

(2:16). The fact that the list of "ones" in this passage begins with the "one body" underscores the importance of the people of God, something that will be developed later in chapter 4. As we noted above, the Holy Spirit not only gives birth to the church, the body of Christ, but also baptizes each member into "one body" (1 Cor 12:13). The oneness of the Spirit provides grounding for diversity in the expression of spiritual gifts (1 Cor 12:7–11). Thus, the association of "one body" and "one Spirit" is based on theological bedrock as well as the actual experiences of Christians in community.

Just as you were called to one hope when you were called (4:4). The Greek of this phrase could be rendered more literally, "just as you were called to the one hope of your calling" (NRSV). In 1:18 Paul prays that his readers might know "the hope to which he has called you." This, as we've seen, points back to 1:10, where God will unify all things in Christ. Thus when God calls us, he calls us to embrace this particular hope as a matter of confident assurance. Apart from Christ we have no hope (2:12). In Christ, our "one hope" with all other believers includes "eternal life," which is much more than life after death for individual believers. Someday we will share together in the transformed new creation, where all things are brought back into wholeness through Christ.

One Lord, one faith, one baptism (4:5). In Paul's writings, "Lord" generally refers to Christ (see 1:2, 3, 15, etc.). First Corinthians 8:6 offers a parallel to this passage: "There is but one God, the Father, . . . [and] one Lord, Jesus Christ." We hear in this text an echo of the *Shema* of Deuteronomy 6:4, the central confession of Judaism: "Hear [*shema*], O Israel: The LORD our God, the LORD is one." It is striking, of course, that the earliest Christians as Jews who called God "Lord" applied this title to Jesus, even to the point that "Lord" usually referred to him as distinct from God the Father, though for the Father's glory (see Phil 2:5–11).[9]

The use of "one Lord" in 4:5 with "one Spirit" in 4:4 and "one God and Father of all" in 4:6 shows in broad outline what would later mature into explicitly Trinitarian theology (see also 1:3, 13–14, 17; 2:18, 21–22; 3:16–17).

The "one faith" shared among Christians has both intellectual content (what is believed) and relational context (whom we trust). The use of "one

---

9. The Christian confession of Christ as Lord put early believers at odds with their neighbors. In Asia Minor, the destination of Paul's letter we call Ephesians, Artemis of Ephesus was a dominant deity; she was acclaimed as "Lady" (*kuria*), the feminine equivalent of the Greek term "Lord" (*kurios*). Moreover, in the latter half of the first century AD, the Roman emperors began to claim the title of "Lord" for themselves. Thus, the confession of Jesus as Lord implied that Caesar was not Lord, an implication that often led to persecution or martyrdom for those who acknowledged the lordship of Christ.

faith" in 4:5, echoed in the unity of the faith in 4:13, points to the basic beliefs that all Christians share in common.

"One baptism" might refer to the Spirit's work of baptizing all believers into the body of Christ (1 Cor 12:13). But it is more likely that "one baptism" signifies the initiation ritual experienced by all who became Christians in the time of Paul. Baptism is one in the sense that it is one basic rite, in which water is central. But more significantly, there is "one baptism" because there is "one faith," signified by baptism, and "one Lord," into whom all are baptized.

One God and Father of all, who is over all and through all and in all (4:6). The final "one" of this passage identifies one "God and Father of all." This affirmation once again echoes the Jewish *Shema* in Deuteronomy 6:4, "Hear, O Israel: The LORD our God, the LORD is one" (see also 1 Cor 8:6).

God has been identified as Father previously in Ephesians (1:2, 3, 17; 2:18; 3:14). In 3:14–15 God is the Father "from whom every family in heaven and on earth derives its name," which draws a connection between God and all groupings of earthly and heavenly beings. Similarly, in 4:6 God is "over all and through all and in all." Though "all" in this context could refer to all church members, it's more likely that "all" picks up the broader connotation found in 1:10 and related verses, where God is uniting all things in Christ. God is "over all" as the sovereign of the universe, the one who created all things. God is "through all and in all." God does not literally dwell in all things, as pantheists believe; rather, he is involved in all things, working his will in all things, and ultimately uniting all things in Christ. Indeed, 4:6 is reminiscent of the doxology of Romans 11:36: "For from him and through him and for him are all things. To him be the glory forever! Amen."

Although Ephesians 4 begins an extended explanation of how we are to live out our calling, the text reminds us that the dos and don'ts of Christian living must never be separated from the theological foundation of our faith. "Live a life worthy of the calling you have received" (4:1) points back to God's story in Ephesians 1–3. Verse 4:3 urges us to keep unity, a directive that could well stand on its own in light of chapters 1–3. But the exhortation to preserve unity is undergirded by the sevenfold elements of Christian theology. Thus the "is" leads to the "ought"; the indicative leads to the imperative. Or, given the story of Ephesians 1–3, we might say that the narrative implies the imperative.

LIVE the Story

As we get into specific moral exhortations, it can seem obvious how to live the story. We do what the text says! So in the case of 4:1–6, we choose to walk worthy of our calling. We could go through this passage bit by bit, illustrating how we might live out each individual imperative. But instead, I would like to focus on two main storylines: *calling* and *unity*.

Do You Have a Call?

As I sat before my church's candidates committee, a member asked me, "Mark, do you have a call?" I knew the right answer. I was taking a first step towards ordained ministry, and for this, I needed to be sure that God was "calling me into the ministry." For its part, the committee needed to validate my "call" if I was to advance as a candidate for ordination.

I grew up in a church that used the language of calling almost exclusively for those who were ordained as pastors. Those who had a "Rev." in front of their names had been "called" by God to "the ministry." Missionaries, too, might have been able to claim a divine calling. But the rest of us did not have a call. We were ordinary Christians.

When Lloyd Ogilvie became the pastor of my church, he brought a new language of calling. Lloyd said that according to Scripture, all Christians have been called by God into the ministry of Christ. Some have a particular calling to ordained ministry, but every single Christian is called.

Lloyd didn't make this up; he got it from Ephesians 4. In his preaching he showed that according to 4:1, all Christians are to walk worthy of their calling. Therefore, all Christians are called. Yet when I appeared before the candidates committee, even though Lloyd had been the church's pastor for ten years, the committee members still used the language of calling as if it applied exclusively to ordained pastors. When I was asked if I had a call, if I had answered, "Of course I do. All Christians are called by God into ministry," I would not have been applauded for my insight. Language traditions do not quickly or easily change.

Why does this matter? Because if our language implies that only a few select Christians are called by God, then the vast majority of believers may fail to hear or respond to the call that is truly theirs. They will not be prepared to walk worthy of their calling because they never knew they had one.

Vocation and Vocations

Our word *call* comes from a Germanic root. *Vocation*, which has a similar meaning, is a Latin-based word from *vocatio*, which means "summons, invitation." In common English we use *vocation* for "occupation, job, career," but in theology too we may speak of a "vocation." In his book *Visions of Vocation*, Steven Garber writes, "The word *vocation* is a rich one, having to address the wholeness of life, the range of relationships and responsibilities. Work, yes, but also families, and neighbors, and citizenship, locally and globally—all of this and more is seen as vocation, that to which I am called as a human being, living my life before the face of God. It is never the same word as *occupation*, just as *calling* is never the same word as *career*."[10]

To be sure, our divine vocation relates to our work, whether it be paid or unpaid. Given that most of us spend the majority of our waking hours working, we must walk worthy of our calling in and through our jobs. But Garber is right. Our vocation, our calling from God, isn't just about work. It touches and transforms all of life. As Mark Labberton writes in *Called*: "The vocation of every Christian is to live as a follower of Jesus today. In every aspect of life, in small and large acts, with family, neighbors and enemies, we are to seek to live out the grace and truth of Jesus. This is our vocation, our calling. Today."[11]

This notion of vocation, expressed so eloquently by Labberton, has had a major impact on my life and, indeed, my occupation. For two years I oversaw The High Calling, a digitally based outreach of the Texas-based H. E. Butt Family Foundation. Our purpose was to help people understand and live out their high calling to serve God in all of life, especially in their daily work.

Meanwhile at Fuller Seminary in California, this ideal of vocation was taking center stage. When Mark Labberton became president of Fuller in 2013, he announced a new, school-wide emphasis on vocation and formation. Fuller would continue to educate pastors, missionaries, and a wide variety of Christian leaders. Yet it would do so with a new focus on helping its students discover their true vocation (following Jesus) and learn how to walk worthy of this central calling in their particular vocations (jobs). Fuller would not just educate its students but would intentionally help them to be formed in Christ for their vocation in the world. Fuller grads who became pastors would be equipped to help all of their people discover their true vocation and learn how to live this out in every part of life, including their occupations. Fuller grads who became entrepreneurs, teachers, filmmakers, and bankers would live out their vocation in the context of their work.

As an example, take Elizabeth, who graduated with a master's degree. Though she had worked in more traditional ministry settings in the past, she sensed that she should live out her calling in a different direction. So Elizabeth founded an educational organization called Mary Lee Kitchen that seeks to help people learn about food and eat in a way that is healthy, sustainable, and inclusive of all people. For Elizabeth, her vocation to love and serve the Lord is expressed in her specific vocation centered in education, food, and health. Her seminary education helped her to discover and live out her calling in a distinctive way.

---

10. Steven Garber, *Visions of Vocation: Common Grace for the Common Good* (Downers Grove, IL: InterVarsity Press, 2014), front matter.

11. Labberton, *Called*, 45.

As I watched this new vision of a vocation-centered seminary education play out at Fuller, I was thrilled, believing it to be one of the most important things happening among Christians today. So in my role with The High Calling, I arranged to have our film crew spend time at Fuller, interviewing Mark Labberton and others who were leading the vocation and formation charge. During this filming, Mark and I began a conversation that led in a most unexpected direction. Six months after our video project at Fuller, I joined the seminary as the Executive Director of the Max De Pree Center for Leadership. One of the main reasons for this change in my occupation was my desire to join the people at Fuller as they seek to instill a biblical vision of vocation among Christians throughout the world. So you might say that my vocation/calling to follow Jesus took me to a new and unanticipated vocation/occupation.

My story is not unique. Millions of Christians have experienced something like this in their lives. As they have sought to live out their calling, God has led them in unexpected directions. This is true of not just those who work in explicitly Christian organizations. The world is full of teachers, salespersons, carpenters, nannies, lawyers, stay-at-home moms, and entrepreneurs whose lives have been redirected when they chose to walk worthy of their calling. Yet at the same time, millions of other believers have not experienced major job changes when they began to take their vocation seriously. Rather, for many, their current situations became infused with new significance and purpose.

I think, for example, of a Chinese man I'll call "Sam." He owns a substantial business with a global reach. Sam has shaped his business as an expression of his faith in Jesus. The fundamental values of his organization, which reflect the exhortations of Ephesians 4:1–6, have allowed Sam to build a flourishing business as well as to bear witness to the gospel. His life as a business executive is an expression of his divine calling every bit as much as what he does in his personal life. Sam is called by God just as you and I are called by God.

Eager to Keep the Unity of the Spirit

Ephesians 4:3 says we are to "make every effort to keep the unity of the Spirit." This means much more than to recognize the invisible, spiritual unity of all Christians. Rather, this verse urges us to eagerly desire and diligently pursue the actual unity of God's people wherever and however we can.

The history of the Christian church is not a glorious tale of unity. Rather, we see the people of God dividing over various matters of faith and practice. Such division often happens in small scale, between two members of a church, and sometimes in large scale, between whole churches or denominations.

My own denomination, the Presbyterian Church USA, is currently in disarray when it comes to unity. For the last several years, many churches have left the denomination over theological disagreements. In the process, dozens of churches have been divided, often splitting lifelong friends and fellow believers.

Because I did some writing about church unity, sometimes people in churches considering leaving the denomination have sought my input. On one occasion I met with a group of a dozen leaders from a church in a discernment process. They began by expressing their unhappiness with the denomination and several of its theological positions. After they were finished, I thought it might be good for them to consider how a commitment to unity might affect their thinking, so I said, "I have one simple question for you. Here it is. Have you made every effort to keep the unity of the Spirit in the bond of peace?"

Now, I expected them to respond with some version of "Yes." After all, many churches have tried for years to maintain fellowship with a denomination that theologically is moving further and further away from biblical teaching. I thought the leaders of this church would tell me about all they had done to keep the unity of the Spirit. Instead, they were angry with me for even suggesting that unity might be a higher goal. When I mentioned that this wasn't my idea, that I got it right from Scripture, they became even more perturbed. It seemed that they wanted out of the denomination without grappling with the very Bible they thought was being ignored by the denomination.

This does not mean, of course, that all those who work for denominational unity do so in a way consistent with Ephesians 4:1–6. I have seen people fight for their version of church unity in a way that is not humble or gentle. They are not bearing with their denominational opponents in love. So while supposedly seeking the unity of the church, their behavior damages that very unity.

Though it's right for us to consider church unity on a global scale, and though denominational reconciliation can be a worthy goal, support for large-scale unity must be matched by small-scale unifying actions. If I contend for institutional unity but fail to be humble and gentle, then I am not living my life worthy of my calling.

Throughout my pastoral experience, I have seen church leaders act in ways that promote unity. These "unifiers" were always seeking to walk worthy of their calling in their daily lives, in their ordinary relationships. They were practicing humility, gentleness, patience, and forbearance.

I think, for example, of an elder named Tim in my former church. Tim is not by nature humble and gentle. He was a fighter pilot in Vietnam before he became a successful lawyer who once argued before the U.S. Supreme Court. Tim is strong and tough. Yet he seeks to live worthy of his calling as one eager to maintain the unity of the Spirit.

Once in a meeting of the board of elders of my church, Tim proposed that the church display the American flag during worship services. Many Presbyterian churches do this, he explained. He did not see the flag as a distraction from the true worship of God. Rather, for Tim it was a reminder to pray for the country. He realized this would be a new step for our church, but Tim thought it would be helpful.

The first elder who responded to Tim didn't like his idea. A man I'll call Dave began his rebuttal, "That's exactly what Hitler did in Nazi Germany." Now in my experience, playing "the Hitler Card" rarely contributes to church unity. Then Dave added insult to injury with several other strongly worded criticisms. Tim was not pleased, yet he managed to hold his tongue. After a bit more conversation, we decided to table the matter.

Tim was angry, not so much because Dave didn't like his idea, but because Dave compared it to Hitler. I encouraged Tim to take time to pray about what he should do in response. As he prayed, Tim received a heart of compassion for Dave. He decided to approach Dave as a brother in Christ, reaching out to him humbly and gently, showing patience and forbearance. Tim did not begin his first conversations with Dave by focusing on the flag issue. Rather, he sought to get to know Dave as a person, learning about his family, his work, his hobbies, etc. As Tim did this, a true friendship began between two men who might well have been at each other's throats. Their personal unity affected the board of elders, and through the elders, the whole church. In the end, our discussion about the flag was not heated, and we found a way to remind ourselves to pray for our country in worship while taking Dave's concerns seriously.

This story has a happy ending because Tim, and then Dave in response, chose to live their lives worthy of their calling. Tim's commitment to being humble, gentle, patient, and forbearing made a difference, drawing Dave into a similar posture. Thus when confronting a disagreement that could have divided the church, these two leaders preserved and enhanced our unity.

No matter what we do in life, every one of us has a chance to live worthy of our calling, to make every effort to keep the unity of the Spirit, and thus to live for the praise of God's glory. We don't have to wait for some momentous opportunity. Rather, we can live out our calling in our everyday relationships at work and at home, among our neighbors and fellow church members, in our towns and cities, and in every part of life.

CHAPTER 9

Ephesians 4:7–16

LISTEN to the Story

⁷But to each one of us grace has been given as Christ apportioned it.
⁸This is why it says:

"When he ascended on high,
he took many captives
and gave gifts to his people."

⁹(What does "he ascended" mean except that he also descended to the
lower, earthly regions? ¹⁰He who descended is the very one who ascended
higher than all the heavens, in order to fill the whole universe.) ¹¹So
Christ himself gave the apostles, the prophets, the evangelists, the pastors
and teachers, ¹²to equip his people for works of service, so that the body
of Christ may be built up ¹³until we all reach unity in the faith and in the
knowledge of the Son of God and become mature, attaining to the whole
measure of the fullness of Christ.

¹⁴Then we will no longer be infants, tossed back and forth by
the waves, and blown here and there by every wind of teaching and
by the cunning and craftiness of people in their deceitful scheming.
¹⁵Instead, speaking the truth in love, we will grow to become in every
respect the mature body of him who is the head, that is, Christ.
¹⁶From him the whole body, joined and held together by every
supporting ligament, grows and builds itself up in love, as each part
does its work.

Listening to the text in the Story: Genesis 1–2; Psalm 68:1–35; Acts 2:1–47;
Romans 12:1–8; 1 Corinthians 12–14; Colossians 3:12–16.

The previous section of Ephesians (4:1–6) invites us to participate in God's
cosmic work of bringing unity to all things in Christ. We are to live out this
calling first of all by acting so as "to keep the unity of the Spirit" in the church
(4:3). We prioritize unity because it is essential to God's plan for the cosmos

(1:10; 2:11–16; 3:10) and because it reflects the core of our faith, including the oneness of God himself (4:4–6).

As we accept our calling to nurture the unity of the church, we may wonder if there is more for us to do. Are there other ways for us to help the church be all God intends it to be? If so, what are these ways, and how can we walk in them? Ephesians 4:7–16 helps answer these questions.

This passage addresses certain questions that emerge from the opening chapters of Ephesians. For example, God's people are a building that "rises to become a holy temple in the Lord" (2:21). How are we as God's building being constructed? Do we have an active role in this process, or are we simply building blocks placed by our heavenly stonemason? Ephesians 4:7–16 helps answer these questions.

Moreover, previous sections of Ephesians have suggested that God is doing something amazing through us. We are "God's handiwork, created in Christ Jesus to do good works" (2:10). God "is able to do immeasurably more than all we ask or imagine, according to his power that is at work within us" (3:20). We wonder: What are the good works God has for us to do? What splendid things might God do by his power working in us? Ephesians 4:7–16 helps answer these questions as well.

It does so by using language familiar from other letters of Paul, language of church, body, ministry, and gifts. As we examine our text from Ephesians, we will keep in mind other spiritual-gifts passages, especially Romans 12:1–8 and 1 Corinthians 12–14. But we should avoid the tendency of some interpreters to miss the unique storyline of Ephesians because echoes of Romans and 1 Corinthians ring too loudly in their ears. In Ephesians 4:7–16 Christ's gifts are not what we might expect, and their primary function is not what we might assume.

EXPLAIN the Story

Summary of Ephesians 4:7–16

In Ephesians 4:7–16 the church as the body of Christ is to grow up. This growth in unity, maturity, and stature comes from Christ himself. He gives grace to each of us so that we might be active in the ministry of building up the church (4:7). Christ also gives to the church gifts of people in different roles who share in the vital task of equipping all of God's people for ministry (4:11–13). As we do our ministry, in which speaking the truth in love is central, we grow up as the body of Christ together and as individual members of that body (4:14–16).

Strictly speaking, Ephesians 4:7–16 is a narrative of Christ's activity as the giver of gifts and source of the church's growth. Yet this story implies several imperatives that elaborate further what it means for us to walk worthy of our calling (4:1). The "is" of what Christ is doing in the church implies the "ought" of our participation in the ministry of building up Christ's body.

Christ Gives Grace to Each One (4:7)

But to each one of us (4:7). Verse 7 continues the use of "one" found in the previous verses ("one body . . . one God"; 4:4–6). Yet the word "but" alerts us to a new sense of "one." Whereas the focus had been on the "ones" at the core of our faith, now we learn what has happened to "each one of us."

"Each one of us" includes all of God's people, not just the apostles, prophets, evangelists, pastors and teachers mentioned in verse 11. This point is underscored by the repetition of "each one" further along in verse 16, which closes our passage in the way it began.[1]

The emphasis placed on "each one" leads some interpreters to claim that Ephesians 4:7–16 explores the diversity of the body of Christ, even as 4:1–6 emphasizes its unity. Yet this reads too much of 1 Corinthians 12–14 into Ephesians. 1 Corinthians does indeed examine the interplay of unity and diversity in the body. Ephesians 4:7–16 does not, however, investigate the diversity of gifts so much as it underscores the gift shared and stewarded by all of God's people.

Grace has been given (4:7). This gift is "grace," from the Greek word *charis*, which is related to but not identical to *charisma*, "gift" (used in the plural in Rom 12 and 1 Cor 12–14). According to 2:8, God saves us by grace, but in 4:7 there is a new expression of God's generosity. In 4:7–16, "grace" empowers God's people for the work of building up the church. Previous passages in Ephesians revealed God's "glorious grace" (1:6) and "the incomparable riches of his grace" (2:7; see also 1:7). God's amazing grace has the capacity not only to save us but also to transform and empower us for a life of service (2:10).

Grace draws us into ministry as it drew Paul into ministry (3:2, 7). In 3:7 Paul "became a servant . . . by the *gift* of God's *grace given* me" (emphasis added). In 4:7 he uses the same Greek words to speak of the gift of grace given to each of us for our own ministry.[2]

As Christ apportioned it (4:7). The NIV speaks of grace "given as Christ apportioned it." The Greek could be rendered more literally, "according to the

---

1. In the Greek, both 4:7 and 4:16 use the phrase "each one" (*heis hekastos*). This parallelism is not obvious in the NIV, which uses "each part" in v. 16 rather than a more literal "each one part."

2. Both 3:7 and 4:7 use all three of the Greek words *dōrea* ("gift"), *charis* ("grace"), and *didōmi* ("give").

measure of the gift of Christ." Though this could refer to God's gift of Christ to us,[3] the following verses make it clear that Christ is the giver in this case, not the gift. Elsewhere Paul uses the word "measure" (*metron*) to underscore God's authority to give as he sees fit or to determine our sphere of ministry (Rom 12:3; 2 Cor 10:13). Yet only six verses after 4:7 in 4:13, *metron* is used in reference to "the fullness of Christ," which is immeasurably vast (1:23; 3:19). Thus we might amplify the sense of verse 7 by adding a word: grace was "given as Christ *generously* apportioned it."

In Paul's discussion of gifts, ministry, and church in 1 Corinthians 12–14, the Holy Spirit is the giver (1 Cor 12:1, 4, 7). In Ephesians 4:7 Christ is the giver. With this thought in mind, Paul moves to show how the giving of grace by Christ reenacts a particular story about God from the Old Testament.

Christ Gives like God in Psalm 68 (4:8–10)

Gave gifts to his people (4:8). Christ's giving of grace was foreshadowed in the story of God in Psalm 68, which appears to be quoted in 4:8: "When he ascended on high, he took many captives and gave gifts to his people." The introduction "this is why it says" suggests a biblical antecedent.[4] Yet when we examine the specific verse, Psalm 68:18, we find a perplexing inconsistency between Paul's quotation and the apparent original: "When you ascended on high, you took many captives; you received gifts from people . . ." In addition to the shift from second person (you) to third person (he), we find a puzzling variation from God receiving gifts in Psalm 68 to God giving gifts in Paul's paraphrase. What might account for this reversal of the direction of giving?

Several commentators explain the variation by pointing to a Jewish interpretive tradition of Psalm 68 that adds an element of giving to verse 18.[5] An ancient Jewish targum (Aramaic paraphrase) of Psalm 68:18 reads, "You ascended to the firmament, *O prophet Moses*; you captured captives, *you taught the words of Torah*, you gave *gifts* to the sons of men."[6] Even if Paul did not know this particular paraphrase, he may well have been aware of Jewish traditions that included giving among the actions of the one who ascended in Psalm 68:18.

These traditions accurately summarize the story of the whole psalm, even if they alter the meaning of verse 18. Psalm 68 celebrates the strength of God. The God who ascended on high did not just receive gifts. He also gave them.

3. Barth, *Ephesians*, 429–30.
4. In 5:14 the same phrase (*dio legei*) introduces what likewise appears to be a snippet from early Christian worship.
5. Lincoln, *Ephesians*, 243–44.
6. Translation of the targum of Psalm 68:19 [v. 18 is here numbered as 19] by Edward M. Cook, http://targum.info/pss/ps2.htm (italics original).

God "gave abundant showers" to the land and "provided for the poor" (Ps 68:9–10). Psalm 68 ends by celebrating the fact that God "gives power and strength to his people" (Ps 68:35). Thus the quotation in Ephesians 4:8 represents a major theme of Psalm 68, the ascendant God giving to his people.[7] The story of God in Psalm 68 prefigures the story of Christ in Ephesians 4.

Ascended . . . descended (4:9–10). Paul's commentary on Psalm 68 in Ephesians 4:9–10 reads: "What does 'he ascended' mean except that he also descended to the lower, earthly regions? He who descended is the very one who ascended higher than all the heavens, in order to fill the whole universe." Most interpreters agree on the basic meaning of Christ's ascent (his resurrection and journey to heaven), but there is little consensus about his descent. Does this refer to his death and burial, to his visiting the underworld after his death,[8] to the giving of the Spirit at Pentecost, or to his incarnation? Given the likelihood that Paul would have thought of the surface of the earth as the lower regions, he probably envisioned Christ's incarnation as his descent (similar to Phil 2:6–8).

The final phrase of 4:10 states that Christ ascended to the highest heavens "in order to fill the whole universe." More literally, the Greek could be translated, "in order that he might fill all things [*ta panta*]." This intentionally echoes 1:10 in which God's cosmic purpose is "to bring unity to all things [*ta panta*] in heaven and on earth under Christ." At the end of chapter 1, Christ is "head over everything [*panta*] for the church, which is his body, the fullness of him who fills everything [*ta panta*] in every way" (1:22–23). Christ's giving of gifts contributes to his effort to unify and fill all things.

Why did Paul choose to include a Christological interpretation of Psalm 68 in his discussion of Christ's giving in Ephesians 4? You could, after all, remove verses 8–10 from 7–16 without affecting the main storyline. Their inclusion, however, highlights the fact that Christ's giving to his people replays the story of God's giving to his people. Christ is faithfully living the story of God as told in Psalm 68.

Christ Gives Gifts to Equip His People (4:11–13)

Ephesians 4:11–13 is the first half of a 124-word Greek sentence that extends from 11 through 16. We will consider this sentence in two sections (11–13; 14–16). The first section reveals that Christ gave gifts of people in particular functions for the purpose of equipping all of God's people for the ministry of building up the church, so that the church might grow in unity, maturity, and stature.

---

7. See Gombis, *Drama*, 139.
8. See 1 Pet 3:19–20.

So Christ himself gave the apostles, the prophets, the evangelists, the pastors and teachers (4:11). In 4:7–10, Christ gave grace to each person. Verse 11 specifies one dimension of Christ's gift that we might not expect if we are familiar with Paul's teaching on gifts found in Romans 12 and 1 Corinthians 12–14. There, the gifts are specific, diverse abilities or empowerments for ministry. In Ephesians 4:11, the gifts are not abilities or empowerments but rather people serving in certain roles: "So Christ himself gave the apostles, the prophets, the evangelists, the pastors and teachers." Some interpreters have suggested that this verse means "Christ gave some to be apostles, some to be prophets, etc." But this reading, though possible in Greek, is not likely. The more obvious sense is that Christ gave people-gifts *to the church*, to the people of God whom they are to serve.[9]

Earlier sections of Ephesians cast light on the list of people-gifts in 4:11. Paul identifies himself as an apostle (1:1). He notes that the household of God is "built on the foundation of the apostles and prophets" (2:20; see also 3:5 and 1 Cor 12:28). The first two people-gifts in 4:11, apostles and prophets, served a foundational role in the earliest church. Yet according to verse 11, the people given by Christ to the church are not just these founders but also those who serve in the present time. All apostles, prophets, evangelists, pastors, and teachers are part of Christ's gift. Other roles might have been included, though Paul does not mention them here.[10]

Verse 11 has stirred up ample conversation about the meaning and relevance of "the apostles, the prophets, the evangelists, the pastors and teachers." There have been debates about whether all of these roles belong in the church today, or whether apostles and prophets were only for the early church. Many have tried to define the precise function of each role. Some have built elaborate missional models based on the five-fold schema of 4:11.[11] The main problem with these sincere efforts is that Ephesians 4 gives us so little to go on. This passage does not explain the distinctive work of each role, only what they have in common, namely their source and their purpose.

We can fashion, however, a rough idea of the roles mentioned in verse 11. Apostles were authorized and sent to preach the gospel and to plant, nurture,

---

9. It is tempting to refer to "the apostles, the prophets, the evangelists, the pastors and teachers" with a generic title such as "leaders." I have refrained from doing so because the word "leader" is laden with meaning that might obscure Paul's argument here. Instead, I will refer to them as people-gifts to underscore the unique nature of the Christ's gifts in Ephesians 4.

10. It seems likely, for example, that Paul would have considered "overseers and deacons" (Phil 1:1) or perhaps leaders (Rom 12:8) as gifts from God who help to equip the church.

11. For a creative discussion of this passage and its implications for today's church, see Alan Hirsch and Tim Catchim, *The Permanent Revolution: Apostolic Imagination and Practice for the 21st Century Church* (San Francisco: Jossey-Bass, 2012).

and oversee churches.[12] Prophets communicated God's truth to God's people, not only concerning the future (1 Cor 14:1–40). The meaning of the word "evangelist"[13] suggests that this role had responsibility to share the gospel with those who had not received it. Pastors were those who oversaw and cared for God's flock, much like literal shepherds with their sheep. In fact, the Greek word translated here as "pastor" means "shepherd."[14] In the New Testament, it is used in the sense of "pastor for people" only here, except for passages that speak of Jesus as the shepherd of his flock (John 10:11–16; Heb 13:20; 1 Pet 2:25).[15] Finally, teachers instructed God's people in God's truth.

The various roles mentioned in 4:11 overlap considerably. Take Paul, for example. He was an apostle (Eph 1:1). Yet he also evangelized (1 Cor 1:17), taught (Col 1:28), and exercised pastoral oversight of his churches (1 Thess 1–5).[16] Moreover, it's likely that Paul prophesied (1 Cor 13:2: 14:3–6, 37). Furthermore, the Greek language used in Ephesians 4:11 suggests a strong connection between the role of pastor and teacher. A literal translation of this verse reads, "[Christ gave] the apostles, the prophets, the evangelists, the shepherds and teachers." While the absence of the definite article in front of "teachers" might be stylistic, it seems more likely that Paul regarded the functions of pastor and teacher as inextricably linked. The emphasis in our passage, at any rate, is not on the distinctions between the roles, but rather on what they share in common. They are all gifts from Christ to the church.

To equip his people for works of service (4:12). And all these roles share in a common work: "to equip his people for works of service, so that the body of Christ may be built up" (4:12). This does not mean, of course, that equipping is the only thing apostles, prophets, evangelists, and pastors and teachers do. But their job descriptions overlap in a key task that is highlighted in verse 12.

The NIV translation of this verse captures its basic sense but obscures some relevant details. "His people" in the phrase "to equip his people" could be translated more accurately as "the saints" or "God's holy people" (as in 1:1 of the NIV). The saints are those set apart by God for his purposes.[17] According to Ephesians, all of God's people are special. All are set apart by God. All are to be equipped by those Christ gives to the church for this task.

---

12. See the discussion of "apostle" in the commentary on 1:1.

13. "Evangelist" in Greek is *euangelistēs*, which means "one who proclaims the good news." See also Acts 21:8; 2 Tim 4:5.

14. *Poimēn*; see Luke 2:8 for example.

15. The verb "to shepherd" (*poimainō*) is used for humans pastoring others in John 21:16; Acts 20:28; 1 Pet 5:2.

16. Some years ago, I wrote my dissertation on the topic of Paul as a pastor to the Thessalonians. See Mark David Roberts, "Images of Paul and the Thessalonians" (Ph.D. diss., Harvard University, 1992).

17. "Saints" in Greek is *hagioi*. For more, see commentary on 1:1, 4.

According to the NIV, God's people are to be equipped "for works of service" (4:12) The Greek text, however, speaks not of "works" of service but of "a work" or "the work."[18] The emphasis is on the work of the saints viewed as a whole, not as individual works. Additionally, the Greek word translated as "service" is *diakonia*. This word can mean "service," that which is done by a servant (*diakonos*). But the NIV often translates *diakonia* not as "service" but as "ministry." So for example, Paul says he takes pride in his "ministry" (Rom 11:13; see also 2 Cor 4:1). God has given us the "ministry of reconciliation" (2 Cor 5:18). The people of God in Ephesians 4:12 are to be equipped not just for works of service but for *the work of ministry*. This verse reveals that all of God's people participate in the ministry of Christ. All of us are his ministers, not in the sense of being "ministry professionals" but rather as people set apart by God to serve him and people in both the church and the world.

Some translations and interpretations of 4:12 disagree. The KJV, for example, says that Christ gave people-gifts "for the perfecting of the saints, for the work of ministry, for the edifying of the body of Christ." In this translation, the saints are the recipients of the ministry done by the apostles, prophets, evangelists, and pastors and teachers. But this translation misses a crucial distinction in the Greek. The original text says that Christ gave people-gifts "toward [*pros*] the equipping of the saints into [*eis*] a/the work of ministry into [*eis*] building up the body of Christ." There are not three parallel tasks here for the people-gifts to do. Rather, they have one major, shared function. They get the saints ready to go into the work of ministry, that is, into building up the body of Christ. The grammar of verse 12 suggests what verse 7 (Christ gave grace to each one) and verse 16 (the body grows when each one does its part) confirm. The people-gifts prepare all of God's people for their work of ministry, which in this passage is focused on the building up Christ's body.

Verse 13 expands upon what this edification entails. The people of God do their ministry and build up the body of Christ "until we all reach [*eis*] unity in the faith and in the knowledge of the Son of God and [*eis*] become mature, [*eis*] attaining to the whole measure of the fullness of Christ." The repeated use of the Greek word *eis* ("to") spells out three crucial dimensions of Christian growth: unity, maturity, and stature.

Until we all reach unity (4:13). The Greek word translated as "unity" (*henotēs*) in verse 13 is the same word used in verse 3: "Make every effort to keep the unity of the Spirit." Interestingly, verse 3 portrays unity as something already provided by the Spirit that therefore needs to be preserved. Verse 13 sees unity as the goal of ministry, something for which we strive. Once again, who we are "in Christ" (united) determines how we are to live (building

---

18. "Work" is *ergon,* singular, without the article.

unity). According to Yoder Neufeld, "Ministry has to do with becoming what we already are."[19]

Notice that church unity is "in the faith and in the knowledge of the Son of God." As we saw in our earlier discussion of Ephesians 2:8, "faith" includes both an intellectual and a relational element, both belief and trust. In 4:13 "*the* faith" emphasizes the believing dimension of faith (like 4:5). The phrase "and in the knowledge of the Son of God" reiterates the importance of what we believe. Knowledge, as we have noted earlier in this commentary,[20] is not just a matter of thinking. There is an inherently relational dimension to biblical knowing.[21] But the kind of knowledge of the Son of God that fosters unity has to do with rightly understanding who the Son of God really is, what he really did, and what he really does. Growth in church unity is nourished by orthodoxy.

Become mature (4:13). The NIV translates the phrase following the second *eis* in 4:13 as "and become mature." This translation captures the sense of the Greek, though the original language is more challenging. In Greek, the phrase *eis andra teleion* means, literally, "to a/the perfect/complete/mature man." The singularity of "man" indicates that this phrase does not refer to the individual maturity of the multiple members of the body of Christ. Rather, the singular "man" points to the church as the body of Christ becoming mature. The use of *eis andra teleion*, however, suggests an even more specific sense. The body of Christ is to grow not just into maturity but into *the perfect man*, that is, into Christ who exemplifies maturity. That Christ is the aim of the body's growth is reinforced by the last part of verse 13 as well as verse 15, which says in Greek that we are to grow up "into Christ in every way." The body is to "become mature" as it grows into the maturity and completion of Christ himself.

Attaining to the whole measure of the fullness of Christ (4:13). The third *eis* in verse 13 introduces the phrase translated by the NIV as "attaining to the whole measure of the fullness of Christ." We have heard language like this before in Ephesians. According to 1:23, the church is the body of Christ, "the fullness of him who fills everything in every way." In 3:19 Paul prays that we might "be filled to the measure of all the fullness of God." The language of fullness evokes a vast reservoir filled to overflowing by Christ. Thus "the whole measure of the fullness of Christ" in 4:13 suggests growth in size. Even as a human body becomes physically larger as it ages from infancy to adulthood, so the church as the body of Christ grows up to the size of Christ's enormous fullness. Once more, what an earlier passage from Ephesians envisions as a

---

19. Yoder Neufeld, *Ephesians*, 184.
20. See discussion of 1:17–18.
21. For a classic explanation of Christian knowing, see J. I. Packer, *Knowing God* (Downers Grove, IL: InterVarsity Press, 1973).

given (the church as the fullness of Christ), chapter 4 portrays as a goal (the church growing to the measure of Christ's fullness). Christ sets the standard for the church's growth, now in stature as well as maturity.

The growth envisioned in 4:13 includes individual members of the body of Christ but is something that the body experiences as a whole. Yet the emphasis in 4:7–16 on corporate growth does not exclude individual maturity, as we shall see in the next section of our passage.

Christ Grows His Body (4:14–16)

Then we will no longer be infants (4:14). Though in English verse 14 begins a new sentence, in Greek the sentence begun in verse 11 continues with the word *hina*, "in order that." The basic grammatical structure of 14–16 is in order that 1) we should no longer be infants and 2) we should grow.

Up to this point in our passage, it is the church, the body of Christ, that grows in unity, maturity, and stature. The growth of individual parts is only implied. But verse 14, by use of the plural "infants," shows that corporate growth and individual growth go hand in hand. If the body of Christ grows, then individuals will no longer be spiritual babies.

Verse 14 employs a mixed metaphor (being infants, being tossed around like little boats) to underline one facet of spiritual immaturity: the tendency to be influenced by false teaching, especially that motivated by deceit. Yet if the people of God do their ministry well, then the church as a whole will grow in true faith and knowledge, not to mention maturity, which means that individual believers will also grow up in Christ. Right belief is essential for corporate and personal growth. It enables us to grow up "in every respect" into Christ, as verse 15 puts it.

Speaking the truth in love (4:15). Orthodoxy and spiritual growth do not happen automatically, however. They come as God's holy people exercise their ministry by "speaking the truth in love" (4:15). Some interpreters translate this phrase as "truthing in love" or "living the truth in love" because the Greek uses the verb *alētheuō* (related to *alētheia*, "truth"). But this reads more into this verb than is warranted. A few verses later in 4:25, Paul uses the verb "to speak" followed by "truth" (*laleite alētheian*). His only other use of *alētheuō* in his letters clearly means telling the truth (Gal 4:16). So *alētheuō* in 4:15 should be translated as "speaking the truth." Yet the addition of "in love" indicates that the truth we speak must also be truth we live.

What is this truth? I have heard some say that this verse has to do with confronting the sin of another Christian. There certainly are times when we need to speak this sort of truth to a brother or sister (see Matt 18:15–17), but this is not what Paul has in mind in Ephesians 4:15. Rather, the truth to be spoken in love is the good news of God's work in Jesus Christ. Ephesians 1:13 identifies "the message of truth" as "the gospel of your salvation." The core of Christian truth speaking, therefore, involves sharing the good news of Christ in all dimensions and implications. The letter of Ephesians itself serves as a prime example of this kind of truth telling. Paul is modeling that which he urges all Christians to do as ministers of Jesus Christ.

Speaking the truth in love undoubtedly involves speaking in a loving manner.[22] But "in love" points to more than just our mode of communication. In 4:25 it says: "Therefore each of you must put off falsehood and speak truthfully to your neighbor, for we are all members of one body." This parallel verse shows that speaking the truth in love means not just speaking kindly but also speaking in the context of our relationships in the body of Christ. God's love in Christ draws us into fellowship with each other and binds together our corporate life (Col 3:14). We speak the truth in love, therefore, when we live in a community in which God's love in Christ determines our way of life (Eph 5:1–2).[23]

We will grow to become in every respect the mature body of him who is the head, that is, Christ (4:15). The Greek reads more literally "we will grow up in every way into him who is the head, Christ." Yes, this means we become the mature body of Christ, as the NIV affirms. But the emphasis of the original is once again on Christ as the goal of our growth, just like in 4:13.

From him (4:16). Yet Christ is not just the target of our growth but also the source. Verse 16 begins with the phrase "from him" as it explains how the whole body grows. Christ as the head of the body is the source of its multi-faceted growth. This sense of Christ's headship was foreshadowed earlier in 1:22–23, where God appointed Christ to be head "over everything for the church, which is his body, the fullness of him who fills everything in every way." As head of the church, Christ is filling it up. Thus when it comes to the growth of the church, we would expect Christ to be the source of its growth, much as nourishment for a human body comes from the head by way of the mouth. Most of all, Christ supplies grace to the church so that it might grow up (4:7).

The whole body, joined and held together by every supporting ligament, grows and builds itself up in love, as each part does its work (4:16). Verse 16 accentuates the importance of each member of Christ's body for its growth. The complex phrase, "joined and held together by every supporting ligament,"

---

22. See 4:29–5:2; see also 1 Cor 4:21; 13:1.

23. For a thorough discussion of how community is essential to our growth in Christ, see Tod E. Bolsinger, *It Takes a Church to Raise a Christian: How the Community of God Transforms Lives* (Grand Rapids: Brazos, 2004).

which is even more complicated in Greek, reveals that every part of the body is somehow connected to and dependent on every other part (similarly, 1 Cor 12:12–27). Therefore, the body will grow up only "as each part does its work" (Eph 4:16). The Greek of this expression echoes verse 7, reminding us that Christ gives grace to each one so that each one can help the body grow.

Thus Ephesians 4:7–16 ends much as it began, with Christ as the one who gives to each one of us. His grace enables all of us to engage in the ministry of building up his body, the church. The church will only grow as it should when each member contributes. Apostles, prophets, evangelists, and pastors and teachers are given by Christ to the church to in order to equip all of God's holy people for our ministry, so that we might help the church grow in unity, maturity, and stature. We do so mainly by speaking the truth in love. When we grow as the body together, we will also grow as discrete members. Christ is both the source and the goal of our corporate and individual growth.

LIVE the Story

The first three chapters of Ephesians tell the story of God's plan to bring to unity all things under Christ. In chapter 4, we participate in God's plan not only as those in whom God graciously acts but also as actors in his drama. We are called to live in light of all God has done, at first by eagerly preserving the unity of the church given by the Spirit. Verses 4:7–16 add to the story by telling how Christ gives grace to all of us so that we all might contribute to the growth of the church in unity, maturity, and stature.

Echoes of the Story of Creation

That God would involve us in such a grand enterprise makes perfect sense when we remember the beginning of God's story in Scripture. In Genesis 1 God created the world, including human beings, who were made uniquely in God's image. God gave us a unique assignment to steward his creation, filling it and caring for it (Gen 1:28; 2:15). Even though we messed up God's creation through sin, God did not abandon his desire to use us for his purposes. Ephesians reveals that in Christ, God forgave us and gave us new life, creating us afresh for good works, similar to what happened in the first creation (1:7; 2:4–10). Even as God created us to tend his world, so he has recreated us in Christ to help mend his world.

Yet we do not do this work of mending in our own strength. Rather, we receive ample divine help. Christ gives grace to each one of us so that we might participate in the ministry of building up his body (4:7, 12), which is the central effort in the cause of cosmic unification. One expression of

Christ's grace comes in the form of people-gifts who equip all of us for our ministry (4:11–12). In Ephesians 4 this ministry is focused on contributing to the manifold growth of the church. But the goal of uniting all things under Christ, not to mention the story of the first creation, reminds us that God is renewing the whole cosmos, and we are participants in that renewal. From the first chapter to the last of God's story in Scripture, human beings participate in God's work in the world.

How God's Story in Ephesians 4 Has Become My Story

Unfortunately, the story of God doing his work through each one of us became confused by a competing story that emphasizes called, trained, and authorized priests, pastors, and preachers. The ministry of all of God's people became replaced by the ministry of the clergy, the professionals. As the King James Version of Ephesians 4:11–12 proclaimed, Christ gave people gifts not to equip the saints for their ministry, but rather to do the ministry for the saints. The church became divided into the clergy who did ministry (and got paid for it) and the laity who received it (and paid for it). Though there were occasional exceptions throughout church history, this became the dominant story of Christendom.

It was certainly the story I accepted until a watershed Sunday in 1972. I had grown up in the First Presbyterian Church of Hollywood, California, a megachurch noted for its exceptional "ministers." In 1972 our newest senior minister, Lloyd John Ogilvie, began his tenure at "Hollywood Pres." I will never forget his first Sunday in our church. Rev. Ogilvie, who looked so young (a plus) and whose voice was so deep (a marvel), stood up and said to the congregation, "I want to introduce you to the ministers of this church." That seemed an odd thing to say, since we all knew the ministers. They were the men in black robes who sat in the front of the church and had "Reverend" or "Doctor" affixed to their names. Rev. Ogilvie was the only minister who needed an introduction, as far as I knew. "I am the new pastor of this church," he said. "And *you* are the ministers. Each and every one of you is a minister of Jesus Christ."

This was something unexpected, strange, and wonderful. How could I be a minister of Christ, given that I had not gone to seminary and didn't own a black robe? Rev. Ogilvie explained, "Scripture teaches that all Christians are ministers. The job of the pastor is to equip you for your ministry. That's why I'm here. And that's why I want to be known as your pastor, not your minister."

I didn't know at the time that he was drawing from Ephesians 4:11–12. Nor did I realize how the truth that *Pastor* Ogilvie shared would utterly change my life.

That change began as I started to take seriously my own calling to be a minister of Christ. I got involved teaching Sunday school, and after a while leading a junior high Bible study. I shared the gospel with my friends at school. I continued to be active in Christian service while in college, long before I considered becoming an ordained "Minister of Word and Sacrament" in the Presbyterian Church.

On the day of my ordination at Hollywood Pres, Pastor Ogilvie looked straight into my eyes and charged me to fulfill my calling to equip God's people for their ministry. I did so for several years under his tutelage, serving on the staff of the Hollywood church before assuming the role of pastor of Irvine Presbyterian Church in Southern California. I had become one of Christ's gifts to the church, a pastor-teacher who accepted the responsibility of preparing the saints for ministry.

Because I had grown up under Lloyd Ogilvie's teaching, I assumed that his approach was commonplace. So when I first preached on Ephesians 4:11–12 in my new church, I was surprised by the reaction. Many had not heard anything like this before. They believed "the ministry" was to be done by professionals like me, paid by their generous giving. Much as I had been in 1972, many who heard for the first time that they were ministers of Christ were intrigued.

But not everyone. After my sermon on "lay ministry," a man I'll call "Steve" cornered me on the steps. His face glowed with anger. He pointed his finger at me and said, "Pastor, you're just trying to get out of your job. You're trying to get us to do it for you. We pay you to do the ministry. So stop telling us to be the ministers of this church."

I was stunned by Steve's reaction to my sermon because I believed that what I had preached was both commonly known and clearly taught in Scripture, not to mention good news for church members. Squelching my defensiveness, I said, "Hey, we aren't going to be able to settle this on the church steps. Let's get together next week and talk about your concerns. Maybe we can figure this out."

When Steve and I met, he had calmed down, so we had an open conversation. I walked him through Ephesians 4:11–12 once again. I listened to his concerns about pastors not doing their jobs. I reassured him that I was not trying to get out of preaching, teaching, praying, and shepherding the congregation. I helped him see that I was doing these things not because I was "the minister" but because I wanted to equip and empower Steve and other members of the church to be ministers. As we talked, Steve's attitude began to shift: "You mean if I wanted to teach a Bible study in this church, I could do that, and you would help me?"

"Yes," I said, "that's a fine example."

"I've always wanted to do something like that," Steve said, "but have never felt like I could because I'm not ordained."

Steve left my office that day excited about the possibilities for his ministry. He did indeed start a Bible study. I helped equip Steve for his work through my own preaching, teaching, and personal discipleship. In time, as Steve lived into the story of his being a minister of Christ, he began to see his ministry as more than just his service in church. He got excited about the possibilities of serving Christ in his professional life as a financial advisor. He began to see his daily work as an opportunity for ministry.

Steve was concerned that pastors might not be doing their jobs. I share his concern today, though not in the form he once expressed it. I am worried that many pastors, in spite of the countless hours they put in, are not doing the work of equipping their people for their ministry. We pastors often see ourselves as the ministry professionals. We don't want the laity to mess up our work or, even worse, to do it for us. We get affirmation and compensation from doing "the ministry." And in many cases our congregations are filled with people who are perfectly happy to let us do the ministry and pay us for what they receive.

Are we pastors really equipping the people of God for ministry? Do our churches reflect the ministry and maturity of Ephesians 4? Are we living into the biblical story of Christ giving grace to all of his people so they can help build the body? Or are we stuck in another story, a story that assumes a biblically questionable distinction between clergy and laity, a story that limits the work of ministry to apostles, prophets, evangelists, and pastors and teachers? And even if we affirm the importance of the ministry of all of God's people, do those of us in positions of leadership in the church really act as equippers, as player-coaches for the team of God's people? How much of our work is intentionally dedicated to preparing the saints for their ministry in the church and the world?

The Story of Laity Lodge

After sixteen years as *pastor* of Irvine Presbyterian Church, I left the familiarity of Southern California to move with my family to the Texas Hill Country outside of San Antonio. I did so to become part of the work of Laity Lodge. Though I was still an ordained pastor, I joined an organization committed to equipping, empowering, and encouraging the laity to be ministers of Jesus Christ in every part of life.

The story of Laity Lodge is the tale of someone who took seriously the truth of Ephesians 4. Howard E. Butt, Jr. grew up as the heir apparent to a large grocery company in Texas. If one's father is Howard E. Butt and his company is HEB, then there's not too much question about what path some-one named Howard E. Butt, Jr. was expected to take.

Yet when Howard Jr. went to college, he discovered that God had power-fully gifted him for evangelism. During his days at Baylor, he and his classmates led thousands of young people throughout United States to faith in Christ. This created a crisis for Howard. A good Baptist boy with such a gift for preaching was surely "called into the ministry." Yet he sensed a divine calling into his family's business. As Howard wrestled with God's will for his life, including the story of Ephesians 4:7–16, he became convinced that he was indeed called into the ministry, the ministry of serving God in the family business, the ministry of serving as a lay leader in the church, the ministry of helping millions of other "laymen" recognize that they were, indeed, ministers of Jesus Christ.

After years of doing his ministry in the grocery company, the church, and the world, Howard founded Laity Lodge, a retreat center on a large ranch owned by his family's foundation and used for camps for underprivileged children. Laity Lodge became a center of theological discovery, authentic Christian friendship, and spiritual renewal. Retreats featured speakers such as J. I. Packer, Eugene Peterson, Henri Nouwen, and Madeleine L'Engle. For more than fifty years, Laity Lodge has been the centerpiece of Howard Butt, Jr.'s effort to help all of God's people, including both laity and clergy, embrace their high calling to a life of ministry.

God's story lived out at Laity Lodge became a vital chapter of my story in 2007 when God's surprising guidance led me to become the senior director of Laity Lodge. Part of what drew me to this work was its founding vision, still vibrantly articulated by Howard. I wanted to join forces with those who had dedicated their lives to seeing Ephesians 4:7–16 become reality. Fittingly, the advice of my former pastor and mentor, Lloyd Ogilvie, was one main reason Laity Lodge wanted me and I wanted Laity Lodge.

As the leader of the Laity Lodge team, I had the privilege of devoting my life to equipping and encouraging the people of God to embrace their God-given ministry. I came to know hundreds of people who do this every day in their ordinary (but really not so ordinary) lives. I think of Kimberly, a contractor in Austin, Texas, who served Christ through her daily work reno-vating houses. I picture Rudy, who cared with faithfulness and excellence for the property of the H. E. Butt Family Foundation, the organizational home of Laity Lodge. (The inspirational stories of Kimberly, Rudy, and others are captured in videos produced by The High Calling, the online outreach of the Foundation.)[24] I am greatly encouraged by the extent to which the story

---

24. Kimberly is featured in "Restoring Homes to Restore a Community," http://youtu.be/okh-2v7tQvtA. Rudy appears in "He Put Me Here for a Reason, Don't You Think?" http://youtu.be/YtNHQm_fuIw.

of Christ's calling and equipping all of his people for all kinds of ministry is being told, retold, and lived out each day by millions of Christians around the world.

For example, I think of what's happening at Abundant Life Church in Cambridge, Massachusetts. When I joined this congregation for worship some time ago, I was warmly welcomed into a vibrant community made up primarily of African-American believers. I was impressed by how the church's mission reflects the vision of Ephesians 4: "The Abundant Life Church exists to introduce, develop and empower people to faithfully follow Christ, in order that each person may fulfill their purpose in the church, the community, and the world." Its pastors, Larry and Virginia Ward, have been equipping God's people in this church for over twenty years. The church website describes Pastor Larry as "a gifted teacher and communicator of God's Word with a heart to see believers equipped and empowered to build God's Kingdom." Pastor Virginia serves in a variety of roles in the church, with a particular focus on youth. She seeks to "inspire, enlighten, and help individuals and organizations equip the next generation of leaders."[25] The Wards see their pastoral work in Abundant Life Church not primarily as doing ministry for their people but rather as equipping their people to do their own ministry in every segment of life. Their efforts have been profoundly shaped by the story of Christ's giving pastor-teachers to the church to equip all of his people for all kinds of ministry.

Rethinking the Language for Ministry in Light of God's Story

Yet as I have spent many years telling the Ephesians 4:7–16 story, watching it play out in the lives of many, I continue to be concerned about some of the barriers that keep all Christians from experiencing it. There are institutional barriers ("The rules say . . ."), cultural barriers ("We've always done it like this"), and preferential barriers ("I want my minister to . . ."). One of the most prevalent and pernicious barriers, it seems to me, has to do with our language for ministry.

For example, a good friend of mine is a pastor. He believes that pastors are to equip God's people for ministry. He does this in his congregation largely through his preaching and teaching. The church he pastors has plenty of members who are living the "ministry of God's people" story throughout their whole lives. Yet my friend persists in using language for ministry that, in my opinion, works against his theology and his passion to see his congregation equipped and deployed as active ministers of Christ. He continues to call himself a "minister," reserving this title only for those who are ordained.

---

25. http://www.alccambridge.org/.

People in his congregation can minister in church or in their daily work, but only he and his ordained colleagues are "in *the* ministry." My friend believes that God calls all Christians to live their whole lives for God's purposes, yet he speaks of being "called into the ministry" as something that happens mainly to ordained pastors or perhaps official missionaries. My friend has a solid biblical theology of ministry. He seeks to equip his people for their ministry. His heart is in the right place. But I believe his language reflects a Christian cultural tradition that is out of sync with Scripture and that inhibits the ministry of all of God's people.

I would propose to my friend, and to all other Christians who embrace the story of Ephesians 4:7–16, that we declare a moratorium on language for ministry that fails to reflect the biblical narrative and that can keep God's people from embracing their ministry. I would suggest that "*the ministry*" should refer to "the ministry of all of God's people." We would rightly say, "Every Christian is called into *the ministry*." Those of us who are called to be pastor-teachers (or apostles, prophets, or evangelists, for that matter) could modify our particular calling with appropriate adjectives. Thus I might say that I have been called to "pastoral ministry" but not to "the ministry." I can truly say that I am a minister of Jesus Christ because this is true of all believers. More specifically, I might call myself a pastor, a pastoral minister, a pastor-teacher, a teaching elder, or a preacher. But even this language can be misleading, since many who do the work of pastors in the church are not officially ordained, even though God uses them to shepherd his flock. I long for the day when our language—yes, including my own—more accurately reflects the biblical story and encourages all of God's people to participate in the ministry of Christ.

If you were to ask me, "When were you called into the ministry?" my answer would be shaped by the story of Ephesians. I might be so bold as to say I was called into the ministry before the creation of the world, since that's when God chose me to be one of his holy people (1:4). But I might also say I was called by God into the ministry when I first accepted his grace offered to me in Jesus Christ. I was called when I heard the good news of salvation and responded in faith. I first receive my vocation when I said "yes" to the gospel. Thus the fundamental calling I have received from God, the calling that guides my life and I share with you and all other believers, is the calling to follow Jesus Christ and to share in his ministry.

CHAPTER 10

Ephesians 4:17–5:2

📖 LISTEN to the Story

[17]So I tell you this, and insist on it in the Lord, that you must no longer live as the Gentiles do, in the futility of their thinking. [18]They are darkened in their understanding and separated from the life of God because of the ignorance that is in them due to the hardening of their hearts. [19]Having lost all sensitivity, they have given themselves over to sensuality so as to indulge in every kind of impurity, and they are full of greed.

[20]That, however, is not the way of life you learned [21]when you heard about Christ and were taught in him in accordance with the truth that is in Jesus. [22]You were taught, with regard to your former way of life, to put off your old self, which is being corrupted by its deceitful desires; [23]to be made new in the attitude of your minds; [24]and to put on the new self, created to be like God in true righteousness and holiness.

[25]Therefore each of you must put off falsehood and speak truthfully to your neighbor, for we are all members of one body. [26]"In your anger do not sin": Do not let the sun go down while you are still angry, [27]and do not give the devil a foothold. [28]Anyone who has been stealing must steal no longer, but must work, doing something useful with their own hands, that they may have something to share with those in need.

[29]Do not let any unwholesome talk come out of your mouths, but only what is helpful for building others up according to their needs, that it may benefit those who listen. [30]And do not grieve the Holy Spirit of God, with whom you were sealed for the day of redemption. [31]Get rid of all bitterness, rage and anger, brawling and slander, along with every form of malice. [32]Be kind and compassionate to one another, forgiving each other, just as in Christ God forgave you.

[1]Follow God's example, therefore, as dearly loved children [2]and walk in the way of love, just as Christ loved us and gave himself up for us as a fragrant offering and sacrifice to God.

Listening to the text in the Story: Genesis 1–2; Psalm 4:4–5; Zechariah
8:14–17; Romans 1:18–32; 6:1–8; 13:12–14; Colossians 2:6–7; 3:9–
17; James 3:3–12.

As Ephesians 4 begins, it seems as if there will be a major shift from narrative
to imperative. But in fact after just three verses of moral exhortation, 4:4–16
returns to the indicative with a description of the seven "ones" of Christian
unity (4:4–6) followed by the story of Christ giving gifts so that the church
might grow (4:7–16). These indicative sections also have ethical implications,
but the imperatives are implied rather than stated.

Ephesians 4:17 appears to reinstate the imperative stance of 4:1–3. Yet
the exhortation not to live as the Gentiles leads once more into a section of
narrative in which Paul describes the sorry plight of the Gentiles (4:17–19).
Yet when Gentiles receive God's grace through Christ and are taught in him
(4:20–21), they learn to put off their former manner of life, to be renewed,
and to put on a new way of living (4:22–24). Finally, in 4:25 Paul returns
to moral exhortation, which continues consistently until 6:20 (though with
didactic interjections along the way).

The beginning of 4:17, "So [*oun*] I tell you this, and insist on it in the
Lord [*en kuriō*], that you must no longer live [*peripateō*, walk] as the Gentiles
do," echoes 4:1, "As a prisoner for the Lord [*en kuriō*], then [*oun*], I urge you
to live a life [*peripateō*]…" This beginning signals the start of a new section
in chapter 4, an impression that is supported by the thematic change from
4:7–16 (growth of the church) to 4:17–5:2 (moral exhortation).

Ending this section at 5:2 is somewhat arbitrary because the injunctions
that come in 5:3 and following repeat the motifs of 4:17–5:2, such as a list of
sinful attitudes and behaviors (5:3–4), and feature a strong contrast of good
versus evil (5:8) like that found in 4:17–5:2. Yet the first two verses of chapter
5 pick up the language of 4:17 (*peripateō*, walk; *oun*, therefore) and point to
the example of Christ. Thus, 5:1–2 serves as a rhetorical bookend for the section beginning with 4:17. Moreover, 5:3–14 adds a striking new perspective
on how Christians are to live in relationship to the "fruitless deeds of darkness" (5:11). Thus, though its boundaries are porous, 4:17–5:2 is a distinct
section in the broader moral instruction of Ephesians 4–6.

The fact that Ephesians 4 contains much more than a laundry list of ethical exhortations reveals that Paul is not wanting simply to give commands.
Rather, he is eager for his readers to understand the true nature of their new
life in Christ and how this life relates to their previous experience as Gentiles.
Furthermore, he seeks to ensure that they do not turn the Christian life into

a legalistic collection of dos and don'ts. Rather, even as salvation comes in Christ and by grace, so it is with Christian living. It is centered in Christ and is a response to God's grace.

EXPLAIN the Story

Summary of Ephesians 4:17–5:2

This section begins with a fervent request that the readers no longer live as the Gentiles (4:17). This leads into a short description of the ignorant and immoral nature of Gentile living (4:17–19) that contrasts sharply with the way of life we learn in relationship with Jesus Christ (4:20–21). From him, we were taught to "put off [our] old self," to "be made new" on the inside, and to "put on the new self" (4:22–24).

Because we exchanged our old self for the new in Christ, we must live out this new life each day, especially in our relationships with others. Specifically, we reject falsehood in favor of speaking the truth (4:25). We must not sin when we are angry (4:26). We should not steal, but work instead (4:28). We should not use words to tear down, but to build up (4:29). We are to replace bitterness and brawling with kindness, compassion, and forgiveness (4:31–32). We are to imitate God by walking in love, as Christ loved us (5:1–2). Most of these exhortations come in pairs, with something to put off and something to put on.

No Longer Live as the Gentiles (4:17–19)

So I tell you this, and insist on it in the Lord, that you must no longer live as the Gentiles do (4:17). Ephesians 4:17 echoes language used in 4:1, thus indicating the return of moral exhortation. Once again, Paul will tell his readers how to live and how not to live. "Live" translates *peripateō*, which means "to walk" and was used in Judaism for living considered from an ethical point of view (see 2:10; 4:1). In 4:1, Paul's moral authority came from his being a prisoner for (or in) the Lord (*en kuriō*). In 4:17, his authority to tell his readers how to live comes from the fact he is "in the Lord [*en kuriō*]."

Given that the readers of Paul's letter are Gentiles (see 3:1), it is striking that he tells them not to "live as the Gentiles do." Though they have not become Jews, these believers in Christ are not really Gentiles anymore either. They have become a new category of people, defined by their relationship to Christ and his people.

In the futility of their thinking (4:17). Though immoral Gentile behavior is in view here, how they act is a reflection of how they think. They lead empty and immoral lives because of "the futility of their thinking" (4:17).

The Greek word rendered as "futility" means "emptiness, futility, worthlessness, vanity, purposelessness."[1] The KJV speaks of "the vanity of their mind," whereas contemporary translations prefer "futility" (NIV, ESV, NRSV). In the Greek translation of the Old Testament, this word shows up thirty-nine times in Ecclesiastes, for example, "'Meaningless! Meaningless!' says the Teacher. 'Utterly meaningless! Everything is meaningless.'" (Eccl 1:2). The Gentiles are living futile lives because they are thinking futile thoughts.

They are darkened in their understanding and separated from the life of God (4:18). The first phrase of 4:18 makes a similar point, using the metaphor of darkness. This language will reappear in 5:8–14. The word translated as "separated" appears in 2:12, "*excluded* from citizenship in Israel." In 4:18, the separation is from God's own life, which implies what was made explicit in 2:1–3, namely, that those who are apart from God are dead.

Because of the ignorance that is in them due to the hardening of their hearts (4:18). Here, the metaphor of hard hearts has less to do with emotions and more to do with willful resistance to God and his truth. We see a classical example of this in Pharaoh's opposition to God in Exodus 7–14. Notice the close connection in Ephesians 4:18 between knowing, willing, and relationship with God. Separation from God comes from not knowing God truly. This is a result of ignorance that comes from choosing not to know or serve God. Earlier in the commentary on Ephesians 4, we noted the importance of right theology if one wishes to have relationship with God (4:5, 13, 15). Verse 4:18 shows the flip side of this equation: ignorance of God leads to separation from God.

Having lost all sensitivity (4:19). Paul uses the perfect participle of a rare verb, *apalgeō*, which appears only here in the Greek New Testament. It suggests a loss of feeling. The ESV translates it as "they have become callous." *The Message* prefers "feeling no pain," which is the literal meaning of *apalgeō*.[2] Ironically, as the Gentiles indulge their lusts, they reflect not an excess of feeling but a lack of feeling and discernment. They have become so used to sin that they do not sense how it wounds their souls and relationships with others.

They have given themselves over to sensuality so as to indulge in every kind of impurity, and they are full of greed (4:19). The Greek word translated as "greed" here means "greediness, insatiableness, avarice, covetousness."[3] In 4:19 it could refer to a depraved desire for material gain, though many interpreters take it to refer to the insatiable desire for "sensuality" and "impurity," that is, immoral sexual behavior.

---

1. BDAG 621 (*mataiotēs*).
2. BDAG 96.
3. BDAG 824 (*pleonexia*).

The "walk" of the Gentiles is not merely a matter of wrong actions. These actions reflect wrong, vain thinking that is itself a result of willful rejection of God. Having lived in ignorance and self-indulgence for so long, the Gentiles have lost their moral sensitivity, even their ability to discern which momentary pleasures actually cause them pain in the long run. For the recipients of Paul's letter, this description of the Gentile plight is not theoretical. Rather, it describes their experience of life before Christ. It is also consistent with earlier sections of Ephesians (2:1–3; 11–12) and other passages in Paul's letters (for example, Rom 1:18–32).

Christ Teaches Us a New Way of Living (4:20–24)

Ephesians 4:17–19 sets up a stark contrast between the sorry state of Gentile life and the new way of living that comes through Christ (4:20–24).

That, however, is not the way of life you learned when you heard about Christ (4:20–21). The NIV translation, seeking to capture the meaning of 4:20 in acceptable English, obscures the stark and surprising nature of the verse. Literally, it could be translated: "But you did not learn Christ in this way."

What does it mean to "learn Christ"? This expression could refer to a "way of life" commended by Christ (suggested by the NIV). Or it could refer to theological and moral traditions passed on by the early Christians. But the awkward bluntness of "learn Christ" should not be reduced to either option. Rather, it underscores the fact that Christianity is focused in a person. This person teaches us how to live. This person exemplifies what he teaches. This person is also someone with whom we have a living relationship. We "learn Christ" by coming to know him through faith. We "learn Christ" by communing with him. We "learn Christ" by living life as part of his body. The essence of the Christian life is not a moral system constructed by a fine moral teacher. Rather, it is life in Christ: trusting him, knowing him, following him, loving him, being created anew in him, learning from him, imitating him, sharing in his work.

When you heard about Christ and were taught in him in accordance with the truth that is in Jesus (4:21). Paul's readers did not know Jesus in the flesh. They "heard" about him from those who preached the gospel and "were taught in him" by the pastor-teachers mentioned in 4:11. The growing Christians were taught "in accordance with the truth that is in Jesus." This is an unexpected phrase, since Paul rarely refers to Jesus without some additional title (Lord, Christ). In fact, this is the only unadorned use of "Jesus" in Ephesians. It could be that it is simply a stylistic variation. It does seem, however, that the appearance of "Jesus" is meant to remind us that our learning "in Christ" is connected to the teachings, actions, death, and resurrection of a real human being. Paul provides an example of "the truth that is in Jesus" a few verses later when he calls us to walk in the way of love, "just as Christ loved us and gave himself up for us" (5:2).

You were taught . . . to put off . . . to be made new . . . and to put on (4:22–24). In the Greek text of 4:22, "you were taught" does not appear. The NIV makes explicit in English what is clear in Greek, where "you were taught" in 4:21 continues to govern the passage from 22 through 24. "You were taught" is followed by three infinitives that reveal the content of this teaching. Some English translations, such as the RSV, read these infinitives as if they were imperatives. They once functioned in this way for those who were just beginning their life as Christians. But the Greek verb tense of the first and third infinitives (aorist) supports the NIV translation. That is, Paul is not presenting new imperatives so much as reminding his readers of what they already learned and experienced.

We were taught to "put off [our] old self" and "put on the new self" (4:22, 24). These verbs were used in ordinary speech for taking off and putting on clothing. Here, as in his other letters, Paul uses this language metaphorically. In Romans, for example, we are to "put aside the deeds of darkness and put on the armor of light" (Rom 13:12). Furthermore, we are to "clothe [ourselves] with the Lord Jesus Christ" (Rom 13:14). Galatians 3:27 tells us we clothe ourselves with Christ in the context of our baptism. It is possible that in the time of Paul, baptized individuals removed their old clothing and put on new clothing.[4] If so, this experience would underlie Paul's use of the clothing metaphor in Ephesians 4:22–24. But too much should not be made of this possibility since it is historically uncertain.[5]

Old self . . . new self (4:22, 24). We put off the "old self" and put on the "new self." The NIV uses "self" as a translation of the Greek word *anthrōpos*, or "human being." Our *anthrōpos* is more than simply a way of life, something external we can easily cast off or put on like a garment. Rather, it is our "self," our core identity. Our old *anthrōpos* connects us to the first man, to Adam and his sinfulness. Therefore, it is "being corrupted by deceitful desires" (4:22), that is, by desires that promise joy but deliver pain. Our new *anthrōpos* links us with Christ the new man and his righteousness (see Rom 5:12–19).

As we consider the meaning of *anthrōpos* in this section, we should remember the depiction of Christ's saving work in Ephesians 2:15. There, Christ's "purpose was to create in himself one new humanity [*kainon anthrōpon*] out of the two, thus making peace." When it says in 4:24 that we are to "put on

4. See Wayne A. Meeks, *The First Urban Christians*, 2nd ed. (New Haven: Yale University Press, 2003), 155.

5. Arnold, *Ephesians*, 287.

the new self [*kainon anthrōpon*], created to be like God," this is not only a new individual identity but also a new relatedness, a new participation in Jesus Christ and his united people who are the "new humanity."[6]

The additional description of the new human being in 4:24 confirms this individual and corporate sense. The new human being is "created to be like God in true righteousness and holiness." To be sure, individuals among God's people are to be righteous and holy. Yet both of these concepts when read in light of the Old Testament are thoroughly corporate. Righteousness is right-relatedness with God and God's people. Holiness means being set apart by God for relationship with him and for membership in his holy people.

To be made new in the attitude of your minds (4:23). Two grammatical points are important to note here. The Greek verb "to be made new" is in the passive voice, indicating that we do not renew ourselves. Rather, the agent of our renewal is God. Yet in some sense we cooperate with God in his renewing work. Second, the verb is a present infinitive, which suggests an ongoing process. Though while it is true that when we put our faith in Christ we put off the old self and put on the new self, the work of internal renewal must still continue. "The attitude of your minds" renders the Greek phrase "the spirit [*pneuma*] of your minds." Some interpreters take this to refer to the Holy Spirit, noting that Ephesians underscores the role of the Spirit in the life of the believer.[7] In 3:16, for example, Paul prays that God may "strengthen you with power through his Spirit in your inner being [*anthrōpos*]." But while it's true that God renews us through the Spirit, the use of *pneuma* in this verse refers to something inside of us that the Holy Spirit renews with our cooperation.

According to Paul, we learned from Christ himself to put off the old human being, be renewed, and put on the new human being. Though Jesus did not use this language as far as we know, he did tell people to "repent and believe the good news!" (Mark 1:15). In place of "repent," he could have said, "Take off your old self, be renewed, and put on your new self." Therefore, Paul's clothing imagery is another perspective on the classic call to repentance, which includes a radical change of life and heart.

Putting Off Old Behavior and Putting on New (4:25–32)

Following the reminder to the readers of how they had been taught to put off the old and put on the new, Paul offers a series of practical examples of what this means in the relationships of everyday life. Most of these examples reflect the twofold form of "put off/put on" by beginning with a negative (don't do this) and ending with a positive (do this instead).

---

6. See Yoder Neufeld, 206–7.
7. See 1:13; 2:18; 2:22; 3:16; 4:30; 5:18; 6:18.

Therefore each of you must put off falsehood and speak truthfully to your neighbor, for we are all members of one body (4:25). Though we learned to put off the old self in the past, we still need to live according to the new self every day. The use of "each" in this verse confirms that individual Christians are in the putting-off and putting-on business as members of the Christian community. The Greek original, echoing Zechariah 8:16, says we are to "speak the truth" with our neighbor. This means more than just not lying; we are also to speak "the truth," that is, the truth of God's grace in Christ, the truth of God's uniting all things in Christ, the truth of God's story in Ephesians 1–3. Thus, 4:25 reiterates 4:15–16; we grow in Christ by speaking the truth in love.

Verse 4:25 gives a reason why such truth speaking is required: "For we are all members of one body." This verse does not say we should speak the truth "because it is right" or "because God commands it," though these may be true. Rather in this verse the rationale for truthfulness has to do with our membership in the body of Christ. What calls forth honesty is the fact that we are connected to each other in Christ. The foundation for truthfulness among Christians is the reality of our oneness in Christ, a unity forged by God through the cross and by the Spirit.

"In your anger do not sin": Do not let the sun go down while you are still angry, and do not give the devil a foothold (4:26–27). Verses 26–27 do not follow the put off/put on pattern found in most exhortations of this section. Rather, we find three prohibitions in a row. The first is a citation of Psalm 4:4. The ancient Greek translation of this verse from Psalms uses the same language as the Greek in our text, which reads, "Be angry but do not sin." Many contemporary translations (like the NIV) and commentators argue that the imperative "be angry" is a concession, not a command: "If you are angry, though you really shouldn't be, then don't sin." This may be true. Yet the main point is clear. When you are angry, do not sin. Anger often precipitates sinful words or deeds that hurt others. We should not say or do them.

The last two prohibitions are connected. We must not let our anger last longer than a day, lest it fester in our hearts. Why limit anger to a day? Because putrefying anger gives the devil a "foothold." The Greek word can also mean "space, room, opportunity."[8] Unresolved anger opens up a place for the devil to dwell in us and in our relationships. Smoldering anger provides a foundation for Satan to do his work of dividing, distressing, and distracting us.[9]

This passage shows that anger is itself not wrong. Soon we'll get to 4:31 where it says we should get rid of "all bitterness, rage and anger." In that context, however, the sort of anger is a base, mean, unjustified kind, not an anger

---

8. BDAG 1011–12 (*topos*).

9. For more on Satan and his work, see the commentary on 2:1–3 and 6:10–20.

that is appropriate, even holy. The Gospels show us that our Lord became angry at times (Mark 3:5; 10:14; 11:15–17). Often in Scripture, God is angry over sin and injustice (for example, Ps 90:7–11; John 3:36). So if Jesus, the Son of God, can be angry, and if God the Father can be angry, then anger must not be intrinsically wrong. Additionally, since human beings were created in God's image, then our feelings of anger are not always wrong either. But we must recognize that anger easily leads to sin. When we're angry, we often hurt people, embrace unforgiveness, or plot revenge. Thus if we're angry, even righteously angry, we should always beware because sin is crouching at the door of our hearts.

Anyone who has been stealing must steal no longer, but must work, doing something useful with their own hands, that they may have something to share with those in need (4:28). This verse affirms one of the Ten Commandments, "You shall not steal" (Exod 20:15), though phrasing the prohibition for those who are already stealing. Like the majority of "don'ts" in this section of Ephesians, it is followed by a "do." Those who have been stealing, and implicitly all believers, "must work, doing something useful with their own hands." This echoes the imperative in the Decalogue where the command to keep the Sabbath is followed by "six days you shall labor and do all your work" (Exod 20:9). The centrality of work to human life is made clear in the creation narratives in Genesis 1–2.

Why should we work? Ephesians 4:28 explains: "That [we] may have something to share with those in need." Rather than taking what is not ours, we should give what is ours to those who need it. Throughout Scripture generosity for the poor is required of God's people.[10] Most commentators rightly note that the purpose of work is such benevolence. But beyond that, many overlook something in the text that is easily missed. The NIV says we are to be "doing something useful," but the Greek reads more literally, "working . . . the good [*to agathon*]." Although *agathon* can mean "useful,"[11] this is the same word that figures prominently in Greek philosophy in discussion of "the good."[12] In the Septuagint, *agathos* is used to describe God in his goodness (Pss 118:1; 135:3; in the LXX these are numbered 117:1; 134:3). Thus the CEB rightly renders Ephesians 4:28 as "they should go to work, using their hands to do good." Work is valuable not just because it makes possible charity for the poor but also because it can do good. Work is central to God's purposes for human beings (Gen 1–2). Work is included among the "good works" that God has for us so that we might walk in them (Eph 2:10). Thus

---

10. For example, Deut 15:7; Prov 22:9; 28:27; Isa 58:6–7.
11. BDAG 4.
12. Plato, *Republic*, 508 b–3.

we work not only because it allows us to help the needy but also because doing good work is central to our reason for living.

Do not let any unwholesome talk come out of your mouth, but only what is helpful for building others up according to their needs, that it may benefit those who listen (4:29). This verse continues the familiar pattern of moral exhortation, beginning with the negative before moving to the positive. The Greek word translated as "unwholesome" can mean "rotten, of poor quality, bad, or harmful."[13] It shows up in a saying of Jesus: "Every good tree bears good fruit, but a bad [*sapron*] tree bears bad fruit" (Matt 7:17).[14] As Christians, we need to put away "bad" words that harm and hurt others, words that tear down rather than building up.

By contrast, we are to use our language positively. Our words should be "helpful [*agathos*] for building others up according to their needs, that it may benefit those who listen" (Eph 4:29). Though in this case *agathos* is fairly translated by "helpful," the basic meaning of "good" is implied. Saying what is good is similar to speaking the truth (4:15, 25). According to this text, there are two ways we can use the power of words for good. First, our words can build up people in reference to their needs. The Greek word translated as "needs" is *chreia*, the same word used in 4:28 for material need. Second, our words can "benefit those who listen." The original Greek is stronger than this: it says that our words can "give grace [*charis*] to those who hear them." Our words can be a source of grace to others. This is especially true if we are talking about what is good and true in any arena, and most of all about the good news of God's grace in Christ.

And do not grieve the Holy Spirit of God, with whom you were sealed for the day of redemption (4:30). The placement of verse 30 links it to verse 29, as does the connective "and." Verse 30 expands upon the danger of unwholesome talk mentioned in verse 29. The verb translated here as "grieve" means "to cause severe mental or emotional distress."[15] Some commentators fret over the notion that our behavior can make God feel badly and emphasize that this is only a metaphor. Yet given that we are created in God's image and given biblical language about God's joy and delight in us (see Ps 147:11; Zeph 3:17), we should not avoid the plain sense of Ephesians 4:30: with our words we can hurt not just God's people but even God's Spirit. We do so in particular by using unwholesome words that wound others and shatter Christian community. Since the Spirit forms the community of God's people, and since the unity of God's people is central to God's cosmic purposes, anything we do that

---

13. BDAG 913 (*sapros*).
14. "Good" in this verse translates *agathos* (see BDAG 4).
15. BDAG 604 (*lupeō*).

divides this community distresses the Spirit. On the contrary and by implication, we can please the Spirit when we use our words as part of making "every effort to keep the unity of the Spirit" (4:3).

Get rid of all bitterness, rage and anger, brawling and slander, along with every form of malice. Be kind and compassionate to one another, forgiving each other, just as in Christ God forgave you (4:31–32). These verses form the last of the "put off/put on" pairs in this section. The word "bitterness [*pikria*]" refers literally to that which has an acrid taste. When the Septuagint wanted to label the place where the Israelites encountered bitter water, it used the word *pikria* (Exod 15:23 LXX). Metaphorically, *pikria* is used when people are inundated with animosity or stagnant resentment. "Rage" and "anger" are close in meaning, though Stoics distinguished between initial rage and long term anger.[16] "Brawling" in this context is verbal, not physical. "Slander [*blasphēmia*]" is any speech that denigrates another, whether or not it is true. Bitterness, rage, and anger are the negative feelings that give rise to brawling and slander, which are two among many forms of "malice" (or "evil," *kakia*). All of these, mentioned explicitly or not, must be put off.

By contrast, we are to "be kind and compassionate to one another, forgiving each other, just as in Christ God forgave [us]" (4:32). Kindness (*chrēstos*) is attributed to God in the Old Testament: "Taste and see that the Lord is good [*chrēstos*]" (Ps 34:8; LXX 33:9). God acts in kindness (*chrēstos*) to all (Ps 145:9; LXX 144:9). Thus to be kind is to express goodness and grace in tangible action, imitating God.

The Greek word translated here as "compassionate" literally means "good bowels" (*eusplagchnos*). The Greek language locates emotions not in our hearts but in other vital organs (stomach, kidneys, intestines, etc.). Another translation of *eusplagchnos* is "tenderhearted" (as in the ESV and NRSV). Tenderhearted people allow the feelings of others to touch their own souls. When people around them grieve, compassionate people feel sad. When people are needy, tenderhearted people sense that need.

Yet no matter our intentions, there will be times when we wrong each other. When this happens, forgiveness is required. Paul says his readers should be "forgiving each other, just as in Christ God forgave you" (4:32). The Greek verb translated here as "forgiving" and "forgave" is *charizomai*, which is related to the noun *charis*, "grace." We are to give grace to people in the form of forgiveness when they wrong us.

The last phrase in 4:32 provides both a motivation and a model for forgiveness. We are moved to forgive not because we're such nice people or because the one who wronged us is worthy but because God has forgiven us

---

16. Lincoln, *Ephesians*, 308. See Rom 2:8; Col 3:8.

in Christ. We learn how to forgive by watching the model of God in Christ. According to Ephesians 1:7–8a, "In [Christ] we have redemption through his blood, the forgiveness of sins, in accordance with the riches of God's grace that he lavished on us." Forgiveness flows from God's grace, mercy, and love. As we receive these gifts, we are to give them away to others.

Walk like Christ in the Way of Love (5:1–2)

Follow God's example, therefore, as dearly loved children and walk in the way of love, just as Christ loved us and gave himself up for us as a fragrant offering and sacrifice to God (5:1–2). Although these two verses appear in chapter 5, they complete the thought begun in 4:31–32. We are to forgive as God has forgiven us in Christ. Modeling ourselves on Christ continues in 5:1–2: we are to be imitators of God and "walk in the way of love," just like Christ.

Ephesians 5:1 is not the first time Scripture says that God's people should be like God. In Leviticus 19:2, for example, God says to Israel, "Be holy because I, the LORD your God, am holy." In Matthew 5:48, Jesus says, "Be perfect, therefore, as your heavenly Father is perfect." A few verses earlier in Ephesians say we are "to put on the new self, created to be like God in true righteousness and holiness" (4:24). Verse 5:1 says our imitation of God is to be rooted in our experience of God's love as his "dearly loved children." As human children imitate their parents, so we are to imitate our heavenly Parent.

We imitate God when we "walk in the way of love" (5:2). The Greek reads more simply "walk in love." This kind of love is not the maudlin sort that shows up on gift-store posters. Rather, it is seen and experienced in the cross of Christ who "loved us and gave himself up for us as a fragrant offering and sacrifice to God" (5:2). Previously Ephesians says God made us alive when we were dead in our sins "because of his great love for us" (2:4). Similarly Romans 5:8 says God "demonstrates his own love for us in this: While we were still sinners, Christ died for us." In our relationships with each other, we are to imitate the love of God revealed in the self-giving, sacrificial love of Christ. The use of sacrificial imagery here highlights the costliness of love. Moreover, it hints that even as God was delighted by the "fragrant offering" of Christ, so he will be pleased when we love in a sacrificial way.[17]

To "learn Christ" and to be taught by "the truth that is in Jesus" (4:20–21) means to take him as our moral exemplar. Through his death, Jesus Christ shows what love is all about. But on another level, we learn to love by participating in him and in his death. As Paul writes in Galatians 2:20, "I have been crucified with Christ and I no longer live, but Christ lives in me. The

---

17. See for example Lev 1:9, 13.

life I now live in the body, I live by faith in the Son of God, who loved me and gave himself for me."

When we walk in love and put off the old self and put on the new, and put away falsehood to speak the truth, and don't sin when we're angry, and refrain from stealing but do good work, and speak in ways that avoid evil and build up people, and get rid of bitterness, choosing instead to forgive, then our actions embody the good news of the gospel. Moreover, actions such as these help to reconcile divided peoples and edify the body of Christ. Therefore, the moral exhortation in Ephesians 4:17–5:2 reflects and enacts God's plan for the fullness of time: to unify all things in Christ (1:10). We learn in detail how we can walk worthy of our calling (4:1).

LIVE the Story

Since Ephesians 4:17–5:2 features a list of exhortations, it's easy for us to begin to grasp how to live the story by doing and not doing what it tells us.

Putting Off and Putting On

The metaphor of putting off and putting on serves as a central ordering principle for 4:17–5:2. In verses 20–24 it represents what has already happened in the lives of those who know Christ. When we are "in him," we "learn Christ" and from him learn to "put off" our old self, to be renewed, and to "put on the new self" (4:22–24). This happens definitively when we receive God's grace through faith and begin to walk as a Christian.

Yet it is also something we continue to do on a regular basis. Though the aorist tense of "put off" and "put on" emphasizes the initial actions of putting off and on when we said yes to Christ and therefore no to our old way of being, the need to put off and put on does not end with conversion. Verse 25 shows that this experience is ongoing: "Therefore each of you must put off falsehood and speak truthfully." Though we once put off the "old human being," we must choose to put off elements of the old self that remain present in our lives. Moreover, the whole structure of the moral exhortations in chapter 4 shows the need for an ongoing put off/put on experience: to put off falsehood and put on truth, put off stealing and put on work, put off unwholesome talk and put on edifying talk, and put off bitterness, rage, anger, brawling, slander, and malice and put on kindness, compassion, forgiveness, and love.

Many Christians seem stuck in a "put off" mode. Recently, I did some consulting for a Christian college as it considered rewriting its policies for student behavior. In the course of this work, I read conduct standards from many leading Christian colleges. I was struck by how much they focus on the negatives, on what students should "put off," to use Paul's imagery. The lists of forbidden activities had certain things in common, like prohibitions against drunkenness. They also included idiosyncratic "sins" like skateboarding on campus or participating in the homecoming parade without proper authorization. As a whole we Christians can be known more for what we're against than by what we're for.

Yet there is also a tendency in other Christian circles to neglect the "put off" element of the Christian life. We are so eager to draw people to Christ and so unwilling to appear to be judgmental that we minimize or even ignore the call of Jesus to repent or the call here to put off the old self and put on the new. Thus Christ becomes not the basis for a whole new way of life but rather an innocuous addition to an otherwise unchanged life. Then we wonder why Christians aren't much different from their secular neighbors.

We don't need "naked" Christians who have put off their old self but are putting on nothing on in its place. Nor do we need more doubly dressed Christians who have put on the new without stripping off the old. Rather, we need to recover the full picture of the Christian life as found in Ephesians 4:17–5:2. This life begins in Christ, not in anything we do. From Christ, usually through members of his body, we hear the good news and receive God's grace through faith. From Christ we are taught to put off our old life and put on the new life. Yet that is not the end of being a Christian, but only the beginning. God continues to work in us, renewing us by his indwelling power. And we continue to choose each day to live the put off/put on life.

We do not literally put on a Jesus costume, of course, though strangely enough, doing so might help. A recent study in the *Journal of Experimental Social Psychology* found that what people wear influences how they feel and act. If, for example, somebody wears a lab coat associated with being a doctor, that person will be more successful in tests that require paying close attention than if he or she were wearing ordinary clothing. Hajo Adam and Adam D. Galinsky call this phenomenon "enclothed cognition."[18] What we wear influences how we think.

Analogously, we can be influenced by the behavior we "put on." Though a changed heart leads to changed living, sometimes the process flows in reverse. When we "put on" a certain action, even when we don't feel like doing it, we can discover that our feelings follow, that our inner lives are formed through our outer behavior. This is one way we cooperate with God in the renewal of our inner lives. We don't change ourselves directly by how we act. But our actions welcome and assist God's work in us.

---

18. Hajo Adam and Adam D. Galinsky, "Enclothed Cognition," *Journal of Experimental Social Psychology* 48.4 (2012): 918–25.

I remember, for example, my interaction with a member of my church in Irvine. This man, whom I'll call "Holden," bugged me. When he talked to me, he would stand too close, invading my personal space. He would often catch me at the end of a long day, asking if we could talk "for just a minute." I knew very well that Holden's minute could last an hour. My heart hardened with dislike for Holden. I knew that as his pastor I should love him, but I could not summon up feelings of love.

When I asked the Lord to help me love Holden, I sensed no magical change in my affections. But I did become convinced that God wanted me to choose to love Holden, to act lovingly toward him no matter how I felt. So out of sheer obedience I did this, however imperfectly. After many months, I noticed that I did indeed feel a smidgen of compassion for Holden. As my heart warmed to him, loving him in action became easier. Moreover, I found that my overall capacity for love seemed to be greater. I was being changed because I "put on" love, dressing up like Jesus, if you will. (In case you're interested, to this day Holden and I engage in pleasant communication. I am no longer his pastor, but he and I are Facebook friends. We message each other periodically with words of encouragement. Yes, Holden often builds me up in the Lord, thanks be to God!) How grateful I am for what God did in my heart as I "put on" Christ in my relationship with Holden.

Putting on Good Work

One of the put off/put on examples in our passage pertains to work. Though 4:28 directly addresses one who steals, what it says about work applies to everyone. All of us must work, "doing something useful with [our] own hands, that [we] may have something to share with those in need."

The work mentioned in this verse is "ordinary" work. It's not limited to some kind of special "spiritual" work, the sort of thing we do on mission trips or in Bible studies. Paul is thinking of work that produces income that enables us to share with those in material need. This is the kind of work God assigned to human beings when we were created. It is being fruitful and multiplying, filling and governing the earth; it is the work of tilling and tending the garden, and even the work of making (and raising) babies. It's the stuff that fills our lives six days a week, if indeed we pause for one day of rest.

Many Christians devalue this sort of "ordinary" work.[19] We believe that what really matters is church work, mission work, evangelistic work, nonprofit work, justice work, and healing work. Pastors and missionaries get to do this sort of thing professionally. So do those who work in NGOs after college,

19. For a delightful exception to this rule, see Kathleen Norris, *The Quotidian Mysteries: Laundry, Liturgy and "Women's Work"* (Mahwah, NJ: Paulist, 1998).

at least before they "sell out" and get "real jobs," which are valued only insofar as they generate income so we can "share with those in need," including our needy churches and mission organizations.

However, throughout the world today Christians are rediscovering the value of "ordinary," "real," daily work. For the last several years, I have participated in the Theology of Work Project.[20] It is an effort to study every single portion of Scripture and ask how each bit relates to work. The result is a commentary on the entire Bible from that perspective.[21] If you haven't thought much about work in Scripture before, you might be stunned to realize just how much the Bible has to say about it and just how much God values it.

Through my partnership in the Theology of Work Project, I have discovered this growing awareness of the importance of work among Christians throughout the world. Several members of the project steering committee come from countries in the Southern Hemisphere where Christians are committed to do their daily work for the Lord. For example, L. T. Jeyachandran is a civil engineer from India who has also served in several Christian organizations. He talks of how Christians in his country hunger to learn how their daily work matters to God. The same is true in New Zealand, Australia, and South Africa, to name three other countries represented in the Theology of Work Project.

Take as an example Ilam Baptist Church in Christchurch, New Zealand. As described by the Theology of Work website, several home groups of this church

> decided to take the daily work of their people more seriously. They began by spending the first part of each evening listening to one person's story of their work history and an explanation of the opportunities and challenges they now face in their work. Where they can, they have decided to visit that person's workplace. They ask questions and end by praying for that person in their work and for the good of the enterprise and people they work with.[22]

Yet in the minds of many faithful Christians, daily work is of secondary value to "God's work." The work of the gospel, they contend, trumps the work of creation. Yes, we still need to do ordinary work, they think, but only

---

20. For information about the Theology of Work Project, check the website www.theologyofwork.org.

21. You can read all of the Theology of Work Bible Commentary online at www.theologyofwork.org. Its commentary on Ephesians is at http://www.theologyofwork.org/new-testament/galatians-ephesians-philippians. A printed version of the commentary is being published in parts. See, for example, *Theology of Work Bible Commentary, Volume 1: Genesis through Deuteronomy* (Peabody, MA: Hendrickson, 2015).

22. http://www.theologyofwork.org/key-topics/the-equipping-church.

to keep food on our plates and to provide charitable support for the work that matters most.

Ephesians 4:28 offers a corrective to this mistaken line of thinking, not only because of what it says but also because of where it appears. Remember, this verse is in a section about "learning Christ." This is part and parcel of the Christian walk. Work is central to what we put off and put on as believers, to walking worthy of the calling to which we have been called (4:1). "Ordinary work" counts among the "good works" God has prepared for our lives (2:10). In fact when we're in Christ, there is no ordinary work just as there are no ordinary people. All of us in Christ are God's holy people. Therefore, all of our work can be holy as well and an expression of living for the praise of God's glory (1:12).

As we saw in "Explain the Story," 4:28 offers two reasons for why we should work. One has to do with helping others. We work so that we may "have something to share with those in need." When we make money through our work and offer some of it to others, doing so gives value to our work even as it expresses love for those in need.

The other reason in 4:28 is often missed by preachers and commentators, partly because of how it is worded in some English translations. The NIV says that we must work, "doing something useful" with our hands. The ESV has "doing honest work." But the Greek reads plainly as in the CEB, "Instead, [thieves] should go to work, using their hands to do good." Work produces good when it is work that honors God. Stealing may take effort, but it is not good work. Oppressing people is not good work. But growing food, raising children, governing people, building homes, investing money, mending bodies, teaching teenagers, all of these and so many other kinds of work can "do good," and therefore are examples of good work that pleases the Lord. Plus, we must not assume that work only counts when we're paid, for this thinking leads us to denigrate much of what we do in life.

We will return to the matter of work when we get to 6:5–9, the instructions for slaves and masters. But for now, we should recognize that one of the ways we put on our new self is through doing good work, work that produces good even as it also allows us to be generous with those in need.

Walking in the Way of the Cross

Several years ago I had the privilege of walking through Jerusalem's *Via Crucis*, Latin for "the Way of the Cross." This is the path through the streets and alleys upon which, according to Christian tradition, Jesus carried his cross. Along the Way of the Cross there are twelve stations that invite us to reflect upon the experience of Jesus in that place and its meaning for us. Christians from throughout the world make pilgrimages to Jerusalem so that they might follow Jesus along the *Via Crucis*.

As meaningful as it was for me to walk the literal Way of the Cross, Ephesians 5:1–2 invites me to walk this way every day, metaphorically speaking. This passage says we are to imitate God "and walk in the way of love." What is this way of love? Paul answers this question by pointing to the death of Jesus: "just as Christ loved us and gave himself up for us" (5:2). Though Jesus loved people in tangible ways during his earthly life (feeding, healing, embracing, teaching, etc.), his most dramatic act of love was giving up his life for us on the cross. Thus, the cross of Jesus defines the center of his love.

Notice what else it says in Ephesians 5:2. Christ's giving up of himself on the cross was "for us." It was an act of love for us, the supreme act of love. But the verse goes on, "as a fragrant offering and sacrifice to God." By walking in the way of self-giving love, Christ not only served us but also his Heavenly Father. By loving others in such a sacrificial way, Christ also offered a beautiful sacrifice to God.

We too can offer sacrifices of love. As we love people in imitation of God, as we seek to walk in the way of the cross, not only are people served but also God is worshiped. Your love for others does double duty. It cares for people and it glorifies God. It meets human need and it honors God. It blesses the recipients of your love and it blesses God, the source of all love.

Ephesians 5:1–2 not only calls us to love as Christ loved but also invites us to experience God's transforming love. If we realize that we ought to be more loving, the place to start is not by trying harder to love. This approach is doomed to fail because our capacity for love is limited. But according to 5:1, we are to follow God's example "as dearly loved children." In Christ, we have access to the God whose love for us is great (2:4). By God's power, we can come to know "how wide and long and high and deep is the love of Christ" (3:18). When we do this, we will know the "love that surpasses knowledge" so that we might be "filled to the measure of all the fullness of God" (3:19).

Thus, if we realize that we need to be more loving to others—and which of us does not need this?—we do not begin with ourselves but with God. We come to God, admit our lack of love, and ask for his help. We open our hearts to a fresh and deeper experience of God's love for us. We turn our attention not to our lack of love but to God's abundance of love poured out on the cross. In God's way and God's time, we will know more fully his love for us and therefore be empowered to love others more fully.

In the short term, it can be hard to love and to see how God is helping us be more loving. Earlier, I told the story of learning to love Holden. I'm looking back on that episode of my life some twenty years later. But during the years in which I sought to love him in spite of my lack of feeling for him, I struggled to love and to believe God was softening my heart.

Recently, I found myself in a situation that once again revealed my lack of love for another Christian. This is possibly the one person I've had the hardest time loving. When I reached out to him, he slapped my hand. When I made myself vulnerable, he attacked. In my darker moments, I fantasized about ways to knock him off his perch. I asked God to help me, and sometimes I felt spasms of compassion. But they didn't last. What did last, however, was my conviction that, as in the case of Holden, I was supposed to love this man through actions, no matter how hard my heart might be. I was called to act with kindness and compassion, to forgive as God had forgiven me in Christ, and to walk in love as Christ loved me.

Today, I bear witness to the fact that this is not easy. Yet I am reminded of the fact that the cross was not easy for Jesus. The way of love walks along the *Via Crucis*, the Way of the Cross. This is what we discover when we "learn Christ." It is the core of "the truth that is in Jesus."

CHAPTER 11

Ephesians 5:3–14

📖 LISTEN to the Story

³But among you there must not be even a hint of sexual immorality, or of any kind of impurity, or of greed, because these are improper for God's holy people. ⁴Nor should there be obscenity, foolish talk or coarse joking, which are out of place, but rather thanksgiving. ⁵For of this you can be sure: No immoral, impure or greedy person—such a person is an idolater—has any inheritance in the kingdom of Christ and of God. ⁶Let no one deceive you with empty words, for because of such things God's wrath comes on those who are disobedient. ⁷Therefore do not be partners with them.

⁸For you were once darkness, but now you are light in the Lord. Live as children of light ⁹(for the fruit of the light consists in all goodness, righteousness and truth) ¹⁰and find out what pleases the Lord. ¹¹Have nothing to do with the fruitless deeds of darkness, but rather expose them. ¹²It is shameful even to mention what the disobedient do in secret. ¹³But everything exposed by the light becomes visible—and everything that is illuminated becomes a light. ¹⁴This is why it is said:

> "Wake up, sleeper,
>   rise from the dead,
>   and Christ will shine on you."

Listening to the text in the Story: Genesis 1:1–5; Psalm 139:11–12; Isaiah 9:2; 42:16; Matthew 5:14–16; John 1:1–14; 3:19–21; 8:12; 12:35–36; Romans 1:28–32; 13:12–14; 1 Corinthians 4:5; 5:9–13; 6:12–20; 14:24–25; 2 Corinthians 4:6; 6:14–7:1; Colossians 1:12; 3:5–8; 1 Thessalonians 5:4–10.

Ephesians 5:3–14 focuses on the question of how we are to live in a world from which we are radically different. We are holy people in the midst of an unholy world (5:3). We are light in the midst of darkness (5:8). So how should we then live?

Verses 5:3–14 continue the exhortation of 4:1: Live (walk) worthy of your calling! This theme is picked up again in 4:17: we are not to live (walk) as the Gentiles do. Verses 5:3–14 go into greater depth about the Gentile way in which we are not to walk and how we are to respond to it. Not surprisingly, we are not to partner with those who live in immorality and darkness. But nonengagement is not the whole story, as we'll see in 5:11–14.

There is a sharp break between 5:2 and 5:3, meaning we should regard 5:3–14 as a new section. Verse 14 concludes the use of dark/light imagery found in this passage, suggesting that the section might end here. Verse 15, however, bridges between what has gone before and what comes afterwards, both summing up 5:3–14 and serving as a topic sentence for 5:15 and following. Thus, the section break between verses 14 and 15 should not obscure the close connection between 5:3–14 and 5:15–20.

EXPLAIN the Story

Summary of Ephesians 5:3–14

Following immediately on the heels of 5:2, which describes Christ's death as a "fragrant offering," 5:3 plunges us into the depths of human indecency. In the Greek text, "sexual immorality" follows right after "sweet smell" without any transitional warning ("but" in Greek comes after "sexual immorality," as is common in this grammatical construction). Verse 5:3 introduces a discussion of the depravity and coarseness of the world and counsel on how we as "God's holy people" are to live in such a world with its disobedient people. The subsection ends with the stark directive in 5:7: "Therefore do not be partners with them."

Ephesians 5:8–14 continues the same theme but now uses the imagery of darkness and light. We are to "live as children of light" (5:8), not by removing ourselves from the darkness but rather by shining into the darkness so as to make visible the things of darkness. Through us, those who live in darkness might be drawn to the light, even being raised from death to life, just as we have been through God's grace (2:4–6).

Living as Holy People in an Unholy World (5:3–7)

But among you there must not be even a hint of sexual immorality, or of any kind of impurity, or of greed, because these are improper for God's holy people (5:3). According to a literal reading of 5:3, sexual immorality, impurity, and greed must not "be named" among God's people. In other words, they should not exist in the church. "Sexual immorality" translates *porneia*, the Greek word used by early Christians for sinful sexual activity, that is, sexual intercourse outside of marriage.[1] More broadly, we are to avoid "any kind of impurity," which includes but is not limited to sexual corruption. The use of "greed" in this context, like in 4:19, could mean material avarice, but may be referring to sexual craving in particular, which is a possible translation of *pleonexia*.[2] In either case, "greed" indicates inordinate desire. "God's holy people" translates the word *hagiois*, meaning "saints," a common designation for believers throughout Ephesians (for example 1:1, 4). God has set us apart from this world for relationship with him and for involvement in his work. Thus, we should not engage in worldly impurities that are inconsistent with our holy identity in Christ.

Nor should there be obscenity, foolish talk or coarse joking, which are out of place, but rather thanksgiving (5:4). This verse moves from improper sexual activity to improper speech. Verse 4:29 already warned against "unwholesome talk" that fails to build up others. Verse 5:4 develops this thought further. The NIV translates the Greek word *aischrotēs* as "obscenity." This includes, but may not be limited to, speech that is shameful before others. The next word, *mōrologia*, confirms that speaking is the focus of this verse. *Mōrologia* is the talk (*logia*) of the fool (*mōros*). "Coarse joking," *eutrapelia,* can mean "lively wit" in secular Greek, but it has a negative connotation here. Christians are not to avoid all humor, only the off-color stuff. All of these verbal activities are "out of place" among God's people. Instead of using words in silly and demeaning ways, we should offer "thanksgiving." The Greek word *eucharistia*, thanksgiving, sounds similar to *eutrapelia*, which may explain the presence of that unusual word in this context. Notice once again the familiar pattern: put off *eutrapelia*, put on *eucharistia*.

For of this you can be sure: No immoral, impure or greedy person—such a person is an idolater—has any inheritance in the kingdom of Christ and of God (5:5). This verse intentionally echoes verse 3, which says, "But among you there must not be even a hint of sexual immorality, or any kind of impurity, or of greed." When we look at the Greek, we find these parallels: sexual immorality/immoral person (*porneia/pornos*), impurity/impure person (*akatharsia/ akathartos*), greed/greedy person (*pleonexia/pleonektēs*). So verse 5 underscores the thought of verse 3 while adding a new perspective having to do with idolatry and God's kingdom.

The phrase "such a person is an idolater" might be taken to apply to someone who is immoral, impure, or greedy. But the grammar suggests that idolatry relates most of all to the greedy person.[3] Greedy or covetous people

---

1. BDAG 854.
2. *NIDNTT* 1:137–39.
3. See also Col 3:5. Arnold, *Ephesians*, 324.

desire things more than God. Their desire so dominates their hearts that they come to "worship" their "idols" rather than the Lord.

The "inheritance in the kingdom of Christ and of God," an unusual identification of the kingdom, seems to refer to the present and the future reign of God.[4] This phrase echoes 1:18, "the riches of his glorious inheritance." There, God is the one who inherits us. In 5:5, inheritance is the heavenly reward we receive if we are not idolaters.

We could read 5:5 as a threat: "If you are a Christian and you engage in any sexual immorality, impurity, or greed, then you will be excluded from heaven." This reading, however, neglects the earlier teaching of Ephesians that salvation is by grace not works (see 2:8). When we receive God's grace through faith, we are saved and newly created in Christ (2:8–10). If after this time we sin, we do not thereby become excluded from the inheritance that is ours in Christ because this inheritance has come by grace.

A better way to read 5:5 is to see it as a promise: "No immoral, impure or greedy person . . . has any inheritance in the kingdom of Christ and of God." From earlier in Ephesians we know that our inheritance is guaranteed, not by our actions but by the seal of the Holy Spirit (1:13–14). So if we do have an inheritance in the kingdom, and if we know that we have this inheritance because of the Spirit, then it must mean that we are not essentially immoral people, impure people, or greedy people. Yes, we may sometimes engage in immoral, impure, or greedy behavior, but we are not defined by these actions. Rather, our essential identity comes from God and his grace in Christ. We are God's special people, God's children, God's creation, God's beloved. So 5:5 is a promise of our future, of the fact that we will be welcomed into God's kingdom and showered with our grace-based inheritance. However, if our lives continue to be characterized by immorality, impurity, and greed even after we have responded positively to the gospel, then we need to ask whether our response to grace is what God intends. Are we living in the good works God has assigned to us (2:10)? Are we walking worthy of the calling we have received (4:1)? Genuine grace received genuinely by faith leads to transformation, which will become complete when we receive our kingdom inheritance.

Let no one deceive you with empty words, for because of such things God's wrath comes on those who are disobedient (5:6). This verse offers a general warning against those who would deceive us with "empty words," that is, with words that lack substance and truth. In Colossians, Paul confronted specific false teachers who sought to bewitch the Colossian Christians with "hollow and deceptive philosophy" (Col 2:8). In Ephesians, however, no particular group of false teachers is in view. Rather, Paul offers a comprehensive and

---

4. Arnold, *Ephesians*, 325; Thielman, *Ephesians*, 333–34.

preemptive warning, no doubt in light of his experience with the Colossians and his awareness of the broad cultural tendency to minimize the wrongness of what Christians identify as sin.

What are we to make of "God's wrath" that "comes on those who are disobedient" (5:6)? Historically, Christians were less tentative than we are today about the wrath of God. Perhaps in your high school English class you read Jonathan Edwards's classic sermon from 1741, "Sinners in the Hands of an Angry God." There Edwards speaks of "the dreadful pit of the glowing flames of the wrath of God" and the fact that we are on our way to this pit apart from God's grace.

In reaction to preaching like this, and in a culture where tolerance is prized, many Christians have backed away from talking about the wrath of God. We have emphasized God's love and grace without mentioning that God is saving us not just from our own hurts but also from God's righteous judgment, what Scripture often calls God's wrath. When we hear the word "wrath," we might envision petty fits of rage. But in the biblical understanding, divine wrath is closer to what we would call "righteous indignation." It is emotion that stems from a deep sense of injustice, from hatred of the hurt that sin does to God's creation and his beloved people.

Paul mentions God's wrath in Ephesians 5:6 to remind us that God doesn't benignly overlook immorality, impurity, or greed. He does not minimize the evil of sin. Rather, God detests it and judges it. Of course, this is not the end of the story. In Ephesians 2 we learn that all human beings are "deserving of wrath" (2:3). God has every right to find us guilty and sentence us accordingly. But "because of his great love for us, God, who is rich in mercy" saved us by his grace (2:4–5). God's plan for us is that we would leave behind a life deserving of wrath and live in the freedom and holiness of his grace.

Therefore do not be partners with them (5:7). This verse sums up the first subsection of 5:3–14 with a simple injunction. "Them" in this context means "those who are disobedient," literally in Greek the "children of disobedience" (5:6). The word translated here as "partners" appears twice in the New Testament and only in Ephesians. In 3:6, the other usage in this letter, it is used in the phrase "*sharers together* in the promise in Christ Jesus" (emphasis added). In secular Greek, it can mean being a joint owner of something with another person.[5] Paul does not say we should never have anything to do with the disobedient. We are not to cut ourselves off from them. Rather, we are to refrain from joining with them in their shameless behavior. Thus Paul's counsel in 5:3–7 parallels that of 1 Corinthians 5:9–11 where he explains that while Christians are not to associate with fellow Christians who regularly engage

---

5. LSJ 1679 (*summetochos*).

in sexual immorality, we should indeed engage with the immoral, greedy idolaters of this world; otherwise as Paul writes, we "would have to leave this world" (1 Cor 5:10).

Thus with regard to the question of how we as God's holy people are to live in an unholy world, Paul's answer is clear: we are not to engage in immoral behavior. Yet we are not to withdraw completely from the world in order to make this easy. Rather, by implication we are to remain engaged with those who are caught in immorality and darkness. The following subsection of Ephesians 5:3–14 explains why we should engage with people of the world.

Living as Light in Darkness (5:8–14)

For you were once darkness, but now you are light in the Lord. Live as children of light (5:8). This verse adds another perspective on how we should live in a world that is not like us. It repeats the "once [*pote*] . . . now [*nun*]" perspective found earlier in Ephesians. Chapter 2 says we were "dead in [our] transgressions and sins, in which [we] used to [*pote*] live" (2:1–2). We lived among those who are disobedient "at one time [*pote*]" (2:3). But God out of his mercy and grace saved us from our former condition. In the second half of Ephesians 2, the "once . . . now" schema is even more obvious. We were "formerly [*pote*]" Gentiles by birth and therefore separated from God and his people (2:11–12). We were "once [*pote*]" far away from the Lord, his life, and hope (2:13). "But now [*nuni*, an emphatic form of *nun*] in Christ Jesus," we have been "brought near by the blood of Christ" (2:13).

In Ephesians, "once" points to our condition before God saved us by his grace. *Once* we were really dead; *now* we are really alive in Christ. *Once* we were really separated from God and his people; *now* we have been brought near through Christ. And in 5:8, *once* we were darkness; *now* we are "light in the Lord." We experience a fundamental reality change when we receive God's grace through faith. We move from *once* to *now* (see also 2 Cor 5:17).

The imagery of darkness and light picks up a major theme in the biblical story of God and takes us back to the first day of creation. God speaks light into existence, sees that the light is good, and separates the light from the darkness (Gen 1:3–5). In the story of the exodus, one of the plagues covers Egypt with darkness as a sign of God's judgment (Exod 10:21–22). Later in the narrative, God leads his people by a pillar of fire at night "to give them light" for safe travel (Exod 13:21). The prophet Isaiah describes the lostness of human beings who have turned away from God and therefore "see only distress and darkness and fearful gloom, and they will be thrust into utter darkness" (Isa 8:22).

But Isaiah also offers hope through a glimpse of the future: "The people walking in darkness have seen a great light; on those living in a land of deep darkness a light has dawned" (Isa 9:2). Someday the Lord will "turn the darkness into light" before his people (Isa 42:16). In that day God will send his servant as a "light for the Gentiles" (Isa 42:6; 49:6). Even though "darkness covers the earth," the nations will come to the light of God's people "and kings to the brightness of your dawn" (Isa 60:2–3). In the future, "the Lord will be your everlasting light, and your days of sorrow will end" (Isa 60:19–20).

Ephesians 5:8 echoes the language of Isaiah. But here, those who live without God are not just *in* darkness. They *are* darkness. And those who live with God are not just *in* the light. They *are* light.

This remarkable use of darkness/light reflects the image of Jesus in the Gospels. In John, for example, Jesus fulfills the prophecy of Isaiah by being "the true light that gives light to everyone" (John 1:9). Jesus as the light "shines in the darkness, and the darkness has not overcome it" (John 1:5). Jesus identifies himself as the "light of the world." He says, "Whoever follows me will never walk in darkness, but will have the light of life" (John 8:12). In a passage that prefigures Ephesians 5:8, Jesus says, "You are going to have the light just a little while longer. Walk while you have the light, before darkness overtakes you. Whoever walks in the dark does not know where they are going. Believe in the light while you have the light, so that you may become children of light" (John 12:35–36).

In the Gospel of Matthew, those who follow Jesus, the light of the world, are not just light-followers. We are more even than "children of light." According to Jesus, we also are "the light of the world" (Matt 5:14). Thus Jesus says, "Let your light shine before others, that they may see your good deeds and glorify your Father in heaven" (Matt 5:16). Of course, it would be a mistake for us to see ourselves as the light of the world in exactly the same way Jesus is the light of the world. Yet as we are in relationship with him, we become luminous reflectors of his divine light. We shine into the dark world through what we do and say, not in order to draw attention to ourselves but that those who live in darkness might "glorify [our] Father in heaven."

Ephesians 5:8 uses the metaphor of darkness and light in the same fluid fashion. Yes, we are to walk (the NIV uses "live" to translate the Greek verb *peripateō* that literally means "to walk") in the light and become children of light (as in John 12). But as in Matthew 5, we *are* light because of what God has done for us in Christ. Thus, we are to "live [*peripateō*, "walk"] as children of light."

For the fruit of the light consists in all goodness, righteousness and truth (5:9). This verse echoes what we hear elsewhere in Ephesians. In 2:10, for example, we learn that we have been "created in Christ Jesus to do *good* works which God prepared in advance for us to do." In 4:15 we hear that we are to help the body of Christ grow by *"speaking the truth* in love." In 4:24, we read that we have "put on the new self, created to be like God in *true righteousness* and holiness" (emphasis added to all). So the imagery of light in chapter 5 offers another perspective on what we have already learned in Ephesians, namely, that we are to be people of goodness, righteousness, and truth.

Of course, these are fundamental characteristics of God himself. The goodness of God is revealed in the opening chapter of Genesis and is reiterated throughout Scripture.[6] God's righteousness, which in this context has to do with God's supreme justice and rightness in relationship to all things, including us, is also a major theme of the Bible.[7] And as we have recently seen in Ephesians 4:24, our new self is like God who exemplifies "true righteousness." Similarly, God is characterized by truth, truth that is incarnate in Jesus Christ.[8] Thus Ephesians 4:21 refers to "the truth that is in Jesus." Using the metaphor of light, Ephesians 5:8–9 reveals that God has redeemed and re-created us to be like him. Even as God is light, so we are "light in the Lord" and "children of light." Even as God is good, righteous, and true, so when we live as the light, our lives will be fruitful, producing "goodness, righteousness and truth."

And find out what pleases the Lord (5:10). In English this sentence seems to hang in the air as an unattached imperative. In Greek, however, "find out" is a participle connected to the imperative in 5:8: "Live as children of light . . . [by] finding out what pleases the Lord." In other words, living and finding out are not two distinct activities, but rather two deeply interconnected ones. The Greek verb translated as "find out" (*dokimazō*) means "to examine, test, approve, or prove."[9] It suggests the use of our mental faculties to consider something carefully and make a wise judgment about it. To borrow the words I often heard from my parents, it means "to use your head." Thus we live as children of light by using our heads to find out what pleases the Lord.

Have nothing to do with the fruitless deeds of darkness, but rather expose them (5:11). Since fruitfulness is a result of living in the light (5:9), it follows that the "deeds of darkness" will be fruitless. They will not lead to goodness, righteousness, and truth. "Have nothing to do with" is not the best translation of the Greek verb *sunkoinōneō*, because it might suggest to the reader that we are to back away entirely from the things of darkness. The last phrase in this verse proves that this is not the case. Whatever it means to expose the deeds of darkness, it surely implies some kind of awareness of them. *Sunkoinōneō*, which is built around the word *koinōnos*, or "partner," means "to participate in

---

6. For example, Pss 25:7; 34:8; 100:5; 107:1; Mark 10:18; 1 Pet 2:3.
7. See Pss 7:11, 17; 11:7; 33:4–5; 145:17; Jer 23:6; Dan 9:7; Rom 1:17.
8. Ps 33:4; Isa 45:19; John 1:14, 17; 14:6.
9. BDAG 255–56.

with someone"[10] or "to have a joint share of."[11] The point is that we must not enter into partnership with these deeds or the people who do them.

Instead, we are to "expose" them. The verb translated as "expose" is *elenchō*. It can mean "expose, examine, convict, convince, correct."[12] It is used in the Septuagint in Proverbs 3:11, for example, "My son, do not despise the Lord's discipline, and do not resent his rebuke [*elenchomenos*]." Sometimes the Greek Septuagint uses *elenchō* to translate the Hebrew verb that means "to decide a case," such as in Isaiah 11:3–4: the shoot of Jesse "decides" by what he hears and "gives decisions" with justice. In the New Testament, Jesus promises that the Advocate (the Paraclete) will "prove [*elenxei*] the world to be in the wrong about sin" (John 16:8). In a passage that is similar in many ways to Ephesians 5:8–14, 1 Corinthians 14:24 says that if an unbeliever comes into the Christian gathering while people are prophesying, that person is "convicted [*elenchetai*] of sin and . . . brought under judgment by all." As a result, the unbeliever falls down and worships God, a clear sign of repentance (1 Cor 14:25).

The use of *elenchō* in Ephesians 5:11 is further elucidated by the next two verses. In 5:12 "it is shameful even to mention what the disobedient do in secret." Thus *elenchō* must not mean "to reveal evil deeds out loud," since this would require shameful speaking. Verse 13 adds, "But everything exposed [*elenchomena*] by the light becomes visible." *Elenchō*, therefore, involves shining God's light on things in the darkness so that they might be seen. We will see how to do this later, under "Live the Story."

It is shameful even to mention what the disobedient do in secret (5:12). The word translated as "shameful," *aischron*, is related to the word translated as "obscenity" in 5:4 (*aischrotēs*). Paul's point is that what people do in secret is so bad that it would be wrong to speak of it. This raises a question about how we are to go about exposing the deeds of darkness if we are not to speak about them. Verse 13 begins to answer this question in a most surprising way.

But everything exposed by the light becomes visible—and everything that is illuminated becomes a light (5:13). The first part of verse 13 is common sense. If you shine a light on something, it becomes visible. The second part of verse 13 is perplexing, if not stunning. What does it mean that "everything that is illuminated becomes a light"?[13] A hint comes from a verse a few lines up. There we are reminded that "[we] were once darkness, but now [we] are

---

10. *NIDNTT* 1:639.

11. LSJ 1666.

12. BDAG 315.

13. Note that the Greek could be translated differently if the participle *phaneroumenon* (found in 5:14 in the Greek) is read as a middle, not a passive. Then the verse would mean "for the light makes everything visible," as in the NLT 5:14. See on this Arnold, *Ephesians*, 333.

light in the Lord" (5:8). What made this extraordinary change in us? God's grace offered in Christ. When we received it in faith, we were brought from death to life (2:4–5), from far away to near (2:13), and from darkness to light (5:8). When the light of the gospel shone on us, it showed us our need for God such that we turned to God, received his grace, and became a light. If we shine God's light toward others who are in darkness so that their deeds become illuminated, then they can see how much they need God and turn to Christ. According to Yoder Neufeld, *elenchō* in 5:3–14 represents love for one's neighbor, an act of "evangelistic exposing" rather than condemnation.[14]

This is why it is said: "Wake up, sleeper, arise from the dead, and Christ will shine on you" (5:14). This verse confirms the redemptive direction of *elenchō* that we found in 5:11–13. "It is said" in Greek is an expression that often introduces a quotation of the Old Testament, as in 4:8. Elements of 5:14 are found in Isaiah: "But your dead will live, LORD; their bodies will rise—let those who dwell in the dust wake up and shout for joy" (26:19); "Arise, shine, for your light has come, and the glory of the LORD rises upon you" (60:1). Yet while both of these passages seem to resonate in Ephesians 5:14, neither one seems to be quoted. This has led many commentators to conclude that Paul is quoting a fragment of early Christian worship, perhaps a hymn used in the context of baptism.[15]

The hymn is addressed to a "sleeper" who also happens to be "dead." This sounds like the description of a human being outside of Christ who is spiritually dead in sin even though physically alive (2:1–3). If used in a baptismal liturgy, this hymn would invite those being baptized to leave their "sleep," their spiritual death, and "wake up" or come to life in Christ.[16]

What happens when someone responds to the gospel by waking up? Paul says, "Christ will shine on you" (5:14). And when Christ shines on someone, that person now illuminated actually becomes light (5:13). Thus, the use of the hymn in 5:14 confirms the "evangelistic exposing" reading of *elenchō* in 5:12–13. Moreover, it connects this passage to 3:10: God makes his wisdom known to the heavenly powers through the church. One way this happens is as the people of God "expose" works of darkness through their light.

What is not clear at this point, however, is exactly how we are to shine our light and expose the deeds of darkness so that those who do them might be redeemed. I will consider this further in "Live the Story."

---

14. Yoder Neufeld, *Ephesians*, 234.

15. Lincoln, *Ephesians*, 331–33.

16. The use of dark/light imagery in 1 Thess 5:4–11 and Rom 13:11–14 has persuaded some commentators that the hymn in Eph 5:14 addresses sleeping Christians, not unbelievers. This reading misses the sense of dark/light imagery in Ephesians 5, as well as the death/life metaphor in chapter 2.

LIVE the Story

Why Bring Up Sex Right after the Cross?

The transition from Ephesians 5:2 to 5:3 can feel like whiplash. One moment our hearts are inspired by the love of Christ who "gave himself up for us as a fragrant offering and sacrifice to God" (5:2). The next moment we are confronted with sexual immorality, impurity, and greed. Why does Paul juxtapose the sweetness of Christ's sacrifice with the ugliness of promiscuity? Paul appears to exemplify the stereotypical Christian who is obsessed with the sins of the flesh. Something in me wants to cry, "Get your mind out of the gutter, Paul!"

If he were around to defend himself, I expect Paul might respond, "We need to pay attention to the gutter because that's where we are!" Though we have been raised and enthroned with Christ in the heavenly realms (2:4–6), we still live in this world with all of its corruption. If we are going to walk worthy of our calling in this world, then we need to know the world accurately, to see its peril and its potential. This means, among other things, we need to speak openly about sex.

But why here? Why put a discussion of sexual immorality so close to the cross?

Because, I would suggest, this is exactly where it ought to be. In fact, when we separate our discussion of sexual ethics from the cross, we land in trouble.

First of all, the cross reminds us that what we do with our bodies really matters. God did not just unveil some magic revelation to save our souls. Rather, he became incarnate, in-flesh. Though the incarnation alone does not save us, it is a prerequisite for salvation. Moreover, it reminds us just how much God values his creation. That's one reason why God's plan for the cosmos is to unite all things in heaven and on earth in Christ. What Jesus did with his body matters exceedingly. And so it is with us. What we do with our bodies matters to God, and it matters to us. If our bodies matter, then sex matters.

Second, we should keep the cross nearby when we talk about sex because most of us need to experience God's love and grace when it comes to our sexuality. Some of us know this all too well because we have done things for which we desperately require God's forgiveness. Apart from the cross, we are stuck in our guilt and shame. Because of the cross, we can be forgiven and set free. We need this good news.

But even if you haven't done things sexually that are obviously against God's intentions, there's a good possibility you have been wounded sexually. Maybe you've felt sexual rejection. Maybe you feel bad about your physical appearance. Maybe your fantasy life is out of control. Maybe you were molested as a child. Maybe you've been sexually assaulted as an adult. There are so many more "maybes."

The reality and diversity of sexual brokenness makes sense if we consider Genesis 3. The very first thing that happened after the man and woman ate the forbidden fruit was that they tried to hide their nakedness (Gen 3:7). Where they had once known the freedom of unabashed sexual intimacy, now things would never be the same. And they haven't been the same ever since. Therefore, we need the cross when we talk about sex because the cross deals with the problem of sin. The cross brings forgiveness, restoration, and healing. The cross enables us, however incompletely in this age, to begin to experience more of the joy God had intended for our sexual lives.

Third, we need to keep the cross nearby when it comes to sex because we must remember what love is really all about. The world tells us love is a matter of romance. It celebrates sexual freedom, encouraging sexual exploration outside of marriage. The world speaks of "making love" as if love could be made through sexual engagement, even between relative strangers.

But this is not real love. In Ephesians 5:1–2, we are told to imitate God by walking in the way of love. The example of such divine love is the self-giving sacrifice of Christ. Then we come to verse 3: "But among you there must not be even a hint of sexual immorality." The juxtaposition shows that walking in the way of love is inconsistent with engaging in immoral sexual behavior.

One of the essential characteristics of sexual immorality is the consuming focus on one's own desires. No matter what we pretend, sex becomes primarily a means for our own gratification rather than a way to love another person in a self-giving way. This is true whether we act on our desires or merely look at another person lustfully, something Jesus calls committing adultery in one's heart (Matt 5:27–28).

Thus when it comes to sexual expression, the cross offers a necessary corrective to the "empty words" of our culture's sexual ethic. It invites us to discover a love that really is love. It offers forgiveness for our past sins and healing for our wounds. It tells us we are loved by God in a way that excels all other loves. In his love, we begin to discover what God intends for our sexuality. As Paul wrote to the Corinthians in response to their sexual misdeeds, "You are not your own; you were bought at a price. Therefore honor God with your bodies" (1 Cor 6:19–20). You and I were bought with a price, the price of Christ's own death. Thus we belong to God. We are beloved by God. And we have been called to honor God with our bodies.

Living the Story Even When We'd Rather Not

Let's be honest: sometimes we'd rather not live God's story. Sometimes we'd rather live our own story, at least for a while.

As one example, each year while I was pastor of Irvine Presbyterian Church, the men went on a retreat in the local mountains. There was plenty of singing, prayer, and Bible teaching. But one of the delightful elements of our men's retreat was humor. We told jokes and stories. We did silly skits and pranked each other. We laughed and laughed.

Once in a while during informal gatherings, one of the men would tell an off-color joke. It was a kind of tradition, a way for the men to feel free from the constraints of ordinary life. When one told a bawdy story, the others would chuckle and forget about it.

That is until one year when a man I'll call "Harry" showed up at the retreat. He was put off by the light tone of the whole event, preferring a more reverent one. And he was horrified by the suggestive stories told after hours. Harry confronted those who told the jokes, citing Ephesians 5:4 as his authority. He challenged the men to avoid "obscenity, foolish talk or coarse joking."

Some of the men wanted to reject Harry's criticism by labeling him as a killjoy. But they were too committed to Scripture to ignore what he had said. Several of the men, including some who had enjoyed a racy joke in the past, knew they couldn't reject biblical truth just because they didn't like it. They wanted God's Word to govern all of their lives, including their language at the men's retreat, *doggone it.*

Harry's criticism launched a wider discussion about the appropriateness of humor at the retreat. Was it right to be silly? Was some of our humor too negative? Someone pointed to the King James Version of Ephesians 5:4, which cautions against "filthiness," "foolish talking," and "jesting." Does this mean that all joking around is wrong?

As we carefully studied both the context and the language of Ephesians 5:4, we saw that Paul is not saying Christians should never tell a joke. This is not a blanket prohibition of all humor and laughter. Rather, we are being cautioned about language that is obscene and impure. We are to avoid words that degrade what God has created for good, including our sexuality (which probably explains the inclusion of bad language in a passage about sexual immorality).

After considering Ephesians 5:4, the men decided that it was fine to continue doing much of what had made our retreats fun. Most of the jokes, stories, and gags were in line with biblical teaching. But the men did make a new commitment to eliminate the off-color language and risqué stories. Their desire to live God's story in Ephesians 5:4 overcame their original preference to ignore this part of the story.

You may not be tempted to say bad words or tell dirty jokes, but I'd guess there are other portions of God's story that you'd rather ignore. I've found that one of the most refreshing and freeing things I can say to the Lord is, "I really don't like this passage very much." Admitting this, I begin to open myself to hearing God's story afresh and living it in new ways.

How Do We Expose the Deeds of the Darkness?

According to Ephesians 5:8, once we were darkness, but now in the Lord we are light. Therefore, we are to "live as children of the light." We do this when our lives bear fruit that is good, right, and true. We do this when we avoid partnership with "the fruitless deeds of darkness, but rather expose them" (5:11).

How do we expose the deeds of darkness? Many Christians think they already know the answer to this question: we expose the deeds of darkness by denouncing them publicly. Believers across the theological and political spectrum take upon themselves the responsibility of pointing out the failings of others. For those on the more conservative end of the spectrum, this often means denouncing "godless Hollywood" or inveighing against sins associated with sexuality. More progressive Christians "speak truth to power" by condemning corporate greed or opposing U.S. military policy. Many Christians, no matter their ideological leanings, indulge in criticism of the moral failings of their family members or neighbors. In these ways we flatter ourselves that we are exposing the deeds of darkness.

Though one might try to construct a biblical case for the kind of pronouncements I have mentioned here, Ephesians 5:11 should not be part of that case. This passage does not tell us to expose the dark deeds of others by publicly denouncing them. In fact, it says the exactly opposite: "It is shameful even to mention what the disobedient do in secret" (5:12). So it seems unlikely that Paul wants us to expose these secret deeds by speaking of them publicly. He must have another sense of "expose" in mind.

Perhaps then we are to expose deeds of darkness, not so much by denouncing them as by letting the light of God shine in and through us. We do this by announcing the good news of God's grace in Christ and by living in such a way that this good news shines forth. The "fruit of the light," after all, is found in "all goodness, righteousness and truth" (5:9). So even if there is a time for us to denounce the darkness in the world, our main task as children of light is to let the light of Christ shine in our words and deeds. We are to live in such a way that deeds of darkness are seen to be fruitless in comparison to the abundant fruit of light that grows in our lives.

Paul didn't make up this idea, of course. He got it from a reliable source. In Matthew 5:14–16 Jesus says, "You are the light of the world. A town built on a hill cannot be hidden. Neither do people light a lamp and put it under a bowl. Instead they put it on its stand, and it gives light to everyone in the house. In the same way, let your light shine before others, that they may see your good deeds and glorify your Father in heaven." There it is. We are to let our light shine by allowing people to see our good deeds and glorify our Father in heaven.

It is surely true that people will not glorify God because of our good needs unless they know why we are doing them, under which authority, and by what power. In other words, there is an implied "telling" part of letting our light shine. But Jesus emphasizes the "doing" part. And so does Paul in Ephesians 5:12–14.

When it is time to speak the light into the darkness, what should we say? We are to deliver the good news: "Wake up, sleeper, rise from the dead, and Christ will shine on you" (5:14). We bear witness to the gospel, to God's grace in Christ, to the story of God that ends with God putting all things back together in Christ.

Is there a time to speak out about evil? Yes, we can find ample biblical precedent for this. But before we get up on our soapbox and denounce the sins of others, perhaps we ought to see how brightly our own light is shining into the darkness. Would anyone be drawn to the light of Christ because of us?

When we think of ourselves as "the light," we must remember the whole phrase. We are "light *in the Lord*" (5:8, emphasis added). We are not light all by ourselves. Rather, we shine with the light of Christ, and all of our light is reflected light.

If you want to internalize this truth, just remember my Christmas Eve sermon from 1998. That year we had two services for children and families in the early evening. As was my tradition, I did a short sermon for the children, using my own kids as my partners. Our text was Ephesians 5:8–10; our title was "Live as Children of Light."

I remember this service well for a couple of reasons. First, it was my son's reading debut in front of an audience. Though Nathan was only six years old, he read the passage on his own. (Of course, he had practiced so much that he had the whole thing memorized.) Second, I remember this service because it included what—I flatter myself—was my greatest moment ever in a children's sermon.

After Nathan finished reading the Scripture, I talked about how God brought us from darkness to light through Christ, the true Light of the World. I explained that we are to shine with his light into the world in part by doing all that is good, right, and true.

Next, I asked our technicians to dim the lights in the sanctuary. In the front, there was a table with a giant, wrapped present on it. I explained how

Christ wanted to give the whole world the gift of his light. Instantly, I turned on a blazing spotlight that illuminated the present so that it glowed. "This spotlight is like Christ. It is truly dazzling," I explained. "That's impressive, but it really doesn't fill the room with light, does it? So how can we get this spotlight to fill this room with light? How can Christ shine his light into the whole world?"

As I walked over to the giant present, I said, "I have an idea," and I lifted the present from the table. Under the box was a mechanized disco ball covered with hundreds of small mirrors. It was spinning rapidly. As the brilliant spotlight hit these mirrors, it filled the whole sanctuary with blazing flashes of light, circling wildly throughout the room. I smiled as the children, and even many of the adults, gasped in wonder.

"You and I are like these mirrors. We reflect the light of Christ into the world. The church is like this disco ball. When all of us 'mirrors' work together, the world will be filled with the light of Christ."

"How can we shine the light of Christ into the world?" I asked my congregation. "We do so through our actions each day. We do so through our words. When we love each other, the light of Christ shines. And when we forgive. And when we serve. And when we build homes for the homeless. And when we are honest in our jobs or at school. And when we love the people at school or work whom everyone else makes fun of. And when we let others know that God's light has come into the world through Jesus. Jesus, the true Christmas light, has come to bring light and life to everyone. You and I as children of light get to live this truth and share it with others. As we do, we shine the light of Christ everywhere."

Ephesians 5:15-20

📖 LISTEN to the Story

¹⁵Be very careful, then, how you live—not as unwise but as wise, ¹⁶making the most of every opportunity, because the days are evil. ¹⁷Therefore do not be foolish, but understand what the Lord's will is. ¹⁸Do not get drunk on wine, which leads to debauchery. Instead, be filled with the Spirit, ¹⁹speaking to one another with psalms, hymns, and songs from the Spirit. Sing and make music from your heart to the Lord, ²⁰always giving thanks to God the Father for everything, in the name of our Lord Jesus Christ.

Listening to the text in the Story: Exodus 32:5–6; Proverbs 1:7; 4:10–14; 13:20; 23:20, 31; 28:26; Acts 2:1–21; Romans 13:11–14; 1 Corinthians 1:20–24; Colossians 1:15–20; 2:2–3.

Ephesians 5:15–20 flows smoothly from the earlier part of the chapter, connected both rhetorically (*oun*, "then" in 5:15) and thematically (*peripateō*, living/walking) to 5:1–14. In fact, 5:15–20 adds to the conversation begun in 4:1, "live a life [walk] worthy of the calling you have received." This theme of living/walking reappears in 5:2, "walk in the way of love" and 5:8, "live [walk] as children of light." Verse 15 begins with "be very careful, then how you live [walk]." It introduces a passage that provides a different perspective on how we are to live/walk, looking from the vantage point of wisdom.

Ephesians 5:15–20 also flows smoothly into what follows. The Greek verb in verse 21, translated in English as "submit," is actually a participle dependent on the imperative of verse 18, "be filled . . . submitting." So breaking the flow of thought between verses 20 and 21 can be potentially misleading, though it makes it easier for the interpreter to grasp what would otherwise be an overly long passage with many themes. When we get to verse 21, we will remember its dependence on verse 18.

EXPLAIN the Story

Summary of Ephesians 5:15–20

Paul begins by urging us to watch ourselves carefully so that we might live wisely rather than foolishly (5:15–17). Wise living includes avoiding drunkenness and instead being filled with the Spirit (5:18). Such filling involves speaking (5:19), singing and making music (5:19), giving thanks (5:20), and submitting (5:21). The passage is structured by three parallel "not this . . . but this" expressions (Greek *mē . . . alla*): not unwise but wise (5:15), not foolish but understanding (5:17), and not drunk but filled with the Spirit (5:18).

Pay Careful Attention to How You Live (5:15–17)

Be careful, then, how you live (5:15). The Greek reads more literally, "Watch carefully, then, how you walk."[1] The Greek verb translated in the NIV as "be careful" is *blepō*, the basic word for "to see."[2] It has the sense of "watch, beware of" in several New Testament passages, most notably in Mark 13, where the imperative of *blepō* is rendered "watch out" (Mark 13:5) or "be on your guard" (Mark 13:9, 23, 33). In Ephesians 5, though the eschatological urgency is not as strong as in Mark 13, Christians nevertheless must watch carefully because, though they are light, they are living in darkness, in the midst of evil days (Eph 5:8, 11, 16).

Not as unwise but as wise (5:15). Verse 17 makes a similar point with slightly different language, "do not be foolish, but understand." These verses connect Christian living to wisdom and thus to one of the major themes in the grand story of God. In the Old Testament book of Proverbs, for example, "The fear of the Lord is the beginning of knowledge, but fools despise wisdom and instruction" (Prov 1:7). A father instructs his son in "the way of wisdom" that leads him "along straight paths" (4:11). Thus the son will not "walk in the way of evildoers" (4:14). Christians join themselves to the Jewish wisdom tradition now interpreted in light of Christ who is the "wisdom of God" (1 Cor 1:24).

Making the most of every opportunity, because the days are evil (5:16). The NIV translation irons out an intriguing wrinkle in the original language. The verb translated as "making the most of" is *exagorazō*, which means to "buy up" or "redeem."[3] It appears in Galatians, where Christ "redeemed us from the curse of the law" (Gal 3:13). Thus a more straightforward rendering of verse

---

1. Some ancient texts change the word order, which might be translated, "Watch, then, that you live carefully." But the evidence for this option, though preferred by a few commentators, is not as strong as "watch carefully" chosen by the NIV. See Bruce M. Metzger, *A Textual Commentary on the Greek New Testament*, 2nd ed. (New York: United Bible Societies, 1994), 540.
2. BDAG 178–79.
3. LSJ 580.

16 might be, "redeeming the time, because the days are evil." Yet what does this mean and how can we do it?

In apocalyptic Jewish thinking, the present age is evil. Although the perspective of Ephesians is more nuanced than the stark visions of the apocalypses, Paul too articulates the evil character of our current existence. In chapter 2, for example, he says we once "followed the ways of this world and of the ruler of the kingdom of the air, the spirit who is now at work in those who are disobedient" (2:2). Chapter 6 identifies our struggle in life as "not against flesh and blood, but against . . . the spiritual forces of evil in the heavenly realms" (6:12). Thus labeling the days as "evil" does not condemn the calendrical days as wicked but expresses the truth that our daily experience is filled with sin and dominated by the powers of darkness.

From the biblical point of view, evil does not reside only in those whose deeds score high on the index of terror and injustice. Rather, we all live in evil days. We all confront evil in our lives. We all are under the domination of evil. And we all live in a time when the battle between good and evil rages. Yet we are not captive or hopeless. Rather, when we acknowledge the evil of these days, we have a chance to do something profoundly good. We can redeem the time.

We do not "buy time" by paying some sort of ransom to the devil, as some interpreters have suggested. Rather, when we are watchful about how we live, when we use our time wisely, when we seize moments that might otherwise be wasted and fill them with wise deeds, we are redeeming time from its diabolical prison. Ironically, 5:16 speaks of redeeming or buying time where we would talk about spending it. To use our English idiom, if we spend our time wisely, not wasting it on worthless or sinful activities, then that time will have been well invested.

Understand what the Lord's will is (5:17). Understanding the Lord's will does not in this context refer to knowledge of God's specific plans for our lives, as in the commonly asked question, "What is God's will for my life?" It means we begin to grasp the magnificent story of creation and redemption. We remember from Ephesians 1 that God "made known to us the mystery of his will according to his good pleasure, which he purposed in Christ, to be put into effect when the times reach their fulfillment—to bring unity to all things in heaven and on earth under Christ" (1:9–10). Thus we will avoid folly and live wisely if we ground our living on the revealed will of God, especially his plan to unite all things in Christ.

Dimensions of Spirit-Filled Living (5:18–20)

Do not get drunk of wine, which leads to debauchery (5:18). Verse 18 contains the last of the three "not this . . . but this" sentences in 5:15–20: "Do not get drunk on wine [*mē methuskesthe oinō*], which leads to debauchery. Instead [*alla*], be filled with the Spirit." We cannot know for sure why Paul mentions drunkenness here. It may be that he was influenced by Proverbs 23:31, which in the Greek Septuagint reads, "Do not get drunk on wine [*mē methuskesthe oinō*], but [*alla*] talk with righteous people."[4] It's possible that Paul wanted to discourage Christians from imitating pagan festivals that included inebriation. Or perhaps Paul like others in his day saw a certain similarity between drunkenness and spiritual inspiration. Philo, a first-century Jewish philosopher, notes in his treatise *On Drunkenness*, "Now when grace fills the soul, that soul thereby rejoices and smiles and dances, for it is possessed and inspired, so that to many of the unenlightened it may seem to be drunken, crazy and beside itself. . . . [I]ndeed, it is true that these sober ones are drunk in a sense."[5] This is exactly what happened on the day of Pentecost when the first followers of Jesus were filled with the Spirit and some witnesses accused them of having had "too much wine" (Acts 2:14).

Whatever motivated Paul to forbid drunkenness, he adds a reason for this directive: drunkenness leads to "debauchery." The Greek word used here can also mean "dissipation" or "profligacy."[6] Though these English terms sound overelaborate, Paul's readers knew what he meant. In the first-century Roman world, as in ours, abuse of alcohol led to folly, immorality, and all kinds of perversity.

Instead, be filled with the Spirit (5:18). The imperative "be filled with the Spirit" is in a passive form both in Greek and in English. Filling with the Spirit is not something we can do by our own power. Rather, the passive reveals God to be the agent who fills us with his Spirit through Christ, "who fills everything in every way" (1:23).

But if God does the filling, then how might we respond to the imperative "be filled with the Spirit"? Since we cannot fill ourselves with the Spirit through some magical formula, Paul is telling us to make ourselves available to God as vessels ready to be filled. We can worship him with openness to the Spirit. We can step out to minister in his name. The more we make ourselves available to God, the more we will be ready to be filled with his Spirit.

Another feature of the Greek imperative "be filled" does not show up in English. The Greek verb appears in the present tense, which signifies an ongoing action, not something that happens once and for all. In English we might represent this sense with "keep on being filled with the Spirit." By implication,

---

4. My translation of the Septuagint, which differs considerably from the meaning of the Hebrew text of Prov 23:31. For a defense of this explanation, see Yoder Neufeld, *Ephesians*, 239.

5. Philo, *On Drunkenness* 145–46, 148 (Colson and Whitaker, LCL). See Lincoln, *Ephesians*, 344.

6. BDAG 142 (*asōtia*).

the filling of the Spirit is something that can happen again and again in the life of the believer.

Elsewhere Paul teaches that we received the Spirit when we put our faith in Jesus Christ as Lord and Savior (Rom 8:15). Yet we who have the Spirit can also be filled with the Spirit so that we might worship or minister with unusual power. Consider the analogy of breath (which is referred to in Greek as *pneuma*, the same word translated as "spirit"). In ordinary life, we have breath within us to keep us alive and well. Most of the time, we don't even think about our breathing. But every now and then, we fill our lungs with extra breath, perhaps because we're planning to swim underwater or because we're hiking up a steep hill. In those unusual times, we are filled with *pneuma*. Similarly, there are times when God fills us with his *pneuma* so that we might serve him with extra vigor. The present imperative "keep on being filled with the Spirit" suggests that this is something that can and should happen often in our lives.

Speaking. . . . Sing and make music . . . giving thanks. . . . Submit (5:18–21). Following the command to "be filled with the Spirit," the Greek text of 5:18–21 contains several participles that are grammatically dependent on that imperative. English translations tend to obscure this relationship in order to make the English flow more naturally. Unfortunately, however, this hides the extent to which speaking (5:19), singing and making music (5:19), giving thanks (5:20), and submitting (5:21) are connected with being filled with the Spirit.

Greek grammar permits various options for understanding this relationship. The participles could be causal, "speaking, singing, etc., will cause you to be filled with the Spirit." Or they could represent consequences of filling, "When you are filled with the Spirit, the result is that you will be speaking, singing, etc." Commentators differ on which interpretation is best. Given the fact that the filling of the Spirit is something God does in freedom, it seems best to regard the participles as results or aspects of filling rather than the causes. But of course the filling of the Spirit often comes when Christians are speaking to each other, singing to the Lord, and so forth. Thus we should not limit too strictly the relationship between the participles and the imperative "be filled."

Psalms, hymns, and songs from the Spirit (5:19). What are these various genres of music? Some commentators believe that psalms, hymns, and songs from the Spirit are distinct musical types. Others argue that Paul is simply stacking up words that overlap in meaning. I believe that psalms, hymns, and songs from the Spirit should not be seen as clearly defined, fully distinct musical genres, though each term may emphasize different qualities of music used in worship.

The word "psalms" (plural of Greek *psalmos*) points to the songs collected in the Old Testament book of Psalms (see for example, Luke 20:42), but may also include spontaneous songs inspired by the Spirit (see 1 Cor 14:26). "Hymns" (plural of Greek *hymnos*) appears only here and in a parallel passage in Colossians (3:16). But the use of the verb "to hymn" (*hymneō*) in the New Testament suggests the singing of a familiar, previously composed song of praise to God (see Matt 26:30; Acts 16:25). "Songs from the Spirit" (plural of *odē pneumatikē*) are perhaps spontaneous numbers sung in the context of Christian worship. Though we cannot identify the precise meaning of "psalms, hymns, and songs from the Spirit," we do know that these are all musical forms used to praise God.

Speaking to one another (5:19). When filled with the Spirit, we will be "speaking to one another with psalms, hymns, and songs from the Spirit." Yet aren't songs of worship meant for the Lord, as it says in the second half of verse 19? In what sense are we to speak to each other with these musical expressions?

One answer to this question points to the different audiences of music used in worship. Some songs address God directly (Psalm 75) while other songs of worship speak to people (Psalm 117:1—"Praise the Lord, all you nations."). Thus we could easily speak to each other with the words of Psalm 117 and the like.

But when Paul urges us to speak to one another with psalms, hymns, and songs from the Spirit, he may have had something more in mind. At several points in his writings, Paul appears to quote or paraphrase a song from early Christian worship; Philippians 2:5–11 would be a salient example.[7] And just five verses earlier in Ephesians 5:14, Paul seems to do this very thing: "This is why it is said, 'Wake up, sleeper, rise from the dead, and Christ will shine on you.'" As we have seen, it's likely that this is an excerpt from a song of early Christian worship. Thus the language of corporate worship fills Paul's own letters in a way that models his exhortation to speak to each other in psalms, hymns, and songs from the Spirit. The language of worship should spill over into our everyday conversation, shaping what we say and how we say it.

Sing and make music from your heart to the Lord (5:19). Moreover when we're filled with the Spirit, we will also find ourselves singing and making music from our hearts "to the Lord" (5:19). Often the lyrics of our worship songs address God explicitly, as in the case of the classic hymn "How Great Thou Art." Yet even if the words of our songs do not speak directly to God, we can still sing these songs for him. We don't have to change "A Mighty Fortress

---

7. See Lynn H. Cohick, *Philippians*, The Story of God Bible Commentary (Grand Rapids: Zondervan, 2013) on Phil 2:6–11.

is Our God" to "A Mighty Fortress Art Thou, God" in order to praise God with this glorious hymn.

Always giving thanks to God the Father for everything, in the name of our Lord Jesus Christ (5:20). This verse identifies one of the most common and appropriate expressions of worship: thanksgiving. Whether in song or speech, when we are filled with the Spirit, we will offer expressions of gratitude to God. We do this "in the name of our Lord Jesus Christ" (5:20), that is, under the authority of Christ and for his purposes. It does not mean that every prayer of gratitude must end with the words "in Jesus' name," though this practice can be a helpful reminder that all of our prayers should be offered under Christ's lordship and for his sake.

Always (5:20). How should we thank God "always"? It's unlikely that the Paul means giving intentional, verbal thanks every single waking moment. Surely there were times when his verbal skills were focused on something other than forming prayers of gratitude. I believe Paul meant at least two things when he said we should be "always giving thanks." First, this verse encourages us to pause often in the midst of our busy lives to perceive God's gifts and thank him for them. Second, Ephesians 5:20 urges us to develop an inner perspective of gratitude, to live each moment with an awareness of the blessings we have from God and our debt to him.

We may also wonder what it means to thank God "for everything." Are we to thank the Lord for heresy and falsehood? For depression and death? For despair and darkness? Common sense suggests that we should not thank God for that which is contrary to God's own will. In 1 John 1:5, for example, we read that "God is light; in him there is no darkness at all." So if we thank God for moral and spiritual darkness, we are giving him false credit for that which is evil and risking outright blasphemy.

But we should also realize that apparently bad things turn out to be parts of God's good plan. God even uses human evil for his providential purposes. In Genesis we read that Joseph suffered many terrible things, including attempted murder by his own brothers, being sold into slavery, false accusation, abuse of power, and unwarranted imprisonment. As he was rotting in jail, Joseph may not have been ready to pray, "Lord, thank you that I am rotting in jail." But in retrospect, Joseph saw how God used it for his own benefit, not to mention the benefit of his family and a whole nation. Thus, later in life Joseph said to the brothers who had once tried to kill him, "You intended to harm me, but God intended it for good to accomplish what is now being done, the saving of many lives" (Gen 50:20).

There are times when we simply don't know how to pray, when we're not sure if the things happening to us are of God or are manifestations of evil. In times like these, we may not know exactly how to thank God for everything. But even then we can still thank the Lord for his presence with us, for his compassion, for never leaving or forsaking us, for saving us from sin and death, and for giving us the sure hope of his future. We can thank God that nothing happens outside of the scope of his sovereignty and that he can and will use all things for his purposes. We can thank him that the most horrible action in all of history—the torture and murder of God's own Son—turned out, in the mystery of his grace, to be the ultimate demonstration of divine love.

The final participle in the collection dependent on "be filled" is "submitting" (5:21). Though we will consider what this means in the next chapter, submitting to other people reminds us of the corporate context of Ephesians 5:15–20. Being careful how we live, redeeming the time, avoiding drunkenness, being filled with the spirit, speaking to one another with music for worship, singing and making music to the Lord, and giving thanks to God are functions of the Christian community. Yes, in the sovereignty of God we can be filled with the Spirit while we are alone. And, yes, we can sing to God in the privacy of our personal devotions. But in general, it is as members of the body of Christ that we are to walk in wisdom and be filled with the Spirit.

LIVE the Story

Redeeming the Time

According to a literal translation of Ephesians 5:16, we should watch carefully how we live, "redeeming the time, because the days are evil," choosing to use well the time that is given to us, filling it with wise, godly actions rather than foolish, diabolical ones.

Most of us feel the evil of the days in which we live. We live in a world pervaded by ethnic violence, human trafficking, global terrorism, exploitative pornography, unjust economics, and entrenched racism. The oppressive evil of our time can debilitate us, discouraging us from trying to make a positive difference.

We can feel like Frodo in *The Fellowship of the Ring*. Early in this novel by J. R. R. Tolkien, Frodo received a visit from Gandalf, the wise wizard. Frodo, an unassuming hobbit, had been given an evil ring of power. After sharing with Frodo the history of the ring, Gandalf observes that Sauron the Great, the Dark Lord, is growing in strength and wants the ring back. This placed Frodo in the crosshairs of evil, since he was responsible for the ultimate destruction of the ring. Understandably, Frodo was concerned.

"I wish it need not have happened in my time," says Frodo.

"So do I," says Gandalf, "and so do all who live to see such times. But that is not for them to decide. All we have to decide is what to do with the time that is given us."[8]

All we have to decide is what to do with the time that is given us. Wise words, words that might well have been spoken by the apostle Paul. Words that were, I expect, shaped by Tolkien's own Christian faith.

According to Ephesians, we too live in evil days. We have not been given a ring of power. But we have been entrusted with the good news of the gospel and called into a way of living that opposes the darkness of our world. When we say yes to Jesus, we join his battle against the forces of evil.

Like Frodo we might also say, "I wish it need not have happened in my time." But we cannot choose to live in another time. We cannot skip immediately to the future when God reigns and all of creation is united under Christ.

Yet we do have a choice about how to live. We can choose to walk worthy of the calling with which we have been called (4:1). We can choose to be careful how we live, to walk wisely, and to redeem the time given to us (5:15–16). As we look at our lives and the world in which we live, "All we have to decide is what to do with the time given us." Will we use it as the world dictates? Or will we liberate time from the clutches of evil and use it for God's purposes? Will we, like Frodo, heed the call given to us and live for the sake of redemption?

Like Frodo, we are not alone in this effort. We also have a fellowship, not the fellowship of the ring but the fellowship of the Lord. He has joined us together in one body so that we might work jointly to fulfill his purposes on earth. As God's people in community, we can redeem the time in ways we could not do by ourselves.

Consider, for example, the case of the First Presbyterian Church of Concord, California. Thirty years ago, the scourge of pornography manifested itself not on the yet-to-be-invented Internet but in countless "adult" bookstores and pornographic theatres. In Concord, a classic downtown theater was purchased by a company that turned it into a pornographic movie house. The "Showcase Theater" was adjacent to the First Presbyterian Church, which committed itself to shut down its evil neighbor.

There were many different ways for the church to "redeem the time" when it came to the blight in their neighborhood. They could have protested. They could have complained. They could have sought to change the laws to prevent a pornographic theater from adjoining a church. Yet what the church did was a more literal kind of redemption: they went out and bought the theater.

---

8. J. R. R. Tolkien, *The Fellowship of the Ring* (New York: Random House, 2005), 55–56.

Ironically, for two years the church technically owned the theater as it continued to show "adult films" under the terms of the lease. The church had no other legal option. But once the lease ran out, the church converted the theater into the Presbyterian Community Center. Soon happier activities filled the space, including YMCA aerobics, Boy Scouts, a music academy, wheelchair soccer, and a counseling center. Twenty years later when those community groups found other places to function, the Presbyterians leased the facility to a Vineyard church, which, as of this writing, fills the former theatre with songs, hymns, and songs from the Spirit.[9] Literally, First Presbyterian Church redeemed the space, turning it from evil to good, "redeeming the time." Also, it contributed in some small measure to God's work of healing the cosmos through Christ, unifying all things in him.

Worship without Wars

About the same time the First Presbyterian Church of Concord was buying that pornographic theater, hundreds of Presbyterian churches throughout the United States, along with thousands of other churches, began to engage in what were called "worship wars." The fight often pitted adherents of traditional Presbyterian worship against those who preferred contemporary praise music, such as that popularized by the Vineyard. To use the language of Ephesians, soldiers on one side fought for "hymns" while their opponents took up arms in favor of "songs from the Spirit." Most of the time the battles took place within congregations, a civil war pitting worshiper against worshiper.

At the risk of oversimplifying matters, I believe that the worship wars could largely have been avoided if combatants on either side had paid closer attention to Ephesians 5:18–20. First of all, they would have noted that God's people are supposed to worship with "psalms, hymns, and songs from the Spirit." Whatever these terms mean, they surely suggest that musical worship ought to include diverse genres and expressions. Those who wanted to sing only hymns or only songs could have recognized that their limited preferences were out of touch with Scripture. They could have chosen another way, the way of psalms, hymns, and songs from the Spirit, the way of unity, the way of Christ.

I'll never forget one battle of the worship wars that was fought by the elders of my church in Irvine. Several of them were advocating the inclusion of praise songs in our traditional worship services. Others were standing their ground in defense of cherished traditions. One of the staunchest advocates of traditional music was an elder named Tim.[10] He sang in the choir and loved

---

9. "A History of the First Presbyterian Church of Concord, California," http://www.fpcconcord.org/history.htm.

10. Yes, this is the same Tim who appeared in the commentary on 4:1–6.

the great hymns of the church. But as the battle of words continued in that board meeting, Tim began to have a change of heart. Finally, he said in his booming voice, "We all know how much I love traditional music in worship. I would prefer not to sing praise songs in our services. But I've decided that if using praise songs helps us draw high school kids into worship, if it allows us to reach even one kid for Christ, then I'll vote for using both hymns and songs in our worship." At that moment, the battle was over.

Notice that Tim was not motivated by these verses about singing "psalms, hymns, and songs from the Spirit" in worship. Rather, his heart was moved by the gospel, by the possibility of reaching out with the love of Christ, by the potential for greater unity and more faithful mission. When we are filled with the Spirit of God, we discover new passion for the things of God and less desire for our own things. You might say it was the vision of Ephesians 1 and 2 more than the musical inclusiveness of Ephesians 5 that captivated Tim's spirit.

Another feature of Ephesians 5:18–20 helps put an end to worship wars. Verse 19 says: "Sing and make music from your heart *to the Lord*." This reminds us that worship, though it edifies the body of Christ as well as individual members, is not primarily for us. Our worship is mainly for the Lord, for his glory and pleasure. If I'm preoccupied by my preference and pleasure in worship, then I'm missing the point.

One of the reasons my elder board was able to avoid a long and divisive worship war was that their notion of worship had been wisely shaped by Irvine Presbyterian Church's first pastor, Ben Patterson. Ben spoke of worship with an analogy he borrowed from Søren Kierkegaard. This Danish philosopher taught that God was the true audience for worship. Congregation members were the performers. Worship leaders were the prompters. And the true measure of any worship service is not whether I liked it or you liked it but whether God liked it.

If God is the true audience of worship, then our personal tastes lose their significance, not to mention their power to fuel battles over music in worship. Moreover, if God is the true audience of worship, and God appears to prefer psalms, hymns, and songs from the Spirit, then who are we to fight for one genre against another?

Ephesians 5:18–20 enables us to prevent or to end worship wars as well as to move beyond them into a wise understanding and practice of worship. We recognize that our worship, in whatever genre, is primarily for God and God's own pleasure. But we are also reminded by this passage that our worship allows us to serve and build up each other. When we let the words and reality of worship fill our minds and hearts, we will speak to each other with psalms, hymns, and songs from the Spirit. The content of our worship will enable us to speak the truth in love so that the body of Christ might grow up to become all that God intends it to be (4:15–16). Moreover, as the church worships in unity, the cosmos will see that God's plan to unite all things in Christ is working.

CHAPTER 13

Ephesians 5:21–33

📖 LISTEN to the Story

²¹Submit to one another out of reverence for Christ.

²²Wives, submit yourselves to your own husbands as you do to the Lord. ²³For the husband is the head of the wife as Christ is the head of the church, his body, of which he is the Savior. ²⁴Now as the church submits to Christ, so also wives should submit to their husbands in everything.

²⁵Husbands, love your wives, just as Christ loved the church and gave himself up for her ²⁶to make her holy, cleansing her by the washing with water through the word, ²⁷and to present her to himself as a radiant church, without stain or wrinkle or any other blemish, but holy and blameless. ²⁸In this same way, husbands ought to love their wives as their own bodies. He who loves his wife loves himself. ²⁹After all, no one ever hated their own body, but they feed and care for their body, just as Christ does the church—³⁰for we are members of his body. ³¹"For this reason a man will leave his father and mother and be united to his wife, and the two will become one flesh." ³²This is a profound mystery—but I am talking about Christ and the church. ³³However, each one of you also must love his wife as he loves himself, and the wife must respect her husband.

Listening to the text in the Story: Genesis 2–3; Psalm 8; Ezekiel 16:8–14; Mark 10:35–45; 12:28–31; John 13:1–17; 1 Corinthians 7:1–6; Galatians 5:13–14; Colossians 3:18–19; 1 Peter 3:1–7.

Ephesians 5:18 urges us to "be filled with the Spirit." Four participles explain the activities that this filling generates: *speaking* to each other worshipfully, *singing* and *making music* to the Lord, and *giving thanks* to God. Yet there is a fifth participle in this string, namely, *submitting* to one another (5:21). Most English translations begin a new sentence with verse 21, opting for the imperative "submit." But in the Greek text, it is a participle ("submitting") that depends grammatically on the imperative ("be filled"). Thus, verse 21 completes the exhortation that began in verse 18.

Yet 5:21 is also a bridge that connects the previous three verses with a new, lengthy section of Ephesians, an extended discussion of household relationships (5:21–6:9). These relationships include wives and husbands, children and parents, slaves and masters. Scholars label Ephesians 5:21–6:9 as a *household code* (sometimes referred to by the German name *Haustafel*).[1] This code lays out the structures and obligations of household members so as to advise them, especially the male head of the household, on how best to live. An early example of such a code appears in Aristotle's *Politics*. He explains that an understanding of "household management" is essential to knowing how a city or state functions. He begins with "the primary and smallest parts of the household," namely, the relationships between "master and slave, husband and wife, father and children."[2] Discussions like that of Aristotle are found throughout the moral discourse of the Greco-Roman world, including Hellenistic Judaism and early Christianity, though most versions do not assume the tidy threefold structure that is found in Aristotle and Ephesians.

Greco-Roman moralists focused on the household because they considered it essential not just for private life but for public life as well. Ephesians, however, is not a tractate on politics. So why did Paul include a household code in this letter (as he did in Colossians 3:18–4:1, but not in his earlier letters)? Scholars have proposed a variety of answers to this question. Perhaps Paul was responding to relational problems that were common among Christians. Perhaps he was defending Christianity against Roman fears about a new religion undermining the social order.[3] At the very heart, he wanted the readers of his letter to understand how the story of God's work in Christ transforms all of life, including household relationships. Moreover, Paul's version of the household code has implications for life beyond the home. As Timothy Gombis writes, "This is something more like a manifesto for how the new humanity is to flourish as a political entity—as God's new community among whom God dwells."[4]

Several aspects of the household code in Ephesians are hotly contested among commentators, including mutual submission (5:21), the submission of wives to husbands (5:22), the idea that the husband is the head (5:23), and the exhortation to slaves to obey their masters, a command that seems to

1. A helpful introduction to the household code can be found in David L. Balch, "Household Codes," *ABD* 3:318–20; and P. H. Towner, "Households and Household Codes," *DPL* 415–19.
2. Aristotle, *Politics* I.II.1–2 (Rackham, LCL).
3. See Craig S. Keener, *Paul, Women, and Wives: Marriage and Women's Ministry in the Letters of Paul*, Part 2: Women's Roles in the Family (Grand Rapids: Baker, 2004).
4. Gombis, *Drama*, 176.

endorse slavery (6:5). Given the controversies swirling around this passage, we may be inclined to approach it with a predetermined sense of its meaning and relevance, thus making it difficult for us to engage the text afresh on its own terms.

Furthermore, though some of us might regard this household code as an indispensable guide for living, others might secretly prefer that it weren't in the Bible at all. Yet, it is here as a part of God's inspired Word and therefore deserves our best effort to discern its truth. I believe this demanding and unsettling passage offers an essential and encouraging example of how the story of God in Christ transforms our lives, relationships, and witness to the world.

The household code in Ephesians covers twenty-two verses, from 5:21–6:9. Though we must keep in mind the whole code as we consider its parts, it seems beneficial to cover this section in three shorter chapters (ch. 13, wives and husbands, 5:21–33; ch. 14, children and parents, 6:1–4; ch. 15, slaves and masters, 6:5–9).

EXPLAIN the Story

Summary of Ephesians 5:21–33

Ephesians 5:21–33 begins with a summons to all Christians: "Submit to one another out of reverence for Christ" (5:21). The next twelve verses explore one kind of relationship in which submission occurs: marriage. Verses 5:22–24 address wives, urging them to "submit yourselves to your own husbands" and basing this imperative on the fact that the husband is the "head" of the wife. Verses 5:25–32 instruct husbands to "love your wives," explaining this love in terms of Christ's relationship with the church. In fact, this section speaks more about Christ than it does about husbands. Verse 5:33 summarizes the practical teaching on marriage, urging a husband to "love his wife" and a wife to "respect her husband."

Submit to One Another (5:21)

Submit to one another out of reverence for Christ (5:21). The Greek actually uses a participle, *hypotassomenoi*, which means "submitting" and relies grammatically on the imperative in 5:18, "be filled with the Spirit." Life in the Spirit includes speaking with words of worship, singing and making music to the Lord, giving thanks to God, *and submitting to one another.*

When the first recipients of Paul's letter heard verse 21 read in the assembly, they might well have been stunned. From their experience in the highly stratified, hierarchical Roman world, they knew all about submission. Submission was how people approached their superiors: their fathers, masters, husbands, and most of all Rome itself. Submission flowed in one direction, from down to up, from the lesser to the greater.[5] But now Paul was urging believers to submit to each other! What did this mean? How was mutual submission even possible?

The verb translated as "submit" has a basic meaning of "subject oneself, be subjected or subordinated, obey." The standard Greek-English lexicon renders the sense in 5:21 as "voluntary yielding in love."[6] Submitting involves placing oneself under someone else in a structured relationship. Today we would speak of this as following the leadership of someone. Submitting is related to obeying (which Ephesians reserves for children, not wives, 6:1), but involves more than merely doing what someone tells you to do.

Whatever Paul means by submission, he must see it as something that Christians can do "to one another," not just from the weak to the powerful. This can seem counterintuitive. Some commentators have tried to solve the puzzle of mutual submission by claiming that Paul did not actually want every Christian to submit to others. The rest of the household code, according to this interpretation, shows that in practice submitting means that wives, children, and slaves submit. Husbands, fathers, and masters receive submission but do not give it. This reading, however, not only contradicts the plain sense of verse 21 but also fails to note the inclusive use of "one another" elsewhere in Ephesians,[7] as well as the inclusive scope of the imperative "be filled with the Spirit" (5:18).[8] No, whatever Paul means by submission, it must be something that all Christians can offer each other, regardless of our social, familial, or economic status. As John Calvin writes, "God has bound us so strongly to each other, that no man ought to endeavor to avoid subjection; and where love reigns, mutual services will be rendered."[9] We can all develop a consistent attitude of submissiveness, actively submitting to others when it is appropriate, even as they actively submit to us on other occasions.[10]

Galatians 5:13 provides an intriguing parallel that uncovers some nuances of submission in Ephesians 5:21. In Galatians, people free in Christ

5. See Cohick, *Ephesians*, 135. For a broad discussion of the lives of women in the Roman world, see Lynn H. Cohick, *Women in the World of the Earliest Christians: Illuminating Ancient Ways of Life* (Grand Rapids: Baker, 2009), esp. ch. 3, "Wives and the Realities of Marriage."

6. BDAG 1042 (*hypotassō*). *Hypotassō* is used here in the middle voice, meaning "submit yourselves."

7. See 4:2, 25, 32, where "one another" includes all believers.

8. Arnold, *Ephesians*, 356–57.

9. Calvin, *Galatians and Ephesians*, Kindle location 4948–50.

10. In this discussion of mutual submission, I am indebted to I. Howard Marshall, "Mutual Love and Submission in Marriage," in *Discovering Biblical Equality: Complementarity without Hierarchy*, eds. R. W. Pierce and R. M. Merrill Groothuis (Downers Grove, IL: InterVarsity Press, 2005), 186–204.

should "serve one another humbly in love" (Gal 5:13). The NIV uses "serve humbly" to translate the Greek verb *douleuō*, which means "to be a slave, to perform the duties of a slave, serve, obey."[11] Though "serve humbly" and "submit" are not precisely equivalent in meaning, serving humbly is an active expression of submission, one that goes beyond mere obedience, moving submission from "voluntary yielding in love" to "voluntary serving in love."[12]

There could be no more essential illustration of submission in the Roman world than the service offered by slaves. Slaves were, if you will, the masters of submission. Thus as we consider the close parallel between Ephesians 5:21 and Galatians 5:13, we realize that Paul does not see submission only as a matter of obeying orders. Slaves did this, of course. But their whole lives were lived in submissive service to their masters. Submission, therefore, involves choosing a posture of humility that leads one to serve others in the mode of a slave. If I'm in a community of mutual submission, I don't just wait around until a brother or sister gives me an order to follow. Rather, I seek out opportunities to serve humbly, to lower myself before other members of the church by serving them as a slave. Thus I follow my Master who stooped to wash the feet of his disciples.[13]

Galatians also highlights the close association of active submission and love. The imperative "serve one another" does not stand alone but is modified by "in love."[14] Moreover, this imperative is followed immediately by an explanatory rationale: "For the entire law is fulfilled in keeping this one command: 'Love your neighbor as yourself'" (Gal 5:14). Love for our neighbor motivates us to serve our neighbor humbly and lovingly. Thus Galatians 5, not to mention the whole flow of Pauline ethics, encourages us to see submission, including mutual submission, as going beyond obedience to a lifestyle of humble, slave-like service to others, service motivated by love and modeled on Christ.

One other Pauline text deserves to be mentioned in this context. In Philippians 2, Paul begins by referring to the unity we have with Christ that ought to be lived out with actions and attitudes that contribute to that unity (Phil 2:1–2). Paul writes: "Do nothing out of selfish ambition or vain conceit. Rather, in humility value others above yourselves, not looking to your own interests but each of you to the interests of others" (Phil 2:3–4). This sounds curiously similar to mutual submission because the imperatives are addressed

---

11. BDAG 259.
12. I'm not suggesting that the dictionary definition of *hypotassō* should be changed. My point is that Paul's creative use of *hypotassō* enriches and expands upon the basic lexical meaning.
13. See John 13:1–17.
14. Greek *dia tēs agapēs*.

to all believers. One expression of submission is humbly valuing others above ourselves, putting their needs about our own.

Why should we act in this countercultural and counterintuitive way? Because of Christ, who "did not consider equality with God something to be used to his own advantage; rather, he made himself nothing by taking the very nature of a servant, being made in human likeness. And being found in appearance as a man, he humbled himself by becoming obedient to death— even death on a cross!" (Phil 2:6–8). As Christ humbled himself like a slave in his incarnation and crucifixion, so we should humble ourselves like slaves in our relationships with each other.

Ephesians 5 does not refer in detail to the humility and slave-like servanthood of Christ as it provides a rationale for mutual submission. But like Philippians 2, Ephesians 5 reveals that Christ motivates us to submit humbly to each other. Ephesians 5:21 says we are to submit to each other "out of reverence for Christ." The word translated here as "reverence" is *phobos* in Greek, the basic word for "fear." "Reverence" captures the subtlety of *phobos* while rightly avoiding the sense of scariness. But we might paraphrase *phobos* as "awestruck reverence and deep respect" for Christ.[15] The more we are overwhelmed by the grandeur of Christ, the more we will submit ourselves fully to him as his servants. This act of reverent submission to Christ will prime our souls to submit to each other. When we are on our knees together before our Lord, we'll find it easier to remain on our knees in submission and service to one another. Moreover, as people filled with the Spirit of God (5:18), we will be empowered to do that which does not come naturally, submitting ourselves to others, even as they do the unnatural thing in submitting to us.

Wives Submit to Your Husbands—Husband as Head (5:22–24)

Wives, submit yourselves to your own husbands as you do to the Lord (5:22). Following the instruction for all Christians to submit to one other, wives receive an added injunction to submit to their husbands.[16] To be sure, if a woman was married to a Christian husband, she should already be practicing submission to him as her brother in Christ according to verse 21. Yet for reasons Paul does not explain, he adds the call for wives to submit.[17]

---

15. See "The Fear of Christ," in Barth, *Ephesians*, 662–68.

16. It's likely that the original version of 5:22 did not even have a verb but carried over the meaning of "submitting" from verse 21. See Metzger, *Textual Commentary*, 541.

17. Commentators suggest various reasons for the special injunction to wives. Perhaps Paul had witnessed Christian wives taking advantage of their freedom in Christ in a way that dishonored their husbands (as had likely happened in Corinth). It is also possible that Paul sought to help his readers uphold honorable aspects of Greco-Roman culture so as to minimize unnecessary offense

Wives are to submit "to your own husbands" (5:22). This verse does not call for women to submit to men in general, beyond the need for both men and women to live out the mutual submission of verse 21. But verse 22 points to a kind of submission that ought to happen within marriage.

Notice also that wives are addressed in this text as moral agents, that is, as people who can choose how they act. Most household codes in the Hellenistic world addressed men as moral agents, leaving women, children, and slaves as those acted upon by the superior men. Yet according to Ephesians, wives have the opportunity and authority to choose to submit themselves to their husbands. In Christ, their moral agency is both assumed and affirmed.

Wives are to submit to their husbands "as [they] do to the Lord" (5:22). Wives should submit willingly to their husbands as an expression of their reverence for Christ.

For the husband is the head of the wife as Christ is the head of the church, his body, of which he is the Savior. Now as the church submits to Christ, so also wives should submit to their husbands in everything (5:23–24). The submission of wife to husband is based on the headship of the husband. What does it mean for the husband to be the head of the wife as Christ is the head of the church? This is one of the most hotly debated topics in biblical interpretation in the last forty years.[18] The closer we stick to what Paul actually says in this and related texts, the more likely we will be to uncover his intended meaning.

The Greek word translated as "head" is *kephalē*, the standard word for a head, or as the Greek lexicon puts it "the part of the body that contains the brain."[19] Yet in our passage, *kephalē* is not meant literally but figuratively. Most English readers have understood "head" to mean "leader, authority."[20] Not only does this understanding follow standard English usage of "head," but it also seems to reflect an obvious reading of the passage. The woman should submit to her husband. One submits to an authority. Thus the husband is that authority because he is her head. Therefore, head equals authority. This interpretation appears to be supported by the added point that "Christ is the head of the church, his body" (5:23). Since Christ is the supreme authority over

---

and maximize potential witness. See Keener, *Paul, Women, and Wives,* Part 2: Women's Roles in the Family.

18. For an in-depth overview of this academic debate, see Anthony C. Thiselton, *The First Epistle to the Corinthians,* NIGTC (Grand Rapids: Eerdmans, 2000), 812–22. See also Gordon D. Fee, "Praying and Prophesying in the Assemblies," in *Discovering Biblical Equality,* 142–60, esp. the section "The Probable Meaning of 'Head' as Metaphor," 149–54.

19. BDAG 541–42.

20. For a strong defense of this interpretation, see George W. Knight III, "Husbands and Wives as Analogues of Christ and the Church: Ephesians 5:21–33 and Colossians 3:18–19," in *Recovering Biblical Manhood and Womanhood: A Response to Evangelical Feminism,* ed. John Piper and Wayne Grudem, rev. ed. (Wheaton, IL: Crossway, 2012).

the church, authority seems to be the sense of his headship here. Moreover, a study of the use of *kephalē* in Greek literature, especially the Septuagint, shows that this metaphorical use of *kephalē* in the sense of authority was not unknown in the Hellenistic world.[21]

However, the actual sense of *kephalē* in this text is not so clear as it might at first seem. The Greek word has a wide range of meanings, including "the noblest part" of something or "source" as in the head of a river.[22] In his writings, Paul uses *kephalē* nonliterally twelve times.[23] Not including the two instances in Ephesians 5:23, only two of the other ten uses have the "authority" sense (Eph 1:22; Col 2:10). The other eight uses of *kephalē* mean something else, either "source" or "preeminence, foremost."[24]

Consider for example the two metaphorical uses of *kephalē* that occur in Ephesians prior to chapter 5. In 1:20–23 God raised Christ from the dead and seated him in the heavenly realms, "far above all rule and authority, power and dominion . . . And God placed all things under his feet and appointed him to be head over everything for the church, which is his body, the fullness of him who fills everything in every way." Here, Christ is head "over"[25] everything, ruling from a heavenly throne. This is the head-as-authority sense of *kephalē*. Notice, however, that Christ is not said to be head over the church, but head over everything "for the church,[26] which is his body." The authority of Christ over the church is not in play in this specific passage, but rather the unity of Christ with the church. (Of course I'm not denying that Christ is the chief authority over the church. But this notion is not present in Ephesians 1:20–23.)

In Ephesians 4:15–16 Christ is once again depicted as the head of the church: "We will grow to become in every respect the mature body of him who is the head, that is, Christ. From him the whole body, joined and held together by every supporting ligament, grows and builds itself up in love, as each part does its work." As head of the body, Christ is the *source of its growth*. Of course he is also Lord over the church, but that is not mentioned here. Rather, the headship of Christ underscores the profound unity of Christ with the church and explains his unique role as the source of the church's growth.

---

21. See Wayne A. Grudem, "Does *Kephalē* (Head) Mean 'Source' or 'Authority over' in Greek Literature? A Survey of 2,336 Examples," *Trinity Journal* 6 (1985): 38–59; and "The Meaning of *Kephalē* ("Head"): A Response to Recent Studies," *Trinity Journal* 11 (1990): 3–72.

22. LSJ 945 (see I.2, also II.d).

23. A metaphorical use of *kephalē* in Paul's writings appears in 1 Cor 11:3 (3x), 4, 5; Eph 1:22; 4:15; 5:23 (2x); Col 1:18; 2:10, 19.

24. *Kephalē* as something other than "authority" is used in 1 Cor 11:3 (3x), 4, 5; Eph 4:15; 5:23 (the verse here under consideration); Col 1:18; 2:19. On *kephalē* as "preeminence, foremost," see Thiselton, *First Corinthians*, 821–22.

25. Greek *hyper*.

26. Greek *tē ekklēsia*.

As in Ephesians 1:20–23, Christ's headship of the church is not a matter of his authority over the church but rather a way of talking about his unity with and service to the church. So the only uses of *kephalē* in Ephesians, outside of 5:23, do not point to Christ's authority over the church. Rather, they emphasize his unity with the church, and as a result of this unity, his being the source of the church's growth.

Thus when we come to Ephesians 5:23 and the statement that "Christ is the head of the church, his body, of which he is the Savior," the literary context of Ephesians points in the direction of head-as-source, not head-as-authority. This interpretation is confirmed by the added claim, "of which he is the Savior." Christ is the ultimate source of the church because of his saving work on the cross, the supreme act of love that brought it into existence (see 2:11–22). If Paul were employing the head-as-authority meaning of *kephalē* here, surely he would have said that Christ is the Lord of the church. But the lordship of Christ is never mentioned in the discussion of marriage in Ephesians 5.

Yet what about verse 24, which says that "the church submits to Christ"? Doesn't this demand a head-as-authority sense of *kephalē*? Not necessarily. It may be that Paul used *kephalē* here with awareness of its range of meanings, including head-as-authority. But the church submits to Christ, the source of its life and growth, by receiving all that he seeks to give (see 4:7–16). The church submits to Christ by allowing him to dwell among its members, filling them with his expansive love (see 3:17–19). Submitting, as we have seen above, involves more than just obedience. The church submits to Christ when it serves him, responding reciprocally to his own servanthood.

Wives, like the church, should submit to Christ "in everything" or better, "in every way"[27] (5:24). Does this really mean that a wife must submit to her husband in every instance, no matter what? Should a wife submit even if he wants her to do something sinful? Of course not. We must always read the biblical text in the wider context of Scripture. A wife's submission to her husband should always be circumscribed by her ultimate and unqualified submission to Christ.

With so much debate about various meanings of *kephalē* in 5:23–24, we can easily neglect the most significant point of the head-body metaphor. The husband's headship of the wife is meant to underscore their profound unity, just as Christ is one with his church, his body (see 5:30–32). The wife submits to her husband-head because she and her husband-head are profoundly one. It's almost as if she is submitting to herself (see the parallel point in 5:28). This emphasis on unity between husband and wife flows in the mainstream of

27. Greek *en panti*.

God's story in Ephesians, the uniting of all things in Christ, as we'll see later. Unity in Christ will be experienced in the cosmos (ch. 1), the church (ch. 2), and marriage (ch. 5).[28]

A paraphrase of 5:22–23 might read: "Wives, submit to your own husbands as you submit to the Lord. For the husband is the head of the wife, and therefore they are unified as one body, just like Christ and the church. When the wife submits to her husband, it's as if she is submitting to herself. Moreover, Christ, the Savior of the church, is the head of the church, that is, the source of the church's life and growth. As the church receives all that Christ has to give, so the wife should receive all that her husband gives for her benefit. Plus, she should seek to serve him as an expression of love."

The claim that the husband's headship of the wife is not mainly a matter of authority runs counter to much of what has been said and written about verses 23–24. (It should be noted, in fact, that headship as a concept does not actually appear in this passage, or any other passage of Scripture. Talking about headship turns metaphorical language into propositional language.) Yet the actual usage of *kephalē* in Ephesians, combined with what the text actually says about Christ as head/Savior of the church, points away from a head-as-authority reading. But what will really help us grasp the sense of male headship in this passage is yet to come, namely Paul's instructions to husbands in 5:25–32. If he urges husbands to exercise authority over their wives, as would be completely typical in his culture, then we have evidence for the head-as-authority reading. But if he exhorts husbands differently, then we'll discover what Paul actually means when he speaks of the husband as head.

Husbands Love Your Wives as Christ Loved the Church (5:25–32)

Popular wisdom in the Greco-Roman world held that husbands should rule over their wives. Aristotle put it plainly: "It is part of the household science to rule over wife and children . . . for the male is by nature better fitted to command than the female."[29] Josephus, the first-century AD Jewish historian, wrote, "The woman, says the Law, is in all things inferior to the man. Let her accordingly be submissive, not for her humiliation, but that she may be directed; for the authority has been given by God to the man."[30]

Given this cultural background and the fact that Paul has just instructed wives to submit to their husbands, we along with Paul's readers would expect his command to husbands to begin: "Husbands, exercise authority over your

28. For a similar understanding of the function of "head" in this passage, see Sarah Sumner, *Men and Women in the Church: Building Consensus on Christian Leadership* (Downers Grove, IL: InterVarsity Press, 2003), 154–90.

29. Aristotle, *Politics* I.V.2, 59 (Rackham, LCL).

30. Josephus, *Against Apion* 2.24 (Thackeray, LCL).

wives." But this is not what the text says. The husband's authority is never mentioned in Ephesians.

In fact, only once in his letters does Paul actually write that a husband has authority over his wife. This appears in 1 Corinthians 7:4, which reads, "The wife does not have authority over her own body but yields it to her husband." That might appear to clinch the case for one-way authority in marriage, the husband over the wife. But Paul is not finished; he adds: "In the same way, the husband does not have authority over his own body but yields it to his wife." Here in Paul's own words is a clear statement of the wife having authority over her husband, even as he has authority over her. This is mutual authority, if you will. The implied flip side is mutual submission. Wives are to submit to their husbands, and husbands are to submit to their wives. Paul couldn't be clearer about this (or more controversial, given his cultural setting. I am sometimes amazed at how many discussions of submission and authority in marriage completely overlook 1 Cor 7:4.)

Husbands, love your wives, just as Christ loved the church and gave himself up for her (5:25). What does Paul want husbands to do, if not to exercise authority? They are to love their wives. The Greek verb "to love" is *agapaō*, which is frequently used in the New Testament for self-giving love, love demonstrated by Christ and expected of all of his followers (5:1–2). Husbands are to imitate Christ by loving their wives as Christ loved the church, a love shown most of all in his giving up of his life for the church. Thus, this kind of love is an expression of the mutual submission to which all believers are called in 5:21. Husbands are called to love in a self-giving, self-sacrificing, self-denying way, the way of Christ. Through his loving sacrifice, Christ became the Savior of the church, the source of its life, and the "head" of the church. The husband acts as the head of his wife when he loves her with Christlike love, thus giving life to her through his love. This is what it means for a husband to act as the head of his wife according to Ephesians.

It's hard to overemphasize the cultural distinctiveness of Paul's command for husbands to love their wives. We can take this for granted because we talk so much about marital love in our culture. But in the Greco-Roman world, exhortations for husbands to love their wives "are fairly infrequent," and no household code written before Paul instructs husbands to love (*agapaō*) their wives.[31] Yet Ephesians not only calls husbands to love their wives but also illustrates the nature of that love by pointing to Christ's loving sacrifice for the church.

Of course, a wife should also love her husband in a Christlike way. This is not mentioned in 5:21–33. But it is clearly stated in 5:1–2 that all believers,

---

31. Lincoln, *Ephesians*, 374. Colossians 3:19 ("Husbands, love your wives") is probably the earliest known example of this kind of statement.

including wives, are to "walk in the way of love, just as Christ loved us and
gave himself up for us." We don't know exactly why Paul chose to exhort
husbands explicitly to love their wives. I wonder if it was necessary given the
patriarchal culture in which the early Christians lived, one in which male
authority was a given and sacrificial love of the husband for the wife would be
unexpected if not culturally alien.

*To make her holy, cleansing her by the washing with water through the word,
and to present her to himself as a radiant church, without stain or wrinkle or any
other blemish, but holy and blameless* (5:26–27). In the next two verses, Paul
leaves his teaching on marriage to reflect further on the relationship of Christ
to the church. His language echoes the opening portion of Ephesians: "For
[God] chose us in [Christ] before the creation of the world to be holy and
blameless in his sight" (1:4).[32] The "washing with water through the word"
is reminiscent of baptism. In 1 Corinthians 6:11 for example, Paul writes,
"But you were washed, you were sanctified, you were justified in the name of
the Lord Jesus Christ and by the Spirit of our God." The "word"[33] associated
with washing with water could be something proclaimed in baptism or even
the gospel itself. It is also possible that Ephesians 5:26–27 reflects the story of
God bathing his people as found in Ezekiel 16:8–14. There the Lord sought
out forlorn Israel, washing, anointing, and dressing her as a bride for her wedding. In language suggestive of Ephesians 5:27, the result of the Lord's care for
Israel was his own international fame "because the splendor I had given you
made your beauty perfect" (Ezek 16:14).[34]

Ephesians 5:26–27 reveals that Christ's love for the church leads him to
prepare the church to be fully holy and radiant. The latter word has a basic
meaning of "being held in high esteem, honored, distinguished, eminent,"[35]
suggesting that the church will shine radiantly for all to see the glorious result
of Christ's love (see 3:9–11).

Are husbands to love their wives so that they also might be glorious, like
the church? The placement of 5:26–27 suggests that husbands should see
their love as a means of their wives becoming more Christlike. The beginning of verse 28 underscores this connection: "*In this same way,* husbands
ought to love their wives . . ." Husbands imitate Christ by loving their wives
sacrificially so that their wives might become all that God intends them to be.

Husbands ought to love their wives as their own bodies (5:28). Verse 28
begins another subsection in Paul's instructions for husbands. To make the

---

32. Both 1:4 and 5:27 use the same pair of adjectives: "holy" (*hagios*) and "blameless" (*amōmos*).
33. Greek *rhēma* (not *logos*).
34. The relevance of the bath in Ezekiel 16 is noted by many commentators. I first encountered
it in Yoder Neufeld, *Ephesians*, 262.
35. BDAG 332–33 (*endoxos*).

point even more strongly, Paul adds, "He who loves his wife loves himself." This sounds like the biblical command to love one's neighbor as oneself,[36] but it makes an even weightier claim. A wife is so united to her husband that when he loves his wife, it is as if he were loving himself.

After all, no one ever hated their own body, but they feed and care for their body, just as Christ does for the church (5:29). The wife's being like the husband's body suggests a bit of commonsense wisdom: we do not hate our bodies but rather care for them. Now, Paul is not dabbling in modern psychology or considering every possible scenario, such as "body hatred." Rather, he is simply reflecting on the fact that people "feed and care for their body." In fact, this is what Christ does for the church "for we are members of his body" (5:30). This language brings to mind Ephesians 4:15–16, where Christ as the head of the body is the source of its nourishment. Again, there is a striking emphasis upon unity here, the unity of Christ and the church, his own body, which mirrors the unity of husband and wife, who is like a body to her husband who is like a head.

"For this reason a man will leave his father and mother and be united to his wife, and the two will become one flesh" (5:31). The unity between Christ and the church, illustrated in the unity between husband and wife, can be seen in Genesis 2:24, where the man "is united to his wife, and they become one flesh." The husband and wife are the same "stuff," not just united as connected head and body but also as one common flesh.

This is a profound mystery—but I am talking about Christ and the church (5:32). Once more, Paul is not satisfied merely to highlight the unity between husband and wife. Again, he turns the spotlight to the relationship of Christ and church. To be sure, the one-flesh unity of husband and wife is also a mystery. But this is not Paul's primary interest. Rather, he sees in the Genesis account a foreshadowing of the "profound mystery," namely, the oneness of Christ and the church.

The language of mystery[37] connects strongly with earlier passages of Ephesians that focus on unity. In chapter 1 God made known the "mystery" of his will, namely, "to bring unity to all things in heaven and on earth under Christ" (1:10). Then in chapter 3 the "mystery" of God is the uniting of Jews and Gentiles in the church (3:3–11). Now in chapter 5 the "mystery" is the unity of Christ with the church. The main point this passage makes about marriage is not the distinct roles of husband and wife but rather the unity between them, unity as seen in the one-flesh-ness of the creation story, unity as between a head and a body, unity as between Christ and the church.

---

36. Lev 19:18; Mark 12:31.
37. Greek, *mysterion*.

Summary for Husband and Wife (5:33)

However, each one of you also must love his wife as he loves himself, and the wife must respect her husband (5:33). The final verse of the household code section on marriage sums up the instructions for husbands and wives. The Greek meaning might be more accurately captured as "each and every one of you must love. . ."[38] Every husband must love his wife as he loves himself.

A wife should "respect" her husband (5:33). The Greek verb translated as "respect" is *phobeō*, which basically means "to fear." It is related to the word *phobos* in 5:21, translated there as "reverence." The point of verse 33 is not that the wife should be afraid of her husband; if he lives out his calling to love her as Christ loves the church, he will be anything but scary. The NIV's "respect" does justice to the original language. Interestingly, Paul does not again use the verb "to submit" to summarize the wife's posture with respect to her husband. Nor does he use the verb "to obey," which comes in the next verse in the instruction for children vis-à-vis their parents. Nor does he get into particulars of fallen married life in which husbands sometimes engage in behavior that is unrespectable. This is because Paul is not writing a detailed marriage manual, considering all possible scenarios, but rather painting with broad strokes a picture of marriage in first-century Greco-Roman culture, marriage transformed and shaped by the story of God.

In this painting, husband and wife are profoundly united, as a head is united to a body. Yet this unity is not just an ideal representation of marriage but also an image of the unity between Christ and the church. Christ is united with the church as its head, even as the man is united to his wife as her head. Christ's headship in this passage is revealed as closely associated with his being the Savior of the church. Moreover, his headship is expressed in action as he loves the church, making her holy, feeding her, and caring for her. Nothing is said here about Christ's authority over the church as her Lord, though, of course, this is true.

How did Christ actually become the source of the church? By offering himself sacrificially in love. He took the form of a slave, becoming human and dying on a cross (see Phil 2:6–8). Thus in one dramatic action, Christ's slave-like sacrifice became the source of the church's life as well as the paradigm of both submission and love. We learn mutual submission through imitating Christ's own humble, slave-like service. We learn how to love each other by imitating his example (Eph 5:1–2). The fact that wives are never told in Ephesians 5:21–33 to love their husbands does not mean, of course, that they aren't to do this. Ephesians 5:1–2 instructs all Christians to "walk in the way of love." And Titus 2:4 explicitly instructs wives to love their husbands.[39] But

---

38. Greek, *kai hymeis hoi kath' hena hekastos.*
39. Titus 2:4 uses the adjective "husband-loving," *philandros.*

the emphasis in the household code section is on the particular duty of the husband as the head of his wife to exercise his headship through imitating the self-giving love of Christ.

Thus when it comes to marriage, both wife and husband are to submit to each other and to love each other. Ephesians 5:21–33 speaks within its own cultural context, emphasizing the submission of the wife and the love of the husband. But the call to mutual submission (5:21) and the call for all to love like Christ (5:1–2) challenge both husbands and wives to a full imitation of Christ within marriage. According to Andrew Lincoln, "In this way, submission and love can be seen as two sides of the same coin—selfless service of one's marriage partner."[40] Moreover, even as Christ's death is God's means of bringing unity to the cosmos, starting with the church, his death also undoes the damage and division sin has brought to marriage, making possible deep unity between husband and wife, a unity that mirrors that of Christ and the church.

Marriage and the Grand Story of Creation, Fall, Redemption, and Restoration

Now that we have examined the teaching of Ephesians 5 on marriage, we are ready to see how it fits into the grand story of God, the story divided in four chapters: creation, fall, redemption, and restoration.

Ephesians 5:21–33 connects explicitly to the first chapter of the grand story when it cites a portion of the creation narrative in Genesis 2: "For this reason a man will leave his father and mother and be united to his wife, and the two will become one flesh" (Eph 5:31). Genesis reveals the original unity between husband and wife. God intends for husband and wife to experience unique oneness, something so profound that it will later serve as an apt picture of the unity between Christ and the church.

According to Genesis 2, God did not create the woman out of the dirt, as he had made the man. Rather, God formed the woman from a part of the man's body. Thus their unity as "one flesh" is based on the fact that the man is the physical source of the woman, though woman is created by God. The man and the woman experience the blessing of their unity in that they are naked yet unashamed, able to share fully who they are with each other, in both body and soul (Gen 2:25).

But this pristine picture of unity is tarnished by sin in the next chapter of the grand story, the fall. In Genesis 3, the first couple choose to eat the forbidden fruit, thus disobeying God. From a theological point of view, sin shatters the perfect relationship between human beings and God. But in the narrative of Genesis 3, the first sign of sin's damage is brokenness in the relationship

---

40. Lincoln, *Ephesians*, 393.

between husband and wife. Whereas they were once so unified that they could be naked together without shame, as soon as they sinned, the first couple "sewed fig leaves together and made coverings for themselves" (Gen 3:7). Sin first rears its ugly head in the shattering of marital unity.

This fracturing of what God had intended for husband and wife is underscored a few verses later when God says to the woman, "Your desire will be for your husband and he will rule over you" (Gen 3:16). In place of unity and collaboration, now the husband will dominate his wife. However we understand God's intention for the relationship of man and woman in marriage, it's clear that sin has warped God's design and given man an evil tendency to rule over woman inappropriately.

If we had the time, we could listen to many stories in the Old Testament that play out the brokenness of marriage and abusive male domination. For example, in Genesis 12 we read that Abram risks the sexual purity of his wife, Sarai, in order to save his own skin.[41] In the most horrifying biblical example of male abuse of power, Judges 19 tells the story of a man and his concubine traveling on a journey. When they lodge with an old man for the evening, wicked men pound on his door, demanding to have sex with the visitor. The owner of the house, desiring to be hospitable to his guest, offers the men outside his own virgin daughter and his visitor's concubine. When the men reject this offer, the male visitor, in order to save himself from abuse, sends his concubine outside where she is raped until she dies. When the man finally arrives at home, taking with him the body of his violated concubine, he cuts her up in pieces and sends a part to all of the areas of Israel as a testimony to the evil in the land.[42]

Even if we have not personally experienced the depravity of sexual abuse and male violence against women, we surely know its victims both in our network of relationships and through the media. Yet if by grace our own marriages are spared from such extreme horrors, all husbands and wives know the relational brokenness caused by sin. None of us experiences fully the unity God intended for husband and wife.

God's story does not end with the fall but with redemption and restoration. Ephesians says the blood of Christ purchases our redemption (1:7), which we begin to experience now as we await the fullness of redemption in the future (1:14; 4:30). Restoration in Ephesians is described in terms of unity. God is restoring all things by uniting everything under Christ (1:10).

God's redemption is centered in Christ, in the shedding of his blood on the cross (1:7). Christ's death not only allows individuals to be saved (2:8) but

---

41. Gen 12:10–20. See also Gen 20:1–16; 26:1–11.
42. Judg 19:1–30.

also brings oneness to divided humanity, as seen in the uniting of Jews and Gentiles through the cross (2:14–18). This newly united humanity forms the church through which God is working out his plan to bring all things together in Christ (3:2–11).

"All things" includes marriage, as Ephesians 5:21–33 discloses. A husband and a wife are united like a head and body (5:23). Husbands are to love their wives as they do their own bodies. Husbands are so unified with their wives that loving their wives is like loving themselves (5:28). The unity between husband and wife that God intended in creation can now be realized, however incompletely, through marriages that embody the story of God's redemption and restoration in Christ.

LIVE the Story

Married people have an obvious opportunity to live the story of Ephesians 5:21–33. The strong exhortation in the summary verse of the passage, which says to husbands, "each one of you also must love his wife," reminds husbands (and wives, too) that we should do more than study this passage. We must also live it in our daily lives.

But this does not mean single people are excluded from living the story. For one thing, Ephesians 5:21–33 assumes that marriages are conducted in the context of Christian community. Wives and husbands live the story in Ephesians 5 not in some private sanctuary set apart from others but rather in relationship with brothers and sisters with whom they are united in Christ and to whom they are called to submit. Thus the teaching on marriage is relevant to single Christians who are members of Christ's body. Moreover, though this portion of the household code in Ephesians speaks directly to wives and husbands, it actually spends more words talking about the relationship between Christ and the church.[43] Thus all of us whether married or not can enact the storyline of Ephesians 5:21–33.

Living the Story of Unity in Marriage

For married people, the more we read Ephesians 5:21–33 through the lens of God's grand story, the more we will examine the unity in our own marriage. Are we growing into deeper oneness through Christ? Or have we settled for comfortable but unbiblical independence? Are we allowing our marriage to be damaged by division? Are we letting past sins putrefy in our marriage through denial or unforgiveness? Are we afraid of dealing with the woundedness in

---

43. About 55% of the words in this passage focus on Christ and the church.

ourselves that keeps us from true intimacy with our spouse? Are we willing to reach out for help when we need it?

Some people worry that unity in marriage might obliterate their individual uniqueness. They have watched weddings with "unity candles" in which the bride and groom each take a candle that represents their own identity. Then together they light a common "unity candle." As this happens, many couples blow out their individual candles. I have been to weddings where the groom snuffs out his candle and his bride's candle. At this point, some of us get understandably squeamish. Does unity require the loss of personhood, the surrender of one's unique identity?

An answer to this question comes from Ephesians 5. Does the unity between Christ and the church mean that Christ and the church lose their distinctiveness? Not at all. They are separate yet also united. Christ is the Savior and nurturer of the church. He does not become the church, even though they are unified like a head with a body. So one of the challenges for married people is to discover how godly unity can be realized in their marriages in the same way, one that does not deny their own identities.

The broader story of God underscores what we learn about unity and distinctiveness in Ephesians 5. God made the woman to be different from the man, even though they share in one flesh. She is not an appendage to the man but a fully separate, unique human being. In coming together as husband and wife, they do not surrender their own personhood, merging so as to become a singular being. Rather, their unity incorporates their distinctiveness.

Yet in many popular teachings based on Ephesians 5, the differentness of husband and wife and their roles has been emphasized to the exclusion of their unity and common calling. Without denying that husband and wife are different and have different assignments in this passage, we ought to put the emphasis where it lies in the text, on the unity between husband and wife, a unity that fits the grand story of God and reflects the oneness between Christ and his beloved church.

What Should a Couple Do When They Are Just Plain Stuck?

Ephesians 5:21 says, "Submit to one another out of reverence for Christ." When Christians first heard this in their first-century gatherings, they would have been perplexed. Mutual submission, whatever it entailed, must have sounded like nonsense to many who lived in the first-century Roman world.

Though reticent to admit it, we might also regard mutual submission as less than sensible. After all, how can a married couple practice mutual submission? Wouldn't this lead to chaos? Doesn't somebody need to be in charge to make things work? If a husband and wife are following the teaching of

Ephesians 5:21, what happens when they come to a disagreement that they can't resolve? What should they do when they are just plain stuck? Somebody has to break the logjam; shouldn't that somebody be the husband?

Before we consider a case of an apparently irresolvable disagreement in marriage, I'd like to share a pastoral observation. I have known couples who prize mutual submission in their marriages, and I have known couples who seek to practice male leadership and female submission. But in reality, all of these couples with thriving marriages practice mutual submission most of the time.

I think, for example, of a couple I'll call "Bill and Teri." They are solidly committed to what they refer to as male headship. At times, Bill might make a decision that Teri accepts because she submits to Bill. But in almost every decision and activity of everyday life, they share leadership. Teri has wisdom about parenting that eludes Bill, so he often follows her lead as they raise their children. Teri is also an exceptional student of Scripture from whom Bill learns much. Moreover, both Bill and Teri serve each other with active submission, going out of their way to care for each other. As a result, their marriage is solid and flourishing. When submission is seen as more than taking orders, when it includes active servanthood, then mutual submission makes obvious sense for married Christians who seek to follow Christ.

Too often the discussion of submission in marriage becomes mired in the swamp of either-or, with couples forced to choose between mutual submission or male leadership. Yet in most of life, submission and leadership are fluid rather than static. Consider my work, for example. I supervise a team of people who submit to me, though we don't use that language; we speak instead of their "following my leadership." In certain matters like performance reviews, I am clearly the one who is in charge. Even then, however, I learn plenty from those I lead. Moreover, on a daily basis I often submit more to my team than they do to me. I rely on their expertise and wisdom all the time. I'm pleased to follow their leadership, and our work flourishes because I do.

This same kind of fluid leadership works well in marriage. One leads while the other follows. Then they switch. But what about when a couple is stuck? They've talked and talked, argued and argued, prayed and prayed, and they still can't come to an agreement. Isn't this the place where mutual submission breaks down? Doesn't the husband need to exercise his authority and make the tough call? Isn't this what the apostle Paul would recommend?

Let's consider a case that is hypothetical, although based in reality. A married couple heard the gospel and became Christians. In the wife's immature understanding of what it meant to be spiritual, she believed that she and her husband should no longer have sexual relations. He was not pleased, but went along with her. In order to satisfy his sexual needs, in his immaturity he began having sex with other women. This betrayal hardened her resolve to abstain from sex with him.

What we have here is classic "stuckness." When it comes to sexual intimacy, the husband says, "Yes. Yes." The wife says, "No. No." Mutual submission seems like a fine idea, but it doesn't appear to work in this situation. So one might wonder, isn't this is a time when Paul would advise the woman to submit to her husband, with wifely submission to her "head" trumping mutual submission?

In point of fact, Paul did face a case like this, but he did not give up on his commitment to mutuality. The story I just told is based on 1 Corinthians, especially chapter 7. It emerges from a close reading of the text, especially 7:1–7.[44] If I haven't rendered the details precisely, the main story is surely correct. For whatever reason, some Christians in Corinth were withholding sex from their spouses. How did Paul advise them, including the hypothetical couple I described? 1 Corinthians 7:3–5 reads: "The husband should fulfill his marital duty to his wife, and likewise the wife to her husband. The wife does not have authority over her own body but yields it to her husband. In the same way, the husband does not have authority over his own body but yields it to his wife. Do not deprive each other except perhaps by mutual agreement and for a time, so that you may devote yourselves to prayer."

Though it's not particularly romantic to refer to sex as "marital duty," Paul sees this duty going both ways. Then he starts with something that would have been commonplace in Greco-Roman society, "The wife does not have authority over her own body but yields it to her husband" (1 Cor 7:4). The verb translated as "have authority" is *exousiazō*, a standard Greek verb based on the noun *exousia*, which means "freedom of choice, power, authority, ruling power."[45] None of Paul's readers would have batted an eye over the claim that the husband has authority over his wife's body. That was the commonplace cultural, legal, and moral standard.

But then comes the shocker: "In the same way, the husband does not have authority over his own body but yields it to his wife" (1 Cor 7:4). Although a few Greco-Roman philosophers spoke positively of women's capabilities, nobody went so far as to claim that a wife had authority over any part of her husband's concerns, let alone his person. The use of "in the same way" shows that the wife's authority is just like that of her husband; both husband and wife have the same authority over each other, and both are also to submit to each other.

---

44. For a trustworthy discussion of this passage and its backstory, I recommend Gordon D. Fee, *The First Epistle to the Corinthians* (Grand Rapids: Eerdmans, 1987), 272–86.

45. BDAG 352–53.

This is the only place in all of Paul's writings, in fact in the whole New Testament, where the Greek verb for "exercise authority" is used with respect to the relationship between husbands and wives. It is noteworthy that in this usage authority is mutual, husband over wife and wife over husband. Among other things, this shows that the submission of the wife to the husband, such as we find in Ephesians 5:22–24, does not preclude her also having authority over her husband in some ways.

Mutual authority in marriage as taught in 1 Corinthians 7:4 does not easily resolve the problem of being "stuck." Paul avoids the easy road in marital relationships both here and in Ephesians 5. What he seeks is not that one member of a marriage exercise sole authority to break the impasse but that both members work together to forge a genuine agreement. 1 Corinthians 7:5 makes this clear: "Do not deprive each other *except perhaps by mutual consent.*" "By mutual consent" renders the Greek phrase *ek symphōnou*, literally, "out of agreement." In times of apparently irresolvable disagreement, both husband and wife are to figure out how to agree together.

Now we're back to our original problem. How can a couple deal with stuckness, especially if they seek to live by mutual submission as found in Ephesians 5 and mutual authority as in 1 Corinthians 7? If we stand back and look at what's happening in 1 Corinthians 7, we realize that our couple is not really stuck. They are getting help from outside the marriage. Paul is offering inspired counsel. He does not assume that their marriage is private and off limits to his pastoral guidance. Rather, he addresses their quandary and shows a way out.

When people say, "Mutual submission doesn't work because if a couple is stuck, then somebody has to make the decision," they are buying into an individualistic, Western view of marriage as the private domain of husband and wife. But Scripture does not support this perspective. On the contrary, the example of Paul's writing in 1 Corinthians illustrates what is confirmed in Ephesians, namely, that marriages "belong" to the church as well as to the couple.

Thus if a husband and wife come to an impasse in their own effort to decide something, they are not actually stuck. They have brothers and sisters in Christ to get them unstuck. Moreover, and here things get uncomfortable for most of us, the husband and wife are called to submit to their fellow Christians even in the matter about which they cannot agree.

I realize what I've just described runs contrary to the way most of us think about marriage. But I believe the biblical story leads us to see our marriages as embedded in the life of the church. Our unity in Christ as members of his body enfolds and supports our unity in Christ as husband and wife.

I know from personal experience how uncomfortable it can be to do what Scripture commends if we're stuck. In the first years of our marriage, Linda and I got stuck repeatedly. We also got lots of help, thanks be to God and his church. On one occasion, we were bound in an apparently unbreakable deadlock. We reached out to two of our Christian friends (single friends, by the way) and asked them to meet with us and help us. I confess that sharing our problem felt unpleasant, not only because it revealed my shortcomings but also because it meant that I was submitting myself to them and their guidance. I couldn't keep insisting on my own way (even though I *knew* my way was best!). After an hour of conversation, it seemed that Linda and I were finding a way out of our bind. Our friends left us alone and prayed for us as we kept on talking. Before long, Linda and I had come to an agreement. We felt relieved and elated, grateful to be members of Christ's body and glad we had taken the risk of submitting our dilemma to others.

Genuine agreement based on mutual submission and mutual authority is hard to achieve, even with help from the church. In a way, effective mutual submission is impossible, impossible for us, that is. Thus we take heart that the English imperative in Ephesians 5:21, "Submit to one another," in Greek is actually a participle dependent on the imperative in 5:18: "Be filled with the Spirit." When we are filled with God's Spirit, God is able to do in us "immeasurably more than all we ask or imagine" (3:20). God is able to help us walk the precarious path of mutual submission and mutual authority. Sometimes God helps us through members of his body. Sometimes God helps us by the inner working of his Spirit. No matter how it comes, God's help enables us to do what we cannot do on our own strength.

Living the Story of the Husband's Headship

Ephesians 5:23 asserts that "the husband is the head of the wife as Christ is the head of the church." The rest of the passage spells out what headship in marriage means based on Christ's relationship with the church. First, Christ's headship is associated with his being the Savior of the church, the one who brought the church into existence through his sacrifice (5:23). The husband is not the savior of his wife in this sense, of course. But the man is a physical source of the woman's physical existence (Gen 2), and husbands are called to be life-giving to their wives. Second, Christ's headship of the church is seen in his self-giving love for the church. Thus the husband is to love his wife as Christ loved the church (5:25). Third, Christ's headship of the church is seen in his effort to make her "holy and blameless" (5:27). Analogously, husbands can help their wives become more fully what God intends them to be. Fourth, Christ as head of the church feeds and cares for it, just as people do for their own bodies (5:29). Husbands in their role as head ought to nurture their wives. Fifth and most importantly, the fact that Christ is head of the church underscores the unity between them and points to the unity shared by husband and wife (5:30–31).

How might husbands live the thread of the story that identifies them as the head of their wife? What might this look like in practice? I will share two stories that illustrate headship as it is portrayed in Ephesians 5.

The first story comes from my own life, once again from an early stage of my marriage to Linda. Among our wedding presents, we received cash gifts that added up to just over $3,000. Soon after our wedding, we began talking about what to do with this fortune. I was clear about what would be best. We should buy a computer. (In 1984, a "portable" Compaq computer, which weighed 28 pounds, cost just over $3,000.) Linda had other ideas. She believed we should use the money to take a trip to Europe. This would be our real honeymoon since our first honeymoon was very short. If we watched our costs, we could backpack around Europe for three weeks for just about $3,000. Linda was certain this was the best use of our stash.

For weeks we talked, prayed, argued, cried, cajoled, pouted, and persuaded. We couldn't agree. Compromise seemed out of the question because either the computer or the trip would require all our money. I wanted to invest in something tangible that we would have long after an expensive trip was over. Linda wanted to invest in our relationship, something we would have long after a computer was obsolete. We were stuck. And at that time, we were too embarrassed about our situation to get help from our Christian community.

Finally, I decided to take time away to pray about our dilemma. I went to the mountains where I could get some distance and work things out with the Lord. In the back of my mind was the notion that I was the head of my wife, and that I should assert my headship by making the decision to buy the computer. I hoped God would help me know how to do this courageously and graciously.

As I walked through the woods, I began to pray, "Lord, I need your wisdom. Help me know what to do."

Then I "heard" inside a "voice" that was almost audible: "You are to love your wife like Christ loved the church and gave himself up for her."

"Wait," I prayed, "are you saying I'm supposed to give in? Am I not supposed to be the head?"

Again I "heard": "You are to love your wife like Christ loved the church and gave himself up for her." At that moment I knew what I should do. I was to affirm what Linda wanted: no computer, but a trip to Europe. I was not happy. But every time I protested, I "heard" an echo of Ephesians 5:25: "Love your wife as Christ loved the church."

Having lost my argument with God, I went home to announce that I had lost my argument with Linda. I told her that I was supporting her choice. We were going to Europe. She was stunned. She also felt deeply valued and loved. (I don't think she realized I was acting out of sheer obedience, not warm feelings.) After thanking me profusely, she said, "Now, we will do everything we can to get your computer as soon as possible. If we scrimp and save, we should be able to scrape together the money fairly soon."

In fact, we did come up with that money. We did buy "my computer" even before we went on our Europe trip, which had to be planned well in advance. Our trip turned out to be more wonderful than I had imagined, not just because Europe is delightful but mainly because Linda and I experienced intimacy far deeper than anything we had ever known. Looking back, I treasure that time as one of the great moments of our marriage. It was worth way more than $3,000.

Depending on your perspective, you might say that I did exercise my headship by making a decision when we were stuck. That's not quite right, though, because the decision was truly a consensus. You might also say that I submitted to Linda, choosing the way of a slave by giving up my rights. That wouldn't be quite right either because I didn't merely give in to her. I chose my course of action based on what I felt called to do as the head of my wife. In fact, my decision was both an act of submission and an act of leadership. I chose to give up my wishes (submission) and provided leadership in the form of self-giving sacrifice. Whether seen as submission or headship, I sought to love my wife as Christ loved the church.

As we saw in the "Explain the Story" section of this chapter, a husband's headship is more a matter of loving than exercising authority. Thus, when I think headship in the mode of Ephesians 5, I remember a man I'll call "Robert."

Robert had been married to Norma for twenty-five years when they first started attending the church I pastored in California. I knew them casually until Norma was diagnosed with serious breast cancer. Soon my pastoral engagement with Robert and Norma grew deeper as I prayed regularly for them, visited Norma in the hospital, and tried to help them find God's peace in a scary time. For a while, Norma seemed to thrive. But then she started getting sick because her cancer had spread to several vital organs. All of the treatments and all of the prayers she received did not help her physically. Before long, she became gravely ill and died.

During the time of her illness, I watched Robert love Norma. He devoted countless hours to her, sitting beside her, helping her take care of everyday needs, and caring for her in deeply intimate ways. Robert sacrificed time to be with his wife even though it hurt his business. He said that Norma was his real business. As Norma came to the end of her life, I heard Robert's prayers for her. I knew that he would do anything for his wife. He would gladly have given his life for her if he could.

As I was writing this section of the commentary, I remembered Robert. I hadn't thought of him in at least ten years. Now, if you are used to thinking of male headship in terms of authority, then this story does not have much to do with Robert's headship. But if we take seriously Paul's explicit instruction for husbands as head—love your wives, just as Christ loved the church—then what Robert did for Norma was a powerful demonstration of headship as it's explained in Ephesians. I suppose he did make decisions for Norma, especially when she became incapacitated. But his headship wasn't of the "someone's gotta make the call" variety. Rather, it was headship modeled on Christ: Christ the Savior, Christ the giver, Christ the nurturer, Christ the lover.

Living the Story of Christ's Love for the Church

Ephesians 5:21–33, though offering instruction on the marriage relationship, actually has more to say about Christ and his relationship with the church than about husbands and wives. This passage reveals truths about Christ and the church that are not found explicitly anywhere else in Scripture. In fact, this is the only place in Scripture where it says plainly that "Christ loved the church and gave himself up for her" (5:25).

Christ's love for the church is seen first of all in his saving sacrifice for her (5:25). His love for the church is revealed in tender washing of the church in order to make her holy and blameless (5:26–27). His love for the church is shown in his feeding and care for the church, which is his body (5:29). His love for the church reflects his unity with her (5:31–32).

Earlier sections of Ephesians show how important the church is to God and God's plan for the cosmos. The church is the body of Christ, "the fullness of him who fills everything in every way" (1:23). The church is the product of Christ's reconciling work on the cross (2:11–22). The church is the means by which God proclaims to the cosmos his eternal purpose in Christ (3:10–11). The church is the locus of God's work in the world today (4:7–16). All of this demonstrates the importance of the church both theologically and strategically. The church really matters in God's plan.

But the church is also in God's heart. God, incarnate in Jesus Christ, doesn't think of the church only instrumentally as a means of accomplishing God's eternal purpose. Rather, Christ loves the church. Out of love, Christ gave up his life for the church. Out of love, Christ washes and sanctifies the church. Out of love, Christ feeds and cares for the church. The church is not just Christ's project but his bride, his beloved.

What difference would make if we really believed this, if we allowed this theme of God's story to shape our own hearts? It's so common these days for people, including Christians, to rail on the church, to focus on its many shortcomings, and to minimize its goodness. Would we do this if we really believed Christ loved the church?

It's also increasingly common today for Christians to minimize the value of the church, to claim that we need Jesus, not the church. Post on Facebook that you love Jesus but not the church, and you'll get a slew of "likes." Yet if we were convinced that Jesus loves the church, would we be so quick to reject his beloved?

"But," one might protest, "the church is a mess. The church is nothing like Christ intended it to be. I can love the church as a theological ideal, but the real church is just not lovable."

I agree that the church has plenty of flaws. I've seen them, felt them, bemoaned them, and added to them. But does this allow us to fail to love the church? Consider the analogy of marriage. It's true that I have plenty of flaws. I make tons of mistakes. Nobody knows this better than my wife, Linda. But if you criticize me in her presence, her blood will boil. She might not take off your head because she's a godly person, but she will be deeply offended. She'll be more upset by your criticism of me than I will be. I expect Jesus knows that the church is flawed, but I wonder how he feels when we put down his bride?

How do we know that Jesus loves the flawed church? Because Ephesians 5 tells us so. This chapter reveals that Christ "loved the church and gave himself up for her" (5:25). In other words, he loved the church that was to come even before he died for her. He did not love the church only after the cross but also before the cross. Furthermore, this passage shows that Christ seeks to make the church holy by cleansing and washing her. Why does the church need this special treatment? Because it's a mess. But Christ loves the messy, flawed, broken church and is in the business of making it fully holy and blameless.

He calls each of us to join him in this work, not just because the church is central to his plan but also because he cherishes the church. Rather than taking potshots at the bride of Christ, shouldn't we find ways to affirm and embrace her? Rather than separating ourselves from the imperfect, wounded bride of Christ, shouldn't we join Christ in his work of washing, cleaning, feeding, and caring for her? If Christ loves the church so much that he gave up himself for her, shouldn't we also?

CHAPTER 14

Ephesians 6:1-4

📖 LISTEN to the Story

¹Children, obey your parents in the Lord, for this is right. ²"Honor your father and mother"—which is the first commandment with a promise—³"so that it may go well with you and that you may enjoy long life on the earth."

⁴Fathers, do not exasperate your children; instead, bring them up in the training and instruction of the Lord.

Listening to the text in the Story: Exodus 20:1–17; Deuteronomy 6:1–9; Proverbs 6:20; 13:1, 24; 23:24; Colossians 3:20–21; 1 Thessalonians 2:7–12.

The second section of the household code in Ephesians focuses on the relationship between children and parents.[1] This section echoes traditional Greco-Roman and Jewish teaching about family life, though Paul reshapes these cultural conventions in light of Christ. He begins by addressing children (6:1–3) before adding counsel for fathers (6:4).

🔨 EXPLAIN the Story

The four-verse section on the relationship between children and parents includes four imperatives: obey (6:1), honor (6:2), do not exasperate (6:4), and bring them up (6:4).

Children Obey Your Parents (6:1)

Each section of the household code in Ephesians begins by addressing those who had less cultural power: women, children, and slaves. This contrasts with the usual Greco-Roman practice of speaking just to the male head of the

---

1. For discussion of the household code in Greco-Roman society, see "Listen to the Story" for Chapter 13.

household. Paul regards women, children, and slaves as moral agents, people who can choose to live in light of God's story in their position in society.

Children, obey your parents (6:1). The first directive for children uses the standard Greek verb meaning "to obey,"[2] found here in the present imperative, which suggests ongoing obedience. That children should obey their parents was widely affirmed throughout the Mediterranean world. The Jewish wisdom tradition stated, "My son, keep your father's command, and do not forsake your mother's teaching" (Prov 6:20). When Ephesians supports the exhortation "Children, obey your parents" with the rationale "for this is right," both Gentile and Jewish readers would have agreed.

In the Lord (6:1). The distinctively Christian element of verse 1, "in the Lord," may or may not have been in Paul's original letter. The words *en kyriō* do not appear in some of the oldest manuscripts of Ephesians. Text critics are unsure whether "in the Lord" was added to the original text of Ephesians, perhaps under the influence of 5:22 and Colossians 3:20, or deleted by early scribes for some reason.[3] Though "in the Lord" is held to be authentic by most translators and commentators, it would be prudent not to put too much weight down on this phrase. But whether "in the Lord" is original or not, the larger context of Ephesians[4] and the mention of "the Lord" in 6:4 indicate that the obedience of Christian children happens in the Lord, that is, in the realm and community of Christ the Lord.

Children Honor Your Father and Mother (6:2–3)

Honor your father and mother (6:2). Following the imperative "obey your parents" comes a citation of a portion of the Ten Commandments, "Honor your father and mother."[5] This quotation is interrupted by a parenthetical comment, "which is the first commandment with a promise" (6:2). Paul wanted his primarily Gentile audience to know that obedience to parents is not just right but also beneficial. It leads to a blessed and lengthy life (6:3).

Commentators have wondered why Paul adds a quotation from the Decalogue after telling children to obey their parents. If just about everyone in the Greco-Roman world would agree that children should obey their parents, why bolster the opening imperative in this way?

I do not believe Paul cited the Decalogue mainly to provide moral support for the imperative "obey your parents." Rather, Paul was moving from the specific and rather passive command, "obey," to something more sweeping and

2. BDAG 1028–29 (*hypakouō*).
3. Metzger, *Textual Commentary*, 541–42.
4. See 1:9, 13; 2:6, 10, 13, 21; 4:17; 6:10.
5. Exod 20:12 LXX.

active, "honor." The Greek verb for "to honor" means "to value, show high regard for, honor, revere."[6] Surely children honor their parents by obeying them. But honor includes much more, not just following orders but living in such a way that parents feel valued by their children and are esteemed by their community because of their exemplary children. In the honor/shame culture of the first century, one of the finest things children of all ages could do was to live so that their parents were praised by their peers.

Thus, "Honor your parents" is more than a reason for "obey your parents." If anything, "honor" is even more important because of its favorable consequences (good life, long life). Yes, by all means children should obey their parents. But they should go beyond obedience to energetically honor their parents, both in how they treat them directly and in how they live in the world.

Fathers, Do Not Exasperate Your Children (6:4)

Do not exasperate your children (6:4). The exhortation to fathers begins with a negative.[7] In the world of the early Christians, fathers assumed primary responsibility for the upbringing of their children, though mothers participated as well.[8] The address to fathers could include mothers as well, but given the switch from "parents" in verse 1 to "fathers" in verse 4, it's likely that male parents are addressed here (with implications for mothers).

The verb translated as "exasperate" appears only one other time in the New Testament and means there "to make angry."[9] Ephesians 4:26 uses a related noun translated in the NIV as "angry."[10] Several English versions of the Bible read "do not provoke your children to anger" (NRSV, NLT, CEB, ESV) instead of "do not exasperate." The point of the text is not that fathers should never do anything to upset their children; sometimes children become angry even when their parents discipline them in a merciful and wise way. Rather, Paul is warning fathers about treating their children wrongly, thus giving them justifiable cause to be angry. What should fathers avoid? According to Andrew Lincoln, this imperative "rules out excessively severe discipline, unreasonably harsh demands, abuse of authority, arbitrariness, unfairness, constant nagging and condemnation, subjecting a child to humiliation, and all forms of gross insensitivity to a child's needs and sensibilities."[11]

---

6. BDAG 1004 (*timaō*). The Hebrew verb in Exod 20:12, *kabed* in the Piel, means "to make heavy, to honor, to glorify." See BDB 457–58.

7. This is similar to Colossians 3:21, "Fathers, do not embitter your children, or they will become discouraged."

8. See Cohick, *Women in the World*, Chapter 4, "Motherhood."

9. *parorgizō*, Rom 10:19.

10. Greek *parorgismos*. In the NT it is used only in Eph 4:26.

11. Lincoln, *Ephesians*, 406.

Though it's unlikely that Paul warned fathers against angering their children in response to some specific incident, he no doubt understood the potential for this kind of mistreatment of children. Fathers in the Roman world, who had ultimate and complete authority over their children, could easily abuse their power. Christian fathers were to avoid such injustice because their parental responsibility should be shaped not just by legal codes or cultural mores but mainly by the gospel of a gracious heavenly Father. Even as families (*patria*) derive their name from the Father (*patēr*) according to Ephesians 3:14–15, so human fathering should be shaped by the activity of God.

Fathers, Bring Up Your Children in the Training and Instruction of the Lord (6:4)

Given the previous instruction to children to obey their parents, we might expect the positive injunction for fathers to be something like "exercise wise authority over your children." But Paul focuses instead on the deeper purpose of parental authority. Fathers are supposed to "bring up" their children "in the training and instruction of the Lord" (6:4).

The verb translated as "bring up," *ektrephō* in Greek, has a literal meaning of "to provide food, nourish" and a related meaning of "to bring up from childhood, rear."[12] It is used only one other time in the New Testament in Ephesians 5:29: "They feed [*ektrephō*] and care for their body." In the Septuagint, *ektrephō* is often used in a material sense, but a couple of metaphorical meanings provide a background for Ephesians 6:4. The Septuagint version of Proverbs 23:24 reads in translation, "A righteous father brings up [children] well [*kalōs ektrephei*], his soul rejoices over a wise son."[13] Moreover, Psalm 22:2 in the Septuagint (our Psalm 23:2) says of the Lord "In a grassy place, there he caused me to settle; he nourished [*exethrepsen*] me by water of rest."[14] Thus, while the English term "bring up" in Ephesians 6:4 captures in part the verb *ektrephō*, it lacks the nuance of nurture. This verse does not picture a father standing back and giving orders to be obeyed but rather investing himself personally in the raising of his children.[15]

The words translated as "training and instruction" have similar meanings in Greek.[16] "Training" might carry an implication of discipline; "instruction" could be rendered as "admonishment."[17] They suggest positive instruction as well as correction when mistakes are made and warning to avoid them in the future.

12. BDAG 311.
13. My translation of Prov 23:24 LXX.
14. My translation of Ps 22:2 LXX.
15. See 1 Thess 2:7–12.
16. Greek, *paideia* and *nouthesia*.
17. BDAG 748–49 (*paideia*); BDAG 679 (*nouthesia*).

"Of the Lord" translates the Greek word *kyriou*, the genitive of *kyrios* meaning "Lord" and used in Ephesians mainly in reference to Christ. The Greek genitive could mean either "training and instruction done *by* the Lord [through fathers]" or "training and instruction *about* the Lord [done by fathers]." Though arguments can be made for either interpretation, the first has stronger support. Paul certainly wants fathers to teach their children the specifics of the faith. This would be in keeping with a centuries-old Jewish conviction.[18] But in our passage, Paul was not focusing only on what we might call religious education. Rather, fathers (and mothers) are participants in God's own work of bringing up their children. This is one specific example of what we saw previously in Ephesians 4:15–16: Christ is the source of the church's growth through the inspired efforts of each member. Similarly, he is the source of the growth of children in every facet of life through the inspired efforts of parents, not to mention the community of which they are members.

LIVE the Story

Living in Obedience

Ephesians 6:1 was the first memory verse I ever learned in Sunday school. Having recently moved, my family and I were visiting a new church in Hollywood, California. In my first grade class with Miss Kane, I learned to recite, "Children, obey your parents in the Lord: for this is right. Ephesians 6:1." I imagine that virtually everyone among the thousands of people attending Hollywood Presbyterian Church that day would have agreed that obeying one's parents is indeed the right thing to do.

Fast forward thirty years. It's Youth Sunday at this same church. Three high school students have been chosen to give the "sermon" that day. The first stands up and reads Ephesians 6:1. Then she begins her exposition, "The Bible says that children should obey their parents. But we don't believe this anymore. We believe that children need to determine for themselves how they are to live." As you might imagine, this didn't exactly sit well with many in the congregation, including the high school director who had invited the young lady to speak.

As scandalous as that moment might sound to some of us, the young "preacher" on Youth Sunday articulated a point of view that is pervasive in our culture. Many of us are so eager for children to be their own people, to find themselves, to follow their dreams, and to make their own choices that we aren't quite so sure about that "obey your parents" stuff, at least for children

18. See for example Deut 6:1–9.

beyond toddlerhood. As a pastor, I have watched well-intentioned parents let their children make choices that, in the long if not the short run, come back to bite them hard. Many of these parents are so busy that they have little time for their children, and they don't want to "waste" this time with the unhappy task of discipline. Others are so eager to be their children's friend that they abstain from the role of teacher, guide, and disciplinarian.

Ephesians 6:1 instructs children to obey their parents and reminds parents that their children's obedience is necessary if they are going to thrive. If fathers and mothers are going to be used by the Lord to raise their children, then they cannot shy away from giving their children guidance that needs to be obeyed. After all, our heavenly Father does this very thing with us.

Of course as children grow, they should take more responsibility for their own lives. We parents will help them do this wisely if we raise them with lessons to be learned, encouragements to be followed, boundaries to be heeded, and admonishments to be accepted. Through obedience to sensible, godly parents, children will learn how to be sensible, godly adults.

Honoring beyond Obeying

As important as obedience is for children, as they grow honoring of parents becomes even more vital. My own children are now legal adults who live away from home most of the year. Apart from our financial support for the one who is still in college, they are almost completely responsible for their own lives. They no longer honor me by obeying what I tell them because I no longer tell them to do things. Rather, they honor me by communicating with me on a fairly regular basis, receiving my advice graciously, sharing their lives with me, and wanting to spend time with me when we are together. More importantly, they honor Linda and me by the way they live their lives each day as people of self-discipline, kindness, holiness, and robust faith. We are honored by our children's achievements, to be sure, but far more by who they are and how they love.

There may very well come a time when their honoring of me takes a different shape altogether. I'm thinking of what happens when parents get old and can no longer care for themselves on their own. If the Lord allows me to "enjoy long life on the earth," perhaps because I have honored my own parents, then my relationship with my children will probably become the inverse of what it was when we started.

As a pastor, I have walked alongside many people who have entered this challenging, sad, sweet, anguishing, rewarding time of life of caring for their aging parents. Many of my peers are in this stage of life as well. I think, for example, of a friend I'll call "Danielle." From all I know of her, she was mainly an obedient daughter to her parents, who were marvelous examples of the kind of parenting commended in Ephesians 6:4. But now because her parents have enjoyed long lives, their relationship with Danielle has changed. If she were to obey everything they told her now, even things related to their own care, this would not always be best for them. So because Danielle so deeply loves her parents and because she honors them, at times she needs to tell them what they need to do. To put it bluntly, sometimes they need to obey her if their last years on this earth are to be blessed.

Honoring one's parents in this season of life is itself an act of obedience. It's doing what Scripture requires. But it is also an act of servanthood, an example of sacrificial service commended earlier in Ephesians. Making wise decisions to ensure your parents' wellbeing might not feel like submission, but it is a telling and moving example of active servanthood that goes beyond acquiescence to a deep offering of yourself in loving service to others.

Bringing Up Children as an Agent of the Lord

As we have seen, it's likely that the expression "bring them up in the training and instruction *of the Lord*" refers not as much to the content of the upbringing as to its divine source. We parents can talk about raising our own children, but in reality the Lord is raising his children through us.

We are not free to do as we please when it comes to our children. We certainly shouldn't exasperate them (6:4). We shouldn't do to or for them anything that dishonors the Lord. On the positive side, we are to do what God commends to us through Scripture and through the wisdom of his church. We are to model our own parenting on the gracious, truthful, just, and loving fatherhood of God.

In addition to parenting our children in God's way, the fact that we "bring them up in the training and instruction *of the Lord*" means that God is at work in and through us as we parent our children. When we lack wisdom, God is there to provide it. When our patience runs thin, God has more available. When our hearts break because our children have chosen a path we would never have wanted for them, we know that our heavenly Father shares our grief even as he gives us faith to pray for another way. Though parenting can sometimes feel like lonely work, the truth is that we are not alone. God is with us.

Surely God is with us through his Spirit. But God is also with us through his people, the church. The household code in Ephesians doesn't appear as an appendix unrelated to the rest of God's story in this letter. Rather, it is imbedded in both the letter and the story. Our parenting, like our marriage, happens in the context of the church. It is an activity of the body of Christ.

I have experienced this reality many times in my life. The first came when our son, Nathan, was baptized. (Presbyterians usually baptize infants.) Though I was the pastor of the church, Pastor Larry officiated in the baptism, and we stood before him as the parents. He asked the members of the congregation if they were committing themselves to join us in raising Nathan to know Christ and be his disciple. The congregation responded with a thunderous, "We do." I sensed more than ever before that Linda and I were not alone in this scary parenting thing. We had dozens of partners. I felt this again when our daughter, Kara, was baptized.

Today, I look back on all of those who lived out the commitment they once made to our family. I feel deep gratitude for my children's Sunday school teachers, camp counselors, youth leaders, mentors, and school teachers. I'm thankful for the parents of their friends who provided places of safety and fun as they grew up. I'm thankful for those who continue to support Nathan and Kara in adulthood, who visit them at school and take them out for dinner, who converse with them on Facebook, and who pray for them regularly. I'm sure Linda and I have contributed in no small measure to who our children are today. But there is no doubt in my mind that God has been bringing them up from the beginning, working through Spirit and church. For this I am filled with gratitude.

CHAPTER 15

Ephesians 6:5-9

📖 LISTEN to the Story

⁵Slaves, obey your earthly masters with respect and fear, and with sincerity of heart, just as you would obey Christ. ⁶Obey them not only to win their favor when their eye is on you, but as slaves of Christ, doing the will of God from your heart. ⁷Serve wholeheartedly, as if you were serving the Lord, not people, ⁸because you know that the Lord will reward each one for whatever good they do, whether they are slave or free.

⁹And masters, treat your slaves in the same way. Do not threaten them, since you know that he who is both their Master and yours is in heaven, and there is no favoritism with him.

Listening to the text in the Story: Exodus 1–15; 20:2–3; Leviticus 25:39–55; Mark 10:35–45; 1 Corinthians 7:21–24; 12:13; Galatians 1:10; 3:26–29; Colossians 3:22–4:1; Philemon; 1 Peter 2:18–21.

The third section of the household code in Ephesians focuses on slaves and masters.[1] Like the previous discussions in this code, and like the parallel passage in Colossians 3:22–4:1, Ephesians 6:5–9 begins by addressing those with less cultural power (slaves) before speaking to those with more cultural power (masters).

As we approach this passage, we face two formidable, interrelated barriers that might easily prevent us from understanding the text and its place in God's story. The first and most obvious barrier is our own aversion to the text's acceptance of slavery. The passage begins by telling slaves to obey their masters (6:5). Later, though masters are urged not to threaten their slaves, there is nothing that tells masters to stop owning human beings (6:9). There is no broad theological critique of slavery. Given the horrible history of slavery in the United States and the fact that many people, including Christians, have used texts like Ephesians 6:5–9 to justify the practice of slavery, we are understandably distressed by the apparent teaching of the passage. Such

---

1. For discussion of the household code in Greco-Roman society, see "Listen to the Story" for Chapter 13.

distress makes it difficult to read the text fairly (though I would suggest such discomfort can help us grasp its meaning more firmly).

The second barrier to our understanding of this passage contributes to the first, namely, our ignorance of slavery in the first-century Roman world along with our tendency to project into that world elements from the American experience that do not rightly belong there. As S. Scott Bartchy, an expert on slavery in the Greco-Roman world, writes, "It must be stressed that for the most part knowledge of slavery as practiced in the New World in the 17th–19th centuries has hindered more than helped achieving an appropriate, historical understanding of social-economic life in the Mediterranean world of the 1st century."[2] Among the differences between first-century slavery and that of the New World, Bartchy identifies the following:

> Racial factors played no role; education was greatly encouraged (some slaves were better educated than their owners) and enhanced a slave's value; many slaves carried out sensitive and highly responsible social functions; slaves could own property (including other slaves!); their religious and cultural traditions were the same as those of the freeborn; no laws prohibited public assembly of slaves; and (perhaps above all) the majority of urban and domestic slaves could legitimately anticipate being emancipated by the age of 30.[3]

Thus while Bartchy in no way minimizes "the inhumanity and aura of terror surrounding Roman slavery,"[4] he helps us to interpret Ephesians in its own cultural context before trying to make sense of its implications for our own day. The fact that Paul, like every other moral philosopher and religious teacher of his day, did not pursue an overt abolitionist agenda should not prevent us from taking seriously this section of the household code in Ephesians.

EXPLAIN the Story

The five-verse section on the relationship between slaves and masters speaks mainly to slaves (four verses). Though the NIV divides the instruction for slaves into three sentences, the Greek original is one sentence governed by

---

2. S. Scott Bartchy, "Slavery: New Testament," *ABD* 6:66. Bartchy's contribution to our understanding of first-century slavery is laid out most extensively in his monograph, *Mallon Chrēsai: First-Century Slavery and the Interpretation of 1 Corinthians 7:21*, SBLDS 11 (Missoula, MT: Scholars, 1973). In addition to the *ABD* article, Bartchy has written other excellent summaries of slavery in the early Christian era: see "Slaves and Slavery in the Roman World," in *The World of the New Testament: Cultural, Social, and Historical Contexts*, ed. Joel B. Green and Lee Martin McDonald (Grand Rapids: Baker Academic, 2013), 169–78; and "Slave, Slavery," *DLNT* 1098–1102.

3. Bartchy, "Slavery: New Testament," 6:66.

4. Bartchy, "Slaves and Slavery in the Roman World" (Green and McDonald), 172.

the imperative "obey" (6:5, Greek *hupakouō*). The next sentence contains one imperative for masters: "Treat" (6:9, Greek *poieō*).

The Behavior of Slaves in Light of Christ (6:5–8)

Slaves (6:5). This verse addresses "slaves" using the plural of the Greek noun *doulos*. Some English translations such as the KJV prefer to use "servants," but this masks the basic sense of *doulos*, which means "slave." Essentially, a *doulos* was the property of another person, not just a servant. Bartchy notes that a slave was "bodily and totally subjected to the practically unlimited power of an owner and the owner's heirs."[5] The Hellenistic historian Polybius associated slaves with cattle and household goods.[6] The Greek philosopher Aristotle taught that a slave is "a live article of property" and "a living tool."[7]

We cannot be sure what percentage of the original audience of Ephesians was composed of slaves, though Christianity counted many slaves among its early adherents. Scholars estimate the percentage of slaves in the Roman world to be around twenty or thirty percent of the population.[8] Millions of other people called freedmen and women had previously been slaves who bought or were given their freedom (manumission). Thus many who first encountered Ephesians would have heard 6:5–8 as speaking to them personally.

Obey your earthly masters with respect and fear (6:5). Slaves are to obey their masters "with respect and fear," more literally, with "fear and trembling."[9] This expression, which Paul used to describe his own attitude to the Corinthians (1 Cor 2:3) as well as the Corinthians' reception of Titus (2 Cor 7:15), suggests humility and deference. For us, the command to slaves to obey their masters is troubling. In contrast, those who first encountered this imperative wouldn't have been concerned by its acceptance of slavery. Rather, they might have been intrigued by the fact that Paul addressed slaves directly. Other ancient moral teachers had plenty to say to masters about ruling their slaves, but nothing by way of instruction for slaves themselves.[10] They were after all lumped in with property, tools, and cattle, which are not usually the recipients of ethical exhortation. Paul, however, saw slaves as moral agents, human beings who could choose to act responsibly. Twenty-first-century readers can easily miss the fact that by addressing them directly, Paul was honoring slaves as real people.

---

5. Bartchy, *World of the New Testament*, 170.

6. Polybius, *Histories* 4.38.4, 4.75.2 (Paton, LCL rev. ed.).

7. Aristotle, *Politics* I.II.5, 17; *Nicomachean Ethics* 8.11.7 (Rackham, LCL).

8. See Bartchy, *World of the New Testament*, 170, who estimates the percentage to be between sixteen and twenty. Lincoln, *Ephesians*, 417, says that "one-third of the population of Greece and Italy was enslaved."

9. Greek *phobou kai tromou*.

10. For a helpful compendium of Greco-Roman writings on slavery, see Thomas Wiedemann, *Greek and Roman Slavery* (Baltimore: Johns Hopkins, 1981).

With sincerity of heart, just as you would obey Christ (6:5). Yet Ephesians does not merely call for obedience by slaves. It also addresses the issue of their motivation. Verse 6:5 adds that slaves should obey "with sincerity of heart, just as you would obey Christ."[11] Verse 6:6 adds that they should not obey their masters "only to win their favor when their eye is on you."[12] Rather according to 6:7, slaves should "serve wholeheartedly."[13] Though many slaves in the Roman world did honorable and rewarding work such as doctoring, managing, or teaching, countless others engaged in difficult and disdained labor. Plus all slaves were working for masters who owned them as property. How would it be possible, therefore, for slaves to serve with pure motivation and genuine enthusiasm?

As slaves of Christ (6:6). The answer to this question comes through the way Ephesians 6:5–9 reframes the slave-master relationship in light of Christ. Verse 5 introduces this change in perspective by referring to the slaves' "earthly masters," implying the existence of another, nonearthly Master. Moreover, slaves should obey their masters "as [they] would obey Christ" (6:5). Verse 6 adds that slaves are to act "as slaves of Christ" rather than to be preoccupied with their human masters. What they do as slaves can, in fact, be "doing the will of God from [their] heart" (6:6). Verse 7 reorients the slaves' perspective even further by urging them to "serve . . . as if [they] were serving the Lord, not people." In this way, they can work "wholeheartedly" and enthusiastically (6:7). Furthermore, according to 6:8, slaves should know that the Lord will reward them for their efforts. The language of this verse, similar to what we find in 2 Corinthians 5:10 and Colossians 3:23–24, suggests an eschatological reward, though this does not exclude present-day blessings. Human masters can receive a similar reward since they share the same heavenly Master with their slaves. Ultimately, all human beings, no matter their earthly station, have one Master. Relationship with him reframes all other relationships.

Thus if slaves obey their human masters as they do their heavenly Master; if they see themselves primarily as slaves of Christ who can do God's will through their work; if they focus on serving the Lord rather than people; if they keep in mind the eternal reward laid up for them; and if they recognize that both they and their human masters have the same heavenly Master, then slaves can do their work with a fresh perspective and a willing attitude. They

---

11. The Greek phrase translated as "with sincerity of heart," *en haplotēti tēs kardias*, refers not so much to feelings as to the choice to serve willingly rather than to do so only by compulsion.

12. Greek *mē kat' ophthalmodoulian hos anthrōpareskoi*, literally, "not according to eye-slavery as human pleasers."

13. "Wholeheartedly" translates the Greek phrase *met' eunoias*, which means "with favor, affection, a good attitude, or willingness." See BDAG 409 (*eunoia*). The NRSV translates verse 7a as "Render service with enthusiasm."

can have "sincerity of heart" and "serve wholeheartedly" because they are serving the Lord more than their lord. They can be assured that their efforts will be rewarded if not by their human masters then for sure by their heavenly Master in the age to come.

The Behavior of Masters in Light of Christ (6:9)

According to Ephesians 6:7–8, slaves should serve their earthly masters wholeheartedly because the slaves "know that the Lord will reward each one for whatever good they do, whether they are slave or free" (6:8). The inclusion of those who are free introduces a transition from instructions for slaves to instructions for masters. Yet "or free" does more than provide a rhetorical shift. It also begins a radical revision of cultural assumptions about what it means to be a slave master.

And masters, treat your slaves in the same way (6:9). Ephesians 6:9 opens with an unexpected injunction to masters.[14] The ESV prefers a more literal rendering, "Masters, do the same to them." The Greek reads quite literally, "the same things do to them" (*ta auta poieite pros autous*). The words are not difficult to translate, but they raise a perplexing question. What are these "same things"? How can masters treat their slaves "in the same way" as slaves have been told to treat their masters?

Though the main verb of the exhortation to slaves is "obey," it seems unlikely that Paul is telling masters to obey their slaves. Yet even if they are the ones who give the orders, masters should nevertheless do so in a manner analogous to the way slaves serve them. Masters can give directions "with respect and fear," knowing that their slaves are really slaves of Christ who is Master of both slave and free (6:5, 8). Masters can exercise their authority "as slaves of Christ" who seek to do "the will of God" both in the content of their directives and in the way these are delivered (6:6). Masters can "serve wholeheartedly" in their oversight of slaves because they know that they will be rewarded by their heavenly Master if they exercise justice and mercy (6:7–8).

Still, given the curious ambiguity of "and masters, treat your slaves in the same way," we wonder if there is even more going on in this text. You'll recall that the household code in Ephesians began with an intriguing and unprecedented imperative, "Submit to one another out of reverence for Christ" (5:21). The exact sense of mutual submission is the subject of vigorous debate among biblical interpreters. Some proclaim quite confidently that, whatever mutual submission means, it certainly doesn't apply to slaves and masters. Clearly, these commentators assert, slaves submit to masters and never the other way around.

---

14. The Greek word for "masters" is the plural of *kyrios*, which means "master" or "lord." It is also the Greek word used in reference to Christ as Lord or Master, as found later in 6:9.

But is this really so clear? We tend to think of slaves in the mode of the American South where slaves were repressed and where educating slaves was illegal. In the Roman world, however, "an important minority of slaves had considerable prestige, social power and influence."[15] Many slaves were able to "take responsibility," serving as "doctors, teachers, writers, accountants, agents, bailiffs, overseers, secretaries, and sea-captains."[16] It's not hard to imagine a master submitting at times to the authority of a slave who happened to be his doctor, teacher, or sea captain.

What's more, it's easy to picture masters submitting to slaves in the context of church gatherings where all members are gifted by the Spirit to minister to the body. If a master and a slave shared a common church experience, there might be times when the slave would be gifted for teaching or prophesying. The master would in those occasions submit to a slave who served as a channel for the Spirit's inspiration. Mutual submission does not necessarily mean *simultaneous* submission. One submits to another in one time and one context. The roles are reversed in another time and another context.

Finally, as we discovered in our examination of Ephesians 5:21, Christian submission entails more than simply deferring to the dictates of another person. It involves choosing to act in the way of a servant, indeed, of a slave. Remember the parallel passage in Galatians, "You, my brothers and sisters, were called to be free. But do not use your freedom to indulge the flesh; rather, serve one another humbly in love" (Gal 5:13). Notice that all Christians, including those who are actual slaves, are called to be free in Christ. Notice too that all Christians, including both actual slaves and actual masters, are to "serve one another humbly in love." The verb translated here as "serve" is *douleuō* in Greek, related to the noun *doulos* meaning "slave." Thus all followers of Jesus, including slaves and masters, are called to exercise their freedom by serving as slaves to each other in love. Surely this means that human masters are called to humbly serve not just other free people but also slaves, including their own slaves.

Do not threaten them (6:9). Therefore, masters should not "threaten" their slaves to coerce them to obey. Such an exercise of power is inconsistent with the servanthood expected of all Christians, not to mention the fact that God regards all people, including slaves and masters, without favoritism.

Thus the instruction to masters to "treat [their] slaves in the same way," though not reversing the economic order of everyday life, suggests a wholly

---

15. Keith Hopkins, *Conquerors and Slaves: Urbanization in Developing Countries* (Cambridge: Cambridge University Press, 1978), 123.

16. Hopkins, *Conquerors*, 123.

different model, one centered in Christ who shows "no favoritism" (6:9), who is the Master of both slave and free, and who rewards all for the good they do, no matter their earthly status. Thus this portion of the household code is similar to that concerning wives and husbands; the work, presence, and example of Christ touches and transforms everything.

LIVE the Story

Ephesians 6:5–9 in God's Bigger Story

Any time we come across slavery in Scripture, we would do well to remember the exodus. In the book by that name, the Lord reveals himself to his people as the compassionate and gracious God: "I am the LORD your God, who brought you out of Egypt, out of the land of slavery" (Exod 20:2). In many ways, the exodus serves as a metanarrative that gives shape to the wider biblical story, a story of bondage to freedom.

Jesus reenacted and embodied this story by delivering us from slavery to sin and death (Rom 6:16–17). Galatians 5:1 boldly proclaims, "It is for freedom that Christ has set us free. Stand firm, then, and do not let yourselves be burdened again by the yoke of slavery." This yoke includes trying to earn God's favor by works of the law.

Yet ironically, Jesus freed us by taking on the nature of a slave (Phil 2:7, Greek *doulos*) and humbling himself even to the point of dying on a cross (Phil 2:8). The irony continues in that when we are set free from sin, death, and the demands of the law, we become "slaves of God" (Rom 6:22). Our service to our new Master involves offering our whole lives to him, including serving as slaves to each other (Gal 5:13). Those who are in Christ form a new community marked by Christlike love and Christ-forged unity: "There is neither Jew nor Gentile, neither slave nor free, nor is there male and female, for you are all one in Christ Jesus" (Gal 3:28).

As we have seen before, a vision of cosmic unity serves as the missional center of Ephesians. God is working out his plan "to bring unity to all things in heaven and on earth under Christ" (1:10). Christ's death on the cross not only offers salvation to individuals but also creates unity between formerly divided people. It formed the church as a unity between Jews and Gentiles. Christ also opened the way for families to sample the unity of God's future. In Christ, wives and husbands can be deeply united not just in theory but also in the day-to-day realities of married life. Parents can relate differently to their children because they are participating in Christ's own nurture of their children.

The wider story of God in Scripture also reshapes slavery, which was both a household structure and an economic system. Not only are slaves and free people united in the community of Christ, but also their way of relating to each other is transformed by Christ. In place of grudging obedience, slaves can discover in Christ an opportunity to serve wholeheartedly as "slaves of Christ" (6:6). Masters are called to treat their slaves in light of the fact that Christ is Master of all who rewards all without regard for their cultural status. Masters and slaves discover how they can serve each other and even submit to each other in the eschatological community of the church.

Why Not Abolition?

Yet we wonder why there isn't more. Why does Paul settle for reforming the relationship between slaves and masters rather than calling for the abolition of slavery itself?

In considering this question, we need, once again, to stretch our minds to grasp the nature of slavery in the Roman world. Not only was slavery in that context more ethically complex than slavery in the United States, but it also was so basic to economic and social life in the Roman Empire that "virtually no one questioned its morality," according to Bartchy. He continues, "Roman jurists and philosophers . . . seemed never to have doubted the practical necessity or moral appropriateness of this practice."[17] It is unrealistic to expect Paul to transcend his own culture and to think as a twenty-first century citizen of a free society. As N. T. Wright explains, "Paul could no more envisage a world without slavery than we can envisage a world without electricity."[18]

Moreover, given the realities of the Roman world, it's hard to make the case that a frontal assault on slavery would have been wise. As Wright explains in a commentary on Philemon, a letter Paul wrote on behalf of a runaway slave, a loud protest against slavery itself would "without a doubt, have done more harm than good, making life harder for Christian slaves, and drawing the young church exactly the wrong sort of attention from the authorities." Such damage to Christians and churches would have been "totally ineffective," according to Wright.

> One might as well, in modern Western society, protest against the mortgage system. Even if all Christians of Paul's day were suddenly to release their slaves, it is by no means clear that the slaves themselves, or society in general, would benefit: a large body of people suddenly

---

17. Bartchy, "Slaves, Slavery," *DLNT* 1098–1102.
18. N. T. Wright, *Paul for Everyone: The Prison Letters: Ephesians, Philippians, Colossians, and Philemon*, 2nd ed. (Louisville: Westminster John Knox, 2004), 70.

unemployed in the ancient world might not enjoy their freedom as much as they would imagine.[19]

Disruption Rather Than Destruction

Yet it's not as if Ephesians 6:5–9 blesses the institution of slavery. When we read carefully, we can see the seeds of slavery's undoing in these five short verses. Yes, they tell slaves to obey, but they also reframe slavery as primarily a matter of a slave's relationship with Christ. Slaves are not defined by being owned by their earthly masters but by their relationship to their heavenly Master. When they choose to serve Christ through their work, slaves begin to "unslave" themselves. As the fourth-century preacher John Chrysostom noted in his homily on this passage, "Serve on principle and by choice, not under compulsion. If you serve freely in this way, you are not a slave. If your service comes from your free choice, from good will, from the soul and on account of Christ, you are no slave."[20]

What Ephesians 6:8–9 says about masters is even more subversive of slavery's mindset. They will be rewarded by the one true Lord for the good they do, just like slaves (6:8). Both masters and slaves have one Master in heaven who shows no favoritism (6:9). This heavenly Master regards earthly masters and slaves equally. Thus human masters are to treat their slaves well, even in discovering how they might serve their own slaves in humble, loving imitation of Christ.

Ephesians 6:5–9 advocates the disruption of slavery, not its destruction. It upsets the assumptions that first-century people, including slaves, made about slavery, beginning with its instructions for slaves and ending with its stunning claim that masters are to treat their slaves "in the same way" because they and their slaves have the same Master in heaven.

Confronting Slavery Today

Although Ephesians does not advocate the abolition of slavery, and though it focuses on the relationship between slaves and masters, we would be remiss if we failed to mention the pressing issue of slavery today. If we live in the United States or Western Europe, it's easy to assume that slavery is a thing of the past. Yet for millions of people throughout the world today, even the Western world, it is a present reality.

---

19. N. T. Wright, *Colossians and Philemon*, TNTC (Downers Grove, IL: InterVarsity Press, 1986), 169.

20. John Chrysostom, "Homily on Ephesians" 22.6.5–8, ACCS 8, 2nd ed. (Downers Grove, IL: InterVarsity Press, 2006), 205.

The Walk Free Foundation publishes one of the most widely respected reports on slavery in today's world. According to their Global Slavery Index (http://www.globalslaveryindex.org), they estimate that 35.8 million people throughout the world lived as slaves in 2014. Though scholars debate the methodology behind this estimate, even if it is on the high side, it nevertheless testifies to the fact that millions upon millions of people in our world are slaves in need of liberation.[21]

Unlike first-century Christians, we are familiar with critiques of slavery. In fact, many of the most notable abolitionist battles have been fought in the name of Christ. Moreover, most of us do not live under the thumb of an empire with no ability to fight for meaningful social and economic change. Even if we individually do not have the resources to wage war against slavery, we can support Christian organizations that do this wisely. World Vision and International Justice Mission are two highly regarded organizations on the forefront of Christian efforts to fight slavery, usually called human trafficking. Such efforts are the outgrowth of the seeds planted in Ephesians 6:5–9 and reflect the wider story of God in which all things are being made right in Christ.

Workers and Bosses

As vital as it is for us to consider how the story of God inspires efforts to confront slavery in today's world, Ephesians 6:5–9 also speaks by analogy to one of the most common relationships in daily life, that of employees and bosses. If Paul were writing today, I wonder if he might say something like this:

> Employees, obey your earthly bosses with respect and fear, and with sincerity of heart, just as you would obey Christ. Obey them not only to win their favor when their eye is on you, but as employees of Christ, doing the will of God from your heart. Work wholeheartedly, as if you were working for the Lord, not people, because you know that the Lord will reward each one for whatever good they do, whether they are employees or bosses. Bosses, treat your employees in the same way. Do not threaten them, since you know that he who is both their Boss and yours is in heaven, and there is no favoritism with him.

If you're used to thinking of the workplace as part of the "real world" that is disconnected from matters of faith, this paraphrase will sound odd, even unduly invasive. But God doesn't divide the world into God's domain

---

21. See, for example, Neil Howard, "Keeping Count: The Trouble with the Global Slavery Index," *The Guardian*, January 13, 2014. http://www.theguardian.com/global-development-professionals-network/2014/jan/13/slavery-global-index-reports.

(church, family, personal life, mission trips) and everything else (work, play, politics, etc.). Rather, God is in the business of bringing to "unity all things in heaven and on earth under Christ" (1:10). All things include work, business, supervision, compensation, annual reviews, hiring, firing, production, marketing, and financing. We would do well to consider how Ephesians 6:5–9 informs our work and especially our relationships at work.[22] As we do, we'll discover that the story of God focused in the work of Christ touches and transforms everything.

---

22. For several years, I have been privileged to participate in the Theology of Work Project (www.theologyofwork.org), an ambitious effort to think theologically about every aspect of work. The main activity of this project has been writing a Bible commentary that examines every portion of Scripture that is relevant to work. I had the honor of contributing to this commentary, writing on Galatians, Philippians, and, yes, Ephesians. If you're looking for a more detailed exposition of the relevance of Ephesians 6:5–9 to daily work, I point you to The Theology of Work commentary on Ephesians (http://www.theologyofwork.org/new-testament/galatians-ephesians-philippians).

CHAPTER 16

Ephesians 6:10-20

📖 LISTEN to the Story

> [10]Finally, be strong in the Lord and in his mighty power. [11]Put on the full armor of God, so that you can take your stand against the devil's schemes. [12]For our struggle is not against flesh and blood, but against the rulers, against the authorities, against the powers of this dark world and against the spiritual forces of evil in the heavenly realms. [13]Therefore put on the full armor of God, so that when the day of evil comes, you may be able to stand your ground, and after you have done everything, to stand. [14]Stand firm then, with the belt of truth buckled around your waist, with the breastplate of righteousness in place, [15]and with your feet fitted with the readiness that comes from the gospel of peace. [16]In addition to all this, take up the shield of faith, with which you can extinguish all the flaming arrows of the evil one. [17]Take the helmet of salvation and the sword of the Spirit, which is the word of God.
>
> [18]And pray in the Spirit on all occasions with all kinds of prayers and requests. With this in mind, be alert and always keep on praying for all the Lord's people. [19]Pray also for me, that whenever I speak, words may be given me so that I will fearlessly make known the mystery of the gospel, [20]for which I am an ambassador in chains. Pray that I may declare it fearlessly, as I should.

> *Listening to the text in the Story:* Genesis 3:1–7; Psalms 11:2; 35:1–3; 120:2–4; Isaiah 11:4–5; 49:2; 52:7; 59:15–19; Luke 4:1–13; Romans 13:12–14; 1 Corinthians 15:24–26; 2 Corinthians 10:3–5; 1 Thessalonians 5:4–11.

After the extended household code of 5:21–6:9, Paul wraps up his moral exhortation with one final section. This is not an afterthought. Rather, it summarizes much of what has been revealed in Ephesians while urging readers to be armed and ready for the struggle of Christian living. If we are to walk worthy of our calling, then we will necessarily wrestle against "the spiritual forces of evil in the heavenly realms" (6:12). This fact could be intimidating except for the reassurance that God's strength is available to us (6:10). We can put on his "full armor" in order to stand firm in the battle against dark powers (6:11).

Verses 6:10–20 are a distinct subsection of Ephesians 4–6. They continue to explain how we are to live our calling (4:1). The warfare imagery sets this section apart from what has gone before. Moreover, 6:10–20 is introduced with the strong rhetorical divider "finally," while the remarks following 6:20 are not only exhortations but also closing greetings.

For the twenty-first-century reader, the biggest challenge of 6:10–20 is not understanding what its words mean, though there are a few verbal puzzles. Rather, our assignment is to decide how we understand our spiritual battle and how we will engage in it.

EXPLAIN the Story

Summary of Ephesians 6:10–20

The first two verses of this section urge us to "be strong in the Lord" by putting on his "full armor" (6:10–11). Verse 12 explains why we need divine power by revealing the spiritual nature of our enemies. Verses 14–17 identify the individual pieces of God's armor that we're to put on. These pieces are basic elements of our faith: trust, righteousness, peace, faith, salvation, and the word of God.

Verse 18 discloses what we should do when suited up for battle. Pray! We should pray not just a little every now and then but "on all occasions with all kinds of prayers . . . always . . . for all the Lord's people." At this juncture, Paul seeks prayer for himself and his work that he might "fearlessly make known the mystery of the gospel" (6:19). For this gospel, Paul is "an ambassador in chains" (6:20).

One could divide 6:10–20 into smaller subsections, such as: "6:10–13—Summons to Divine Warfare; 6:14–17—The Divine Armor; 6:18–20—Prayer as Struggle and Solidarity."[1] Yet such divisions may not be helpful. Since 6:14–17 is an explication of verses 11 and 13, it seems better to keep 10–17 together. Though the NIV begins a new paragraph with verse 18, supplying the imperative "pray," this is not supported by the Greek grammar. "Pray" is actually a participle, "praying," that is dependent on "take" in verse 17. If we were to make 6:18–20 a discrete subsection, we easily miss the profound connection between putting on spiritual armor and prayer.

---

1. So writes Yoder Neufeld, *Ephesians*, 292.

Fighting Our Spiritual Battle in God's Strength (6:10–20)

Finally, be strong in the Lord and in his mighty power (6:10). "Finally" makes it clear that we are beginning a new section and getting to the end of the moral exhortation in Ephesians. The present-tense imperative "be strong" suggests an ongoing process, "keep on being strong." This imperative comes in a form that can mean either "strengthen yourselves"[2] or "be strengthened" (middle/passive in Greek). Though the passive makes more sense here, there isn't much actual difference between these two options since we are to be strong "in the Lord and in his mighty power." No matter the grammar, our strength comes from God. "Mighty power" emphasizes the supremacy of God's power. It echoes what we read in 1:19, "his incomparably great power for us," and in 3:20, God is able to do "immeasurably more than all we ask of imagine, according to his power that is at work within us."

Put on the full armor of God (6:11). In order to be strong in the Lord, we must "put on the full armor of God" (6:11). "Put on" is the same verb found in 4:24, "put on the new self." It suggests that even if "be strong" means "be strengthened," there are things we can do so that God's power might fortify us: we can put on God's armor.

"Full armor" renders the Greek word *panoplia*, which has the diction-ary definition "all armor" (and is the root of the English word "panoply"). "Armor of God" could mean "the armor God supplies" or "God's own armor." At first glance, "the armor God supplies" seems like the obvious meaning. Yet Paul was drawing from Old Testament imagery that portrays God as an armed warrior. In Isaiah 59, for example, the Lord "put on righteousness as his breastplate, and the helmet of salvation on his head; he put on the gar-ments of vengeance and wrapped himself in zeal as in a cloak" (Isa 59:17).[3] In Psalm 35 the psalmist cries out to God to fight against his enemies: "Take up shield and armor; arise and come to my aid. Brandish spear and javelin against those who pursue me" (Ps 35:2–3). Thus while the "full armor" of God is that which God supplies to us, "of God" also indicates that we are wearing God's own armor. We are fighting God's battle with God's weapons.

So that you can take your stand against the devil's schemes (6:11). Only when we are clothed in God's armor will we be able to "take [our] stand against the devil's schemes." The term "devil," *diabolos* in Greek, appears only twice in the Pauline corpus outside of the Pastoral Epistles, here and in 4:27 ("do not give the devil a foothold"). *Diabolos* means "slanderer" in Greek and is regularly used in the Septuagint as a translation of the Hebrew *satan*, meaning "adver-sary," from which we get the name "Satan." In 2:2 the devil is identified as "the

---

2. Bruce, *Colossians, Philemon, Ephesians*, 403.
3. See also Isaiah 11:4–5; 49:2.

ruler of the kingdom of the air, the spirit who is now at work in those who are disobedient." In 6:11 the devil has his "schemes," the same Greek word found in 4:14 for "deceitful scheming" done by people outside of Christ. We can oppose the devil's schemes effectively only if we are wearing God's armor.

For our struggle is not against flesh and blood, but against the rulers, against the authorities, against the powers of this dark world and against the spiritual forces of evil in the heavenly realms (6:12). The word translated as "struggle" in 6:12 is *palē*, which appears only here in the New Testament. In secular Greek, it usually refers to a wrestling match, though it can also mean "battle."[4] Paul may have chosen this unusual word to emphasize the personal nature of our fight against evil. Yes, the battle against these powers is something that all of God's people share in together, but it is also true that each of us individually has been drafted into God's army.

These enemies are not "flesh and blood." They are not human. Though we might have conflicts with human beings and earthly institutions, behind them are myriad "spiritual forces of evil in the heavenly realms" (6:12). We encountered these forces and the "heavenlies" before in Ephesians. Verses 1:20–21 say that God "seated [Christ] at his right hand in the heavenly realms, far above all rule and authority, power and dominion, and every name that is invoked." Verse 3:10 says the church makes known God's wisdom "to the rulers and authorities in the heavenly realms." Though these powers are in the heavenly realms, they influence things on earth.[5]

Ephesians does not offer much detail on how this influence happens. In 2:2 the ruler of the air is "at work in those who are disobedient." In 4:26–27 anger can "give the devil a foothold." According to 6:11 the devil has "schemes" to hurt us. In 6:16 the evil one shoots "flaming arrows" at us. The whole passage from 6:10 onward makes it clear that the devil and his evil cohort are attacking us, so that we need God's strength to stand firm.

In his other writings, Paul gives hints about how Satan and his minions affect our lives. Satan can tempt us sexually (1 Cor 7:5). He can urge us to not forgive others (2 Cor 2:10–11). He can torment us through "a thorn in [the] flesh" (whatever that means, 2 Cor 12:7). Once, Satan blocked Paul's effort to visit Thessalonica (1 Thess 2:18). Satan uses "all sorts of displays of power through signs and wonders," just like the "lawless one" who will come as his representative (2 Thess 2:9).

From Paul's writings, we receive only tantalizing tidbits on how the devil works to oppose us. This lack of information about Satan is no accident. For Paul, an encyclopedic knowledge of the devil is not needed precisely because

---

4. LSJ 1291.
5. Plus, because of God's grace, we too inhabit "the heavenly realms in Christ Jesus" (2:6).

Christ has defeated him and his powers (Eph 1:20–21; Col 2:8–15). Our struggles with evil forces matter, but we don't need to worry about how the story will end. Christ has already secured victory, and we get to participate in it both in our current struggle and in our future celebration.

The list in Ephesians 6:12 of spiritual entities that oppose us is not meant to be a catalogue of all possible powers or a map of demonic hierarchy. Rather, it represents all evil spiritual powers. As Yoder Neufeld observes, "Whatever the origins of these terms, they are intended to be shorthand for the myriad of powers, great and small, personal and impersonal, individual and systemic, that resist the saving activity of God among humanity."[6]

Contemporary readers might stumble over the idea that there are supernatural evil powers affecting our lives on earth. In the last fifty years, an alternative understanding of the powers has grown in popularity among interpreters of the New Testament.[7] This interpretation demythologizes the powers by seeing Paul's language as an ancient way to describe what we talk about with the language of politics, economics, psychology, and social theory. Even if Paul believed that the powers were actual supernatural beings, it is contended, we know better because such beings do not exist. Yet militarism, materialism, nationalism, and a variety of others "isms" do exist and do exercise power through cultures and institutions, which Paul portrayed as demonic powers. This reading of Paul's language may appeal to modern thinkers, but it fails to do justice to Paul's understanding, and it has failed to convince millions of Christians whose worldview is not shaped by Western philosophical materialism.[8]

Therefore put on the full armor of God, so that when the day of evil comes, you may be able to stand your ground, and after you have done everything, to stand (6:13). Verse 13 begins with an imperative similar to that of verse 11: "Put on the full armor of God." The NIV is not the most precise, since the Greek verb is more in the direction of "take up, take along, take in hand."[9] We must pick up God's armor because of the nature of our opposition and so that we may be able to stand "when the day of evil comes." "The day of evil" could refer to all the time before God unites everything in Christ. In this case, it would be

---

6. Yoder Neufeld, *Ephesians*, 296.

7. See, for example, Hendrik Berkhof, *Christ and the Powers* (Scottdale, PA: Herald, 1977). For enlightening introductions to the question of the cosmic powers, see D. G. Reid, "Principalities and Powers," *DPL* 746–52; Craig Keener, "Paul and Spiritual Warfare," in *Paul's Missionary Methods: In His Time and Ours*, ed. Robert L. Plummer and John Mark Terry (Downers Grove, IL: InterVarsity Press, 2012), 107–23; Gombis, *Drama*.

8. In several writings, Walter Wink sought to reinterpret the biblical language of powers without affirming their supernatural character. Wink summarizes his academic writings in *The Powers that Be: Theology for a New Millenium* (New York: Doubleday, 1999).

9. BDAG 66–67 (*analambanō*).

another way of saying that the days are evil, as in 5:16. Alternatively, "the evil day" might point to a particularly difficult time of eschatological wrestling, a time when we need God's armor more than ever.

Stand (6:13). Verse 13 uses two verbs related to standing. The first is *anthistēmi*, which means "stand against" and is translated in the NIV as "stand your ground." It suggests standing firm in the face of an attack. The second standing verb in 6:13 is *histēmi*, the basic Greek word for "stand." This picture of standing firm in the face of attack suggests to many interpreters that Christians should adopt a defensive posture and a "turn the other cheek" response to cosmic attack. After all, verse 13 does not say, "stand when attacked and then hit back." But, as we'll see, standing in the face of evil means more than merely withstanding the onslaught of evil.

And after you have done everything (6:13). The Greek verb translated as "you have done" is *katergazomai*, which has a common meaning of "to achieve, accomplish, do, bring about, prepare."[10] In Paul's other writings, it always has this meaning. But *katergazomai* can also mean "to overpower, subdue, conquer, prevail upon."[11] Given the particular context in which this word functions in verse 13, such a meaning is possible. Yoder Neufeld renders the last part of verse 13 as, "And having conquered completely, to be standing."[12] In this case, standing is not a defensive posture but a celebration of a victorious offense in battle.

Stand firm then, with the belt of truth buckled around your waist, with the breastplate of righteousness in place (6:14). Verse 14 begins with the imperative, "stand" (*histēmi*), which is followed in verses 14–16 with four grammatically dependent participles in the aorist tense, each participle being connected to a specific piece of armor: *having wrapped around*—belt of truth; *having put on*—breastplate of righteousness; *having fastened under*—shoes of the gospel of peace; *and having taken up*—shield of faith. The two pieces of armor in verse 17 are covered by another imperative.

Paul's use of armor imagery was inspired by the Old Testament, especially Isaiah 59:17: the Lord "put on righteousness as his breastplate, and the helmet of salvation on his head." Both of these pieces of armor appear with the same sense in Ephesians 6:14–17, which shows clearly Paul's dependence on Isaiah. Yet in 1 Thessalonians 5:8, he writes about "putting on faith and love as a breastplate, and the hope of salvation as a helmet." The variations in the meaning of the armor indicate that Paul does not have one fixed schema whereby one piece of armor always has the same meaning. Rather, his use of

---

10. BDAG 531.
11. LSJ 924.
12. Yoder Neufeld, *Ephesians*, 298.

armor imagery is fluid.[13] Thus we must beware of injecting too much allegorical meaning into Paul's choice of armor (for example, "The helmet of salvation shows that salvation protects our thinking capacity").

We should pay close attention, however, to what is represented by the armor. It matters considerably that truth is numbered among the pieces of armor and is mentioned first. Throughout Ephesians, truth is an indispensable element of Christian faith and life.[14] This is not truth in general or ordinary truth-speaking. Rather, it is the truth communicated in the gospel (1:13) and embodied in Jesus (4:21). This is our first piece of armor.

The "breastplate of righteousness" is mentioned explicitly in Isaiah 59:17 as something the Lord put on to bring judgment and justice to his people. Thus it's not likely that the "breastplate of righteousness" in Ephesians refers to the righteousness of Christ applied to us. Rather, in this context righteousness is acting rightly according to God's standards. It is being in right relationship with God and people. It is righteousness in individual relationships and justice in social structures.

And with your feet fitted with the readiness that comes from the gospel of peace (6:15). A participle meaning "having fastened under," which depends grammatically on the imperative "Stand" in verse 14, is translated here as "fitted." Footwear is not mentioned explicitly but is implied by the verb and the mention of feet. Fitting our feet with "readiness" suggests intentional preparation for battle. A soldier would not want to go to war barefooted. The CEB captures this well: "Put shoes on your feet so that you are ready to spread the good news of peace."

The phrase "gospel of peace" associated here with feet echoes Isaiah 52:7, "How beautiful on the mountains are the feet of those who bring good news, who proclaim peace, who bring good tidings, who proclaim salvation, who say to Zion, 'Your God reigns!'" Peace plays a central role in Ephesians as that which Christ forges through his death. Verses 2:14–16 read, "For he himself is our peace, who has made the two groups one and has destroyed the barrier, the dividing wall of hostility, by setting aside in his flesh the law with its commands and regulations. His purpose was to create in himself one new humanity out of the two, thus making peace." Even as Christ preached peace to people far and near (2:17), so we are to be ready to do the same as we prepare for battle with cosmic powers (see also 3:7–11).

---

13. See also Wisdom 5:17–20 NRSV: "The Lord will take his zeal as his whole armor, and will arm all creation to repel his enemies; he will put on righteousness as a breastplate, and wear impartial justice as a helmet; he will take holiness as an invincible shield, and sharpen stern wrath for a sword, and creation will join with him to fight against his frenzied foes."

14. See 1:13; 4:15, 21, 24, 25; 5:9.

In addition to all this, take up the shield of faith, with which you can extinguish all the flaming arrows of the evil one (6:16). The metaphor of flaming arrows appears in the Old Testament, though not with reference to Satan (see Ps 7:13; Prov 26:18). In Ephesians 6:16 "flaming arrows" represent whatever Satan and his minions are able to "shoot" at Christians to hurt them. The use of "extinguish" to describe the function of a shield might seem odd to us. We might imagine a shield blocking the flaming arrows but not quenching them. The language of this verse would have made sense in its original context, however. Roman soldiers used large shields covered in leather. Since their shields were vulnerable to flaming arrows, the soldiers would wet their shields before battle. Thus the shields would actually quench the flames of the arrows. Craig Keener observes that since the protection of a Roman army required all the shield bearers to march together in formation, verse 16 underscores something implicit throughout this passage, namely, that Christians must fight together, not alone.

How does faith extinguish demonic attack? If the particular attack is doubt, then faith will effectively quench it. But more is intended here. The Greek phrase behind "shield of faith" could also be translated "shield of *the* faith." It points to faith not just as trust in God but also as the core of Christian belief, as in 4:5 and 13. Thus the shield of the faith enables us to extinguish flaming arrows, not just of doubt but also of unbelief and false belief. It extinguishes "all" of the devil's arrows.

Take the helmet of salvation and the sword of the Spirit, which is the word of God (6:17). This verse includes a new imperative, "take" (*dexasthe*). "The helmet of salvation" appears as part of God's armor in Isaiah 59:17. 1 Thessalonians 5:8 mentions "the hope of salvation as a helmet" that encourages us in times of trial. In Ephesians the "helmet of salvation" refers mainly to our experience of salvation by grace through faith (2:8). When we remember that once we lived subject to satanic power (2:1–2) but God saved us because of his "great love" and "grace" (2:4–5), we can have confidence that we are protected from ongoing demonic attack.

When we hear "the sword of the Spirit, which is the word [*rhēma*] of God," we naturally think that it must symbolize the Bible. No doubt there is a close relationship between the sword/word of 6:17 and Scripture, but this is not what Paul means in 6:17. For one thing, the Bible as we know it didn't exist in his day. The Old Testament canon of inspired writings may have been known through the Septuagint, the Greek translation of the Hebrew Scriptures. But the New Testament was in the process of being written. Moreover, earlier in Ephesians Paul identifies the "message [*logos*] of truth" with "the gospel of your salvation" (1:13). In Romans 10:8 he wrote, "'The word [*rhēma*] is near you; it is in your mouth and in your heart,' that is, the message [*rhēma*] concerning faith that we proclaim." A few verses later Paul adds, "Consequently, faith comes from hearing the message, and the message is heard through the word [*rhēma*] of Christ" (10:17). So Paul was lifting up the core truth of God's work in Christ, something closely related to the truth that is buckled around our waist and the gospel we wear as a helmet. The gospel, the word of God, may be the most powerful weapon in our spiritual arsenal.

The "sword of the Spirit" is the only obviously offensive weapon in God's armor. The Greek word translated as "sword" is *machaira*, which was the smaller of two blades carried by Roman soldiers.[15] This has led some interpreters to claim that the "sword of the Spirit" is not actually an offensive weapon at all, but rather a defensive one.[16] But in fact the *machaira* functioned both defensively and offensively, especially in hand-to-hand combat.[17] Yoder Neufeld points out that *machaira* is used in the Septuagint for the sword God uses as the Divine Warrior.[18] So the sword of the Spirit, the word of God and all that goes along with it, enables us to engage in spiritual warfare not just defensively but offensively too.

It's curious that Ephesians 6 does not appear to instruct us to fight with the armor we have put on, including the sword of the Spirit. According to the text, we are to put on the armor and take up our weapon in order to stand (6:13–14). Many interpreters believe this means we are simply to resist attack, not to fight offensively. But this interpretation is inconsistent with the image of God as a warrior. Since we are wearing God's armor, shouldn't we also engage in God's battle? Has God given us truth, righteousness, peace, faith, salvation, and his word simply to protect us from attack? Or are these also to be used offensively as well?

The fact that we have been given a sword points in the direction of offense. Plus, when we remember that God plans for the church to demonstrate his wisdom to "the rulers and authorities in the heavenly realms" (3:10), this surely suggests something more than merely standing in a defensive posture. The last part of 6:10–20 shows us yet another way we are to do battle, one of the most powerful tools in our arsenal.

And pray in the Spirit on all occasions with all kinds of prayers and requests. With this in mind, be alert and always keep on praying for all the Lord's people (6:18). In the NIV and many other translations, 6:18 starts a new paragraph beginning with the imperative "pray." The Greek, however, features a

15. BDAG 622. See also Heb 4:12, "For the word [*logos*] of God is alive and active. Sharper than any double-edged sword [*machairan*]."
16. Berkhof, *Christ and the Powers*, 43.
17. Keener, "Spiritual Warfare," 113.
18. Yoder Neufeld, *Ephesians*, 303.

participle dependent on the imperative from verse 17: "Take the helmet . . . praying." In other words, verses 18–20 do not introduce prayer as a new subject. Rather, they complete the thought of verses 10–17. They help to answer the question of what we do once we've put on God's armor. How do we engage in God's battle? We pray.

We don't just pray a little bit, either. Verse 18 contains four different uses of the Greek word meaning "all": "And pray in the Spirit on *all* occasions with *all* kinds of prayers and requests. With this in mind, be alert and *always* keep on praying for *all* the Lord's people."

Three additional phrases in verse 18 explain how we are to pray. First, we are to pray "in the Spirit [*en pneumati*]." This could refer to praying in an unknown language (see 1 Cor 14:13–19) but should not be limited to praying in tongues. According to Romans 8:26–27, the Spirit helps us as we pray and even intercedes for us.

Second, we are to "be alert." This doesn't simply mean that we shouldn't fall asleep while praying. Rather, it urges us to be attentive to what needs prayer and how God wants us to pray. With the same verb as in Ephesians 6:18, Jesus urges his disciples to "be alert" to the eschatological signs of the times (Mark 13:33). The fifth-century theologian Theodoret put it this way: "Those who have wars continually pressing on them do not even sleep. Therefore, the holy apostle tells them under conditions of battle to keep awake and pray constantly, not giving in to the pains of the body but to bear them with the utmost fortitude."[19]

Third, we are to "always keep on praying." The original reads more literally "being alert in all perseverance and prayer." The Greek noun *proskarterēsis*, meaning "perseverance, patience," occurs only here in the New Testament.[20] But a related verb, *proskartereō*, is often linked with prayer. Acts 1:14, for example, says the disciples of Jesus "joined together *constantly* in prayer." Romans 12:12 urges us to be "*constant* in prayer" (ESV; emphasis added).

Pray also for me, that whenever I speak, words may be given me so that I will fearlessly make known the mystery of the gospel (6:19). The readers of Ephesians should pray for "all the Lord's people [*pantōn tōn hagiōn*]," including Paul. He used the general exhortation to pray as an occasion to seek prayer for himself. He desired prayer in support of his evangelistic mission, asking that a word (*logos*) be given him when he opened his mouth. The passive implies that this word would be given from God. Also Paul's readers should pray that he "will fearlessly make known the mystery of the gospel." "Fearlessly" renders the Greek phrase *en parrēsia*. "Boldly" as found in the NRSV, ESV, and KJV is

19. Theodoret on 6:18 in "Epistle to Ephesians," ACC 8:214.
20. BDAG 881.

preferable. *Parrēsia* appears in Ephesians 3:12 in reference to our freedom in relationship with God. In 6:19 it describes the manner in which Paul sought to proclaim the good news. Even as first-century secular philosophers prized their *parrēsia*, their freedom to speak with boldness, Paul desired this very thing in his preaching.

For which I am an ambassador in chains. Pray that I may declare it fearlessly, as I should (6:20). Paul uses the same verb "to be an ambassador" in 2 Corinthians 5:20 where he says, "We are therefore Christ's ambassadors." But in Ephesians, Paul's ambassadorial role is ironic. He claims to be serving as an ambassador, a position worthy of honor in the Roman world. Yet in fact he was in chains and a socially dishonored prisoner because of his ambassadorial effort (see 3:1; 4:1). The final part of verse 20 reiterates in slightly different language what Paul had requested in verse 19, namely, that he declare the gospel fearlessly or boldly, adding "as I should." To the Corinthians Paul wrote, "For when I preach the gospel, I cannot boast, since I am compelled to preach. Woe to me if I do not preach the gospel!" (1 Cor 9:16). He was under compulsion not only to preach the gospel but also to do it boldly. Such boldness comes from God, which is why Paul asks his readers to pray for this specific need.

In 6:10–20 prayer is not identified with a piece of armor. Rather, it is portrayed as what we do once we have put on our armor. We fight not just defensively but also offensively through prayer. Yes, we also fight by wielding the sword of the Spirit, the good news of God's work in Christ. But as Paul demonstrated by his own request for prayer, even this offensive effort depends on prayer because it requires God's power. Prayer is arguably the most important activity in our battle with the powers of darkness.

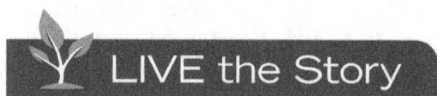

LIVE the Story

As we have seen throughout the ethical sections of Ephesians 4–6, we live the story by doing what the text urges. Thus we live the story of 6:10–20 by being strong in the Lord, putting on his armor, and praying.

Dodging the Devil

I grew up in a Bible-believing family. We were deeply engaged in a Bible-believing church. Yet I rarely heard about the devil, and never to my recollection heard one word about "the spiritual forces of evil in the heavenly realms." I thought of the devil mainly as a frowned-upon Halloween costume or the antagonist of comedian Flip Wilson's famous one-liner, "The devil made me do it." During my boyhood, I never gave Satan or his demonic minions a second thought.

That is, until I read *The Exorcist*.[21] Because of the popularity of the movie, when I was a junior in high school I decided to read William Peter Blatty's bestselling novel. The fact that it was based on a true story augmented my curiosity. I started this 300-plus page book one evening at about ten o'clock, figuring that I'd read for an hour before bed. Seven hours later, at five in the morning, I finished *The Exorcist*. I was exhausted, terrified, and utterly unable to sleep. If this book really was based on a true story, then the devil was horrifyingly real and nothing to make fun of through silly costumes or funny jokes.

Yet my juvenile fear of the devil disappeared before long. I majored in philosophy in college, learning to understand the world without recourse to "naive supernaturalism." I believed in God and the basic doctrines of Christian faith but managed to steer wide of "the devil" as I studied the Bible. I happily avoided passages like Ephesians 6:10–20 with its primitive idea of how the cosmos worked.

Then, in grad school, I discovered a way of reading the New Testament that didn't ignore the principalities and powers but rather reinterpreted them in a mode that made sense to my rationalistic and scientific worldview. Theologians like Hendrik Berkhof[22] and John Howard Yoder[23] convinced me that the language of cosmic powers was a prescientific way of talking about what we describe with the language of sociology, economics, psychology, and social theory. There really were powers beyond individual human beings, the powers of culture, militarism, materialism, racism, and sexism. Paul talked about these powers as if they had personalities. We now understand that they are real and truly evil, but not supernatural so much as cultural.

When I shared my new understanding of the powers with my Christian friends, some were relieved. They could be biblical Christians without having to believe all that weird stuff about demons. Other friends were concerned that I had abandoned a central doctrine of the faith. "Even if I have," I responded, "what's the big deal? What difference does the reality of the devil make in your life?" My friends had no answer.

But when I left the insular life of graduate school, my devil-free worldview began to be threatened. Partly, I got to know servants of Christ who served in places around the globe where the demonic was unmistakable. One told me, "Don't even think of doing mission work in Brazil unless you're prepared to cast out demons." This man wasn't a spiritual extremist but a deeply mature, wise, biblical, and rational servant of God. I couldn't dismiss what he told me. And I certainly wasn't ready to do mission work in Brazil!

---

21. William Peter Blatty, *The Exorcist* (New York: Harper and Row, 1971).
22. Berkhof, *Christ and the Powers*.
23. John Howard Yoder, *The Politics of Jesus* (Grand Rapids: Eerdmans, 1972).

Moreover, as I became familiar with people who were not, like me, products of Western rationalism and philosophical materialism, I realized just how much my worldview was shaped by my limited culture and experience. Who was I to dismiss those who took demonic reality seriously just because it didn't reflect my own cultural bias? Was it time for me to learn from those whose experience and wisdom exceeded my own?

As I began to embrace a broader understanding of reality, one that included personified evil powers, I found that I could make sense of Scripture without dismissing the supernatural elements. When Jesus cast out demons, he really did cast out demons. And when Paul mentioned "the spiritual forces of evil in the heavenly realm," he wasn't just using old-fashioned language to identify socioeconomic realities. Yes, powers such as materialism, nationalism, and racism truly exist among human beings. But these powers can be animated by something beyond collective humanity. They can be instances of genuine supernatural evil.

At this point, you may be inclined to quote C. S. Lewis to me, the part from *The Screwtape Letters* that warns us against feeling "an excessive and unhealthy interest" in devils. Indeed, I know some Christians who pay so much attention to evil powers that they have almost misplaced Christ as the center of their faith. But in my slice of the Christian world, we would do well to pay more attention to the demonic reality, not less. In fact, here's what Lewis actually wrote in the preface to *The Screwtape Letters*: "There are two equal and opposite errors into which our race can fall about the devils. One is to disbelieve in their existence. The other is to believe, and to feel an excessive and unhealthy interest in them. They themselves are equally pleased by both errors and hail a materialist or a magician with the same delight."[24] Thus I no longer dodge the devil intellectually, though I certainly try to dodge him as I live my life.

Learning Not to Demonize the People Who Oppose Us

What difference would it really make if we were to acknowledge the reality of our spiritual warfare against the powers of darkness?

First of all, if we take seriously the fact that our struggle is not against flesh and blood, then we'll avoid "demonizing" human beings who appear to be our opponents. Whether we're fighting global terrorism, denominational disagreements, or neighborhood battles, it's easy for us to imagine that the people who oppose us are the real enemy. From there our hearts can slip into hatred; we cannot bring ourselves to love those who disagree with us and we justify our contempt for others. But if we recognize that our true battle is with spiritual

---

24. C. S. Lewis, *The Screwtape Letters* (New York: Macmillan, 1943), preface.

powers, not with flesh and blood, then we will find it easier to love both our neighbors and our enemies.

Not long ago, I found myself tempted to demonize someone who was making my life extremely difficult. As I tried to honor God in my ministry, this person stood in my way time and again. He viciously spurned my efforts to reach out to him. As he looked at me with animosity in his eyes, I was tempted to return the same. Yet I would tell myself—or perhaps the Spirit of God would remind me—that this man was not my real enemy. I'd beg the Lord to give me compassion for this brother.

Surely it was crucial for my own soul not to be filled with hatred for another human being for whom Christ died. Yet it was also crucial for my leadership. When I found myself demonizing this man, I was not able to make wise, balanced, godly decisions about how best to move forward in ministry. My thinking was twisted by my contempt. On the contrary, when God helped me see that my apparent opponent was not really my opponent, then I could make better strategic decisions. I could even choose to love him through my actions no matter what I felt in my heart.

Seeing our true opponents as other than flesh and blood does not mean we minimize the reality of evil. Quite to the contrary! It means that we see people accurately and can confront the evil they do without turning them into personified evil. It means our hearts can remain open to loving our human enemies and treating them in a loving way, all without abandoning the battle for the gospel.

Fighting Our Spiritual Battle in God's Way

If we acknowledge that our struggle is not against human beings but against demonic powers in the heavenly realms, then we should be eager to fight this battle in the right way. More to the point, we will want to fight it in God's way, in the way God commends and fights.

In some segments of the church today, believers easily, even eagerly, recognize the demonic dimension of our battle. Our fellow believers don't buy the passive standing position advocated by some interpreters of Ephesians 6:10–20. Rather, they go on the offensive against evil. Some focus on exorcism and deliverance, casting out demons as a centerpiece of their ministries. Others practice an unusual sort of prayer that concentrates on rebuking the devil and his demonic minions, taking authority over these powers in the name of Christ. I have "prayed" with some people who spend more time talking to the principalities and powers than they do talking to the Lord.

Now, the practices I have just described may be godly and wise, at least when practiced by godly and wise people. The example of Jesus and the early church shows that there are times when demons need to be cast out of people. But this is not taught in Ephesians 6:10–20. Plus there is nothing in this text to support a battle plan that revolves around speaking to the fallen heavenly powers. Nothing in this passage suggests that we are to fight against the spiritual forces of evil primarily by rebuking them, commanding them, or otherwise using our words to claim authority over them. Yes, we are to engage in the struggle against the dark powers but in ways that seem much more mundane than we might expect.

According to Ephesians 6:10–20, we are to fight principally by putting on God's full armor. And what is God's armor? It consists of truth, righteousness, peace, faith, salvation, and the word of God. If we are to fight God's battle in God's way, here are the majors in which we need to major both as individuals and as God's people together.

These pieces of God's armor are certainly less exciting than engaging in verbal warfare with demonic powers. Plus, you're probably not going to write a bestselling novel about someone who rather than exorcising demons devotes his or her life to the unglamorous fight of truth, righteousness, peace, faith, salvation, and the word of God. This sounds more like a Sunday school curriculum than a hit movie. But Ephesians 6:10–20 is clear, even if it feels at first rather lackluster.

In the previous section I spoke of how this passage challenged me not to demonize someone who was making my life miserable and my ministry less effective. I have no doubt that my engagement with this man was part of a spiritual battle. I don't imply that he was the only one being influenced by spiritual forces. I'm quite sure I was also as some of the flaming arrows of the evil one got by my lowered shield. There were times I did and said things I now regret.

But there were also times when I put on the armor of God. In prayer I would ask the Lord, "Am I really committed to the truth of the gospel? Am I acting in righteousness? Am I seeking peace? Am I putting my faith in you? Am I remembering your salvation? Am I wisely believing, speaking, and living your word?" As I pondered these questions, I would commit myself once again to these basics. Sometimes the Lord would show me where I had let his armor slip and how I could wear it more faithfully.

As I describe this experience, I do not want to imply that fighting in God's way is something we do only as individuals. To be sure, each of us contributes personally to the battle. But this battle isn't my private battle or your private battle. Rather, it's a battle we share together as God's holy people. We put on God's armor as individuals and also as a community. As I struggled with the piece of the battle assigned to me, I had fellow soldiers standing with me.

I had righteous advisors who helped me discern God's truth when I could not on my own. In one particularly challenging time, I had chosen to move forward in a direction that seemed like the only possible course. My wife was not convinced. "You need to take this before the Lord and sit with it and with him for a while," she said. "You need to release it to him. You need to spend more time in prayer about this." I did as she advised, offering the situation to the Lord and reflecting intentionally on what truth, righteousness, peace, faith, salvation, and the word of God meant in this instance. As I did, slowly another way unfolded before me, a better way, a gospel way.

When You're All Armored Up, Pray!

It's no accident that when I set aside ample time for prayer, I was able to fight God's battle in God's way rather than in my way. Prayer is central to spiritual warfare according to Ephesians 6:10–20.

You will not find this claim in most commentaries on this passage. Partly this is because as I mentioned in "Explain the Story," most translations turn verse 18 into a whole new paragraph, as if Paul had moved on from spiritual warfare to a different topic. But the grammar of this passage requires that spiritual warfare and prayer be kept together. Far from introducing another topic, verse 18 is the climax of the passage beginning in 6:10. Once we have donned the armor of God, we are to fight by praying.

In one of my grad school seminars, we carefully studied Ephesians 6:10–20. My professor, a brilliant scholar, believed that this passage commends a passive approach to spiritual warfare. He argued that all of the armor in 6:10–20 is defensive, even the sword. "What do we do when we put on the armor?" he asked one day in class. "Nothing! We just stand there. Standing firm is what we do."

At this point I raised my hand nervously. "I have to disagree," I said. "There is something more for us to do here, something vital. Verse 18, as you know, is not separate from the armor passage. It is all part of the same argument, the same sentence beginning in verse 17. So when we have put on the armor, we don't just stand there passively. We do something active. We pray. We pray with all kinds of prayer, all the time, for all people. Prayer is how we fight."

When I finished my comment, the room was quiet, filled with tension because I had so plainly disagreed with my professor. He looked at me and stroked his chin thoughtfully. "You may be right," he said finally. "I haven't seen that before." On the outside I appeared to take his positive response in stride. Inwardly, I was cheering.

I had not figured this out on my own; I learned it in a course I had audited at Fuller Theological Seminary called "The Body of Christ in Ephesians." It was taught by Don Williams, an adjunct professor (who also happens to be my uncle). Don was the one who first showed me the connection between putting on the armor and praying. He convinced me, and I convinced (well, almost convinced) my Harvard professor.

I believe there are three main reasons why we overlook the centrality of prayer in the teaching on spiritual warfare in Ephesians 6. First, we miss the connection because prayer is not identified as a piece of armor. If Paul had said, "Grabbing the lance of prayer," then we'd be sure to get the point. Second, we miss the linkage between putting on God's armor and praying because translators often turn verse 18 into a separate command, even a separate paragraph.[25] If you don't read Greek, you would never see what is so clear in the original text. Third, we discount the centrality of prayer in spiritual warfare because our own prayer lives are so insipid. Perhaps if we learned to pray "in the Spirit on all occasions," and if we prayed "with all kinds of prayers and requests," and if we learned to "be alert" when we pray, and if we kept on "praying for all of the Lord's people," we'd begin to see how central is prayer to our battle.

To sum up, prayer is what we do once we've put on God's armor. It is one of the main ways we fight spiritually. It has both defensive and offensive capability. But prayer is not alone in this regard. Every bit of God's armor equips us both to defend against spiritual attack and to go on the offensive. As we do, let us remember that in this war, we are seeking not to defeat or decimate people but to lead them to the Savior. To mix the metaphors of Ephesians, when we go on the offensive, we shine the light of the gospel into the world so that those who are in darkness might become light, so that those who sleep might awake to new life in Christ.

---

25. The following translations begin a new paragraph with verse 18: NLT, CEB, NRSV. The ESV does not do this: "(17) and take the helmet of salvation, and the sword of the Spirit, which is the word of God, (18) praying at all times in the Spirit."

LISTEN to the Story

²¹Tychicus, the dear brother and faithful servant in the Lord, will tell you everything, so that you also may know how I am and what I am doing. ²²I am sending him to you for this very purpose, that you may know how we are, and that he may encourage you.

²³Peace to the brothers and sisters, and love with faith from God the Father and the Lord Jesus Christ. ²⁴Grace to all who love our Lord Jesus Christ with an undying love.

Listening to the text in the Story: Acts 20:1–6; Philippians 4:14–23; Colossians 4:7–18; 2 Timothy 4:12; Titus 3:12.

The final section of Ephesians begins with details about Tychicus, the person who is delivering the letter on behalf of Paul. Then the last two verses of the letter offer a closing benediction. In this section Paul mentions none of the letter's recipients by name. He includes no travel plans. Comparing this section of Ephesians to other Pauline letters shows how brief and impersonal it is. This would make little sense if Paul was writing only to the Christians in Ephesus whom he knew well because of his time spent with them. The unusual ending of the letter lends support to the notion that it was meant to be read beyond Ephesus by people who did not know Paul personally.

EXPLAIN the Story

What Tychicus Will Do (6:21–22)

Tychicus, the dear brother and faithful servant in the Lord, will tell you everything, so that you also may know how I am and what I am doing (6:21). Paul introduces Tychicus, who we assume was the one carrying Paul's letter to those who received it. He appears elsewhere in the New Testament as a travel companion of Paul (Acts 20:4) and as someone Paul sent as his representative

(2 Tim 4:12; Titus 3:12). But by far the most intriguing reference to Tychicus in Paul's letters appears in Colossians 4:7–9:

> *Tychicus will tell you all the news about me. He is a dear brother, a faithful minister* and fellow servant *in the Lord. I am sending him to you for the express purpose that you may know about our circumstances and that he may encourage your hearts.* He is coming with Onesimus, our faithful and dear brother, who is one of you. They will tell you everything that is happening here. (emphasis added)

If you were to examine the Greek behind this passage and compare it with the Greek of Ephesians 6:21–22, you'd find that the words I have italicized are exactly the same in both letters. Many commentators take this as sure evidence for the fact that whoever wrote Ephesians had access to Colossians. This is certainly possible, especially if Paul wrote Ephesians.

The verbal similarity between Colossians 4:7–9 and Ephesians 6:21–22 by no means requires that a disciple of Paul wrote Ephesians. In fact, one might naturally assume that such close similarity indicates the same person wrote both letters.

Paul describes Tychicus as "the dear brother and faithful servant in the Lord." Colossians adds "fellow servant [*sundoulos*]" (4:17), which is not mentioned in Ephesians. We wonder why if the writer of Ephesians was copying Colossians directly this was not included. A variation like this calls into question the copying theory.

I am sending him to you for this very purpose, that you may know how we are, and that he may encourage you (6:22). In addition to delivering Paul's letter to the churches for which it was intended, Tychicus is charged with bringing these churches up to date on Paul's life, especially his imprisonment. In 3:13 Paul urged his readers "not to be discouraged because of my sufferings." Presumably, Tychicus reported that Paul was doing well and was using his imprisonment for the advance of the gospel so that his readers would be encouraged (see Phil 1:12–14).

The word "also" in the phrase "will tell you everything, so that you also may know how I am doing" (6:21), suggests that Paul sent Tychicus to another church or other churches with the letter and with news about Paul. It's likely that Tychicus carried Colossians to the Christians in Colossae (Col 4:7–9) and perhaps other churches in the area. In these churches he made sure Ephesians was read, and he passed on news about Paul.

Closing Benediction (6:23–24)

Peace to the brothers and sisters, and love with faith from God the Father and the Lord Jesus Christ. Grace to all who love our Lord Jesus Christ with an undying love

(6:23–24). The closing benediction of Ephesians reiterates dominant themes of the letter: peace, love, faith, and grace. It echoes the greeting in 1:2, "Grace and peace to you from God our Father and the Lord Jesus Christ," though adding love into the mix. Given the centrality of love throughout the letter (1:4, 15; 3:17–19; 4:2, 16; 5:1–2, 25, 28, 33), this addition comes as no surprise.

The use of "brothers and sisters" in the benediction is unexpected in two ways. First, up to this point Paul has not addressed his readers as "brothers and sisters," something he did in all of his other letters sent to more than one person (not Philemon or the Pastoral Epistles). The lack of "brothers and sisters" points to a kind of formality throughout Ephesians. Second, when Paul uses sibling language in verse 23, he does not say "peace to you brothers and sisters" but "peace to *the* brother and sisters." This also reveals a lack of familiarity between Paul and his readers and the likelihood that his letter was going to many brothers and sisters throughout a wide region rather than to one church.

The final verse confirms this observation. Rather than saying something like "grace be with you" as he usually does when closing his letters (see, for example, Gal 6:18; Phil 4:23), Paul writes "grace to all who love our Lord Jesus Christ" (6:24). This is both more inclusive and less personal than Paul's standard benediction.

The phrase translated in the NIV as "with an undying love" includes *en aphtharsia*, which means "in/with immortality" or "in/with incorruptibility."[1] Paul has not used this language before in Ephesians. Most translations link this phrase with the love that people have for Christ. The NLT, however, connects the phrase with grace: "May God's grace be *eternally* upon all who love our Lord Jesus Christ" (emphasis added). This option is supported by some commentators.[2] It is not possible to decide definitively for either reading, though the emphasis on God's grace throughout Ephesians points, I believe, in the direction of eternal grace. God's grace is present for us forever, without being corrupted.

Yet no matter which interpretation one prefers, it's crucial to note that *en aphtharsia* are the last two words in Ephesians. The letter began with God choosing us before the foundation of the world. It ends with the hope of an endless future, one that is indeed filled with God's grace for us and our love for Christ. Yoder Neufeld is right when he observes that *en aphtharsia* is "intended to place the whole of God's interaction with redeemed humanity into the context of hope and permanence—a fitting benediction indeed."[3]

---

1. See BDAG 155 (*aphtharsia*).
2. See Lincoln, *Ephesians*, 466–68; Arnold, *Ephesians*, 482–83.
3. Yoder Neufeld, *Ephesians*, 321 (emphasis in the original).

LIVE the Story

How can we live a story that features the introduction of the deliverer of Paul's letter who would have also let the recipients know how he was doing? As I've considered this question, I've come up with an unexpected answer. No, I'm not going to send someone to deliver this commentary to you and fill you in on my life. But I am going to follow Paul's lead in a different way.

Paul assumed that the recipients of his letter would want to know how he was getting along. Yes, this might be mainly about his imprisonment. But as we read through Paul's letters, we find he was often filling in his readers on his personal life, his travel plans, and his struggles and victories. He assumed it was not enough for him to deliver the message entrusted to him, whether in person or by letter. Rather, he sought also to share his life with his readers, even those who don't know him.

Paul explained this practice in 1 Thessalonians in a description of his ministry in Thessalonica: "Because we loved you so much, we were delighted to share with you not only the gospel of God but our lives as well" (1 Thess 2:8). What Paul did in person, sharing the gospel and his own life, he sought to do through his letters, both through what he wrote and through the messenger who delivered the letters. Ephesians contains relatively little about Paul's personal life, no doubt because of its unusual nature as a circular letter to churches, several of which Paul did not plant. But to compensate for that, Tychicus, as he delivered the letter, let the churches know more about Paul.

You and I are in a rather similar situation to that of Paul and his readers. A few who read this commentary know me personally; most do not. I've put enough of my Christian experience in this volume that if you've read it, you actually know quite a bit about me. I have been delighted to share with you not only the gospel of God in Ephesians but my own life as well.

Yet perhaps I need to live the story of 6:21–24 a little more intentionally. Though I can't send Tychicus, I can finish this commentary by sharing with you a bit about how I have lived the story of Ephesians while writing about it. I realize that most commentaries don't do this. But most commentaries aren't charged with trying to help us live the story, either. A unique purpose deserves a unique conclusion.

How I Have Lived the Story of God in Ephesians
When I first agreed to write this commentary, I was the senior director of Laity Lodge, a retreat center in the Texas Hill Country outside of San Antonio. Part of what had drawn me to Laity Lodge in the first place was its explicit theological grounding upon truths from Ephesians. Howard E. Butt, Jr., the

founder of Laity Lodge, passionately believed that all Christians are saved by grace through faith and created in Christ Jesus for good works (2:8–10). Inspired by Ephesians 4:11–16, Howard committed his life to encouraging the ministry of the laity in the church and the world. Hence the name "Laity Lodge."

When Zondervan offered me the opportunity to write this commentary on Ephesians, Howard was quite enthusiastic since he understood how essential this letter is for a right understanding of how God works in the world through all of his people individually and through his church. Howard affirmed my own conviction that the story of God in Ephesians needs to be heard and lived today now more than ever. Thus Howard and the other top leaders of The H. E. Butt Family Foundation, the "mothership" of Laity Lodge, encouraged me to take on this project as a central part of my work.

Another facet of that work was writing devotions for The High Calling, the digital outreach of the Foundation and a sister ministry to Laity Lodge. These "Daily Reflections" were published online and emailed to more than 20,000 subscribers each morning. For two years my reflections were based on Ephesians. As I worked slowly through the text, studying each word and praying through each verse, God made himself known to me in fresh ways, and I was grateful to be able to share what I was learning with my "online congregation." During our slow walk through Ephesians, many of my readers shared with me their insights and questions, which shaped the writing of this commentary.

As I studied Ephesians both exegetically and devotionally, I was moved once again by the grand story of God in this letter. I saw as I never had before just how central to the whole story is God's plan for the fullness of time, "to bring unity to all things in heaven and on earth under Christ" (1:10). I wrestled with what it means for me to "be for the praise of [God's] glory" (1:12). I recommitted myself to walking in the "good works" God had prepared for me, whatever those works might be (2:10). I longed to "live a life worthy of the calling" I had received and to help others understand and embody this calling in their lives (4:1). I wondered what might happen in my life if I really believed that God "is able to do immeasurably more than all [I] ask or imagine" (3:20).

My engagement with these truths from Ephesians, as well as the God who inspired them, ended up taking my life in a very different direction from what I had expected. This detour began when I discovered how Mark Labberton, the new president of Fuller Seminary, was articulating a fresh expression of the mission of the seminary. He framed this mission using the language of calling or vocation. Fuller's purpose is to help its students understand their primary calling to follow Jesus and then to help them discern how to live out this primary calling in their "derivative" callings or vocations. For many students, according to Labberton, these "kingdom vocations" are not necessarily what we normally associate with seminary grads (pastoring, missionary work, etc.). They might well use their Fuller education to serve the Lord as teachers, lawyers, mayors, entrepreneurs, or artists. If they become pastors, then one of their chief tasks is helping members of their flock understand their primary vocation and how they might live this out in their own diverse vocations.

I had never heard anything like this from a seminary president. I was thrilled by what I was hearing. Not only was it in tune with our work at Laity Lodge and The High Calling, not only was it a fulfillment of dreams Howard Butt and I had shared about seminary education, but it also was an extraordinarily inspired expression of the story of God in Ephesians. Mark Labberton and Fuller Seminary really "get" God's cosmic purpose to unify "all things" under Christ (1:10), not just "churchy things" or "spiritual things" but *all things*. They truly believe that all of God's people are ministers of Christ and that pastors and other leaders are to equip all of God's people for ministry (4:11–12). They articulate their core purpose right along the lines of Ephesians 4:1, which urges us "to live a life worthy of the calling [we] have received."

In my excitement about what was going on at Fuller, I called Mark Labberton and asked if I might be able to bring a film crew from The High Calling to document the movement of God at Fuller. And so, a few months later, my crew and I spent an afternoon with Mark, hearing his vision for not just seminary education but also for God's work in the world through people called to follow Christ and live out this primary calling in a wide range of "kingdom vocations." As I listened, I believed that God's work at Fuller was one of the most important things happening in the world today. I was pleased to be able to support this effort by partnering with Fuller while I was working at the Foundation.

That's when my life took a different turn. A short time after our day of filming, Mark asked if I had any interest in joining his team at Fuller, something I had never anticipated. My immediate response was negative, given my commitment to The H. E. Butt Family Foundation and its excellent work. I was excited about the possibility of a partnership between the Foundation and Fuller. A conversation began on those terms. But with God you never know where a conversation like that will lead.

At this same time, I was asked to provide leadership for a Christian organization that was in a major crisis. Without going into details, I knew that if I took this assignment it would be one of the most difficult and potentially explosive of my life. It could be very costly to me personally and professionally. Yet I also knew that God wanted me to do it. So I consented, in fear and trembling.

The next few months were some of the craziest and most stressful of my life as I sought to walk in the good works God had prepared for me. I agonized over what it meant for me in my professional life to lead a life worthy of the calling I had received. Was it time for a major job change? I was reminded once again that when God does "immeasurably more than all we ask or imagine" in our lives, we may not at first be thrilled. God's grace often feels like an unwelcome disruption. Only later can we see clearly the unmistakable print of God's own finger in the struggles of our lives.

In time, I came to believe that God was indeed leading me to join Mark Labberton's team at Fuller as the executive director of the seminary's Max De Pree Center for Leadership. In this role I would be able to serve leaders in diverse fields by helping them understand their true calling to Christ and discover how they might live out this calling in their own life and leadership. I accepted the position partly because of my desire to proclaim, teach, and encourage people to live the good news of Ephesians, including: God is uniting all things in Christ (1:10); we are partners in this work because God has saved us by grace and created us anew in Christ Jesus for good works (2:10); we are invited to live lives worthy of our calling (4:1); all of God's people are called into his ministry (4:11–12); leaders are to equip God's people for their ministry (4:11–12); God's story transforms our understanding and practice of work (4:28; 6:5–9); we are children of light who shine God's light into the darkness so that those living in darkness might become light (5:8–14); and our core purpose in life is to exist for the praise of God's glory (1:12–14).

Yet before I began work at Fuller, I needed to complete the writing of this commentary. The support of The H. E. Butt Family Foundation enabled me to do this so that I might finish the project we had taken on together. For this I am deeply grateful.

As I worked my way slowly through Ephesians, I was struck once again by how much the story of God in this letter has become my story. I'm not saying I live it perfectly, or even adequately. I am continually in need of "the immeasurable riches of [God's] grace" and glad this grace is so central the story of God in Ephesians (2:7). But I do know from personal experience that the narrative of Ephesians isn't just something to behold with wonder. It is also something to live and breathe, something to proclaim, something to cherish, something to embody, and something to guide us through all of life. We do this as individuals who have been saved by God's grace and as members of the body of Christ, the church through which the truth of the gospel is demonstrated to the cosmos (3:10).

If you take Ephesians seriously, it will change your life. How do I know this? Because the God whose story fills the pages of this letter is able to do far more than anything you might envision for yourself. It seems only fitting to close this commentary with the inspiring, encouraging, and sometimes intimidating benediction from Ephesians 3:20–21:

> Now to him who is able to do immeasurably more than all we ask or imagine, according to his power that is at work within us, to him be glory in the church and in Christ Jesus throughout all generations, for ever and ever! *Amen.*

Scripture Index

1 Corinthians

2 Corinthians

Galatians

Subject Index

abolition of slavery, 234–35. *See also* slavery

"always giving thanks," 187. *See also* giving thanks

"anger/rage" metaphors, 153–54, 156

apostles, 95–97

"appointed by lot" phrase, 33

"armor" metaphor, 151, 238–54

ascension of Jesus, 24, 52, 128, 131–32. *See also* Jesus Christ

baptism
  hymns and, 174
  of individuals, 151, 204, 226
  of Jesus, 27
  one baptism, 116, 120–22

barriers, 87, 144–45, 227

benediction, 256–57, 262

Berlin Wall, 85–90

"bitterness" metaphor, 153–54, 156

blamelessness, 26–27

blessings, 23–32, 44–46

blood of Christ, 75, 78, 170, 208

body of Christ
  church as, 1, 14, 42–43, 50, 82, 103, 111, 120, 217, 225, 261
  good works and, 59, 74
  love and, 137–39, 157–58, 172
  marriage and, 225
  as metaphor, 82
  parenting and, 225
  spiritual growth and, 74, 120–21, 128–30, 134–38

breastplate of righteousness, 238, 243–44

"bring up" metaphor, 222

"building" metaphor, 83–84

Called: The Crisis and Promise of Following Jesus Today, 118, 124

"calling" metaphor, 117–18

calling, worthy of
  choices and, 189
  evil and, 238–39
  good works and, 162
  meaning of, 13, 116–27, 156–62
  participation and, 13, 259–61

view of world and, 175
  wise living and, 166–68, 181–85

career, 123–25

children
  exasperating, 221–22
  honoring parents, 220–21, 224–25
  obedience of, 219–20, 223–24
  raising, 219–26
  training, 222–23, 225–26

"children of light," 101, 165–66, 170–72, 178–81, 261

"chosen" phrase, 32–33

Christ. *See* Jesus Christ

church
  as body of Christ, 1, 14, 42–43, 50, 82, 103, 111, 120, 217, 225, 261
  early church, 3
  example of, 101–3
  fullness of, 49–50
  glory in, 104, 110–14, 262
  introduction of, 47–50, 58
  laity in, 140–44, 259
  love for, 204, 214, 217–18
  ministry of, 140–44
  mission of, 99–101
  role of, 13–15, 94, 98, 100
  setting of, 3
  unity of, 126–29, 136, 139, 200, 205

circumcision, 75, 77, 80–81, 88, 201

"clothing" metaphor, 151

Colson, Chuck, 71

community, 15, 56–57, 61

consequences
  cross of Christ and, 75–76
  for Gentiles, 83–85
  metaphor for, 83–85
  of sin, 35, 62, 207–8

"cornerstone" metaphor, 83–84

creation, story of, 31–32, 139–40, 183, 207–9

cross of Christ
  consequences of, 75–76
  crucifixion, 47, 55, 119, 157–58, 198
  meaning of, 11–12
  peace and, 79–83, 87

Author Index

Adam, Hajo, 159

Aristotle, 194, 202, 229

Arndt, W. F., 18, 23, 27–30, 32–34, 49, 65, 77, 95–96, 106, 109, 117, 119, 149, 153–55, 167, 172–73, 182, 184, 196–97, 199, 204, 212, 220–22, 230, 242–43, 246–47, 257

Arnold, Clinton E., 1, 49, 81, 95, 108–9, 151, 167–68, 173, 196, 257

Baker, Dana, 90

Balch, David L., 194

Barclay, John M. G., 65

Barnett, P. W., 95

Bartchy, S. Scott, 228, 229, 234

Barth, Markus, 1, 22, 84, 131, 198

Bauer, W., 18, 23, 27–30, 32–34, 49, 65, 77, 95–96, 106, 109, 117, 119, 149, 153–55, 167, 172–73, 182, 184, 196–97, 199, 204, 212, 220–22, 230, 242–43, 246–47, 257

Bellah, Robert N., 54, 55

Berkhof, Hendrik, 242, 246, 249

Betz, Hans Dieter, 96

Blatty, William Peter, 249

Bolsinger, Tod E., 138

Boring, M. Eugene, 96

Boublil, Alain, 71

Briggs, Charles A., 45, 221

Brooks, John Rives, 112

Brown, Francis, 45, 221

Brown, Raymond E., 29

Bruce, F. F., 1, 240

Butt, Howard E., Jr., 52, 124, 142–43, 258–61

Calvin, John, 1, 107, 196

Campbell, Constantine R., 25

Catchim, Tim, 133

Chrysostom, John, 235

Cohick, Lynn H., 1, 6, 22, 66, 67, 186, 196, 221

Cook, Edward M., 131

Crouch, Andy, 97

Danker, F. W., 18, 23, 27–30, 32–34, 49, 65, 77, 95–96, 106, 109, 117, 119, 149, 153–55, 167, 172–73, 182, 184, 196–97, 199, 204, 212, 220–22, 230, 242–43, 246–47, 257

DeYmaz, Mark, 90

Dickens, Charles, 19

Driver, S. R., 45, 221

Dunn, James D. G., 25

Edgar, C. C., 17

Edwards, Jonathan, 169

Edwards, Mark J., 1

Evans, C. A., 95

Fee, Gordon D., 199, 212

Felix, Minucius, 102

Flow, Don, 40

Foulkes, Francis, 98

Galinsky, Adam D., 159

Garber, Steven, 123–24

Gingrich, F. W., 18, 23, 27–30, 32–34, 49, 65, 77, 95–96, 106, 109, 117, 119, 149, 153–55, 167, 172–73, 182, 184, 196–97, 199, 204, 212, 220–22, 230, 242–43, 246–47, 257

Glover, T. R., 102

Gombis, Timothy, 47, 98, 132, 194, 242

Grudem, Wayne A., 199, 200

Hillenbrand, Laura, 37, 38

Hirsch, Alan, 133

Hoehner, Harold W., 1, 5, 7

Hopkins, Keith, 232

Howard, Neil, 236

Hugo, Victor, 70, 71, 73, 74

Hunt, A. S., 17

Jones, H. S., 169, 173, 182, 200, 241, 243

Josephus, 202

Julian, Roman Emperor, 102

Keener, Craig S., 194, 199, 242, 245, 246

Kierkegaard, Søren, 191

Knight, George W., III, 199

Kretzmer, Herbert, 71